Networked Publics and
Digital Contention

Oxford Studies in Digital Politics

Series Editor: Andrew Chadwick, Royal Holloway,
University of London

Using Technology, Building Democracy: Digital Campaigning and the Construction of Citizenship
Jessica Baldwin-Philippi

Expect Us: Online Communities and Political Mobilization
Jessica L. Beyer

The Hybrid Media System: Politics and Power
Andrew Chadwick

Tweeting to Power: The Social Media Revolution in American Politics
Jason Gainous and Kevin M. Wagner

The Digital Origins of Dictatorship and Democracy: Information Technology and Political Islam
Philip N. Howard

Democracy's Fourth Wave? Digital Media and the Arab Spring
Philip N. Howard and Muzammil M. Hussain

The MoveOn Effect: The Unexpected Transformation of American Political Advocacy
David Karpf

Taking Our Country Back: The Crafting of Networked Politics from Howard Dean to Barack Obama
Daniel Kreiss

Bits and Atoms: Information and Communication Technology in Areas of Limited Statehood
Steven Livingston and Gregor Walter-Drop

Digital Cities: The Internet and the Geography of Opportunity
Karen Mossberger, Caroline J. Tolbert, and William W. Franko

Revolution Stalled: The Political Limits of the Internet in the Post-Soviet Sphere
Sarah Oates

Disruptive Power: The Crisis of the State in the Digital Age
Taylor Owen

Affective Publics: Sentiment, Technology, and Politics
Zizi Papacharissi

Presidential Campaigning in the Internet Age
Jennifer Stromer-Galley

News on the Internet: Information and Citizenship in the 21st Century
David Tewksbury and Jason Rittenberg

The Civic Organization and the Digital Citizen: Communicating Engagement in a Networked Age
Chris Wells

Networked Publics and Digital Contention

THE POLITICS OF EVERYDAY
LIFE IN TUNISIA

MOHAMED ZAYANI

FOREWORD BY JOHN D. H. DOWNING

Published in Collaboration with
Georgetown University's Center for International and Regional Studies,
School of Foreign Service in Qatar.

OXFORD
UNIVERSITY PRESS

OXFORD
UNIVERSITY PRESS

Oxford University Press is a department of the
University of Oxford. It furthers the University's objective
of excellence in research, scholarship, and education
by publishing worldwide.

Oxford   New York
Auckland   Cape Town   Dar es Salaam   Hong Kong   Karachi
Kuala Lumpur   Madrid   Melbourne   Mexico City   Nairobi
New Delhi   Shanghai   Taipei   Toronto

With offices in
Argentina   Austria   Brazil   Chile   Czech Republic   France   Greece
Guatemala   Hungary   Italy   Japan   Poland   Portugal   Singapore
South Korea   Switzerland   Thailand   Turkey   Ukraine   Vietnam

Oxford is a registered trademark of Oxford University Press
in the UK and certain other countries.

Published in the United States of America by
Oxford University Press
198 Madison Avenue, New York, NY 10016

Library of Congress Cataloging-in-Publication Data
Zayani, Mohamed, 1965–
Networked publics and digital contention: the politics of everyday
life in Tunisia/Mohamed Zayani.
pages   cm
Includes bibliographical references and index.
ISBN 978-0-19-023976-3 (hardcover: alk. paper)—ISBN 978-0-19-023977-0 (pbk.: alk. paper)
1. Social media—Political aspects—Tunisia.   2. Online social networks—Political aspects—Tunisia.
3. Social movements—Tunisia.   4. Youth—Political activity—Tunisia.   5. Tunisia—Politics and
government—2011-   I. Title.
HN784.Z915693   2015
320.961109051—dc23   2014050092

9 8 7 6 5 4 3 2 1
Printed in the United States of America
on acid-free paper

To Sonia, Aymen, Malek and Yasmine

Contents

Foreword

If ignorance indeed is bliss, then inside the general run of the Western commentocracy at the time of the upheavals that began in 2011 in the Arab region, verily bliss it must have been in that dawn to be alive, trilling tweets, firing off op-eds, and doing pundit TV. Instant sweeping political change, the drama of day-by-day twists and turns, magically omnipotent mobile media, "our" Facebook, the ever-mysterious Orient: "they" don't hate us after all; why, look how they are suddenly *becoming* "us" . . . at last!

From 2011 onward, the pundits divided broadly into two groups. There were those who knew very little about the region but were mesmerized by then-new information technologies, and who gushed with frothy optimism about the digital transformation of Arab-hood. The stereotype of Arab emotionalism fused with the instantaneity of "social" media.

The second group was in some ways even more impregnably invincible than the first. Dismissing information and communication technologies as somewhere between epiphenomenal and incomprehensible, they sought comfort in caressing continuity. The Middle East was still irrevocably what it was and would always be. The region's oft-quoted demographic skew toward the under-25s somehow stayed a statistical abstraction. Yet those younger citizens were the most likely to be actively exploring fresh communication hardware and software avenues.

Mohamed Zayani's detailed study of how these upheavals took shape in one country in the region before, during, and since 2011 whisks us away from both these reductive frameworks. Drawing upon Henri Lefebvre's analyses of the sociology of daily life, Michel de Certeau's explorations of subterranean challenges to the official order, Asef Bayat's discussions of "social non-movements" and Béatrice Hibou's "historical sociology of the political," Zayani traces out the intricate web of unanticipated consequences that over the decades led up to 2011's explosion.

Anchored in his own experience of Tunisia, but armed equally with the insights of distance through being based elsewhere in the region, Zayani generates a rigorous and convincing narrative of events—one that heavily underscores the need for comparably penetrating studies in Egypt, Syria, Yemen, Bahrain, and Libya. Whether focusing on the regionally distinctive roles of Tunisia's legal profession and labor union activism, or on the lure of new communication technologies for well-educated younger Tunisians in search of entertainment, or on the sterility of most of Tunisia's official media up until 2011, or on the advanced Internet surveillance techniques that went hand in hand with the country's embrace of the Internet as a key component of modernity, Zayani forms a composite picture, piece by piece, of a digitally connected social movement, which to almost everyone's astonishment evolved into powerful challenges to Zine El Abidine Ben Ali's despotism.

It is, frankly, a fascinating account. The author also takes care to include the story's international dimensions, particularly the role online activists in the diaspora played. This historical, on-the-ground yet subterranean exploration of how these trends and processes gradually and unexpectedly grafted themselves on to each other, or clashed, leaves the commentocracy's simplistic shibboleths by the side of the road.

Tunisia's story continues. But to have this exceptionally well-grounded case study provides a marvelous foundation for understanding what may now transpire there, and possible repercussions within the region. It also offers a highly suggestive model for a multilevel approach to the complex dynamics of social movements *over time*, their numerous communication formats, their relationship to the state and economic change. It moves decisively beyond hitherto conventional models of social movement actors that characterize them as mute, noncommunicating pieces on a Rational Social Actor chessboard.

Particularly, this account fleshes out the enduring importance of carefully studying the various roles played by small-scale media of all kinds within the genesis, apogee, and recomposition of social movements. It does so by using sociological, historical, and political analysis, and by resolutely avoiding the standard media studies vice of media-centrism. These nano-media today include uses of smartphones, Facebook, Twitter, YouTube, blogging, and other digital connective media. Ten and twenty years from now, perhaps, a whole fresh array of digital titles and options will dominate debates on the nano-media generated within social movements.

Social movement media, to be found past and present all over the planet, are only recently coming to be taken with the seriousness they deserve, no longer dismissed out of hand as ephemeral trivia. They range from street theater and popular song, body art and murals, dress and satire, dance and demonstrations, cartoons and poetry, posters and mime, all the way into the legacy media of radio, recorded music, television, print, and cinema. They do not work magic—to my surprise, having spent much of my career sociologically investigating such media, I frequently found myself in 2011–12 inveighing against their *overestimation* by one wing of the commentocracy. But, going back in time, these media have often played very significant subterranean roles. Subterranean, that is, to the far observer; not to those on the ground, whether activists or surveillance agents, possessed of alert eyes and ears.

I confidently expect readers to benefit considerably from this study, whether they are specialists in digital connective media, social movements, international affairs, the anthropology of daily life, the Arab region, and/or Tunisia itself. There is much here to plumb and to spark further reflection.

John D. H. Downing
Editor of *Encyclopedia of Social Movement Media*

Acknowledgments

This work would not have been possible without the invaluable help of a number of people and tremendous institutional support from the Georgetown University School of Foreign Service in Qatar. A considerable part of this project was carried out in the course of a research fellowship with Georgetown University's Center for International and Regional Studies, which also provided me with the valuable release time to complete my book. I thank the director of the center, Mehran Kamrava, for his intellectual stimulation and generous support. The Office of Research has also been instrumental in facilitating my work; I thank in particular Valbona Zenku, Ivanka Hoppenbrouwer, and John Crist. From the Office of Scholarly Publications, I would like to thank Carole Sargent, and from Georgetown University Press, I thank Richard Brown. For research assistance, I am grateful to Abdullah Ahmad, Jana Al Okar, Sophia Vogel, Salar Khan, and Dalia Elsayed. Thanks should also go to the following librarians for their help and resourcefulness: Frieda Wiebe, Robert Laws, Susan Fahy, Donna Hanson, and Stefan Seeger. Finally, I would like to especially recognize the support and inspiration I received from three colleagues at Georgetown University and to warmly thank them for helping bring this project to fruition: Gerd Nonneman, Robert Wirsing, and Patricia O'Connor.

I owe a special debt to a number of scholars who were generous with their time and who read earlier drafts of the manuscript, either in full or in part, and provided invaluable critical commentary and insightful feedback to sharpen the book's claims: Paul Musgrave, John Downing, Annabelle Sreberny, Marwan Kraidy, Amy Nestor, Gary Wasserman, Mark Farha, Rogaia Abusharaf, and Joe Khalil. Their critical comments and valuable advice improved the formulations of this work tremendously. Needless to say, the book's shortcomings are entirely my own. I am also grateful for stimulating conversations with a number of scholars at various conferences, research meetings, and academic settings: Jon Anderson, Michael Hudson, Kristina Riegert, Deborah Wheeler, Dale Eickelman, Mohamed Kirat, Noureddine Miladi, Hamid Nafisi, George Joffe, Rikke Hostrup Haugbølle, Adel Jendli, Lahra Smith, Sofiane Sahraoui, Larbi Chouikha, Fatima El Issawi, Muzammil Husain, Sadok Hammami, Philip Seib, Salem Labiadh, Walter Armbrust, Riadh Ferjani, Romain Lecomte, Nouri Gana, Francesco Cavatorta, Noureddine Jebnoun, John Chalcraft, and Randy Kluver. From Al Jazeera Center for Studies, I would like to especially thank Ezzeddine Abdelmoula and SalahEddin Elzein for providing a stimulating forum to present and discuss research formulations. My thanks also go to a number of my colleagues who assisted in other ways: Suzi Mirgani, Zahra Babar, Patrick Laude, Amira Sonbol, Daniel Westbrook, Christine Schiwietz, Johnathon Chapman, Jeremy Koons, Salah Troudi, Max Oidtmann, Clyde Wilcox, James MacGregor, Daniel Stoll, Matthew Tinkcom, Joe Hernandez, Carina Lawson, and Virginia Jones.

Many of the ideas in this book were developed and discussed in the context of the "Media, Culture and Politics in the Middle East" seminar I conducted at Georgetown University and the CCT Summer Institute on Media, Technology and Digital Culture in the Middle East I codirected with J. R. Osborn. I especially thank my students in the Media and Politics Program for their critical engagement with preliminary thoughts and discussion of key formulations. A note of thanks also goes to the anonymous readers who provided useful commentary and constructive readings of the manuscript and to Rene Carman for her marvelous editorial input.

I am also grateful for a great many individuals who provided assistance in the course of my fieldwork in Tunisia. In particular, I thank the activists, bloggers, Internet users and political players who agreed to be interviewed, often more than once, and who gladly shared with me their insights, experiences, and views. I owe much gratitude to Lilia Weslaty for assisting with the field research and Zouheir Makhlouf for connecting me to several activists in Tunisia and facilitating many of the interviews I conducted in Tunis and Sidi Bouzid. Likewise, I am most appreciative of the support I received from Sabeur Zayani, Karim Zayani, and Fatma El Ayech while undertaking fieldwork for this project.

Research for this book was supported by generous funding from the Georgetown University School of Foreign Service in Qatar. Grateful acknowledgment goes to Qatar Foundation for its support of research and scholarly endeavors.

Finally, I am deeply grateful to my dedicated editor and series editor at Oxford University Press, Angela Chnapko and Andrew Chadwick, respectively, who believed in this project and diligently and enthusiastically saw it through to its completion. Last but not least, I would like to thank my wonderful wife, Sonia, for her generosity and support while writing this book.

Networked Publics and
Digital Contention

1

Introduction

On Digital Contention and Everyday Life

Media and the Arab Predicament

No account of the Arab uprisings is complete without reference to digital activism. In the popular imagination and academic circles alike, the revolutionary fervor and momentous changes some Arab countries witnessed in the second decade of the twenty-first century were intimately connected to an unprecedented media momentum that fueled "networks of outrage and hope,"[1] forced a number of dictators from power, and altered what had seemed to be an immutable political reality. The Arab uprisings set off intense debates about the relationship among communications technology, revolutionary dynamics, political activism, and social movements. Initially, these debates centered on the role that social media played in the revolts and the extent to which the uprisings were powered by social networks. But the events also sparked interest in the implications that digital media and social networks have for political dissent, collective action, and street protests. The presumed relationship between citizen-led action and youth-driven movements, on the one hand, and the adoption of a wide range of communication tools and information technologies, on the other, gave media in the Arab world an added relevance and a pointed political significance.

This judgment about the centrality of technical innovation to political change in the Arab world stands in stark contrast to the predominant narrative of only a few years ago, which emphasized the region's aversion to change. Although the advent of transnational satellite television in the 1990s and the widespread adoption of the Internet in the first decade of the new millennium undermined the hegemonic control of Arab governments over information, such transformations appeared to be politically inconsequential in the face of the region's entrenched authoritarianism. Nor, for that matter, had digitally networked technologies and participatory media paid democratic dividends for a region that has long been marked by non-participatory political systems. At best, the vibrant Arab media scene was deemed by some scholars to have created a space of interaction that is akin to what Habermas calls the public sphere—an inclusive mediated space of interaction that thrives on reasoned positions, critical debate, and public deliberation.[2] But attempts to conceptualize the political implications of media in an undemocratic Arab context are fraught with theoretical difficulties, not least because they are embedded in normative claims about democratic politics and mass media workings. Even though the energized media sphere helped break the state monopoly over public discourse and the new culture of connectivity helped democratize the right to access information and interpret events, the effect on the region's political culture remained either constrained or impalpable. In spite of its vibrancy, media in the Arab world did not seem to have affected power relations or to have changed the region's political reality.

Neither the story of technologically enabled revolutions toppling Arab dictators and bringing in sweeping political changes nor the narrative of authoritarian rulers determinately controlling information and stifling online dissidence provide a nuanced understanding of the media experience in the Middle East and North Africa (MENA) region. Although the energized media environment in the Arab world and increased access to information and communications technologies (ICT) have attracted considerable attention in academic and policy circles, the focus has been largely on the political effects. One of the key issues informing Arab media and communication scholarship pertains to whether media could play a transformative political role and have a democratizing potential or whether the altered media environment is undermined by evolutionary adjustments and non-democratic alterations geared toward shoring up regime stability.[3] The security implications of the wide adoption of the Internet for the region's political systems have made this issue even more insistent.[4]

Underlying these formulations is an analytical perspective that leaves a number of significant dynamics unexplored with regards to the nature and workings of changing media practices. Taking heed of these limitations calls for a reformulation of the inquiry into the sociopolitical dimension of media in the MENA region in a way that opens up the possibility of reexamining the complex, subtle, and ingenious ways in which media have been experienced, adopted, and appropriated within the particular context of a rapidly changing Arab world. Capturing the intricacies of these mediated experiences requires a better understanding of the processes that have shaped media usage over the years, in particular the significance of the communication possibilities the adoption of new information and communications technologies affords for imagining and negotiating one's lived reality.[5] Such an endeavor also calls particular attention to the way the media experience intersects with broader social contexts, cultural dynamics, and political realities.

The Youth Factor

Studying the media experience in a complex region like the MENA poses considerable challenges. The region, as Sreberny reminds us, "reveals remarkable differentiation among almost any indicator one cares to choose."[6] Still, one can point out common trends and general tendencies that operate across the Arab world, the most obvious perhaps being the demographic transformation. The MENA region is marked by an unprecedented youth bulge, with half of the population being less than twenty-five years old.[7] This sizable generation grew up at a juncture of Arab histories that has been shaped less by the kind of pronounced ideologies that had dominated earlier decades (whether pan-Arabism or communism) than by a set of disparate constellations induced by the increasing interpenetration of the local, the regional, and the global with new defining vectors ranging from social modernization to commodified consumerism and from religious revivalism to a deeply fascinating cyber-culture. While these forces can be observed throughout much of the Arab world, they are far from being uniformly experienced. What is common though is the seeming inability of youth to effect change. Despite the generation's size, Arab youth have been largely marginalized from institutional political life—a sphere of action that is clearly demarcated and vigilantly guarded as the purview of the authoritarian state. The perceived political irrelevance of Arab youth, though, is only an obvious instance of understudied changes that are affecting an entire generation. Arab youth, as one sociologist put it, "are caught in a poignant and unsettling predicament: the undermining of traditional vectors of stability and loyalty (family and the state) as opposed to the modern alternative sources of education, employment, security, and public opinion that have proved unable to fill the void."[8]

Nurturing these tendencies, Dale Eickelman argues, are various sociocultural developments that have been greatly intensified and significantly shaped by two important vectors: mass education and mass media.[9] Mass higher education has fostered a break with earlier traditions of authority. The educated express their beliefs more publicly and in ways that relate more directly to political action, entailing shifts in the political consciousness of a younger, educated generation in many parts of the Middle East and North Africa.[10] Improved levels of education coincided with notable changes in the reach and nature of mass communication. The advent of the satellite era in the 1990s and the development of a remarkable transnational television industry that spawned hundreds of Arabic-language channels offering a rich repertoire of programs have arguably altered audience experiences, habits, and expectations.[11] If the advent of the satellite era opened the eyes of Arab publics to new experiences and alternative views, the wide adoption of the Internet favored the rise of an even more vigorous and interactive space of engagement for a larger Arab cyber-public.

The changing media environment in the MENA region is having notable effects on society and traditional forms of authority, but it is also affecting the political sphere in unique ways. What is interesting to note in this context is not so much the extent to which growing public access to and intense use of various forms of information and communications technologies are eroding state control over political life, but the way they are changing the nature of political engagement itself. While the latter trends may not be readily or uniformly observed throughout the Arab world, they are nonetheless indicative of new sensibilities and dispositions. New ways of creating, consuming, and using information have arguably brought about subtle and dynamic forms of political engagement that are engendering alternative forms of citizen action and reconfiguring the relationship between citizens and the state.

In spite of these innovations, the dynamics and implications of the region's reconfigured communicative space remain largely understudied, bringing up a number of questions: How are the mediated sociocultural practices that emerged in recent years at the intersection of the real and virtual world affecting agency? How is the changing communication culture altering subjectivity? How do forms of online engagement bear on identity negotiation? Are participatory media harbingers of new or different forms of sociality and to what effect? And how have communication practices that are embedded in social networks redefined the practice of politics and the meaning of citizenship?

Cracking the Carapace

Answering these questions with sufficient depth necessitates moving beyond facile generalizations to study specific contexts. As Kalathil and Boas point out in their study of the impact of the Internet on authoritarian rule, "assertions about the technology's political effects are usually made without consideration of the full national context in which the Internet operate in any given country."[12] Context matters because, as Axford reminds us, "the affordances supplied by communication technologies in general and participatory media in particular impact differently in countries with diverse histories, constitutions, political cultures, and policies towards freedom of expression."[13] Despite such potential, though, studies of the Arab media experience remain mired in generalities. There have been few extensive country-specific studies that delve into the subtle nature of the mediated changes in the MENA region,[14] and even fewer studies that explore the evolutionary dynamics of the Internet in the Arab world. North Africa in particular has received scant attention despite its rich digital experience.[15] Focusing on individual cases is valuable to help us avoid a pervasive tendency to homogenize the Arab digital experience. Grounding the analysis in contextual realities and highlighting the specificity of particular experiences can also create the basis for a much-needed comparative theorization of media practices and experiences.

I contribute to the debates on the political sociology of media in the region through my in-depth study of the Tunisian digital experience. The project is based on extensive fieldwork that I conducted in Tunisia between 2011 and 2013, during which I met with journalists, college students, militants, politicians, online activists, bloggers, cyber-dissidents, new media players, and ordinary Internet users. By delving into the Tunisian experience, I sought to bring into focus the intricate relationships among digital culture, youth activism, cyber-resistance, and political engagement. Anchored as it is in the Tunisian experience, this book is also necessarily about digital activism in an authoritarian Arab context. It takes a close look at an array of forms of online communication that arose within the larger sociopolitical context of the authoritarian state. The book explores the various forms of digital contention and different modalities of online resistance that authoritarianism breeds within an increasingly intense communication environment that is conducive to new kinds of sensibilities, experiences, and actions. It tells the story of the coevolution of technology and society in a specific Arab setting in which the aspirations of digitally empowered publics were often at odds with the instincts of a repressive regime.

A central question motivating my investigation is what happens when networked Arab publics are shut out of the political arena under an authoritarian political system. I find that significant forms of political engagement developed outside of conventional politics and institutional frameworks, giving rise to a digital culture of contention. Exploring how this culture of contention took hold can bring to light evolving forms of political engagement—in particular, the tendency of digital communication to reconfigure political action within ordinary, everyday experiences. Accordingly, this study redirects our attention from the formal institutional politics of the Arab world to the informal politics of everyday life. Of particular interest is the extent to which mediated practices that developed at the margin of institutional political life shaped political consciousness and altered power relations. No less significant are the dynamics of seemingly depoliticized youth becoming politicized in the digital era and the proclivity of networked publics to negotiate agency and reimagine citizenship. In this respect, Tunisia's digital culture constitutes a laboratory for examining the changing state-society relationship.

Embracing the Unthinkable

In late 2010 and early 2011, Tunisia experienced an extraordinary historical moment that took the world by surprise. A spontaneous youth-led movement put the country on a new course, overthrowing an entrenched regime that had enjoyed more than two decades of unchallenged rule in the course of a few weeks. The revolution was unexpected but not inexplicable. The country's apparent political stability, its much-vaunted development model, and its much-touted modernism obscured unsettling changes in society. The movement started on December 17, 2010, when Mohamed Bouazizi, a young street vendor from the provincial town of Sidi Bouzid, doused himself with gasoline in front of the local government building before setting himself ablaze in protest. His action came after he was barred from appealing to the local government when a municipal police officer seized his unauthorized vegetable stand under disputed circumstances. News of Bouazizi's self-immolation produced a wave of sympathetic protests that was met with massive police intervention. The violent clashes between security forces and townspeople, and the subsequent siege of the city of Sidi Bouzid, made Bouazizi's tragedy into a galvanizing symbol of the uprising. The discontented masses and the disaffected youth took to the streets in neighboring towns and provinces. As images and information about the unrest captured on mobile phones circulated on the social Web, the news found its way to widely watched transnational Arab satellite channels. More people started to identify with the grievances of the protesters and joined the popular movement. As the protests became self-sustaining, massive collective action started to take place throughout the country. In a police state where public dissent was not tolerated and where people internalized fear, the protesters' collective public display of anger and frustration stood out.

The regime's instinctive response was to crack down on the protesters. However, increased repression (including the use of live ammunition) only fueled the movement further, widening the scope of the protests and raising new popular demands. What started as regional street protests of specific socioeconomic grievances soon evolved into countrywide protests with a revolutionary momentum. By the time the protests reached the capital city of Tunis, where they drew in the urban middle class, the regime considered deploying the army to quell the revolt. Crucially, keen on maintaining a distinction between the state and the regime, the military refused to be dragged into the clashes—a position that effectively meant the siding of the army with the people. Emboldened, the protesters rejected the concessions the president made in his televised speeches and demanded nothing less than his departure. And thus, some four weeks after the outbreak of protests, Tunisia witnessed a dramatic moment as one of the iconic figures of modern Arab authoritarianism fled the country on January 14, 2011, on board a plane bound for Saudi Arabia, where he sought asylum. These unprecedented events proved to be a turning point in the history of the Arab world that brought hopes of enduring social and political changes (as well as fears of the unknown consequences of such changes). Within a matter of days, massive demonstrations broke out in Egypt, followed by popular protests in Libya, Yemen, Algeria, Bahrain, and Syria.

The Technology Conundrum

Since the outbreak of the Arab uprisings, a wealth of studies has emerged on how, why, and where Arab publics engage in collective mobilization and on the modalities through which they initiate various forms of collective action.[16] While some of these works extend old arguments about what is often conceived as ongoing technology-enabled democratization processes, others are more interested in the dynamics of social movements by digitally enabled and globally connected actors. During the early months of the Arab uprisings, many pundits hailed the centrality of media to the revolution, attributing massive importance to its role in circulating information, raising consciousness, and coordinating protests. Deeming social media as a potent force, a cause of action, and a game changer, they effusively described the events in Tunisia as a social media revolution, portraying Facebook and Twitter as engines of regime change and political transformation.[17] For a few weeks, a narrative developed that explained what happened in Tunisia in 2011 as being an information technology-induced political change.

That narrative reflected a tendency among communications technology optimists and digital enthusiasts to champion the emancipatory potential of technology. Their position recalls Daniel Lerner's *The Passing of Traditional Society*, which considers mass media as a driver of economic and political modernization.[18] Some of the more recent accounts also see new media technologies as engines for political change and enablers of democratization. By eroding governments' ability to control information, the argument goes, new communication technologies have helped build a freer and more open society. Those who espouse this view further point out that modern movements and revolutions have had, in one way or another, a communications technology dimension.[19] During the 1979 Islamic revolution in Iran, for instance, cassette tapes were instrumental in ending the rule of Shah Mohammad Reza Pahlavi.[20] In 2009, new media played a prominent role in promoting political activism and advancing political change in the case of the Green Movement following the disputed presidential elections in Iran, where the micro-blogging service Twitter is believed to have greatly facilitated political mobilization.[21] For Clay Shirky, Iran's Green Movement suggests that social media can potentially incite revolutionary movements and provoke political uprisings: "just as the Protestant Reformation was shaped by the printing press, the Iranian insurrection was shaped by social media."[22] Increasingly, this narrative holds, the emergence of new digital spaces for dissent and the intensification of online struggles are becoming a source of challenge to closed political systems, autocratic leaders, and authoritarian regimes, at times even tipping the balance of power in favor of the people.[23] By enhancing the ability to organize protests, coordinate action, synchronize movement, disseminate information, share video footage, and amplify events, increasingly affordable communication technologies and accessible media are viewed as helping people under authoritarian systems acquire a "net advantage."[24]

Not everyone shares the technology enthusiasts' optimism. For skeptics, reducing social movements to a media effect smacks of technological determinism. Some analysts have argued that connectivity to interactive social networking tools and media platforms during times of unrest could hinder rather than facilitate collective action.[25] For Malcolm Gladwell, social media are not sufficient to maintain social revolutionary movements because social activism requires deep roots and strong social ties, which they are incapable of producing.[26] As many have commented, the ease of sharing a news story on social networks means that such a gesture is not genuine activism but a form of slacktivism or clicktivism. Furthermore, the glorification of social media as a tool of revolution obscures the simple fact that revolutions predate the Internet and that movements are about actual grievances, demands, and aspirations.[27] Arguing against "the Internet freedom agenda,"[28] Evgeny Morozov labels the idea that media technologies are driving revolts and that governments are made vulnerable by technology-empowered citizens as a form of cyber-utopianism.[29] For Morozov, the Internet does not necessarily spread freedom, nor is it the antidote to tyranny. If anything, new information and communication technologies make it easier for governments to monitor their citizens and track political activism, thereby enhancing the ability of authoritarian regimes to monitor what citizens access, stifle dissent, and tighten their grip over their societies.[30]

Authoritarian states in the Middle East may have lost their monopoly over communication, but they have not relinquished their determination to fight back. They have learned to adapt using all means at their disposal, from old-fashioned cyber-police to sophisticated data mining to expensive surveillance equipment.[31] Although new developments in information and communication technologies may have put governments on the defensive,[32] they are far from profoundly altering societal dynamics or irremediably reconfiguring political power. Although the centralized and hierarchical nature of authoritarian regimes and repressive environments makes them rigid and reactive compared to nimble networks and creative digital activists, it does not necessarily disempower them.[33] In fact, authoritarian states are cognizant of the need to transform themselves to better deal with the threats posed by advances in information and communication technologies and to attenuate the impact of fast-changing communication technologies.[34]

Digital Citizens in Contention

In the months after the uprisings in Tunisia and Egypt, corrective accounts to the technology-centric narrative started to emerge. Moving away from the facile analysis of the Arab uprisings, many scholars questioned the extent to which the changing information environment caused the Arab revolutions, pointing out the deep social and economic roots of the protesters' discontent as well as the weight of the region's authoritarian political tradition. For others, this counter-reaction risked overlooking the potentially consequential emergence of non-hierarchical and networked forms of sociality as well as the unintended consequences of new technologies. Significantly, the views of the media skeptics and media enthusiasts alike are premised on functional or instrumentalist approaches toward media that obscure the complex nature of media use and the significance of the broader contexts within which media habits develop. Not only is Internet use embedded in specific contexts that cannot be ignored,[35] but the Internet is itself the space of social participation where the various aspects of sociality interact and intersect, where power dynamics are articulated, and where power relations are constructed.[36] In this perspective, what people do *on* the Internet is as important as the question of what they do *with* the Internet.

Taking heed of these complexities calls for a reformulation of the terms of inquiry in a way that refocuses the analysis away from causation to dynamics. We need to explore how Internet usage and digital communication technologies matter in a complex and interconnected way instead of just looking at their immediate effects. That necessarily entails eschewing the emphasis on the instrumentalist use of the Internet, treating it not so much as a tool to coordinate dissent and mobilize people but as a set of practices and processes that are embedded in everyday life. I am less interested in writing yet another postmortem about the role and impact of the media during the Arab uprisings than in explaining the gradual emergence of a contentious mediated culture. The specific questions that follow from this formulation pertain to the altered sensibilities that developed in tandem with the evolving communication culture. Rather than attempt to tell the story of the region's political changes in a media-intensive era, this case study probes how Internet usage and mediated interactions allowed changes to the category of the political itself—not political communication but the politics *of* communication.

I thus leave behind the comfort zone that has marked the literature on the relationship between information and communication technologies and sociopolitical change to examine the emergence and development of what I call "digital spaces of contention." Throughout this study, I use the terms "digital culture of contention," "digital spaces of contention," and "contentious digital culture" interchangeably to designate an amalgam of social interactions, citizen forms of engagement, cultural practices, ordinary activities, and mundane pursuits that intersect with and are embedded in media experiences, anchored in participatory networks, and intertwined with processes of communication. Contentious digital culture describes dynamics that take shape within an evolving communication culture encompassing a variety of information technologies, media platforms, and communication tools. Contention emerges less as overt dissidence or resistance and more as forms of assertiveness. Contention invokes a set of practices, interactions, engagements, articulations, contestations, and rejections that are not necessarily politically framed but they are political in other ways. Grasping these political dynamics in their full complexity necessitates an interdisciplinary investigation of less formal spaces of engagement and dispersed practices that are associated with everyday life.

Politics and Everyday Life

Tunisia provides a rich and interesting case study that stands out as much for its singularity as it does for its commonality with other Arab nations. It was the first Arab country to connect to the Internet and also the site of the first Arab uprisings. The country also illuminates the acute dilemma of Arab authoritarianism in the age of digital media. On the one hand, Tunisia subsisted for nearly a quarter of a century under the rule of a recalcitrant regime that proved adept at modernizing authoritarianism and ensuring durability. On the other hand, the country adopted an avant-garde Internet development model through which it purposefully sought to build a digital infrastructure capable of positioning it as a model in the age of globalization. Balancing the unlimited promises and subversive potential of new technologies was not easy for a state that considered societal empowerment a threat. Its desire to connect people to modern information and communication technologies while simultaneously striving to keep those same people politically disconnected would prove untenable. The incongruous nature of these two factors contributed to the development of a digital culture of contention that moved from the margins of society to occupy its center stage.

Understanding the lineaments and contours of the contentious digital culture that developed in pre-revolutionary Tunisia calls for a historically grounded and theoretically informed analysis of micro-processes, cultural practices, and societal interactions that intersect with and are embedded in media usage, production, and consumption and anchored in evolving trends of socialized communication that are indissociable from everyday experiences and practices.

The unsuspected complexity of such experience has not received the attention it deserves. A number of social scientists had studied contemporary Tunisia only because it was a case of a phenomenon they were otherwise interested in, the most common being women's rights and authoritarian stability.[37]

One notable exception to what came to be a dominant trend in political science scholarship about Tunisia is Béatrice Hibou's *The Force of Obedience*. Hibou examines the political economy of repression, specifically how the exercise of domination is infused in economic dynamics that permeate people's daily lives and subjects them to a regime many came to view as their only option. Steering clear of an analysis of Tunisia's authoritarian system that focuses on government structures, political institutions, or economic organizations, Hibou proposes "a historical sociology of the political"[38] that unravels the socioeconomic basis for the exercise of power. The central question driving her analysis is how people come to accept or even support practices of domination. Using a Foucaultian approach that takes heed of "the hymn to small things" and favors an "anatomy of political detail,"[39] Hibou sheds light on "everyday domination,"[40] and the way techniques of discipline are woven into everyday social practices. What makes Tunisia particularly interesting is the way the effective exercise of power is associated less with coercive repression and despotic inclinations than it is invested in a set of apparatuses that are ensconced in complex social relations and articulated around "banal kinds of economic and social behavior,"[41] such that subjection and economic security, acquiescence and wealth creation are inextricably linked.

The value of Hibou's work lies in its attempt to complicate our analysis of the system under consideration by reformulating the question of power along the lines developed by Foucault. By privileging the question of the "how" over the "what" and the "why," Foucault shifts the analysis from institutions to techniques. To talk about power is to talk about relationships that are ensconced in a system of social networks: "Power as such does not exist.... Power exists only when it is put into action, even if it is integrated into a disparate field of possibilities brought to bear upon permanent structures."[42] Following Foucault, Hibou re-inscribes power, and the analysis of power, within productive apparatuses ensconced in the realm of everyday life rather than associate them with localizable repressive institutions.

Insightful as it may be, Hibou's work is more concerned with the application of power and the processes though which subjects are constituted than the subversive potential subjects develop under such a system. Despite the affirmation that the system of subjection she outlines is far from being seamless and the exercise of power she meticulously describes is anything but absolute, the emphasis is clearly on the state's domination over its subjects.[43] Although the account she offers pays particular attention to "tensions" and "small scale confrontations"[44] in everyday life by everyday actors that render control more "utopian" than real, it nonetheless affirms the prevalence of the force of obedience over than the force of disobedience. Even if people are at times disposed to reject the system or object to its workings, they inevitably conform to it, and in doing so reaffirm their subjection to the authority and domination of the state. If the force of obedience is susceptible to either "weaken" or "vanish," as Hibou put it, it is not because the system "provided the dominated with significant room for maneuver" but because the "positive elements" upon which repression rested—the socioeconomic well-being of political subjects that clientelism underwrites—became either less obvious or less concrete.[45]

The authoritarian predicament notwithstanding, subjection did not necessarily preclude the development of an impetus that is capable of yielding dynamics, dispositions, and actions that could be potentially consequential. For Foucault, relationships of power are far from being stable or static insofar as configurations of power can potentially induce resistance. "There is no relationship of power without the means of escape," Foucault writes. "Every power relation implies, at least *in potential*, a strategy of struggle."[46] These counter-dynamics are more explicitly and more extensively described in Michel de Certeau's *The Practice of Everyday Life*, which is concerned with the way subjects negotiate their position of power within a particular system. While reiterating Foucault's conceptualization of the way disciplinary technologies, productive apparatuses, and microphysics of power could become extensive and all-encompassing, de Certeau also brings to light "clandestine forms taken by the dispersed, tactical, and makeshift creativity of groups or individuals already in the nets of discipline."[47] For de Certeau, what is important to note is not simply the web of discipline that technologies of power create but also the "network of an anti-discipline"[48] they engender—how marginality is renegotiated and how subjects who are otherwise weak or dominated re-appropriate spaces, discourses, and practices using various tactics, which he dubs the "art of the weak"—a formulation that is echoed in what James Scott terms "the arts of resistance."[49] If these tactics are articulated in everyday life, it is not only because everyday life practices are tactical in essence but also because they are political in nature. In the words of de Certeau, "the ingenious ways in which the weak make use of the strong lend a political dimension to everyday practices."[50]

For a sociologist of the Middle East like Asef Bayat, the everyday life of ordinary people constitutes a de facto site of resistance. It breeds dynamics of change that often go unnoticed because they are associated with "unconventional forms of agency and activism"[51] and articulated around alternative venues of resistance that have the proclivity of reinventing prevailing norms through creative innovation.[52] In *Life as Politics*, Bayat draws attention to a variety of social practices, primarily in urban settings, through which ordinary people either resist or subvert domination. These "social non-movements," as he calls them, "interlock activism with the practice of everyday life,"[53] bringing together "fragmented and inaudible collectives"[54] and devising varied strategies of the "quiet encroachment of the ordinary"[55] on the authority of the autocratic state. In the age of social media, Bayat argues, the ability to connect with other unknown potential actors is enhanced. What social networking sites like Facebook afford is the ability to transcend physical space thus connecting atomized individuals on the social Web in ways that are conducive to the formation of both passive actors and active networks.[56]

What is of interest for this project is not so much the propensity of everyday digital practices to generate social movements or non-movements but the very experience of politics that everyday life tends to inscribe networked publics in, irrespective of whether they see themselves involved in politics or not. To the extent that it is enmeshed with everyday life practices that could potentially affect power relations, the digital experience is inherently political. Yet the political dimension of these practices is often elusive. For the sociologist Henri Lefebvre, the concept of everyday life is constitutive of and intrinsic to social reality, which is tantamount to saying that it is hard to think of culture outside the everyday. At the same time, everyday life refers to a sense of being, to a lived experience that is hard to capture or describe. By definition, the everyday is that which escapes us, being marked by both opacity and ambiguity.[57] Paradoxically, the significance of everyday life rests precisely in its seeming insignificance.

This double bind is also what gives added importance to the digital experience this book discusses. The fact that subtle dynamics of contestation "are not easily observable," as Kurzman points out, makes them all the more worthy of study.[58] Mapping out those spaces of contention calls for a reconceptualization of the digital experience as a revealing feature and a rich dimension of the cultural politics that permeate a changing society. Sreberny perceptively argued that "especially within repressive regimes, when there appears to be no public space for political activity, media foster the politicization of the cultural."[59]

The mediated form of culture that emerges in such context is inherently political, though often in intricate and unsuspected ways.

Accordingly, this study aims to redirect attention from the formal political institutions of the Arab world to the politics of everyday life. It explores the relationship between everyday mediated practices and the subtle sociopolitical dynamics such digital experiences set in motion, while paying special attention to the counter-hegemonic tendencies these experiences encompass and the "counter-publics" they engender.[60] Of particular interest are the evolving forms of contention and modalities of resistance that authoritarianism breeds that are conducive to the reformulation of power relations independently of the institutional framework of formal politics. Such endeavors call for us to retrace the development of contention and to account for its evolution over time. This study takes heed of longer and broader forms of media engagements and communication practices. It privileges a historical investigation that explores the emergence and development of an active Internet culture through which a young generation sought to negotiate its existence over the narrative of the more immediately tangible changes media is believed to have contributed to during the Arab uprisings. I do so not only because the latter aspect has already attracted considerable attention but also because I wish to underscore the significance of less formalized processes that took shape in an increasingly complex media environment over an extended period of time within diffuse, everyday contexts. The attention to the mediated experience of everyday practices has enormous potential for highlighting the way networked publics under authoritarian conditions contest their lived reality and resist a system that grew anachronistic in a globalized culture of connectivity.

Political Mediations

A sociopolitical inquiry into the workings of the digital experience calls for a particular attention to the political dimension but also a reconceptualization of where the latter manifests itself and what it encompasses. I argue that the focus on formal or institutional politics writes off the nonpolitical nature of the political; in doing so it impoverishes the category of the political. In this regard, the case at hand helps shed light on the ways in which online communications, interactions, practices, usages, and interrelations foster what may be termed, after Sreberny, "creative adaptations to the political possibilities of the moment"[61] and thereby reshape power dynamics as such.

A set of interrelated questions arises from this formulation: What are the sociopolitical underpinnings of Internet use in an authoritarian political system? How are political sensibilities articulated in such a context, what form do they take, and under which conditions do they become pronounced? If we assume that the Internet helped nurture political consciousness, stimulate interest, and increase engagement among the youth, through which mechanisms did this reinsertion occur and what were the arenas, spaces, and modalities of this engagement? What is not well understood is how young people develop political interest on the Internet and how they become politicized in a controlled environment that is characterized by the absence of political freedoms. If we concede that the Internet offers a new terrain for political engagement for Arab youth who are believed to have abandoned politics, how do they move from political apathy to involvement? How are they drawn to activism? How is the evolving digital environment redefining the nature of resistance and what kind of experiences figure behind this repositioning? Last, how do seemingly nonpolitical, not to say mundane, actions acquire a political valence?

Answering these questions requires broadening our understanding of politics beyond institutional politics and conventional forms of political involvement. Delimiting the "public political sphere," as Sreberny argues, "often obscures the relationship between communication, culture and politics."[62] Taking heed of the undefined and less demarcated configurations of the political compels us to identify practices and discourses that may not be readily associated with politics or relegated to the realm of the political but which nonetheless structure the political. A re-conception of the category of the political along those lines is amenable to "displacing any unified and stable sense of 'the political' in favor of a more contingent and constitutive set of elements."[63] This line of analysis draws attention to the richness and complexity of everyday culture and gives prominence to otherwise obscure aspects of contemporary mediated everyday experiences. Dissecting how online activities, usages, and interests are integrated into mundane experiences and infused in everyday practices can yield an informed understanding of the significance of incipient trends and changing dynamics.

Central to these dynamics is the notion of citizenship—not so much the legal definition of formal rights, responsibilities, and obligations emphasized in political theory, but in its sociocultural import, which includes participation, engagement, identification, association, recognition, belonging, and inclusion. As used here, citizenship describes certain dispositions, practices, and activities through which individuals attempt to renegotiate—even if unwittingly at times—their relationship with the state. Citizenship is thus less a matter of status (who one is) and instead a category of action (what one does). In this perspective, citizenship manifests itself less in the specific demands of Internet users than in the kind of public engagement those demands favor. An analysis of these forms of engagement can help provide a concrete understanding of how networked publics renegotiate the congealed and delimited notion of citizenship in the absence of political freedoms and democratic governance. Significantly, the case at hand reveals how the growing desire by a substantial segment of the population to renegotiate its relationship with the state helped reclaim the political sphere the regime sought to monopolize. By trying to reposition themselves as citizens rather than mere subjects, networked publics ended up reinventing the category of the political.

Research Design and Interpretative Framework

This book examines an aspect of digital culture that has not been treated with the attention it deserves. The changes and reconfigurations that favored the rise of a more pronounced and potentially consequential digital culture of contention went unnoticed prior to the Arab uprisings. In part, this was because conducting research on such a topic was fraught with difficulties. These included the paucity of systematic and reliable data, the risks to prospective participants of being involved in such research, the lack of trust in the purpose of the research and the intentions of the researchers, the prevalence of anonymity on the Net, and the dearth of studies about the Internet outside the field of communication studies. No less problematic was achieving the necessary critical distance for a researcher to understand these dynamics. Field research in the period following the Arab uprisings often lacked reliability and depth. During the euphoria of the first few months after the ousting of Zine El Abidine Ben Ali, there was a tendency on the part of the interviewees to either favor particular narratives about cyber-activities or to inflate their own importance. The fact that open political engagement became the "norm" after the revolution made it particularly difficult to study older processes of political engagement online. The ephemeral nature of some digital communication and online material constituted yet another complication as some archives and previously posted material were deleted or otherwise became inaccessible. Moreover, Tunisian cyberspace is distinctly multilingual (users communicate in Tunisian dialect, standard Arabic, and French, often concurrently) deterring researchers who are not steeped in either those languages or society. The subject also requires the ability to read the digital culture that emerged from the standpoint of a cultural perspective that is localized, contextualized, and historicized.

As someone who is based in the MENA region and has been studying the changes in the Arab media scene over the past several years, I offer a unique perspective on the developments Tunisia experienced. Long observation of the sociopolitical reality of the region, immersion in everyday life in the Arab world, and native knowledge of the local cultures and languages give me a more nuanced perspective on the intricacies and complexities of the wealth of mediated practices during these periods of change. Retracing this digital culture starts with observing first-hand accounts of users' experiences online and exploring original writings, then immersing oneself in the archives of digital networks, and finally analyzing the contributions of online participants. This study's attention to actual users as empirical subjects and the adoption of a multilayered and historically anchored engagement with the digital experience allows it to analyze and assess changes that manifested themselves gradually and appreciate their rapport with the lived totality. The project therefore weaves together secondary source material and insights gained from field research carried out in Tunisia with textual and content analysis of blogs, online postings from discussion groups, Facebook pages, and other forms of Web-based conversations. Primary material was also collected through an online ethnography, which highlights the richness of the digital experience. This added level of immersion helped contextualize the online conversations and virtual discussions that animated cyberspace.

Using this wealth of research to investigate the development and consolidation of a digital culture of contention yields a compelling account of what happens when digital media takes root in an authoritarian context. While the proposed interpretative description offers a "focalized"[64] understanding of the phenomenon under consideration, it also attempts to push the field in a new direction. Drawing attention to the significance of the unassuming and making visible hidden differentiations challenges the tendency to reify the Arab uprisings using a narrative that essentializes undemarcated communities. In this regard, the case at hand probes the complexity of the lived experience in the digital era as it manifests itself in its ordinariness and unmarkedness.[65] This endeavor necessarily means stepping back from the formal, the immediate, and the revolutionary and putting in perspective the relevance of the cultural, the ordinary, and the everyday.

Scope and Organization

I have organized this book topically and chronologically into two parts. The first provides the sociopolitical context and the historical depth necessary to understand the changing markers of state-society relationship, while the second part focuses on the dynamics, forces, and subtexts that informed the digital culture of contention that developed over time. It is worth noting that the core chapters of the book have a thematic unity that often prevents a lengthy treatment of overlapping media dynamics and communication habits in a single chapter or section. The reader will notice, for instance, that the popular social networking site Facebook and the influential news channel Al Jazeera, which constitute the focus of the penultimate chapter, are only briefly discussed throughout the book. Similarly, the chapter on blogging does not address Facebook in any depth, although, with the intensification of censorship in the two years prior to the revolution, bloggers migrated to Facebook, using the "wall" section of their pages as blogs (which has since been surpassed by the site's emphasis on its "news feed"). If these interlaced dynamics do not often figure side by side in the analysis, it is because focusing too much on individual platforms and media players early on would slow down the narrative. This said, it is important to emphasize the increasingly integrated role of information and communication in the politics of everyday life, which makes the distinction between different media contexts, platforms, and logics increasingly blurry.

A preview of the claims animating the individual chapters will give the reader a sense of what to expect. Chapter 2 provides an overview of the social, economic, and political conditions that characterize contemporary Tunisia with a particular focus on the authoritarian architecture of the system. Paying special attention to the ways in which the modernization of authoritarianism bred exclusionary politics that contributed to the evacuation of the notion of citizenship, this chapter offers pointers for understanding the broad context under which the culture of contention, which came to mark online activism, gradually took hold. Exploring the contextual variables that shaped the authoritarian information environment helps situate the dynamics of contention within a broader framework. The digital culture of contention this study maps out developed in tandem with intermittent instances of civil disobedience and scattered pockets of resistance within society, which are discussed in chapter 3. Curiously, scholars of the MENA region have been keener on theorizing authoritarian resilience and regime durability than on understanding the potential implications of latent forms of resistance—which effectively meant "underestimating the forces for change that were bubbling below, and at times above, the surface of Arab politics."[66] Although these forms of resistance often manifested themselves in a political sphere that was not part of the overall experience of ordinary people, they were important in shaping popular consciousness.

Focusing on offline activism, then, chapter 3 highlights the various challenges the regime faced, pinpoints cracks in the system, and underscores people's growing disposition to question the system. It focuses on a range of contestatory dynamics and militant actions by new and traditional social forces, professional groups, civil society actors, union activists, and political players. Their attempts to voice discontent, seek redress of grievances, and advocate change helped foster a pointed political consciousness, expose the authoritarian nature of the regime, shake off the ingrained culture of fear, and accentuate the crisis of authority that culminated in the popular uprising. These forms of resistance also helped bridge the gap between conventional political activism and digital contestation, thus creating a closer affinity between offline groups and online communities.

Understanding how these dynamics took hold on the Internet necessitates an exploration of structural enabling conditions associated with the state's approach to information and communication technologies. Accordingly, chapter 4 identifies important determinants of Tunisia's emergent digital culture. It outlines the state's Internet strategy and its active promotion of an information society. It then highlights the challenges facing the authoritarian state with the spread of the Internet and the changing patterns of usage and retraces the evolution of digital contention during the early phases of the Internet. Going back in history to the inception of cyber-activism in Tunisia and reconstructing the development of online activism can help identify the contestatory potential of the Internet and map out early forms of digital activism among the first generation of cyber-dissidents who capitalized on the opportunities that Web 1.0 afforded. This contestatory momentum developed around popular and often intersecting online forums with loose dynamics and structures. I focus on five noteworthy experiments during this early phase: TUNeZINE, Reveil Tunisien, Takriz, Tunisnews, and Nawaat. These Net players also deserve attention because they shed light on the contribution of the diaspora to the digital culture of contention that started to take shape.

Chapter 5 examines the rise of blogs with the evolution of the Internet and the advent of Web 2.0. It features authentic voices, changing experiences, and reconfigurations of action—the coming to being of a formative space of contention that later became more expressive, more engaging, and more vocal. While admittedly the blogosphere constituted a small component of the Tunisian Internet, it was arguably one of the most engaging and most revealing about a reconfigured alternative space of freedom that was induced by network-based communication. In a context of shrinking freedoms and increased repression, the critical space blogging fostered helped raise a new consciousness and articulate new expectations. Examining the growing assertiveness of the blogosphere will help point out the contestatory dynamics that started to coalesce and take shape but also accentuated the salience and inevitability of politics.

Encouraging modernization by actively promoting an information society to draw in a young and aspiring population presented an intractable dilemma for the regime. The state's desire to join the global information revolution and promote Internet use and communication was all along tinged with apprehensions about how the intensive use of information and communication technologies could erode the legitimacy of the regime, undermine the hierarchical bureaucracies of the state, displace structures of control, and reconfigure power relations. Increasingly, this balance became hard to maintain. Chapter 6 explores the consolidation of digital networks and the emergence of cyber-movements through examinations of online social networking activities that highlight youth agency and assertiveness. This analytical focus enables us to see how, while responsive to the people's local needs and motivated by the users' frustrations with the kind of Internet control the state practices, youth activism is enacted within a context of globalization in which ideals of freedom and notions of justice become markers of a shared youth culture. Consequently, censorship became one of the rallying causes that helped bridge the gap between dissident bloggers who discussed political issues and often adopted a confrontational approach toward the regime and citizen bloggers who preferred to steer clear of political topics. The regime's attempt to limit the use of media and to stifle digital traffic backfired by generating online initiatives to resist censorship. Although not inspired by overtly political motivations, these small-scale movements were nonetheless rife with political potential. The battle over Internet control helped transform private grumblings about the persistent tendency of the state to impinge on people's right to have open access to the Internet and to communicate freely into a context for forming communities of resistance and enabling a collective movement. Significantly, claiming Internet rights became a context for advocating broader civil and political rights.

Throughout the anti-censorship movement, social media platforms emerged as instrumental in building effervescent forms of digital contention. Thus, chapter 7 identifies micro-Internet practices that favored the silent entry of the youth into the political arena. Focusing on the immersive use of social media platforms, it sheds light on how Facebook became a truly massive phenomenon and a political tool for lay users who had previously steered clear of sensitive issues or political topics. It identifies dynamic forms of political action and highlights the emergence of media-induced counter-politics that appealed to a generation of aspiring digital natives who resented the state's intrusion in their everyday lives. Having mapped out the extent to which social media took hold among a segment of the population, this chapter then shifts its attention to the popular protests that swept the country at the end of 2010 and the beginning of 2011, paying particular attention to the ways various forms of media were used and consumed during the revolution. It provides an analytical narrative of the unfolding of events that toppled Ben Ali, focusing on the mechanisms through which social grievances quickly evolved into political demands and on people's determination to assert their rights, reclaim their citizenship, and redefine their relationship with the state. Of particular interest is the emergence of a new communication environment that was defined by the increased interpenetration between social media networks, citizen journalism, and satellite television. The chapter concludes with an examination of the relationship between new and old media, focusing on how Al Jazeera's antiestablishment inclination and openness to new information and communication technologies connected with cyber-activism.

The book's concluding chapter provides a discussion of the post-revolutionary context and an exploration of what happened to the digital spaces of contention as the country attempted to build a democratic system. It explores the adaptations various contentious voices have undergone since the revolution and reflects on the significance of these changes. More specifically, it looks at the extent to which those who played a role in digital contention prior to the revolution affected and were affected by the changes the country witnessed since 2011 and asks whether they lost their relevance or became embedded; whether they were marginalized or developed the ability to shape the emergent media systems and enhance democratic engagement. While writing about changes that are unfolding and identifying full-fledged trends requires caution, pondering the significance of nascent trends shows the continued relevance of the Tunisian case as it embarks on a new democratic experience.

2

The Mirage of Progress

A Nation's Unfulfilled Promise

The revolution that toppled President Zine El Abidine Ben Ali and forced him into exile after more than two decades of autocratic rule was unexpected. Judging by political considerations, economic factors, and social indicators, Tunisia was not poised for change. Elected political system and modest progress toward democratization, combined with measured economic liberalization and a progressive social orientation, made Tunisia appear stable and even progressive to outsiders and the regime alike. In his address to the World Summit on the Information Society in 2005, Ben Ali boasted to the world of the achievements of his country:

> In Tunisia, we opted for a development model that is guided by the principle of complementarity and correlation between the political, economic, and cultural dimensions as part of a vision that takes into consideration the needs of the current phase and the deep changes the country is witnessing. We have concentrated our efforts on building a modern and developed society, through a reformist project aimed at enlarging the scope of individual and public freedoms, promoting up-to-date legislation, reinforcing democratic practices, protecting human rights, guaranteeing political pluralism, materializing the value of social solidarity, encouraging private initiative, and consolidating the competitiveness of our economy.[1]

For Ben Ali, Tunisia's success story was a testament to the beneficence and wisdom of his rule.

For the regime's opponents, however, this diagnosis was far from accurate. Writing in 2001 about Ben Ali's schemes to cling to power after the end of his constitutional terms, dissident journalist Taoufik Ben Brik lamented that "Ben Ali has done away with the country, criminalized the state, subjected people, fragmented society, dismissed values, broken souls, and mutilated tongues. What can we expect? Nothing. Nearly everything is off track."[2] Many activists agreed. The opposition figure Moncef Marzouki frequently appeared on the widely watched pan-Arab channel Al Jazeera to deliver a similar verdict, audaciously arguing that the Ben Ali regime was beyond salvation.[3] In 2009, shortly after the presidential elections that gave Ben Ali a fifth term in office and a year before the outbreak of the protests that ignited the revolution, Sihem Ben Sedrine, an outspoken journalist and human rights activist, posted an open letter to the president on the Internet. The document was a withering critique and a powerful plea for Ben Ali to step down and spare the country further misfortune. The opening lines depict a bleak image of Tunisia at odds with the official and international appraisal of the country:

> You have misgoverned Tunisia for over twenty years and you just claimed a fifth term of absolute power over our lives and our future. In the eyes of the people, your rule stands for injustice, the deprivation of citizen dignity, nepotism, corruption, and the dilapidation of the country's human and material resources. The country is drifting.... You have disavowed a long-standing tacit ethos which holds that, in Tunisia, the powerful cannot be too powerful and the poor cannot be too poor.... The "consume and shut up" formula your regime prescribed has broken this deal, giving rein to all excesses, plunging a wide section of the middle class into destitution, and favoring the illicit enrichment of a few beneficiaries of the clientelism of the state.[4]

Before the openness of the Arab uprisings, such a public disavowal and unequivocal condemnation was eye-catching.

Understanding how Tunisia got to the desperate state of affairs outlined by Ben Ali's detractors is instructive. Tunisia was ruled by the authoritarian regime of Zine El Abidine Ben Ali for twenty-three years. The regime lacked political and popular legitimacy, because it had seized power in a bloodless palace coup on November 7, 1987. It was also devoid of ideological underpinning, since Ben Ali's regime subscribed to no grand credo and stood for no cause.

His rule was simply a fait accompli that eventually became self-perpetuating. In this chapter, I explain how Ben Ali turned to authoritarian strategies that carefully preserved the appearance of democratization by creating a Potemkin opposition even as the regime cracked down on an Islamist opposition movement that was popular and therefore threatening. The regime's political credo made political dissent and difference unpatriotic. The state's inculcation of a discourse of so-called "responsible freedom" as the basis of good citizenship necessarily meant that public criticism was considered a sign of disobedience. Building a pseudo-consensus and privileging political uniformity over diversity was deemed key to shoring up national unity, maintaining political stability, and consolidating the regime's insincere promises of democratization further down the line. Such strategies also helped contribute to Tunisia's economic growth, through which the regime sought to placate restive internal opponents and also to secure legitimacy on the world stage. Finally, I demonstrate that the West, especially the European Union, was willing to take Ben Ali's representations about his measured "democratization" at face value, thereby justifying their own moves to integrate Tunisia into the Mediterranean world and to use it as a bulwark against Islamist movements.

The Authoritarian Impulse

After its independence in 1956, Tunisia was led by Habib Bourguiba, a French-educated lawyer and charismatic leader who had played a key role in the anti-colonial liberation movement against France (which had governed Tunisia as a protectorate since 1881). Inspired by the Turkish reformer Mustafa Kemal Atatürk, Bourguiba instituted a revolution from above, favoring secularization and social and economic modernization. Under his liberal rule, Tunisia invested in social programs, promoted education, and championed women's freedom. In this effort, Bourguiba was aided by the country's "tradition of national unity."[5] Historically, as an autonomous province under Ottoman rule and a distinct protectorate under French colonization, Tunisia was ruled by privileged families that maintained "centralized and cohesive administrative networks" extending throughout much of its territory.[6] The relative integrity of the country's territory itself endowed the state with legitimacy among the Tunisian people. The tradition of state bureaucracy the country had acquired under Ottoman and French rule led to the development of an urban political elite that was autonomous from kin-based tribal social structures.[7] Having abolished the monarchy and proclaimed the country as a republic following independence, Bourguiba (who, according to his critics, pursued "despotic developmentalism")[8] then took measures to efface tribal identities and dismantle kin-based solidarities as part of his project to establish a cohesive, centralized modern state. As Entelis explains, his success in displacing traditional institutions meant that "the major structures of government... had all become little more than appendages to Bourguiba's system of personal rule."[9]

Despite its moves to modernize Tunisian society, then, Bourguiba's regime was no simple liberal success story. As Tunisia emerged into its post-independence phase and sought to mobilize popular support to consolidate nation-building efforts and achieve socioeconomic development, Bourguiba transformed himself into what Noyon calls a "paternalist authoritarian,"[10] limiting political liberties, pursuing his own political self-interest, and cultivating an imposing cult of personality that was reinforced by his proclamations of himself as president for life in 1974. The late 1970s and early 1980s brought about economic and political challenges that fed instability and intensified uncertainty. With an aging president, the country was spiraling out of control. Given that the political climate was stale, political institutions were in decay, and the state of the economy was deteriorating, the future of the country looked uncertain.[11] With his authority and leadership undermined, the ailing president grew more erratic. The troubled 1980s were the lowest period in Bourguiba's three decades in power.

The wave of unrest and dissidence that erupted in the country in 1984 and was attributed to the Islamists prompted the leadership to crack down on all of its opponents. The regime's choice to implement a more repressive strategy was Ben Ali, a middle-aged general who had previously served as director of national security. He quickly rose to become a minister of state in charge of National Security and then Minister of Interior in 1986. In 1987, he was unexpectedly promoted to prime minister, replacing Rachid Sfar, a technocrat who only a few months earlier had succeeded the long-standing Mohamed Mzali, who had fled the country after he was relieved of his duties. Barely a month into his premiership, Ben Ali seized power in a bloodless coup, installing himself in the presidential palace in Carthage. Many Tunisians were more relieved than enthused about the advent of the new regime. Some saw in the self-proclaimed president a savior and liberator; others deemed him to be an acceptable interim figure who could at least put the country back on track during a transitional phase to an electoral democracy. For his part, the new president portrayed himself as an agent of change and promised a number of reforms. In his maiden speech, he pledged to build a new republic and laid off an agenda for change and reform that seemed well-designed to steer the country away from the authoritarian direction that marked Bourguiba's one-party rule.

The new era was initially marked by a climate of openness and tolerance. There were encouraging signs of liberalizing initiatives and a will to foster a pluralistic political environment and to prioritize the rule of law. Bourguiba's presidency-for-life provision was purged from the constitution, a law regulating political parties was passed, and a few parties were even legally recognized. Likewise, the stringent press laws were relaxed, the security apparatus eased its hold, the state security court was abolished, political prisoners were released, and political dissidents exiled abroad were welcomed back to the homeland. In 1988, the government's engagement with the country's political forces culminated in the signing of the much-touted National Pact, which was to serve as a binding document for all political parties, national organizations, and civic forces in pursuit of reform during the country's transition to democracy.[12] At the beginning of his rule, Ben Ali was not merely open to the opposition's demands; he seemed to incarnate them.

The new regime's relationship with the signatories of the National Pact and other rivals soon curdled. The year 1991 marked what Cavatorta terms an "authoritarian turn."[13] Gradually but unmistakably, the transition period gave way to a restrictive environment marked by resistance to pluralism and the regime's determination to weaken or eliminate dissent. The gulf between the official discourse on participatory politics, democratic progress and rule of law, on the one hand, and the political reality of the country, on the other hand, widened. While advocating an agenda of political change, claiming openness, promising pluralism, and announcing democratizing measures, Ben Ali placed limits on the exercise of democracy, making sure that the political establishment was both structurally and effectively unchallenged.[14] As the regime grew more repressive, Ben Ali's policies differed from Bourguiba's more in their tactics than in the outcomes they sought to realize. Ben Ali tolerated reform only to the extent that it did not challenge the status quo or undermine his absolute control. Despite his pro-democracy rhetoric, Ben Ali ruled with an iron fist. Political rivals and competing voices were either controlled or eliminated. The modest institutional openings provided for by the constitution were either co-opted or strangled: the Parliament (the Chamber of Deputies) had no meaningful voice, the judicial system was subordinated to the regime, the unions were weakened, undesired political parties were banned, and the press was brought under strict control. Being wedded to "exclusivity" and "singularity," as Sadiki put it, Tunisia's political culture precluded power sharing.[15] Citing political stability as the key to economic liberalization and growth, the regime abrogated the National Pact, ending the short period of political tolerance and reform, which were deemed now both disruptive and destabilizing. Thus, genuine political reform and progress toward democratization were deferred in the name of economic growth—although in reality only limited progress was made on the economic front.[16] Over time, it became clear that democratic reform was not on Ben Ali's agenda and that the prospect of his relinquishing control over the political sphere was out of the question.

The Political Game

One of the instruments that consolidated Ben Ali's grip on power was the ruling party, the Democratic Constitutional Rally. The party's genealogy stretches back to the pre-independence Neo-Destour Party, which emerged in 1934 from Abdelaziz Al Thaalbi's more traditionalist anti-colonial Destour Party. After independence, Bourguiba changed its name to the Destourian Socialist Party and made it central to his rule. Ben Ali climbed to the top echelons of the party to become a member of its executive committee and then its secretary general. Once in power as president, rather than sidelining the party for its long association with Bourguiba and its permeation with Bourguibists, Ben Ali renamed it the Democratic Constitutional Rally in 1988 and employed it as a tool of his regime. He recruited a young generation of well-educated advocates of progressive social programs who rejuvenated its regional and local bureaus, widened its base, and consolidated its mobilizational function. The ruling party expanded its national infrastructure, growing a presence in every urban and rural district and boosting its membership base to more than two million people. Shorn of the political vision and authority Bourguiba had, Ben Ali fell back on the institutional legacy of the ruling party. His centralizing strategy was successful and the party dominated Tunisia politically, ideologically, and structurally.

Unlike Bourguiba, Ben Ali lacked both charisma and a grand vision, and the Democratic Constitutional Rally reflected those qualities. The party lost its ideological dimension; its new leaders were technocrats, not visionaries. Furthermore, it became difficult to distinguish the ruling party's apparatus from that of the state. The party's homogenization of politics marginalized nearly all other political institutions. The appropriation of the party by a business circle associated with the regime meant that the party grew to become identified with problems in the economy and polity.[17] The increasing imbrication of the president's opportunistic business circle into political life and their exploitation of prominent party positions to reinforce their hold on the economy took away some of the political prerogatives of the ruling party and aggravated the problem.[18]

Cognizant of the need to project an image of tolerance toward political pluralism, Ben Ali orchestrated the creation of a façade opposition to enable him to claim that he was undertaking political reform and thereby satisfying the West's expectations of democratic progress. In effect, the regime instituted a political pseudo-pluralism.[19] Not surprisingly, although six parties were officially recognized, the opposition was never allowed to organize freely, develop effectively, or play a significant role in the political process. Reforms to the electoral code compelled parties to compete among themselves rather than with the ruling party, which weakened the opposition. Owing their status as political opposition to the regime, lacking financial independence or a popular base, and being dependent on a quota system for their parliamentary presence, the few legal credible opposition parties—like the Progressive Democratic Party and the Democratic Front for Labor and Liberty—operated with great difficulty under a regime that confined their activities to the role that was prescribed for them: a moderate opposition that criticized but could never replace the regime.[20] The Islamist party Ennahda was banned while secular parties that adopted a confrontational approach, like the Congress for the Republic, were not legally recognized or allowed to function.[21] Through such constrained opposition parties, Ben Ali eliminated his more formidable opponents (i.e., the Islamic movement) while keeping the less than threatening official opposition under his thumb.

Although the electoral code was amended to allow the opposition to be represented in the Parliament, the number of seats that went to the opposition in the 1994 and 1999 legislative elections remained insignificant. The ruling party was guaranteed a disproportionate share of seats, precluding the legislature from instituting any checks and balances. Ironically, introducing deputies from the opposition in the Parliament went a long way toward discouraging the formation of alternative views, making the ruling party's exercise of power even more authoritarian.[22] In a political environment where power centered on the figure of the president, supposed reforms aimed at infusing the system with a slightly varied parliamentary representation lent "a veneer of pluralism," as Angrist described it, at the expense of meaningful pluralistic and participatory politics.[23]

In his capacity as head of state, and in addition to presiding over the ruling party and nominating the party's top officials, the president held power over the military, the administration, the diplomatic front, the constitutional outlook, and the legislative body. The controlled pluralism Ben Ali engineered ensured a perpetual monopoly over the presidency. Elections were mostly for show. In 1989 and 1994, Ben Ali ran unopposed and obtained 99 percent of the votes. In the 1999 and 2004 elections, he faced only handpicked challengers, and was re-elected with 99.44 percent and 94.48 percent of the votes, respectively. In 2002, the Parliament approved constitutional changes designed by the president's close advisers that lifted the term limits on the presidency and raised the maximum age limit for the candidates. Following a staged referendum designed to display a popular adoption of the constitutional amendments, Ben Ali was re-elected in 2009 for a fifth consecutive term with 89.62 percent of the votes. For many, this appeared to be a prelude to a presidency for life. Ben Ali further reinforced that perception by adopting a law giving the president immunity from prosecution for acts carried out while in office. The national mythology of change Ben Ali promoted to eclipse Bourguibism was giving way to sameness. Over the years, invoking the need for gradualism and claiming some progress in political reform became a way of perpetually delaying genuine reform while consolidating the power of the regime. Significantly, even as these measures guaranteed the continuity of the Ben Ali rule, his legitimacy eroded. The regime's monopoly on power, the immovability of political players, and the absence of a system of checks and balances succeeded in neutralizing political threats but also made the regime incapable of evolving.[24]

The Islamists' Challenge

In contrast to the regime's carefully calibrated regulation of the secular opposition, the Islamic opposition was outlawed and its members persecuted. The perceived threat of Islamist revivalism in the 1990s was used to consolidate Ben Ali's autocratic rule and defend its regime against critiques of intangible democratic progress, infringements on citizen rights, and human rights abuses. For the regime and its apologists, more political liberalization could bring the well-organized Islamist movement to power and undermine real democratic progress given its ideological positions. The rise of Tunisia's Islamist opposition can be situated in the context of the country's ideological indeterminacy, political evolution, and socioeconomic realities, which favored the rise of a movement that advocated a sense of rectitude based on religious values, contested the government's economic choices, and demanded more political openness.[25] Initially taking the form of a cultural and religious renewal movement with no explicit political agenda, Islamist activism crystallized in 1981 with the founding of the Movement of the Islamic Tendency. Conceiving of themselves as modernizers, the Islamists actively sought to expand their influence. The Islamic movement may have drawn strength from the success of the Islamic revolution in Iran, but it could also be viewed as a political counterculture that emerged in the 1970s as a reaction to Bourguiba's growing authoritarianism and as an articulation of the unfulfilled expectations of people in the face of economic hardship and social inequality, particularly as the government's determined attempt to weaken the unions left a political void.[26] As a comparatively moderate, peaceful, and democratic organization, the Islamic movement acquired a popular base, particularly among the middle and lower classes.[27]

In the post-independence era, Bourguiba purposefully limited the influence of Islam because religious based dissent was antagonistic to his vision. When dealing with the rise of political Islam, he adopted a pragmatic mixture of conciliation and pressure.[28] However, the movement's attempt to assert itself at the end of Bourguiba's rule was met with a firm and brutal government response. Many Islamist sympathizers and activists were arrested, tortured, and sentenced to prison. The 1987 coup altered these dynamics temporarily. For Ben Ali, the Islamist movement could be better controlled if it operated within the country's political structure; for the movement, in turn, the change presented an opportunity to be a formal player in the national political scene.[29] And so the regime and the movement—which changed its name to the Renaissance Movement Party (known as Ennahda) in the run for official political party status—attempted to engage each other within the framework of the National Pact the country's political players signed in 1988. Thus, while the government took some measures aimed at conciliating state and religion and allowed Ennahda to publish a newspaper, the latter agreed to the liberal principles of the Personal Status Code, which banned polygamy and gave women civil rights and social status unparalleled in the Arab and Muslim world.

It soon became clear that reestablishing dialogue with Islamists and making overtures for their support were political maneuvers made by a new and unsteady regime seeking survival, not genuine reforms. Once in control, Ben Ali feared that Islamist competition could endanger Tunisia's system of political conformity, challenge the ruling party's dominance, and jeopardize the regime.[30] Ennahda's political potential as a mass party was evident in its members' performance in the 1989 parliamentary elections and 1990 municipal elections. Although the party did not win seats in the Parliament under the country's winner-take-all electoral system, it showed a significant ideological, mobilizational, and organizational strength.[31] Wary of the increased political activism of the Islamists and the emergence of Ennahda as a potentially important player and a significant force in the political realm, Ben Ali sought to discard the Islamists,[32] positioning himself, as Perkins describes him, as "the defender of a progressive, secular republic under threat from religious chauvinism while melding his vision of constrained political pluralism with a modified version of his predecessor's authoritarianism."[33]

Ben Ali's decision not to recognize Ennahda in 1989 radicalized the movement. The period between 1990 and 1992 was one of increased tension marked by demonstrations and waves of arrests and repression. The confrontation instigated a level of indiscriminate political violence unseen since Bourguiba's turbulent years. At the same time, Ennahda's support for Saddam Hussein during the 1991 Gulf War raised Western concerns and brought about the resentment of the Gulf monarchies. Confronted with the eruption of violence and alarmed at the strength of the Islamic Salvation Front in neighboring Algeria, the regime adopted a hard line against the Islamist movement, arresting, torturing, and imprisoning its members; monitoring its followers; harassing its sympathizers; and forcing its leaders into exile. In the absence of a tradition of political contestation,[34] those who had an Islamist affiliation or inclination were declared enemies of the state. Official discourse portrayed Ennahda as a setback to modernization, framed its politics as a threat to democracy, and characterized its project as an attempt to impose Islamic law through the ballot box. The regime's determination to marginalize the Islamist movement and eradicate its networks forced Ennahda to go underground by the mid-1990s.

Legitimacy through Growth

A key counterpart to the regime's political repression was its goal of reinforcing its legitimacy by delivering on the economic front.[35] Ben Ali understood full well that democratic pretensions without economic achievements would make his political authority both hollow and untenable. The vitality of the economy was crucial to shore up a politically closed regime and generally more people were willing to forsake political liberty and participatory politics for stability, economic prosperity, and quality of life.

In this, Ben Ali was not oblivious to two key incidents in the country's recent history. The general strike of January 26, 1978, which descended into violence that culminated in Black Thursday, and the bread uprising of January
1984, which erupted following the government's elimination of subsidies on
basic consumer goods, were fresh memories when Ben Ali came to power. The
instability the country witnessed during the last few years of Bourguiba's rule
underscored Tunisia's deteriorating economic situation and the urgency of
introducing economic reforms.[36] While oil revenues fell, investment levels
and public expenditures remained high. Similarly, the government's heavy reliance on the public sector was not conducive to economic development. To
address these issues, the government reluctantly adopted structural economic
reform. This meant the implementation of an IMF and World Bank structural
adjustment plan aimed at increasing privatization and privileging a market
economy. However, the economy continued to deteriorate, and in the mid-
1980s the country found itself with mounting debt and an overvalued currency,
which risked engendering an acute shortage of foreign exchange reserves.[37]

In an attempt to halt the economic slide, Ben Ali accelerated the implementation of the structural adjustments that started by taking measures that would
help control spending and boost private investment. Reducing government
spending meant cutting deficits, decreasing government debt, and carefully
reducing consumer subsidies as well as reforming the tax system and privatiz-
ing wasteful state-owned companies. Similarly, the government pursued an
export-led growth that was amenable to integrating it more fully in the liberal
global economy. This was evident in the continued efforts to attract off-shore
companies and foreign firms lured by an educated though cheap labor force,
fiscal advantages, and good infrastructure, but also in the association agreement it signed with the European Union (EU) in 1995 and the bilateral trade
agreements it signed with a number of Arab countries. To prepare itself for the
challenges that come with global competition, particularly in the industrial sector,
Tunisia implemented an industrial upgrading program. It also embarked on a
gradual dismantling of trade protection, took trade facilitation measures to
increase the efficiency of its administrative structures, and pursued fiscal reform.

These measures, along with the stability that defined Ben Ali's rule, transformed the economy. Overall, Tunisia did relatively well throughout much of
the Ben Ali era. Since the mid-1990s, growth rates have been consistently above
5 percent per annum, inflation held at around 4 percent, and the budget deficit
kept at manageable levels. Debt service declined, private sector investment
rose, exports and foreign exchange reserves increased, income distribution

was relatively balanced, poverty rates were reduced, population growth was controlled, and home ownership rates grew.[38] Tunisia had a steady annual growth in GDP per capita (in purchasing power parity), which reached $6,859 in 2006, second in the Maghreb only to Libya.[39] Steady investment in human capital development, particularly in the education and health sectors, went a long way toward enhancing productivity growth and increasing competitiveness.

The country's economic growth impressed many foreign analysts and observers. According to a 2008 World Bank Report, Tunisia was "among the best performers in the region and in emerging countries."[40] In her effusive book *Tunisia: A Journey through a Country that Works*, Georgie Anne Geyer summarized a commonly held Western view: "What characterizes Tunisia more than any other country in the region is its movement.... In Tunisia, people have good jobs, they own their homes, there is education for everyone, social insurance, a representative government, a responsible leadership, a practical set of principles behind the state, a poverty that is diminishing every day, planned economic moves and virtually unlimited hope for the future."[41] Indeed, the aggregate indicators and socioeconomic factors looked reasonably good. The country's stability, economic dynamism, and social modernity were particularly enchanting for its Western allies, who trumpeted its development story. Tunisia was proclaimed to be a success story and a trendsetter, representing "a rare model that works in the developing world."[42] President Jacques Chirac of France even declared Ben Ali's Tunisia a "miracle" on the basis of its economic progress, social success, and apparently radiant future.[43]

These much-touted economic growth statistics came at a price. They emanated out of what Entelis refers to as a fused system of political oppression and social-economic liberalization[44] that defied the premise upon which the engagement of Western liberal establishment with Tunisia rested. Contrary to the widespread view about the relationship between market reforms and democratic political developments, market-oriented reform and favorable economic performance in Tunisia did not bring about political reform or democratization; if anything, as King has argued, "they contributed to the hardening of authoritarianism and provided the material basis on which authoritarianism was reconfigured in a less populist form."[45] In essence, the durability of the Ben Ali regime rested on a ruling bargain often referred to as a "security pact,"[46] "social pact,"[47] or "bread pact."[48] The ruler promised a profitable economy and modern consumer lifestyle in return for his subjects' political deference. The pact that was forged necessarily wedded development to authoritarianism, pitted economic growth against democratic progress, and combined economic laissez-faire with societal control. Underlying the strategy of economic reform was a security component. Economic development could garner the kind of business and popular support necessary to ward off social unrest and foreclose alternative political visions or competing programs. The regime also used its control of the economy to favor the economic players and to win their support, neutralize the power of organized labor, provide reasonably good living conditions for a relatively large middle class to secure their acquiescence, and support the unprivileged class to make them beholden to the regime.

The strategy did not benefit all players equally. Business fared better than labor, for instance. Cognizant of the importance of controlling the labor movement and the need to forge alliances with viable economic players, the regime moved to tame the labor organization while courting the business elite. Although the Tunisian General Labor Union, the country's main labor organization, had a long history, a militant tradition, and a broad legitimacy, its power and influence often went through ebbs and flows. Advancing market reforms, entering into international economic agreements, and increasing the power of private capital undermined the Union's bargaining power and contributed to diminishing labor's influence, eventually prompting the central leadership to support Ben Ali and the state party. Although the rank and file remained militant, state coercion hindered collective organization and unified action.[49] The regime thus faced little resistance from a historically potent political force that had traditionally been a strong advocate of a welfare state.

While the liberalization of the economy further vitalized the economy, it concretely favored a business community that was dependent on the regime for patronage.[50] The business sector was a natural constituent of the government's economic reform program, which meant that the palace closely managed the economy to serve its political ends. As Christopher Alexander explains, "President Ben Ali and a small circle of insulated technocrats have done more than design a prudent sequence of reforms. They have micro-managed the day-to-day implementation of those reforms—picking the players, actively shaping the relations between them, cajoling them to behave in ways that support the government's agenda."[51] A relationship of clientelism developed whereby the regime privileged those economic players who were close to it and designated preferred business partners based on their support for and allegiance to Ben Ali. The system's reliance on a combination of patrimonial ties and corporatist ties meant that key business players became supporters of authoritarian perpetuity.[52]

The regime's appropriation of the economy for political gains went beyond its influence on the business elite. For the urban middle class, the thriving economy translated into individual financial success and the attainment of a fairly good standard of living. The development of consumerism and the facilitation of credit enabled many people to expand their purchasing power while luring others to live above their means.[53] Ben Ali was keen on making the country's economic achievements under his rule palpable not only to the middle class but also to the poor and the unprivileged. Accordingly, he established a number of initiatives aimed at enhancing the redistribution of the generated growth. In 1999, he established the National Solidarity Fund 26/26 to ease economic distress in the less privileged regions, provide basic services, and impact the daily experience of low-income families. In the same year, the National Solidarity Bank was set up to finance small projects. In 2000, the National Fund 21/21 was established to deal with unemployment. The fact that many people benefited from these initiatives should not obscure their real nature. The prevailing logic of what Saïdi calls "the criminalization of poverty" that was adopted by the state was more impelled by political calculations than it was dictated by economic exigencies.[54] Although these initiatives did help reduce inequality, improve the living conditions of the poor, and support the lower middle class, they were aimed principally at boosting Ben Ali's popularity, shoring up public support for the regime, and undermining the Islamists whose situation threatened to impinge on the country's guarded political sphere.[55]

While pursuing what Ayeb terms "a systematic clientelistic policy of selective redistribution of resources,"[56] the regime also made the well-being of a segment of the population inextricably linked to their support of the regime. With the levels of consumption rising among the middle class, most people were indebted and therefore not in a position to protest or criticize the government for fear of economic reprisals. In order to tighten its control over socioeconomic life and further the system of clientelism, the regime used the ruling party, which had a membership base of 2.5 million—roughly a quarter of the total population, even though many of these were not willing members. To a large degree, the party was successful in its endeavor "to extend its influence across a great proportion of the population by promising social mobility, professional success and an increase in wealth."[57] Still, maintaining a delicate balance between economic progression and political regression would prove to be challenge. Midway through Ben Ali's rule, one commentator noted the degree to which the regime's stability rested on economic growth: "As long as the economy picture remains reasonably positive, regime stability may be assured. But in the event of an economic downturn, the lack of peaceful and effective means for citizens to voice discontent suggests that over the medium to long term, instability could well loom on Tunisia's political horizon."[58] Thus, it is to the economic challenges that we now turn.

An Illusionary Stability

In spite of the social achievements the regime touted, the economic strategy the country adopted was not without challenges. Underneath the surface of positive macroeconomic performance indicators, notable challenges were evident. For one, although the growth rate of the Tunisian economy was relatively high when considered in the context of North Africa, it was rather low when compared to the growth rate in other developing countries. The emphasis on the overall economic indicators is also problematic because it does not account for the distribution of economic growth across different classes and regions, which turned out to be consequential. Accelerating the pace of structural adjustments that started in the early 1980s and embarking on liberal economic reform had social implications, the most significant of which was perhaps increased inequality.[59] Overall, the policy choices and the unrealized potential of the economy engendered socioeconomic deprivation, class disparity, rampant social inequality, regional imbalance, and uneven development. The regime's economic policies privileged the capital and favored the development of the prosperous big coastal cities, which benefited from a concentration of tourist resources and industrial projects; it also increased the gap between the country's affluent north and impoverished south. Although the south and southwest region were not lacking in natural resources, such as phosphate, the revenues from the latter were diverted to urban centers in the north and the east. While coastal cities benefited from decades of intensive extraction and geographical transfer of wealth from the inner regions, most of the local populations in these resource-rich towns were reduced to the status of impoverished laborers.[60] The fact that this marginalization was simultaneously regional, economic, social, and political left many people in these regions resentful. Both real and symbolic discrimination against those who inhibit the more marginalized interior of the country became a pointed manifestation of a system that grew to be increasingly more exclusive.[61]

Tunisia's annual growth level was not sufficient to bring down unemployment, which according to official figures stood at a steady 14 percent. Contributing to the problem was the nature of the new jobs. For example, growth in key sectors like agriculture and the textile industry generated low-wage jobs.[62] Equally problematic was the favoring of low-risk sectors like tourism and trade for growth and job creation over economic sectors that could yield high levels of good-paying employment. Focusing on exporting cheap manufactured products to European markets contributed to the country's economic growth but failed to take economic development to a new level. The structure of the economy was not amenable to developing skill-intensive sectors that would provide high-skilled jobs for youth with university degrees. The adoption of a quasi-rentier economy that revolved around the country's natural resources, cheap tourism, and export-destined agriculture did not keep up with the exigencies posed by the changing demographic structure of the country, which yielded a highly educated workforce waiting to be absorbed into the labor force. Overall, the economy remained fragile, relying to a great extent on sectors that could only offer low economic–added value.

The economy's structural difficulties were made all the more complex by the interpenetration of the world economy. Not only did some economic sectors rely on a set of fluctuating external variables (such as oil prices and migrant labor remittances from Tunisians in Europe and the oil-rich Gulf countries) and volatile conditions (like rainfall), but the global integration policies also made the country vulnerable to the European economic conditions.[63] Tourism in particular suffered disproportionally after 9/11 and the global war on terror. As the first decade of the twenty-first century drew to an end, the global financial crisis brought an added level of uncertainty to the tourist industry and the economic woes in the northern shores of the Mediterranean reduced the purchasing power of potential European tourists, thus harming the economic well-being of thousands of families whose livelihood depended on tourism. The country's foreign currency reserves were also considerably reduced as tourism fell. With cutbacks also affecting international development programs, the opportunities for the economy to rebound grew slim.

These problems raised questions about the viability of the country's much-vaunted economic model. The negative social impact of the IMF- and World Bank–prescribed economic reforms cannot be underestimated. Not surprisingly, promoting exports over self-sufficiency in the agricultural sector made the country vulnerable to increasingly volatile international markets for food,[64] which in turn contributed to the economic plight of the average Tunisian family.[65] In theory, the neoliberal prescription advocated liberalization and building strong supportive state structures, which allowed reforms to work effectively and take hold. In practice, the failure to vigorously implement those supporting structures in the absence of democratic institutions and practices—a reality

Western donors and international monetary institutions disregarded—provided a favorable terrain for the emergence of a moneyed elite who would reap economic benefits and political dividends from structural adjustment.

The deterioration of living standards and the shrinking of the middle class went hand in hand with the concentration of wealth in the hands of a select few. Deepening inequality between classes, mounting social and economic grievances, increased debt, reduced purchasing power, bleak employment prospects, and steadily growing impoverishment were made all the more obvious by the unprecedented rise of ostentatious consumption by the small and economically privileged urban class. Endemic problems of lack of transparency, economically distorting bureaucracy, and mismanagement were compounded by economic clientelism and rampant corruption. The second decade of Ben Ali's rule was marked not only by the strengthening of autocratic rule but also by the deepening of nepotism. Over the years, the regime developed "a culture of crony capitalism,"[66] as Murphy calls it, that fostered an aggressive extractive mentality and led to the concentration of wealth in the hands of a few. As Benalism become synonymous in the popular imagination with oligarchic power, the image of the state degenerated into a group of profiteers. The president's family and in-laws had a near monopoly on viable economic sectors and lucrative businesses. Their accumulation of economic privileges was accompanied by their flaunting of power, which translated into more wealth.

Corruption has been a constant feature in Tunisia, but as the regime grew more rapacious it reached intolerable proportions. There was an obsession with the accumulation of wealth and the pursuit of personal enrichment through extortion, shady deals, and unlawful activities such as the acquisition of privatized state companies substantially below their real value, the takeover of public sector institutions and companies, and the institutionalization of monopolies inhibiting free-market operations. Not surprisingly, Tunisia fared poorly in integrity indicators.[67] Inevitably, the enrichment of a small group at the expense of the rest of the population generated widespread resentment.[68] Economic competitiveness was reduced, giving rise to a monopolistic mindset that bred uncertainty in the business environment and curbed foreign investment, leading to a sluggish domestic investment and contributing to the weakness of the private sector.[69] Socially, the rise of a patronage system favoring a small and inner circle undermined the rule of law and sanctioned the circumvention of state institutions, constituting a threat to society's values and morals. Considering that "corrupt authoritarian regimes are generally brittle,"[70] these tendencies were ominous. The economic, social, and moral dimensions would bear strongly on the protests, demonstrations, and convulsions that shook the country in 2010.

Cheated Dreamers

The shaky situation of the middle class was revealed by the intersections between social and political problematics. Although the protests initially took place in the marginalized southeast and the unprivileged populations in the interior cities, they were closely associated with the middle class, which was larger and more ingrained in the northern region and the urban centers. To some extent, the Tunisian dream, as traditionally envisioned by the state, was to aspire to be part of a comfortable middle class—a goal that had been intimately connected with the country's post-independence modernization. The interlaced social, economic, and political nature of this popular pursuit is instructive. With the failure of the Socialist experiment in the early 1960s, Tunisia sought to widen and bolster the middle class in a way that preempted class antagonism and fostered social homogeneity. With the country's economic problems in the first half of the 1980s and the subsequent adoption of a structural adjustment program, this vision—as much a political maneuver as it was an economic choice—was no longer sustainable. The liberal economic policies that were put in place enriched a small class but negatively affected the economic well-being of the middle class and led to its perpetual shrinking. Compounding this trend were both the declining effectiveness of the trade unions and the changes in labor laws that were enacted in the mid-1990s favoring contractual employment and term contracts over lifetime employment. This created a substantial category of workers who were not included in labor negotiations and therefore did not have full entitlement to social security benefits.[71] Diminishing opportunities also favored the rise of a massive informal economy centered on clandestine activities and illegal trans-border trade, creating an entire subclass whose situation was precarious at best.[72] Fiscal policies contributed to this disparity, particularly the adoption of a strict tax policy toward the salaried segment of society while exercising a lax approach toward the entrepreneurial and business class.[73] Rising inflation further reduced the purchasing power of an already indebted population. The worldwide price rises in basic commodities in 2010 constituted an added burden. In this context, the dramatic increase in unemployment and underemployment among college graduates was a development that struck at the heart of the value system of meritocracy upon which the country was erected and the model of social mobility that had reigned since independence. For many people, the fear of downward mobility and of losing one's social standing, irrespective of one's educational level, was more than an economic matter.[74] What prevailed henceforth was the specter of what may be termed, after Bayat, "the paradoxical class of 'middle-class poor.'"[75]

A key element in the equation is the potential of education. After independence, Tunisia made education a national priority. For the state, the opportunities education afforded served its development strategy. For the middle class, education has been the principal instrument for social mobility. Families believed and invested in the education of their children in the hope of positioning them for a better future. For decades, one of the hallmarks of the national education system was rigor and competitiveness. However, in the uncertain 1980s, the state's tendency to forego selectivity and specialized pedagogical training as criteria for hiring schoolteachers affected the quality of education. Over the years, this deterioration was felt within high school education as the level of rigor decreased and pedagogical mentoring ceased to be a priority. Enrollment expansion in schools took precedence over quality.[76] The 1990s marked the real onset of diminishing expectations as the state pursued a more lax educational policy guided in part by narrow political calculations and in part by reform expectations of donor international financial institutions. Successful education and degree earning were marketed as accomplishments of the regime, which inflated success rates for political gains. Similarly, the implementation of World Bank recommendations and the favoring of increased graduation rates meant giving less weight to national exams, incrementally transforming what had traditionally been a determining role of the latter from gatekeepers to floodgates. As a consequence, the percentage of high school graduates with a baccalaureate degree jumped from around 30 percent in the 1990s to more than 50 percent in the first decade of the twenty-first century. During presidential election years, the success rate was as high as 66 percent. Within the span of a decade or so, the number of college students doubled, and by 2010 fully one-third of Tunisians ages nineteen to twenty-four were enrolled in institutions of higher education.[77]

Both quantitatively and qualitatively, the education policy was out of sync with the country's needs and job market.[78] As structural adjustment proceeded, the state ceased to be a massive employer and the role of the public sector in employment receded. As noted earlier, the private sector could not

create high-skilled jobs fast enough to keep pace with rising numbers of degree holders. Nor could graduates easily go abroad. The degradation in the
quality of public schools devalued Tunisian academic and professional degrees
on the international job market as they had been debased at home. Because
curricula had not been linked to evolving professional requirements and market expectations, most university graduates lacked practical training or professional experience. The educational system did not promote creativity and
institutional research and development lagged behind, stifling innovation and
considerably affecting the value of education as a social asset. Education no
longer offered a defense against social exclusion because more education
meant a lower probability of employment and decreasing chances for social
mobility and economic improvement.

Unemployment was a daunting challenge. With 60 percent of the population under twenty-five years of age, the Arab world is one of the most youthful
regions in the world.[79] Nearly half of Tunisia's population is under twenty-
five.[80] This "demographic gift"[81] or "youth bulge"[82] proved to be a complex
asset. More than ever before, youth unemployment and exclusion became
pressing problems for the government, which found itself unable to effectively
boost job creation, particularly among the better educated youth. As estimated
by the World Bank, while the general unemployment rate was 14 percent, the
unemployment rate among individuals below twenty-five years of age was
twice that much, and among college graduates three times as much.[83] According to some reports, in 2008, unemployment among young people aged between fifteen and twenty-nine was as high as 31 percent, representing 72
percent of the unemployed population.[84] During the first decade of the twenty-
first century, the number of college graduates who entered the job market
increased substantially from 20 percent in 2000 to 55 percent in 2008,[85] while
the economy could absorb only a quarter of the country's eighty thousand annual university graduates. The private sector could not reduce unemployment
in any significant way, being able to absorb only 5 percent of the graduates.
Similarly, the public sector's capacity to provide employment was considerably reduced by neo-liberal policies. With a young population, the problem of
unemployment (and of social marginalization) was bound to worsen.

Increasingly, people looked away from Tunisia for solutions. The surge in
illegal emigration to developed countries highlighted the shrinking opportunities at home. The development gap between the southern and northern
shores of the Mediterranean tempted droves of young people to risk their lives
in search of a better future. The development of lucrative networks of illegal

emigration to favorite European destinations like the Italian island of Lampedusa and the dramatic increase in the number of deaths among illegal immigrants during their wretched sea journeys are indicative of the prevalence of this phenomenon. No less notable was the country's growing brain drain (as many of the students who studied abroad preferred not to return home upon graduation) and legal immigration among the active workforce, the more educated middle class, and the professional elite desirous of better opportunities overseas. For those who found Europe inaccessible, the contractual employment opportunities in the resource-rich Gulf countries were particularly attractive. For the government, these worrying trends conveniently eased the pressure on the national labor market, kept unemployment at a steady—even if relatively high—rate, and provided an important source of remittances in hard currency. Although emanating out of economic strains and indicative of the structural limits of the economy, these orientations came to constitute an economic policy that left structural problems unaddressed.

A Captive Society

Ironically, as politics grew more oppressive and the country's economy more straitened, the more sanitized the national media sphere became. So intense was the atmosphere of denial that a casual newspaper story dealing with beggars in the streets of the capital city would be censored on grounds that it could harm the image of the country and affect foreign investment and tourism. During the global financial meltdown, the government claimed that the country had weathered the crisis thanks to Ben Ali's sensible leadership. Given the importance of economic performance for the stability of the regime, the government also went out of its way to silence critical voices. Despite an already draconian press code, the government-controlled Parliament approved measures criminalizing statements to foreign organizations that were deemed harmful to Tunisia's vital interests.[86] The vague formulation of these measures was such that any voices that were critical of the regime and its policy choices and human rights record could be silenced.

The stifling of dissent and intolerance toward criticism went hand in hand with the weakening of associational life and the containment of civil engagement. To reinforce its stranglehold on society, the regime extended its control beyond formal politics, forging *liaisons dangereuses* with civil actors at the expense of freedom while never allowing civil society to put down grass roots or exert real pressure.[87] A 2009 Amnesty International report noted that, among the country's nine thousand or so registered civil society organizations, only a handful were fully independent and none were free from government interference.[88] While several organizations and associations were denied legal status, many of the authorized ones were permanently kept in a precarious political and material state.[89] Independent organizations that were predisposed to resist government interference—like the Tunisian League for Human Rights, the Association of Tunisian Judges, the National Union of Tunisian Journalists, and the General Union of Tunisian Students—were weakened, co-opted, and infiltrated. In order to manipulate critique, independent governing boards were in some instances replaced by pro-government members, resulting not merely in a crippling lack of autonomy but a relationship of cooperation with the regime at the expense of the interests of the constituents.[90] Although a handful of active organizations with recalcitrant voices emerged, they were not officially recognized as with the Association for the Support of Political Prisoners, the Association for the Fight against Torture, the Center for the Independence of the Judiciary, the Observatory for the Freedom of the Press, the National Council for Civil Liberties, and Equity and Liberty—all of which were denied official status, which left them operating precariously as illegal entities that were often subjected to harassment by the authorities and smear campaigns by the pro-government press. Throughout the years, noted one report, "the distance between government and civil society actors has become greater and as a result, positions on each side have become more radicalized."[91] Significantly, the targeting of associational life, the weakening of organizational activity, and the cowing of civil society dried up the channels for effecting peaceful societal change. In the absence of mediating channels and political alternatives, communication between the government and the people—in fact, public debate as such—was nearly nonexistent. The regime became intent on closing down all nonconformist spaces of expression, thus precluding venues for true engagement, honest debate, and the expression of healthy difference.

The regime discouraged active citizenship outside structures it could control. The muzzling of independent voices, views, and visions helped perpetuate a monolithic, univocal, and exclusionary discourse. Under Ben Ali, Tunisia was reduced, at least publicly, to a country that was devoid of struggle, stripped of diversity, and denuded of difference. Significantly, acquiescence to this prescribed and circumscribed reality was induced by the adoption of a fused system of instrumental social liberalization and systematic depoliticization. The political survival of the regime impelled a modernization of authoritarianism through the adoption of progressive social policy choices, which, if dissociated from political appropriation, could have been real assets for development. This included the unassailable adoption of the liberal 1956 Personal Status Code—a code Bourguiba strongly advocated in his endeavor to build a modern state and consolidate state power in the face of kin-based solidarities.[92] Ben Ali's capitalization on the Personal Status Code entailed added measures for the protection and expansion of women's rights, the integration of women in the workforce, and an insistence on their centrality to the nation's development. No less important was the regime's emphasis on the role of education, its adoption of information and communication technologies, and, most prominently, its promotion of youth. The regime actively associated its agenda of change with these modernizing impulses, branding itself as a champion of women's freedom, a promoter of the networked society, and an avatar of youth empowerment. Underlying these progressive policy choices was a commitment to the secularization of society intended to marginalize those who have conservative impulses and Islamist affinities. While playing down religiosity in public and pursuing a systematic depoliticization of the young generation through the policing of the universities, the infiltration of organizations, and the manipulation of cultural production, the regime also promoted a hedonistic lifestyle and encouraged a consumerist culture.

An Ingrained Culture of Fear

The net effect of these regime strategies was the progressive but pervasive instillation of a culture of fear. The government's confrontation with the Islamic movement not only eliminated a formidable opponent and discarded a real political threat to the durability of the regime in the long run, it also institutionalized repression by providing a justification for a security policy to eliminate practically all forms of dissent. In this sense, the tug of war between the government and the Islamists was as much political as it was ideological. The conservative agenda of Ennahda made many people with a liberal orientation unsympathetic to their movement, to the point of identifying with the government's determination to purge the country of Islamism. For the liberal segment of society, Ben Ali was a defender of the country's achievements and an upholder of its commitment to moderation and modernization. And so, when the government cracked down on the Ennahda movement as it grew more radical and brought its members to mass trials, there was a general willingness to look the other way on human rights abuses, legal irregularities, and disregard for the rule of law. Initially, the general public was not aware of the scope of arrests and abuses; those who did know about the mistreatments of the detained Islamists were afraid to speak out.[93] Regional and international events provided a favorable environment to reinforce the security imperative and extend repression. The civil war in Algeria of the mid-1990s, the threat of terrorism, and the specter of extremism as well as the Bush anti-democratic policies, which legitimated tyrants in many settings in the aftermath of the September 11 attacks, gave the regime a pretext for maintaining its crackdown on the Islamists. Increasingly, there was an interpenetration between the state and the security apparatus, resulting in state-led oppression. The more Ben Ali distanced the country from the vision of the development and welfare state Bourguiba had promoted during his rule in favor of a more liberal socioeconomic orientation, the more repression took root. Relieved of its paternalistic trait and its protective role, the state was made to adopt a repressive dimension designed to serve the ruling establishment.[94]

The majority of people did not feel the effect of the crackdown immediately. The prevailing sense of indifference went a long way toward redefining the state-citizen relationship in favor of the regime, which progressively but methodically used its heavy-handed approach as a deterrent to dissent. Repression became an instinct, security an obsession, and social control a policy. What had started as a persecution of a politically motivated Islamist movement developed into a more systematic repression of all dissent, whether religious or secular, and a wider intolerance toward critical voices, whether they were opposition political parties, civil actors, human rights groups, trade unions, or student movements.[95] Hardened with the Islamists, the regime's security approach widened and intensified, eventually morphing into managed repression. Gradually, the security approach the regime used against political opposition and civil rights activism became a more generalized *modus operandi*, collectively experienced as a form of social control that grew more insidious over the years and encroached on all parts of sociality, extending even to cyberspace. As a 2008 report put it, "the regime allowed for no space of contestation, whether social or political."[96] Violation of individual and collective civil rights became routine, inviting a growing public revulsion at central authority.

Under Ben Ali, Tunisia developed into a police state with an extensive and vindictive security apparatus, which became the linchpin of the regime's survival, durability, and prowess. As intense repression became routine, many people internalized the culture of fear. Resigning themselves to the idea that the political reality of the Arab world was immutable, they learned to live with a security-intensive environment that often infringed on their individual liberties. After all, while the state's coercive and repressive practices were felt most injuriously by political opponents and militant elements, most people, as Hibou pointed out, led normal lives: "while people may suffer from the absence of freedom of expression, from the weight of a single, often unrealistic rhetoric and sometimes from a somewhat over-massive police presence, they still appreciate the solicitude of the state and its economic voluntarism."[97] Algeria's example went a long way toward muting any sentiment for replacing the Ben Ali regime or taking steps that could lead to an Islamist victory. Those who were mindful of the civil war agreed to the tradeoff between security and freedom that the regime offered them.

Although the exercise of surveillance by the security apparatus was not new, it took on an added dimension and a more elaborate articulation. At the center of this operation was the Ministry of Interior, an immense bureaucracy upon which was grafted formal agencies and informal mechanisms of surveillance. The most obvious facet of the security apparatus was the police, which operated in such a way that ensuring public order became contingent on intruding into people's private lives. Policing also worked through auxiliary channels, ranging from ruling party cells and local government community offices to neighborhood watch groups and municipal services, which constituted an elaborate network of surveillance. The coexistence of a centralized and structured police apparatus with banal and informal policing practices intimately connected to everyday life allowed for a refined modality for the exercise of power.[98] Surveillance, intimidation, and repression became stabilizing factors. As a consequence, the culture was contaminated by suspicion and mistrust, discouraging critical views, association, and collective action. Acquiescence and obedience became the desired traits of citizenship—even though, as will became clear later, these normalization techniques came with a degree of maneuverability in which people did exercise some form of freedom.

Looking the Other Way

The Ben Ali regime depended on the support it received from the West. Since the 1970s, Bourguiba had favored the integration of the country into a Mediterranean-European context over a pan-Arab orientation.[99] Under Ben

Ali, Tunisia maintained this orientation. To that end, he played the Islamic card to its fullest. The anti-Islamist campaign not only helped consolidate Ben Ali's rule, it went a long way toward assuaging the fears of Western allies and partners wary of the increasing popularity of the Islamic political project on the southern shores of the Mediterranean basin. The fact that Tunisia was very close to Italy's toe made the potential dangers more acute. Ben Ali's hard line against Islamists branded the regime as a valuable, moderate, and pro-Western ally. Accordingly, the regime faced little criticism for its repressive policies. Western fears of political Islam lent Ben Ali support as he constructed a bulwark against genuine political liberalization.

But the Islamic threat was not the only factor at work. Tunisia's economic choices and political arrangement cannot be adequately understood independently of the European—in particular the French—and US strategic geopolitical interests and foreign policy considerations in North Africa. The convergence of interests between Western stakeholders in the region and Maghreb states like Tunisia led to a multidimensional quid pro quo policy approach impelled by economic interests, political stakes, and security considerations.[100]

Western interests in preserving the existing power structure trumped the advancement of human rights and the institutionalization of democracy. Although EU states became more attentive to the human rights practices of the Ben Ali regime after Tunisia signed trade accords with Europe in 1995, these probings were put on the back burner with the advent of the US-led global war on terror. The bombing of a synagogue in 2002 on the island of Djerba in the southeast of Tunisia made the Islamist threat a common security issue.[101] The Western inclination to prioritize stability over the promotion of democracy favored a de facto complicity that was in line with national interests. Although concerned about human rights violations, the West was disinclined to exert real pressure to reform or undermine the regime. For France in particular, support for Ben Ali was a matter of strategic interests.[102] Although they welcomed more substantial progress on the political front, the major Western partners, as Cavatorta put it, generally considered Ben Ali a "responsible leader" with sufficient "democratic credentials."[103]

Likewise, the regime's lack of progress toward—indeed, conscious moves to undermine—real democratic reform and its imposition of constraints on individual liberty and on civil society did not lessen European support for Tunisia's bid for an advanced status within the EU. Given its geographic proximity to and historical ties with Europe, Tunisia sought to deepen its relationship with the EU which, in turn, was keen on promoting sustained development in the southern Mediterranean countries, in the hopes that economic prosperity would both limit migration to Europe and undermine the appeal of Islamism. While the EU looked favorably at Tunisia's bid, the association agreement came with expectations. It called for Ben Ali to make progress in democratic reform and to undertake political and institutional transformations. A degradation of human rights and lack of progress on democratic reform would be out of sync with the values of the EU and would prevent a rapprochement between the two parties. The 2005 Action Plan for realizing this status called for more democratic progress, freedoms, rule of law, and justice.[104] Wary that the country's economy could not be sustained without such partnership, and cognizant that the rules of the game necessitated showing signs of commitment to these values,[105] Ben Ali pledged to abide by EU norms—or, at least, gave his concrete intention to comply with the European expectations. Soon though, the regime reneged, passing a law that prohibited contact with foreign agencies or institutions that could potentially affect the country's image, harm its vital interests, or impact its economic security. The new law opened the door for the systematic prosecution of local activists, NGO members, and others with international networking capabilities. As a 2010 policy report concluded, "The desire to obtain new economic and political privileges from the EU emboldened the Tunisian regime to apply further measures of repression. In this sense, the EU's strategy of including political liberalization through incentives and integration had backfired."[106]

Conclusion

Ben Ali's rise to power had been justified as a repudiation of the abuses that became manifest during the late period of Bourguiba's rule. In the end, however, Ben Ali and his clique revitalized and overhauled the strategies of authoritarian rule that Bourguiba had implemented. In politics, economics, and social relations, the regime's drive for survival dictated the adoption of a variety of policies toward that end. For domestic clients, Ben Ali's rule relied on classic rentier strategies as well as a degree of repression that was more (as with its treatment of Islamists) or less (as with its domestication of the legal opposition) apparent. For international audiences, the government carefully crafted an image of success and modernization—the appearance of liberalizing without ever reaching a liberal endpoint—that proved attractive to observers who saw the regime's propaganda and impressive economic statistics but were willfully blind to the processes that sustained such growth. The contradictions of Ben Ali's rule, however, would soon prove unsustainable.

3

A Crisis of Authority

Offline Activism and Simmering Discontent

As I already described, within months of taking power, Ben Ali began to quell dissent, control civil society, silence independent voices, and co-opt traditional centers of power to discourage political opposition to the government and the ruling party. But the country's memory of activism remained. Tunisia has a rich history of anti-colonial struggle, trade union activism, student mobilization, political movements, and civil society involvement. That activist spirit was kept alive by political dissidents, human rights activists, and professional groups. Although the political sphere was tightly controlled, there was a margin for political involvement that emboldened a number of actors. A handful of nongovernmental organizations, unauthorized parties, independent voices, and victims of the regime helped develop an anti-regime stance. Each might have seemed inconsequential on its own, but cumulatively they had a significant effect. Although the regime could weather many individual challenges to its durability, it increasingly suffered a crisis of authority.

This chapter focuses on people's determination to push back when they began to distinctly feel the authoritarian impulses of the state and the intransigence of the regime. Scattered popular resistance operated on two distinct planes—one overtly political in nature, the other enmeshed within the social sphere. Each obeyed different logics, enlisted different actors, and claimed different spaces. Accordingly, this chapter unfolds along two levels of analysis: formal politics (i.e., conventional political action) and informal politics (i.e., emerging contexts and sites of social action). The first part of the chapter outlines how the regime's attempt to co-opt or repress potentially militant groups and political actors backfired. This is most evident in the growing radicalization of labor activists, the perseverance of the opposition press, the confrontational approach of professional groups like lawyers, and the defiant attitude of unauthorized civil society actors. Less obvious but no less important were emerging forms of social contention anchored in people's ordinary lives. The second part of the chapter highlights a number of significant moments and incidents that speak to this different kind of activism. These developments are particularly significant; studying them can help shed light on a gestation process that took place on the margins. A close analysis of a number of protest movements in deprived regions during the years immediately preceding the revolution reveals increasing interpenetration between the social and the political. Three sites of struggle merit particular attention: the short-lived social movement in the undeveloped mining region of Gafsa, which advocated the right to employment and regional development; the riots in the small town of Ben Gardane on the border with Libya over the scarcity of economic opportunities in the forgotten deep south; and the organized protests of the farmers in the southwest agrarian town of Regueb against a debt economy that relied on state corruption. These limited actions and circumscribed protest movements do not bestow a narrative coherence on the events leading up to the revolution. Nor do they provide a causal explanation for the specific events of the end of 2010. Instead, they help unravel the mechanisms and dynamics through which limited social demands gradually became more political in nature, as well as demonstrate how local issues could have a broader significance. Increasingly, people beyond the traditionally militant core were becoming outspoken, active, and in many ways politicized. Two key implications of these subtle developments emerged: the dissipation of the culture of fear and the disposition of the people to rise up. These changes are discussed in detail in the third and final part of the chapter, which also provides an analytical account of the street protests that culminated in the revolution.

Pockets of Resistance

In this section, I review how the regime was unable to fully quash opposition among labor unions, professionals, parts of the media, and activists. In some cases, the government's repressive measures even stimulated more opposition. I begin with one of the rare dynamic arenas of activism, the labor movement.

The Tunisian General Labor Union had traditionally acted as a mediator between the government and the nation. Its rich history, iconic figures, and long association with the country's sociopolitical scene made it hard to fully control or easily manipulate. Labor activism in Tunisia goes back to the establishment of the General Confederation of Tunisian Workers by Mohamed Ali El Hammi in 1924 and the foundation of the Tunisian General Labor Union in 1946 under the leadership of Farhat Hached. One of the defining characteristics of the Union is the interpenetration of the social and the political. From the outset, the struggle for labor rights could not be disassociated from the larger political struggle against French colonial rule. Protecting Tunisian workers from economic exploitation and improving their social conditions would require a political struggle against the tyranny of the colonizer. This positioning favored a close association between the vision of the Union and the orientation of the Destour Party under the leadership of Habib Bourguiba and Salah Ben Youssef.

After independence, however, a tension developed between the government and the Union over social and economic policy choices. Initially, the political leadership was wary of the Socialist program the Union advocated because it would impact the country's liberal orientation. Even though faltering economic development in the 1960s led to the state's adoption of a more Socialist orientation, Bourguiba's dominance over the country's political and economic life alienated the Union and prompted it to oppose the government.[1] Counterintuitively, the country's turn away from the unpopular and short-lived Socialist experiment to a more liberal model in the early 1970s improved the relationship between the labor organization and the political leadership. However, the economic recession and declining growth rates that marked the end of the 1970s unsettled the partnership that had developed between the government and an increasingly powerful Union. The latter's ability to strengthen its base and attract new members from among the many workers who were affected by the government's economic strategy intensified labor struggles, heightened protest movements, and increased strikes. Rising tensions culminated in the bloody riots of January 26, 1978. This led to a clampdown on the independent Union leadership and a takeover by a more docile top leadership, which ensured that the Union remained under the thumb of Bourguiba and his government, putting an end to its broader ambitions.[2]

Consequently, when Ben Ali came to power, he faced a weak and fractured Union. In his attempt to consolidate his position against the face of the perceived Islamist threat, Ben Ali sought to subdue the Union even further by co-opting its leadership and adopting neo-liberal reforms that undermined the bargaining power of organized labor. He largely succeeded, making the

1990s the lowest point in Tunisia's history of labor activism.[3] To the dismay of the labor forces and the Union base, the alliance with the regime and corruption at the highest level weakened the Union's ability to play a significant role in shaping the government's sociopolitical choices. The country's adoption of neo-liberal measures made the declining influence of the Union more profoundly felt. Over the years, the state's role as the prime employer and the grantor of lifetime employment receded significantly in the face of a private sector energized by a privileged business elite. This weakened the credibility of the Union and divided the co-opted leadership from the principled rank and file.

The fact that the Union toed the government line, adopted pro-regime positions, and engaged in political manipulation should not obscure its fundamentally activist nature. The Union had a strong nationwide network of relatively more militant local cells or sections, and some of the sector-specific unions (particularly in the education sector) were assertive and vocal. The membership's relative radicalism meant that the union was still a credible organization that could not be reduced to a state apparatus.[4] The Union was thus a complex and contradictory totality.[5] While the leadership of the Union sought to adhere to a loyal, pro-government position, labor officials had also to take heed of the demands of its constitutions and the general inclination of its members. For Ayari and Geisser, what distinguishes the Union is "the existence of contestatory debates, internal resistances, and various forms of dissidence and dissonance, alongside localized social conflicts which contribute a positive feedback effect, thus compelling the central leadership to permanently oscillate between a neo-corporatist accommodating line and a more discreet line of support of the protest movements which are animated by the base."[6] Constant acts of contestation at the local level sustained the organization's legitimacy and preserved its image as a vehicle of popular demands and a voice of popular aspirations.[7] Increasingly, it was difficult for the Union to serve two gods—maintaining its credibility among its constituents while preserving its ties to the regime.

Complementing the activism of the labor movement was the increasing political involvement of certain professional groups, especially lawyers. Politically aware lawyers were not a new development: Bourguiba was a lawyer by training, for instance. As traditional defenders of civil liberties, human rights, and the rule of law, lawyers could pose a political challenge for the regime. Lacking Bourguiba's credentials and legitimacy, Ben Ali remained apprehensive of those associated with the legal profession given their political inclination. For their part, the lawyers adopted a strategy of cooperation with the new regime. This orientation was evident in their general tendency in the 1990s to favor a National Bar Association—the quasi-union organization representing lawyers—that would attempt to create a good working relationship with the government in the hope of promoting the interests and professional expectations of the lawyers.

Toward the end of the 1990s, however, both sides moved toward more direct confrontation. Ben Ali sought to limit lawyers' power by instituting a parallel representative structure constituted by pro-regime lawyers. However, the regime's attempt to co-opt this sector would prove difficult and would eventually contribute to lawyers' increased politicization. Growing disillusionment and a pressing desire to regain autonomy and independence prompted lawyers to elect an independent leadership of the National Bar Association in 2001. The new leaders adopted a more confrontational approach, which was evident in the number of protests, sit-ins in courthouses, demonstrations, and strikes lawyers undertook throughout the first decade of the twenty-first century.

Empowered by their legal knowledge, their consciousness of civil rights, and their social status, lawyers grew more vocal and assertive. Among the actions that drew the ire of the regime because of their political significance were the protests and sit-ins in the cases of the hunger strike of Taoufik Ben Brik in 2000, the unfair trial of the dissident political figure Hamma Hammami in 2002, the politicized trial of the outspoken lawyer Mohamed Abbou, and the Parliament's adoption of a law to increase the power of the executive branch over the legal profession in 2006. The government responded with coercion and infringement on legal immunity. Significantly, although regime intransigence prevented the contestatory activities of the lawyers from developing into a wide and cross-sector movement, it could not bring them under its control. Instead, the regime's targeting of lawyers favored the rise of a de facto political arena of contestation.[8]

The opposition press constituted another source of pressure. Nearly all opposition political parties had their own official newspapers, but most of these publications toed the government line and had an insignificant circulation. Three newspapers associated with the officially recognized opposition were not under the thumb of the regime: *Attariq Al Jadid* ("The Renewal"), the oldest, had been the voice of the Communist Party since 1980 before the latter changed its name in 1993 to Ettajdid Movement; *Al Mawqif* ("The Stance"), which was founded in 1984, was the newspaper of the Democratic Progressive Party; and *Mouwatinoun* ("Citizens"), which emerged in 2007 as the voice of the Democratic Front for Labor and Liberties.[9] These papers adopted a critical approach that emboldened them to cover pressing socioeconomic issues and flirt with the red lines proscribed by the regime—even if some topics, like corruption and the Islamists, remained taboo. Running an opposition paper was a frustrating endeavor. The newspapers published irregularly as they struggled to overcome government-imposed hurdles, financial reprisals, lawsuits, defamation trials, banned issues, occasional confiscation, and press card suspension. For the editor-in-chief of *Al Mawqif*, Rachid Khechana, the conditions under which the opposition press operated were lamentable: "We go to print on a Tuesday. The government then vets the copy. Depending on the content, they may or may not release it by Friday. So by the time it reaches the public, it's old news. It's worse than operating in the former Soviet Gulag."[10] Constant bureaucratic obstruction left the newspapers in a precarious financial situation and undermined their ability to build a loyal readership. Newspaper stands avoided carrying them, and the ones that did so hid them between other publications in an unreachable corner. Although caution nurtured a tendency toward self-censorship among readers,[11] the news published in these papers by outspoken writers was sought after because they reported on domestic issues that were typically not covered by the national media. Informed sources estimated the circulation of *Al Mawqif* in 2010 to be ten thousand copies, *Attariq Al Jadid*, three thousand copies, and *Mouwatinoun*, one thousand copies,[12] but readership figures were higher, as copies of these newspapers were often read and then passed along to interested family members and friends, making the information sphere for the curious richer than it might have seemed.

The regime's stranglehold on political life energized part of the opposition. The year 2005 was a turning point. Tunisia's hosting of the World Summit on the Information Society (WSIS)—which Ben Ali meant to use as a showcase of Tunisia's Internet achievements and a propaganda victory for his regime— was a rare opportunity for high-impact activism. The significance of this event for cyber-activism will be discussed in detail in chapter 4. Suffice it for now to point out the more pointed political opportunity the event opened up for the opponents of the regime. A month prior to the summit, eight national figures representing different political parties and civil society organizations went on a month-long hunger strike in the law office of the dissident lawyer Ayachi Hammami. They sought to alert the national and international opinion to the deteriorating state of liberties in the country, deplore the continuing degradation of the political situation, and advocate for more rights and liberties.[13]

They called for freedom of expression, civil liberties, human rights, freedom of organization, and the release of political prisoners. It was political theater par excellence that drew many supporters and sympathizers from within and outside Tunisia.[14] It was called off on November 18, 2005, after international human rights delegations intervened, promising the protesters that they would support their demands.[15]

For a few months after the summit, the various forces of the opposition continued to engage one another in an active dialogue. Eventually, their initiative coalesced into a movement that came to be known as the 18 October Coalition for Rights and Freedoms, a pragmatic alliance seeking to develop a movement that would force a transition to democracy. Transcending political rivalries and putting ideological differences aside in favor of immediate political interests, the movement sought to form a unified front against the regime's entrenched authoritarianism. This coalition drew together disparate elements from the country's political scene, including the unauthorized opposition and the Islamists. Given the state's hard line against Ennahda and the skepticism of some of the ideological adversaries of the Islamists (mainly leftist opposition parties), the marriage between Islamists and secular opposition forces—"not so much over the question of modernization, but rather to achieve democratic progress"[16]—was an achievement of sorts in itself.[17] By the fourth year, personal differences, opposition strategy, and political positioning had undermined the coalition. The 2009 legislative and presidential elections proved especially divisive. While some opposition parties decided to take a shot at the elections, others boycotted them, which effectively shattered the movement. Further undermining the 18 October Coalition was the fact that it was isolated from the people, comprising mainly political elites and members of the urban opposition. Interestingly, their focus on the pragmatic nature of the coalition prevented them from seeing the real sources and forces of opposition that were developing throughout the country. Incidents in inner towns and provinces, examined in more detail later, point to situations in which people beyond the militant core were becoming radicalized.

Cracks in the System

By the turn of the twenty-first century, Ben Ali had consolidated his power base. For most people, his rule appeared unshakable. However, the regime's stability was relative. A degree of organized activism, a series of incidents, and a number of events, which intensified over the years, dented the myth of Ben Ali's immutability. Examining the nature and extent of these moments and incidents helps point out the regime's unsuspected vulnerability.

Over the years, the weight of the regime's repression kindled a public reaction, even if it was measured and limited. By the turn of the twenty-first century, criticism of Ben Ali's political wisdom had started to find its way into the public sphere. Among the early incidents, the Ben Brik affair stood out. Taoufik Ben Brik, a correspondent for the French daily *La Croix*, was one of the few journalists who dared to speak out against Ben Ali. In 2000, he went on a hunger strike to draw attention to the politically motivated infringements on his citizen rights, to compel the government to return his confiscated passport, to allow him to travel, and to cease the harassment of his family. The much-publicized case of Ben Brik was a significant victory because the regime yielded to international pressure. Equally embarrassing for the regime was public criticism from a high-ranked civil servant. In 2001, Mokhtar Yahyaoui, a judge, posted an open letter on the Internet in which he lamented the state of freedoms in the country and called for the president to reinstitute the independence of the judiciary. His bold action was unprecedented, as was his choice of the Web as a venue. The magistrate's risky action brought punishment and Yahyaoui was relieved of his duties, harassed, and ostracized. Commenting on the significance of the letter, *Le Monde*'s Florence Beaugé noted:

> Not only did the man make patently clear to his fellow citizens that "citizenship" was not a vain word in Tunisia, but he revealed the true nature of the regime. By publicly denouncing the judicial power's lack of independence in an open letter to Ben Ali, Judge Yahyaoui struck the hardest blow yet to the Palace of Carthage.... The news came as a surprise for many people who, for a while, could not believe it. All these years, contestation has been widening, slowly but surely. While it may be premature to talk about "a Tunisian spring," there is a general *prise de conscience* among people that they deserve better.[18]

For a "quiet country" like Tunisia, as Dakhlia calls it,[19] such incidents stood out. They tarnished the image of the regime both at home and abroad. Throughout the first decade of the twenty-first century, more public criticism of Ben Ali would be registered, mostly originating from outside the country. These ranged from embarrassing international human rights reports to critical discourses by dissident figures and from unflattering press articles in the

French press to probing books of investigative journalism. Particularly noteworthy was the publication in 2002 of a scathingly critical book by two French
journalists called *Our Friend Ben Ali*, which exposed the other side of the so-
called Tunisian miracle.[20] The notable increase in Internet access since 2005
meant that subversive material circulated widely, ranging from YouTube clips
of the dissident figure Moncef Marzouki on Al Jazeera to pirated copies of
banned books like *La Régente de Carthage*, a riveting investigative report
describing the scandalous dealings of the first lady and her clan. Ironically, the
kind of connectivity that had helped the regime win the bid to host the WSIS
was now making it easier to play up opposition. While cyberspace became another site where everyday life took place, it also generated new spaces for online engagement, allowed the rise of citizen journalism, and prompted the
emergence of cyber-activism. The study of these trends constitutes the focus
of subsequent chapters.

THE MYTH OF INVINCIBILITY

The first serious challenge to Ben Ali's system of control was the Djerba
bombing. On April 11, 2002, a Tunisian man drove a truck loaded with gas
cylinders into the historic El Ghriba synagogue on the Mediterranean resort
island of Djerba. The synagogue, which serves some two thousand Tunisian
Jews, half of whom live on the island,[21] is a destination for many pilgrims and
an attraction for many foreign tourists. The bombing killed twenty-one people, the majority of whom were German tourists. Initially, the authorities were
guarded about the bombing, and tried to pass it off as an accident. They feared
it would have a negative impact on the country's tourism, a vital economic
sector and a leading source of hard currency. Under pressure from the Germans,
and after Al Qaeda had claimed responsibility, the authorities admitted that it
had been a terrorist attack. Beyond the embarrassment and economic implications, the attack had a more serious meaning: it pointed to deficiencies in Ben
Ali's security system. These would become more evident in the armed attacks
four years later by what came to be known as the Soliman group.

In April 2006, five armed Tunisian militants and one Mauritanian slipped
across the Algerian-Tunisian border to take refuge in a mountainous region in
the northwest of the country. They were associated with Al Qaeda in the
Maghreb, which grew out of the Salafi Group for Preaching Combat. After the
police accidentally arrested two of its members, the remaining members
moved out to enlist the help of other Salafi cells. Reinforced by dozens of

members from other towns, the group moved to the southern suburbs of the capital, initially setting up camp in the remote mountains of Ain Tbornog in the adjacent region of Grombalia. Police discovered one of the group's hideouts, leading to a shootout between the group and the military on December 23, 2006, in Hammam Lif, a suburb of Tunis, that resulted in the death of two of the attackers, the capture of a third, and the seizure of weapons and ammunition. In the following days, roadblocks were set up as security forces hunted for the group. On January 3, 2007, heavily armed members of the Salafi group clashed with security forces in the town of Soliman in a series of gun battles that left twelve assailants, one soldier, and one police officer dead, according to official sources (more than thirty according to estimates of the French press).[22] The fifteen or so remaining members of the group were captured.[23]

The Soliman group's attack raised a number of issues. Publicly, the authorities downplayed the gravity of the armed clashes, issuing a press communiqué that described the armed group as outlaws and a gang of dangerous criminals. Rumors circulated that one of the supposed targets of the group was the presidential palace, which presumably explained why the regime tried to cover up the incident. Only after the European media implicated Al Qaeda did the government reluctantly disclose the possibility of terrorism. As in the Djerba Synagogue incident, the government was initially reluctant to concede that the Soliman group was in fact a terrorist group even if there was a reason for it to use the justification of the war on terror. For a closed regime, even releasing information that could help them was considered threatening. Justifying its actions would require engaging people in a debate—something it refused to do given its repressive nature. The regime could not admit that it worried about anything.

Even after the terrorist nature of the attacks was established, there was a clear divergence on what the incidents meant. The ability of a small group to mount such an attack rested not only on its operational link to Al Qaeda but also on its ability to attract, recruit, and organize young people. For the regime, this growing radicalism and the activities of jihadist groups was a regional articulation of global terrorism in the post–September 11 era, which necessitated a tighter security approach and justified increased repression. For civil society, though, the encroaching radicalism was the symptom of problems caused by authoritarian repression creating a gaping sociopolitical void that favored the rise of extremism.[24] A communiqué published in the aftermath of the Soliman events by the Committee for the Respect of Liberties and Human Rights in Tunisia took pains to point out that the real issue was not security but freedom:

These incidents, which mark a new phase in the history of the country, have long been dreaded given the suffocating atmosphere the Tunisian society lives in and the strategy of political, associative and cultural desertification that is breeding despair and disillusionment, particularly among the youth. The political opposition and civil society organizations have repeatedly warned the authorities to the undesired consequences of the savage repression which all the democratic, peaceful and reformist forces in the country have been afflicted.[25]

Resentment of the government's security policies intensified over the next few years. One manifestation of this discontent could be pointed out in the popular movements in the mining region of Gafsa, the border town of Ben Gardane, and the farming community of Regueb. These incidents showed different kinds of fissures in the system that called into question the whole system of governance.

THE RAGE OF THE UNDERPRIVILEGED

The wave of protests that shook the provincial region of Gafsa in 2008 was the most important social unrest since the bread riots in 1984. In a country where street upheavals and social unrest were rare, the rather protracted protests in the mining region indicated a new reality. Situated in the southwest region of the country, on the border with Algeria, Gafsa is rich in phosphate, which was discovered at the end of the nineteenth century. For more than a century, the Gafsa Phosphate Company was the economic engine and principal employer in a region with a rich history of labor militancy. After independence, the company (still the region's largest employer) was an economic asset to the country, a development anchor for the region, and a social stabilizer for local communities with historically deep clan roots. Even today, Tunisia is one of the world's largest suppliers of phosphate, which is concentrated in and around the towns of Oum Larayes, Redeyef, Mdhila, and Metlaoui, known as the mining region, with an estimated population of 150,000 inhabitants. World Bank–mandated economic restructuring that began in the late 1980s gradually but surely altered the traditionally strong link between the people of the region and the company. Increased modernization and the decision to shift phosphate extraction from deep mines to surface mines led to increased productivity but also dramatically reduced the company's labor force. The reforms benefited elites instead of promoting a more socially equitable redistribution of wealth. For the overwhelming majority of the locals, whose lives revolved around mining in a region that lacked economic diversification, these changes were deeply felt. The region's growing number of college graduates with high expectations but no jobs would exacerbate tensions in an already harsh environment suffering from land overexploitation, water resources abuse, chemical pollution, and chronic diseases resulting from decades of mining activities.

These problems simmered for years before boiling over in the first few months of 2008. On January 5, 2008, the Gafsa Phosphate Company released the results of a recruitment contest. The company's proclamation disregarded an agreement to allocate a certain quota of the jobs to the local community and families of laborers who had been injured or killed in the mine—an issue of extreme importance to a region where unemployment was twice as high as the national rate. A higher proportion of jobs would instead benefit those close to the regime. Several unsuccessful applicants and unemployed youth converged on the regional head office of the labor union in Redeyef. Many of those who participated in this action had been associated with a local committee of the officially unrecognized Union of Unemployed Graduates, which was formed in 2007. They were joined by other unemployed young people, lay citizens, and local activists who took to the streets to contest the results, condemn the corruption of the company's management, and denounce the complicity of the local authorities.

The initial protests were spontaneous, but collective action was soon organized and supported by local unions, in particular the union in Redeyef. These local unions were at odds with the management of the regional labor union, which they saw as part of the problem. The management of the regional union was compromised by their close ties to the regime and some even had direct financial interests in the mining operation.[26] The local union stood by the protesters who forced the company and local authorities to negotiate. In addition to insisting on the cancellation of the announced results of the recruitment contest and reiterating the right to employment, the protesters formulated broader demands for social justice and human dignity. They called for the implementation of employment programs for unemployed degree holders, state commitment to the creation of industrial projects in the region, the improvement of basic public services, the provision of basic amenities for the poor, adherence to international environmental treaties, and compensation for environmental damage.[27]

Over the next few weeks, protests spread throughout the mining region, joined by family members of the unemployed, miners' widows, dependents of miners handicapped on the job, workers, angry and frustrated locals, students, and even professionals. The unprecedented mass mobilization included not only sit-ins and protests but even the dismantling of a portion of the railroad, bringing the transportation of the phosphate to a halt. The participation of women gave the movement an added significance. In Oum Larayes, the widows of a dozen former company workers who had died on duty set up tents near company headquarters to assert the right of their children to be employed by the company—an entitlement provided for by an existing agreement, but never implemented. For some time, the tents of these women became the epicenter of the movement. The widows did not give in until they received a presidential promise to settle their situation.

Partial concessions and official promises helped ease some of the tension for a while. The more adamant the protesters grew, the more uncompromising the company officials were, and the more alarmed the authorities became. The lack of progress suggested to the protesters that the authorities were not serious about the negotiations, while the massive presence of anti-riot police forces was a constant reminder of the state's predisposition to resort to force. Initially, the police force had a calibrated interference, only monitoring the situation and controlling access to the towns to ensure that the protests did not spread. Three months into the conflict, the authorities, who had counted on the inability of the protest movement to sustain its momentum, fell back on coercion. A night attack on the police office in Redeyef in early April by unidentified individuals gave the authorities a pretext to launch a massive security operation. They raided homes, attacked locals, and jailed leaders of the protests, including Adnene Hajji, a charismatic union figure who united the protesters in a region distinguished by clanism and rivalries.[28] Repression backfired on the regime, leading to a general strike, a procession involving hundreds of women, and more clashes with the anti-riot police, which retreated. Baffled by the reaction of the protesters, the authorities released the detainees. In early May, a group of protesters occupied the site of the company's electrical generator and cut off its power supply, bringing phosphate production to a halt. The authorities' interference to forcibly restore electricity led to the electrocution of one of the protesters. The protests then turned into confrontations with police, who did not now hesitate to use live ammunition, resulting in the fatal shooting of a demonstrator at a procession. In early June, a curfew was imposed and the army was deployed. The protests were violently and ruthlessly repressed. Some three hundred protesters, activists, and family members of striking miners were arrested, and thirty-three heavy sentences were pronounced against leading figures in the movement.[29] The trials were meant to serve as a lesson for those who may have dared to challenge the regime and a reaffirmation of the regime's ability to keep the situation under control.

The protests that wracked Gafsa were arguably the most enduring and most serious challenge during Ben Ali's two decades in office until the 2010 riots. Significantly though, they remained "a local protest movement"[30] and failed to spread beyond the mining region. It is not that the word did not get out about Gafsa. In spite of the national media blackout about the events, information did circulate. The foreign-based satellite channel Al Hiwar Ettounsi, in particular, helped publicize the events, thanks to the activist journalist Fahem Boukadous, a correspondent for the opposition website Al Badil who was living in the region at the time.[31] These reports and images found their way to transnational channels like Al Jazeera and France 24 and were also recirculated on the Internet. Some locals also passed on mobile phone recordings and snapshots of protests to unionists and friends; others posted amateur video footage of the protests on YouTube. Citizen journalism, Internet activism, blogging campaigns, and solidarity webpages helped foster a degree of popular consciousness about Gafsa. Supporting the movement on the Internet were also committees of immigrant communities in France, most notably in Nantes and Paris, which have a large community of Tunisians originating from the mining region.[32] No less important were the communiqués issued by several European human rights organizations condemning the events and expressing solidarity with the people of Gafsa.

The crucial element that circumscribed the story of Gafsa and prevented it from spreading was political. The regime's ability to co-opt the leadership of the Union went a long way toward limiting the scope of the movement. The other local and regional unions neither decisively nor sufficiently supported the movement. Nor did the political opposition, which was preoccupied by the presidential elections that were due to take place in 2009. Although civil society organizations and others expressed solidarity with the people of the mining region through press releases, the protests failed to take a broader political dimension. The general resignation to an eventual regime victory quashed any hopes that the events would take on a larger political significance. Moreover, those who attempted to connect more with the movement did so from the capital city, far from Gafsa. The one exception was the illegal Communist Party of the Tunisian Workers, which had taken a deep interest in the movement since the outbreak of the protests. Historically, Gafsa had been a Communist stronghold, and although party members were not present in the region in large numbers, there were activists who either took part in the protests or relayed news about the events through the Internet and foreign TV networks.[33] Ironically, the presence of the Communist Party in Gafsa deterred some opposition parties from supporting the protests, as they did not want to appear to bless far-left activists.[34]

Nevertheless, the events did have a larger significance. More than an isolated case or a regional issue, the situation in Gafsa pointed to flagrant structural problems in the country's development model. Those problems stood out all the more in the context of the regime's keenness on vaunting the country's social and economic progress. Beneath the demands for social justice stood a more basic demand: life with human dignity. Even if the protests in Gafsa were quelled, the underlying reason for the discontent refused to go away. The state's employment of repression altered the meaning of the protests because the act of repression obscured the protesters' underlying causes. Gradually, the public's perception of the Gafsa protests shifted from being a matter of socioeconomic local issues to become a more generic issue of police brutality and state repression.

Despite the fierceness of repression and the criminalization of protests, people found a way to reassert their constitutional right to express themselves and to protest peacefully. Although the slogans did not evolve beyond the socioeconomic sphere of action to acquire an overt political dimension, the mining revolt signaled a latent unwillingness to tolerate the status quo. More significantly, the unfolding of the events in Redeyef showed how people, once radicalized, were able to blur previously delineated red lines. This emboldened people beyond the activist core and encouraged those who would not otherwise have had an activist inclination to shake off their accommodating attitude, stand up for their rights, and show their solidarity with the regime's victims. Despite their suppression, the Gafsa protests thus made manifest an accumulation of problems and deep resentments that would only grow over time.

THE NEGLECTED DEEP SOUTH

Tunisia's forgotten south became another site of discontent. Unrest in this region had an unusual beginning: new Libyan taxes on border crossings levied in mid-August 2010. Located some twenty miles from the Ras Jeder crossing point between Libya and Tunisia, the town of Ben Gardane had become synonymous with smuggling. For years, the southern borders had been buzzing with traders acquiring merchandise and commodities in Libya for resale in Tunisia. Situated five hundred kilometers from the capital, lacking development projects, and deprived of infrastructure, the town of eighty thousand depended on quasi-illicit trade.[35] The new taxes that were levied by the Libyan government brought the town to a standstill.

Although harsh, the Libyan authorities' actions were not surprising. While there was no official word on the reasons and parties that stood behind the new measures, there were speculations that the Libyan authorities acted at the behest of the Tunisian regime.[36] Giving credence to these speculations and deepening the people's anger was the widely held perception that these measures were designed to help the inner circle of the president lay claim to this trade.[37] As townspeople continued to cross the borders while refusing to comply with the new regulations, the Libyan authorities started to confiscate their merchandise, prompting protests that were met with police hostility. In the midst of these tensions, the Libyan authorities decided to close the border, leading to new protests and prompting more decisive police intervention.[38] Adding to the grievances that ignited the protests was the escalation of violence by the security forces, inciting people to seek vengeance.[39] Alarmed at the escalation, the Tunisian authorities attempted to reach a settlement with the Libyan government while exercising a media blackout. After a month, the Libyan president Moamar Gaddafi intervened, repealing the previously imposed tax and reopening the Ras Jedeer crossing.

The Ben Gardane events were significant for a number of reasons. People's determination to fight back and to stand for their rights pointed to the limits of the security approach the Ben Ali regime employed. Particularly noteworthy was the way the culture of fear started to dissolve when people's livelihoods were at stake. Equally important were the increased proclivity toward mobilization and the evolving strategies of contestation that developed outside institutional party politics. Finally, the Ben Gardane events pointed to the ominous (for the regime) interpenetration of the social, the economic, and the political. Significantly, the demands of the protesters were as much political as they were economic. During the protests, people chanted slogans that drew attention to economic deprivation, decried unemployment, and demanded that the government provide greater employment opportunities.

These cracks in the system and the sense of uncertainty they produced helped project what Ayari and Geisser call "a diffuse perception of the vulnerability of the ruling elite,"[40] which was reinforced by the release of documents concerning Tunisia by WikiLeaks in the fall of 2010. The specific charges in the documents—that Ben Ali was aging, that his regime was sclerotic, and that his family was corrupt—were hardly secrets. What was new, though, was that the charges were public. Until then, people had discussed such matters only in private. That US State Department classified correspondence made the same observations was thus important. The diplomatic cables not only confirmed the rumors, they emphasized the moral degeneration of the regime and the erosion of its Western support.

Breaking the Code of Silence

People's greater intolerance toward social injustice was even more evident in the case of Sidi Bouzid, which came to be seen later as the cradle of the revolution. The regional socioeconomic context is important in understanding what happened in Sidi Bouzid in 2010. There was a long history of regional prejudice and uneven economic development that privileged the coastal regions over the inner provinces. Over the years, increased levels of education made the endemic problem of unemployment, particularly of college graduates, even more acute. For the natives of the region, the government's systematic policy of disengagement, marginalization, and impoverishment bred a feeling of economic repression that in turn fed popular discontent.

In the few months preceding the revolution, these deep-seated feelings of resentment were brought to the surface in the controversy surrounding the Regueb farmlands and the ensuing protest of the farmers of Sidi Bouzid. In the early years of the twenty-first century, the government unveiled a plan aimed at boosting the development of the agricultural sector, promoting entrepreneurship, and creating investment opportunities for young graduates. A number of individuals and families in Sidi Bouzid used the government incentive to set up farms in Regueb, a small nearby town with an abundance of fertile farmlands. To finance their projects, they obtained credit approval from the National Agricultural Bank but quickly found themselves ensnared in bureaucratic hurdles, legal provisions, and unethical dealings. These difficulties were caused by a closely knit system of interests designed to privilege the business community, whose members came from wealthier regions. The loans (which averaged $150,000) were designed to finance the purchase of the land and farming machinery, irrigation equipment, and pesticides. Because these loans were disbursed in installments, the farmers had to borrow from vendors and suppliers. Drought, crop failure, hikes in fuel prices, and increases in the cost of production contributed to the financial difficulties of the farmers who eventually found themselves unable to pay back their debts. Attempts to re-schedule their payments with the bank were unsuccessful. When they defaulted, the bank swiftly foreclosed on the properties.

As one union activist in the region points out, there was a general feeling among the implicated farmers that the bank had been both "uncooperative" and "dishonest" in its dealings.[41] The interest rates were exorbitant and the ad-ministrative hurdles for releasing the loans were enormous, often leading the farmers to lose their initial agricultural investments. Equally problematic for the farmers was the bank's inflexibility in rescheduling the payments or reach-ing partial settlements—even though the country's tolerance for "bad debts" had been a de facto state policy.[42] Because uncontrollable variables often made farming a volatile sector, banks had typically been lenient with farmers who encountered financial difficulties. In the case at hand, though, the bank took decisive and swift action against the farmers.

Having failed to collect the payment from the landowners, it moved to auc-tion the land. Both symbolically and concretely, this hostile action signified a breach in the state-society relationship. Credit constituted "the mainspring of the security pact," an arrangement premised on the state's ability to forestall uncertainty and risk while providing order and well-being for citizens.[43] Seen from a macro-economic perspective, these difficulties pointed to the impact of problematic development policies. Over the years, the impact of the structural adjustment program on agriculture squeezed small farmers. While the gov-ernment liberalized the agricultural sector in ways that subjected the prices of seeds, chemical products, fertilizers, irrigation, and animal feed to market forces, it nearly froze the price of key agricultural products, thus accruing the farmers' financial problems.[44] Additionally, the fact that most of the invest-ment in the agri-food industries was concentrated in the coastal cities consti-tuted an added burden that hiked the cost of production as the burden of shipping and transportation fell on the farmers' shoulders.[45] These trends led to the gradual impoverishment of the small farmers and the shrinking of the rural middle class.

The case of the Regueb lands not only demonstrated the problematic nature of the development policy the country pursued but also highlighted a whole mentality that people came to resent. Among the native Sidi Bouzid farmers, there was a perception that they had been cheated out of their lands and their families' livelihoods. Their farms were extremely attractive because the land was fertile and water was abundant. The prospects of acquiring these lands at a price that was considerably below their market value fueled a wave of land-grabbing by wealthy investors and speculators, who were mostly from economically privileged coastal regions. The land-grabbing also required the complicity of the judicial system. The unusual expediency of the land seizure and the irregularities that marked the manner of takeovers left many with the conviction that the land had been wrangled away from them through shady legal procedures.[46] For the people of Sidi Bouzid, the issue was symptomatic of the government's dismissive policy toward the entire inner region. The local population was left in an economically unfavorable situation made all the more precarious by the shrinking opportunities for employment, irrespective of educational level.[47]

Feelings of socioeconomic injustice and exclusion were grounds for collective action. Determined to fight for their rights and to protect their interests, a number of concerned families—with people from different age groups—organized a sit-in on June 23, 2010, setting up tents and occupying what they considered their lands. In support of the protest movement, local activists formed a solidarity committee and set up a dedicated Facebook page. Having failed to draw the authorities' attention to their problem by mid-July, a group of farmers headed to the regional government office to lay their case before the governor. Being denied access to officials, the group, which grew to a crowd of a few hundred people, started to chant slogans and lift banners pleading to the president to support the farmers and redress the injustices they had suffered.[48] The protesters were met with indifference. The police used force to disperse the crowd, causing more anger and resentment among the farmers and their families. Eventually, the governor gave in to the pressure and agreed to receive a delegation representing the farmers. The latter had four basic demands: launch an official investigation into the matter, hold to account those who were involved in the land scandal, return the seized lands to their rightful owners, and force the bank to reschedule the payment of the loans without collecting the accrued interest.[49] Before any progress could be achieved, a new governor unexpectedly took office in a government reshuffle. Most of the transactions were deemed legal, and the farmers were ordered to evacuate the lands or else face eviction by force.

The concerned farmers and their families came together a few weeks later to express anew their grievances. On Earth Day, a few hundred people protested in front of the regional government headquarters. The protestors' degree of anger and resentment was evident in their defiant attitude toward the security forces. Even more telling was that fear among these ordinary people—who were not political activists—was starting to dissipate with the loss of faith in the system.[50] Significantly, the socioeconomic nature of controversy over the Regueb lands went a long way toward uniting the political actors, forces, and activists. Gradually, the line between the socioeconomic and the political—between what Hibou calls "financial repression" and "political repression"—was starting to be blurred.[51]

The Cradle of the Revolution

The repercussions of the land controversy were felt a few weeks later as the culture of protest in front of the government building started to take hold.[52] This same building was to be the site of another protest, one that would decisively alter Tunisia's history and affect the Arab world's political configuration. Among the people that took part in the farmers' protest was Mohamed Bouazizi, a street vendor whose extended family included farmers who had a claim to disputed farmlands.[53] On December 17, 2010, Bouazizi got into an argument with municipal police over his unlicensed fruit stand. Although it was not the first time the police had hassled him, the situation became tense as the police officer attempted to confiscate Bouazizi's scale. To protest police harassment, he headed toward the regional government building. Having unsuccessfully attempted to lay his case in front of the governor's office, he dowsed himself with petrol, struck a match, and was quickly engulfed in flames. It was unclear whether the act of self-immolation was intentional or accidental. He was rushed to the hospital but his wounds were fatal.

This was not the first case of immolation, but it had an unprecedented effect, which, according to Bishara made it a "manifesto of sorts."[54] When Bouazizi immolated himself, his family, friends, and fellow vendors flocked to the site of the incident.[55] Soon, droves of people joined them, including not only enraged family members and ordinary citizens but also alarmed unionists and activists. The police—who were fully aware of the depth of people's anger and the delicate nature of the events—monitored the situation from a distance. Toward the end of the afternoon, squads of police forces in armored vehicles started to amass. By nightfall, the police presence was overwhelming.[56] The town was cordoned off from public access to become a closed security zone. It was clear to the townspeople that the situation was likely to escalate.

In an agrarian and semi-rural setting like Sidi Bouzid where kinship ties are still strong, social cooperation and support are common. But clanism was not a driving force in the ensuing events, and the revolutionary momentum that developed later was not tribal in nature. Nor were the dynamics of the protests wholly spontaneous. From the outset, local activists and union members attempted to intervene, including many who had been involved in the controversy over the Regueb lands.[57] These activists coalesced around the Bouazizis. While the tragic incident induced a spontaneous reaction, the gravity of the situation impelled the intensification of local activism. The emerging political dynamics soon took on a life of their own.

The following day, a Saturday, was also the weekly market day—a natural context for gathering. Soon, what had started as a small town's outpouring of support for the Bouazizis and a peaceful protest against a lamentable situation degenerated into violence. The unprecedented mobilization of police forces and their deployment by the thousands further provoked the resentful protesters into throwing stones and burning tires. The police responded with tear gas and sticks, arresting several locals and injuring many more. Multiple street confrontations ensued, which carried over into the night and overwhelmed the police. The protesters were coordinated and determined to carry on the fight.[58] Their persistence encouraged the enraged citizens, who believed they were fighting a just cause, and frightened the regime's security apparatus, which found itself on the defensive.

Protests Gather Strength

These shifting dynamics constituted a favorable terrain for anti-regime politics. Within three days, local activists formed the Citizen Committee for the Defense of the Victims of Marginalization, which comprised some two dozen political figures including lawyers, members of the unrecognized opposition, unionists, local activists, representatives from the unemployed, and some members of the Bouazizi family. A peaceful march from the Café Samarkand, where the committee was established, to the regional government headquarters to demand the release of the protesters was met with police repression, hardening the group's resolve.[59] In the early phases of the crisis, the committee's demands centered on issues of accountability, employment, economic reform, and regional development. These demands, which reflected the aspirations of ordinary citizens, also resonated with people across the social divide. Doctors, lawyers, and other professional groups lent their voices in support, as did regional human rights activists and also some local Internet activists, who worked diligently to draw attention to their grievances, expose the practices of the police, and embarrass the regime.[60]

Just as the protests started to lose momentum, another young unemployed man from Sidi Bouzid committed suicide by climbing an electricity post and holding on to a high-voltage wire. His death deepened people's anger and further incited the protesters. The authorities' efforts to confine the demonstrations proved unsuccessful. On December 24, unrest spread to the neighboring town of Menzel Bouzaïene, where unionists and activists in the local trade unions held meetings and organized sit-ins in support of Sidi Bouzid. Attempts to cordon off the protests instead prompted skirmishes, which started to spread and intensify. During the confrontations, one of the protesters was shot dead by the police. News about the use of live ammunition and stories about snipers shooting at the protesters started to circulate, causing more street demonstrations. The escalation of protests was met with yet more repressive security measures. Gradually, the riots diffused to neighboring towns like El Miknasi, El Mezzuna, Regueb, and Jilma. Ten days after Bouazizi's self-immolation, the protests engulfed the southwest region, resulting in further clashes with the police and more victims of their brutality. The authorities' repressive reaction was met with a sense of righteousness and adamant refusal to be subdued. The flaring up of the protests throughout the region emboldened people, while videos of defiant protesters chanting anti-regime slogans and images of clashes with the police circulating on social media alerted the public to what was happening in the inner cities.

The glaring discrepancy between images of the protests that were captured on mobile phones, passed around on the social Web, and retransmitted by channels like Al Jazeera, on the one hand, and the official story that was broadcast on the national media, on the other hand, accentuated the deepening nature of the crisis. On December 28, the president gave a televised speech in which he denounced the exploitation of what he described as isolated incidents by those who harbored ill will to the country. The president enumerated his regime's achievements and its commitment to equitable development, including poor and underprivileged regions. He also threatened that the actions of what he called a small, delinquent group of mercenaries that employed violence would be met with a decisive and firm response. These were not empty words. In the face of continued unrest and widespread agitations, the state cracked down on the protesters. The latter's distrust of the state made the situation all the more delicate. The disconnection between the state and its people favored the emergence of a rebellious spirit and a revolutionary momentum that would be hard to formalize, channel, or control.

For a few days toward the end of December, the popular unrest seemed to ease. The events ceased to make the headline news on Al Jazeera. Nearly two weeks after the self-immolation incident, state television showed an image of Ben Ali standing beside the badly burned fruit seller with his entire body swaddled in bandages save for an opening around his mouth. Whatever Ben Ali's intentions for the visit had been, it came off as a cynical photo opportunity rather than a sign of genuine compassion. Protests intensified as schools and universities resumed classes in early January. By the time Bouazizi died on January 4, the whole region was again in turmoil. Protests erupted in Tala, Kasserine, and Sebitla, leading to increased violence. Several video clips circulated showing a flow of wounded protesters in the emergency room of the hospital of Kasserine receiving medical attention. One disturbing hospital scene that circulated widely on the Internet featured a man lying on a gurney with a wound to his skull that exposed his brain.[61] The intense emotions these images provoked became important in sustaining the movement's momentum.

Supporting protests broke out in many towns and cities. Gradually, the claims to social justice specific to Sidi Bouzid and the other inner provinces were replaced by broader demands relevant to the whole society. Protests against social inequality and marginalization were not a new phenomenon, but the political demands that evolved were. Initially, the revolution took a social valence, with the demands involving social integration and social justice. People who took to the street wanted to express dissatisfaction with their situation. They called for job opportunities, a better future, more freedoms, and citizen dignity. Soon, social and economic grievances were transformed into demands for political change. The slogans quickly started to revile the regime, its corruption, and its icons, before they targeted the head of the regime, expressing their rejection of Ben Ali himself. "The people want the downfall of the regime" (*ash sha'b yurid isqat an nidham*) became the mantra of the revolution.

The rage that fueled the protesters had been long in the making. Its motivations cannot be reduced to a socioeconomic imperative. This was not a bread riot writ large. The fact that the protests extended to well-off regions and attracted people from across social classes suggestsed that what was developing was less a social revolution than a revolution that strongly articulated social demands.[62] The social, economic, political, and human dimensions were interlinked in complex ways. One of the central demands of the protesters was regaining dignity, which cannot be realized without economic opportunity, social justice, political freedom, moral rectitude, and ethical responsibility. These demands were symptomatic of a new mindset. On the eve of the revolution, one commentator warned: "Ben Ali and his government must realize that people do not live by bread alone. They also live as social actors with aspirations for free speech, organized political activity, civic and social capital, and political dynamism."[63] This yearning for liberty was even more insistent among an aspiring young generation that was increasingly more educated, better connected, and more in tune with global trends. The trade-off between liberty and security that the regime had maintained for nearly two decades would not satisfy a generation that demanded both.[64]

More and more people were ready to adopt the protest movement, while others were caught in the drama of the moment. A logic of collective creative improvisation gave the movement a life of its own.[65] Some protests were connected by union members and activists enlisting the help of people they knew in various towns, while others were simply inspired by the defiant attitude of the many angry citizens who took to the streets. Noticeably, police brutality increased, violence escalated, and confrontations intensified. A spiral reaction ensued as funerals were met with police restrictions that quickly devolved into clashes between grieving townspeople and hostile forces, which bred added violence, led to more deaths, and resulted in new funerals.

The pace and intensity of these developments shook the country. Increasingly, the popular protests were developing into chaos. A number of government buildings and security headquarters were ransacked. Several offices belonging to the government and the ruling party were set ablaze. It was evident that the regime was losing control and that the protests were entering a new phase. Beginning January 7, the army could be seen in some inner towns. It was evident from the limited scale of this measure that the deployment of the army was mainly to protect government buildings. The lack of organic links between the ruling party and the army had historically left it outside the sphere of political influence.[66] Concerned that a sizable and well-funded military could pose a challenge to his rule, Bourguiba had kept the military small, under control, and out of politics.[67] Ben Ali was even more concerned with the potential challenge the military could pose and so he adopted the same strategy, sidelining the military and strengthening the police force instead. As a result, the army, dominated by a professional officer corps, was a cohesive professional organ that was loyal to the republic and not the regime. The deployment of the army was reassuring to people. Rumors swirled about mounting tension between the top commander in the army, General Rachid Ammar, and the president. The decision of the army not to take sides altered the dynamics. By refusing to fire on the protesters, it cut its ties with the Ben Ali regime.

By the second week of January, the protests spread northward to cities like Bizerte, Beja, Jendouba, Silyana, and El Kef; southward to cities like Kbelli, Tozeur, Douz, Medenine, and Ben Gardane; and eastward to reach affluent coastal cities like Nabeul, Sfax, and Sousse. To help circumscribe the protests and minimize contexts for mobilization, the government suspended classes in all educational institutions on January 10. On the same day, Ben Ali delivered another televised speech in which he attempted to appease the demonstrators with promises of economic development, announcing a program to create three hundred thousand jobs over the span of two years. But these promises were widely perceived as empty. Typical official responses to the crisis— reshuffling the government, making sweeping pronouncements, and visiting the zones of unrest—failed to bridle the revolutionary forces that were gathering momentum by the day.

Increasingly, the protests were supported by a broad spectrum of society. The movement encompassed not only the unemployed and the unprivileged in the inner towns and cities but also extended to the middle class and encompassed various professional groups, including journalists, artists, and lawyers.[68] The active participation of and supporting activities by labor unions deserve special attention. The Tunisian General Labor Union played an integral part in the contestatory dynamics. Unlike the clientelist mentality it displayed during the Gafsa protests, the Union was far more involved in 2010.[69] With the movement in the mining region fresh in their memory, the Union's members were less willing to compromise. Although the national leadership of the Union remained cautious, the local unions, which were outspoken and networked, had supported the demonstrations since the beginning. The escalation of violence and the regime's targeting of the unions, particularly as the situation got worse, further ignited the Union's combative spirit and impelled unionists and union activists at the local level to mobilize people. The unprecedented scale of popular unrest altered the relationship between the unionists at the local sections and the regional and national union leadership. As the protests swelled, the latter succumbed to pressure to endorse the people's movement. On January 11, the top leadership of the Union reluctantly gave the green light to the regional unions to organize rotating strikes supporting the demonstrations around the country. On January 12, demonstrations reached Sfax, the biggest city in the south and traditionally a union stronghold, which organized a huge two-hour demonstration. People came out by the thousands. Notably, the demonstration was even supported by the business elite, who resented the excesses of the president's entourage.[70] The Union called for the resignation of the government, the formation of a transitional government that would prepare for early elections, and the release of political detainees. Confronted with the unexpected and fast-unfolding events, the opposition also attempted to position itself, albeit in a measured way. On January 9, a number of political parties issued a statement in support of the people's right to peaceful demonstration, free speech, and freedom.

With the protests engulfing much of the country, it became clearer by the day that the security forces had been overwhelmed by the events. The use of force proved ineffective in ending the unprecedented wave of protests. As the protests neared the capital, the Ministry of Interior imposed a curfew in Tunis, which was both the capital and the country's largest city. Initially, the heavy police presence helped insulate the capital from what was happening elsewhere. Toward the last week of December, some attempted protests could be registered, but these were met with police hostility. Similarly, a show of solidarity by union activists in front of the Union headquarters in Tunis was thwarted and the protesters were violently dispersed. However, by the second week of January, the flaring of the protests throughout the country had taken its toll on the security forces, who were spread too thin. The continuous need for the redeployment of police forces elsewhere and everywhere started to ease the tight control over the capital.

While the protests deepened the resentment of the regime across social classes, they had a strong effect on those who felt marginalized. Many of the people in the inner city and in the poor suburbs had ties to and relatives in the towns and provinces that were hit hard during the protests. They resented the violence against their people and the targeting of their native towns. In the densely populated and economically unprivileged suburbs like Cité Ibn Khaldoun and Cité Al Intilaka, people were charged and ready to burst. On the nights of January 12–13, Cité Ettadhamen saw violent confrontations with the police forces, and the people put up a fierce resistance, assaulting police forces, burning tires and busses, and closing the main roads. Much of the people's anger was a spontaneous reaction to the increased state repression of protesters with legitimate demands for dignity and economic opportunity. Emerging demographic realities also played a role. Many of the inhabitants of these urban conglomerations had left their rural homes to settle there in search of better opportunities during waves of migration beginning in the 1970s. An entire generation was born and raised in these suburbs, many of whom were perceived as provincial by virtue of their social class, regional background, and spoken dialect. For this segment of the population, the riots reawakened regional identities, which then impelled support for the plight of the people in the inner regions, particularly as police violence toward the protesters intensified. These significant urban-rural linkages also manifested themselves in the pointed efforts of activists from towns that were hit hard, like Sidi Bouzid and Kasserine, to stoke events through university students from the region who were pursuing their studies in the capital city as well as other activists.[71]

Mobilization in the capital provided a significant morale boost to the movement. The tipping point was the president's third speech on January 13, in which he promised to reduce the prices of basic food items and ordered the police to stop using ammunition on the protesters. He also vowed not to run again for a new term, announced that he would revise the electoral and press laws, and declared the end of Internet censorship. The speech, which was delivered in Tunisian dialect rather than formal standard Arabic, showed a nervous and desperate president. Such token concessions and half-measures were too little, too late. Rather than appease people, the president's last speech alarmed them. Thousands of active Internet users spent hours on Facebook alerting friends that this was a distraction and that the regime was waiting to get them after the dust settled.[72] By this point, even though the national TV showed jubilant pro–Ben Ali supporters taking to the street in celebration of his speech, few trusted the president.

The following day was a turning point in Tunisia's history. The government was to be dissolved and the prime minister was charged with constituting a new government. On January 14, while the protests continued throughout the country, a massive rally calling for Ben Ali's departure took place in front of the headquarters of the Ministry of Interior. The police used force to disperse the peaceful protesters. By late afternoon, a curfew was imposed and the air space was declared temporarily closed for all air traffic. Under unclear circumstances, the president and his immediate family boarded the presidential plane and flew to Jeddah. In a televised speech, the prime minister announced his assumption of power due to the president's temporary inability to assume his duties. The following day, the Constitutional Council declared a power vacuum and, following the constitution, moved to proclaim the Speaker of the House of Parliament president, thus dashing any hope for Ben Ali's return to power.

Conclusion

This chapter examined how fissures in society allowed pockets of resistance to exist even under an authoritarian regime. In some cases, this resistance had organized and institutional form, as with local labor unions, professionals, and opposition newspapers. The more significant forms of resistance, however, were manifest in the expressions of discontent that emerged from the frustrations and repressions that people endured in everyday life. Understanding the protests that led to Ben Ali's departure in the context of simmering discontent, scattered activism, and sporadic protests could shed new light on the beginnings of the Arab uprisings. Significantly, though, these pockets of resistance and forms of discontent did not cohere. Nor did they seem to pose a real threat to the regime, which grew adept at controlling public life and stifling dissent. Far from suggesting that these various manifestations of resistance had a cumulative effect that culminated in the revolution, the foregoing analysis provides a broader context for understanding the kind of digital contention that emerged and evolved in what was largely considered a marginal space. The online world constituted a site of contestation that was less overt and more diffuse, but one that portended dynamics and challenges of a different nature. The regime knew how to manage discontent offline, but was less adept at dealing with discontent online or developing the ability to reach accommodation with networked publics. While proving skillful at renovating an autocracy he had usurped from his predecessor, Ben Ali was unable to adjust to the expectations of a changing and predominantly young society. It is instructive to explore how these expectations were articulated in a loose space of interaction that the evolving technologies of the 1990s and the first decade of the twenty-first century brought about.

4

Cyber-Activism Comes of Age

Activists, Diasporas, and Networks

Modernization via the Internet

While traditional forms of politics had been present in Tunisia for a long time, emergent forms based more on digital networks were also coming into play. Tracing the development of contention on the Internet and understanding how these dynamics emerged and evolved over the years is instructive. Such an understanding, though, needs to be contextualized within the communication development strategy the Ben Ali regime adopted.

From the early 1990s, the Tunisian state took a keen interest in the Internet. In 1991, it was the first country in Africa to establish a connection to the Internet, although public use of the Internet would not be authorized until 1996. The forward-looking strategy the state adopted in developing the information and communications technologies (ICT) sector is part of its long history of modernization. As Bras notes, the image of the state as an advocate of technological progress and a champion of modernization has been "a constant feature of the Tunisian political formula since its independence."[1] Bourguiba's vision of an educated and enlightened society was partly premised on opening the country toward the West and linking it to technologies of modernization. Under Ben Ali—an avid Internet user who embraced technology to project an image of himself as a modernizer—the country made the development of a viable information and communication infrastructure a priority, enacting a digital leap forward that made it stand out as an emerging ICT leader in the region. From the outset, the Internet had a special appeal to Tunisia's relatively well-educated population. High literacy rates, liberal gender roles, and the general population's ease with the Latin alphabet further facilitated the growth of Internet use. The demographics of the country, especially the youth bulge (with roughly two-thirds of the country's population being under the age of twenty-five), meant that Tunisia had a sizable Net generation. Cognizant of the potential of information technology for economic development, the government sought to build a sophisticated Internet infrastructure to promote the rapid adoption of digital technologies. On the tenth anniversary of his coming to power, Ben Ali reaffirmed his commitment to bringing the country online, promising a qualitative leap in the field of communication to help economic development and attract foreign investors.[2] ICT investment was complemented by measures aimed at strengthening regulation in this new sector, including the creation of the Tunisian Internet Agency in 1996 to provide state-of-the-art Internet services,[3] the licensing of private Internet Service Providers in 1997, and the establishment of El Ghazala Information and Technology Park in 1999. Going hand in hand with these initiatives was the launch of the e-dinar—a secure and convenient electronic payment tool aimed at adapting the economy to the Information Age.

To ingrain a digital culture in the Tunisian populace, the government took a number of steps to improve access to the Internet. During the first decade of the twenty-first century, the percentage of the population with access to the Internet increased from 1 percent to 33.4 percent.[4] To promote Internet use, in 1998 the government authorized the establishment and licensing of Internet cafés and telecommunication centers, commonly known as publinets (formally Public Internet Access Centers), and even provided subsidies to help defray the cost of establishing such public facilities. As one of the objectives of this initiative was the generalization of access throughout the country, publinets were also licensed in rural areas and remote regions. Initially, because of the relatively high cost of computers and Internet services, most people gained access to the Internet through these modestly priced publinets. The number of licensed publinets in operation rose from fewer than 170 in 2000 to 306 in 2002 to 317 in 2004, frequented mainly by high school and university students.[5] Nearly half of these publinets were concentrated in and around Tunis.[6] The state also pledged to wire schools and institutions of higher education, established a number of Internet access points in youth clubs and cultural centers, and created a program for professional development in the area of ICT.

Gradually, access to the Internet through publinets started to give way to subscription-based access. As Internet subscription rates became more affordable, the number of subscribers grew from an estimated 1,200 in 1997 (.09 percent of the population) to 100,000 in 2000 (1.0 percent of the population) to 953,000 in 2006 (9.3 percent of the population).[7] Contributing to this surge in subscriptions was a young generation's appetite for the Internet, which was further fueled by the state's purposeful attempt to encourage computer literacy, disseminate computers, and connect the middle class to the Web. In 2001, the government launched the household computer program, an initiative aimed at helping middle-class people acquire their own personal computers at a reduced price with flexible terms of payment. This was further enhanced by a decrease in the cost of Internet subscriptions. Such initiatives expanded Internet use beyond elite middle-class youth in urban centers, while those who could not afford to subscribe continued to access the Internet through publinets.

According to a 2005 study on the Internet in Tunisia, the majority of users were between eighteen and thirty years old.[8] After 2006, Internet penetration increased dramatically and a significant segment of society plunged into cyberspace. Rapidly expanding Internet connectivity, access to high-speed Internet (known as ADSL or asymmetrical digital subscriber line), improved international bandwidth capacity, and dropping subscription costs meant that the Internet became mainstream media for a broad swath of the population. Between 2007 and 2009, the number of users doubled from 1,618,440 (15.6 percent of the population) to 3,500,000 (33.4 percent of the population).[9] Similarly, between 2008 and 2009, the number of high-speed Internet subscriptions doubled from 178,000 to 354,000.[10] By January 2011, the number of high-speed Internet subscribers stood at 547,763 while the number of users reached 3.9 million,[11] more than one-third of Tunisia's population of approximately 11 million, placing it above average for developing countries and ahead of other Arab nations.

The First Generation of Cyber Activists

From its early days, the Internet in Tunisia was a space that different forces and players tried to control. Although the Internet was initially a controlled and managed space, it evolved to be a dynamic arena of engagement and interaction that gradually favored contention. Despite governmental censorship, several forms of online engagement emerged over the years. For the curious and disenfranchised youth alike, the virtual world was simply fascinating. Cyberspace offered them a refuge—a public space where they could connect to others, experience a different reality, or claim a voice while rejoicing in anonymity. For many young people, the Web was a convenient way of partaking in the digital revolution and globalization. This development was not unprecedented. Just as an earlier generation had turned en masse toward satellite TV in the 1990s, so a desire to be connected (and the fear of being left out) translated into youth's special attraction to, active engagement with, and appropriation of the Internet. The Web was particularly appealing because it facilitated social contacts and enhanced the ability to go beyond prescribed boundaries. In a country that limited access to information, exerted strong control over the media, and imposed severe constraints on the freedom of expression, the Internet was a repository of information, a freer space of engagement, and an open forum for debate.[12] As in much of the Arab world, people's appropriation of cyberspace broke the limitations on who could speak in public and expanded what can be talked about publicly.[13] With a growing mass of Web enthusiasts and Internet users, this open environment favored the rise of spaces of contestation, some of which were enduring and others more experimental and short-lived. Progressively, these spaces of interaction also connected Tunisians in the homeland with their countrymen and women in the diaspora in ways that would prove transformative for some users.[14]

The sites that users created varied in form and structure, ranging from relatively anarchic chat groups and Internet forums to more organized mailing lists and independent news services. Among the early online experiments that were developed by the first generation of cyber-activists, several sites—Takriz, TUNeZINE, Reveil Tunisien, Tunisnews, and Nawaat—deserve special attention. Empowered by low-cost information and communication systems, they operated as loose semi-anonymous entities. Being online initiatives, they were less constrained by traditional structures, physical location, financial resources, or formal expertise. As a result, they produced novel forms of communicating, engaging, organizing, and resisting.

Where Pop Culture Meets Politics

One of the early loci of cyber-activism was an online forum called Takriz. The recalcitrant and provocative nature of the forum was evident in its name, a Tunisian slang word designating the state of being deeply aggravated, as well as suffocation. The name evoked the mindset of a young generation frustrated by a system that held them back.[15] Founded in 1998 by two students who operated under the pseudonym Fœtus and Waterman, and hosted on a server in Canada, Takriz provided its members with a "free zone," as Fœtus described it, to rant about the dysfunctional aspects of everyday life.[16] Underlying this initiative was a desire to configure a relatively free space of interaction away from family control and state repression.[17] Initially, Takriz used a simple mailing list to exchange personal reflections about a wide range of issues and social commentary on a number of taboo topics. They adopted a distinctive style, "writing in an imperfect French that is often bold, rough and insolent, echoing both a deep anger and an appetite for life."[18] As Waterman explains, driving the group's streetwise style is the desire to shake things up and to be provocative:

> We use a "trashy" style and we speak like uncouth people, but we are not such. The foul language we use is not a sign of disrespect or inso-lence. All we wanted was to provoke young people, shake them up, and get them to rid themselves of their fear. The first step in this en-deavor was to untie their tongues, to dare them to talk about taboo things, and to get them to speak their minds. This is the enduring legacy of Takriz.[19]

The subjects that animated the forum were varied and included government bureaucracy, university malpractice, state media, Internet control, nepotism, gender relationships, virginity, and religion.

From its inception, Takriz was an exclusive group that operated clandes-tinely. Even after the revolution, their operation remained secretive. Although I managed to interview the two founding members of the group (Fœtus and Waterman) in the course of my fieldwork, the Skype interviews were con-ducted with the image feature turned off. Except for the cofounders who were childhood friends, and Sux and Furax, who were trusted members of the core group, Takriz's initial group of twenty-two active members—who were based in Tunisia—did not know one another.[20] Only trusted individuals were invited to join the group. In subsequent years, recruitment of new members followed a more rigorous process that involved initiation rituals.[21] Typically, the mem-bers of the group do not physically meet or know one another's real identity.[22] In fact, one of the guiding principles of the group is a commitment to working in strict anonymity. This principle has implications for the group's modus op-erandi. Structurally, Tarkiz is a cyber-movement with no centralized leader-ship.[23] As envisioned in its eccentric charter, "Takriz is decentralized and intentionally disorganized. The dynamics of the movement and its members

are a source of creativity and innovation."[24] Operationally, the group empha-
sizes secrecy and exclusivity: "The fact that we refuse to deal with those who
are not free increased our readership base and drew in more fans who gladly
but discreetly pass on our messages."[25] Takriz conceives of itself as "a group of
cyber-reflection and collective intelligence"[26] committed to liberty, truth, and
justice. The group's outspokenness against state propaganda, systematic disin-
formation, media monopoly, and blatant censorship emanates out of their
firm belief that the fight against authoritarianism requires freedom of speech
and Internet freedom.[27]

These ideals proved to have a special appeal. By the end of 1999, Takriz
could claim more than two hundred subscribers, although not all of them
were active contributors.[28] The growth in the subscription base of the group
prompted a discussion on whether Takriz should go public. Many members
objected to the idea. While some did not feel comfortable acting in the open,
others felt that revealing their identities would make them vulnerable to official sanctions. Consequently, the email list remained private, but Takriz
reached out to the general public by launching a website and an e-magazine in
2000. The fresh tone, no-holds-barred discourse, indulgent style, down-to-earth
idiom, and the unstilted—even crude—language of Takriz's members and
"amateurish reporters"[29] contributed much to its popularity among a section
of the young population, particularly in university settings. Some of their fans
made copies of the newsletter and circulated them clandestinely to other students who lacked access to the Internet. Word of mouth publicized the movement further, and soon enough Takriz became a counterculture.

Takriz's appeal did not go unnoticed by the authorities, who were quick to
censor it. The development of Web search engines extended Takriz's audience,
but also enhanced the surveillance ability of the state. Among the many Web
search engines that were operative in 1998, Yahoo was particularly popular,
with about 100 million page views a day worldwide.[30] Its database at the time
was organized hierarchically, which meant that the search function used
to provide Web (sub)directories, rather than listing full webpages the way a
Google search started doing in subsequent years. Because Takriz was based in
Tunisia, it was indexed as "Tunisian media." Inevitably, the site's enhanced
searchability drew the attention of the Tunisian Internet Agency. Within days,
it was blocked. As the existence of censorship was officially denied, the group
received no formal notification or legal justification for such action.

Takriz was more contestatory than revolutionary or anarchist.[31] Its members were animated by their desire for a critical discussion of everyday issues

rather than political debates. As Fœtus put it, "In Tunisia, everything is controlled and that goes for what people think. So we do not pretend to do politics.... The purpose of the site is to express ourselves freely on issues which we face as Tunisians."[32] Since members of Takriz considered themselves less as "enemies of the regime" than as "militants for the freedom of expression,"[33] political commentary took the form of light and oblique critiques often in a humorous or sarcastic vein. Even though some of the members of Takriz were aware of the political situation in the country, the "anti-intellectual" orientation of the movement[34] was such that discussions of political topics were muted and conversations along ideological lines eschewed.[35]

Initially, Takriz was more of a subculture than a thorn in the side of the authorities. Individual liberty and free speech were causes célèbres of the group, partly because infringements on these rights most directly affected the everyday life of the group members. Their motivation came from a desire "to free the Net and expression."[36] Perhaps unsurprisingly, one of the group's early campaigns was against Tunisie Telecom, the national communication company. Subscription rates to the Internet were relatively expensive and the only two existing providers, PlaNet and Global Net, were either owned by the president's family or controlled by individuals associated with the regime. Gradually, these forms of calibrated engagement evolved into cyber-dissidence and became overtly militant. In the words of one of Takriz's founding members, "the group was pushed to adopt a more overt political orientation."[37] Two years of interaction on the e-forum steered the discussion about the issues facing young Tunisians from individual manifestations of the problems—such as censorship and Internet control—to the source of the problems: Ben Ali's regime.[38]

The authorities' decision to censor Takriz's site in 2000 hardened the group.[39] Its members expressed their indignation at being citizens of a country that did not respect the freedom of speech.[40] Undeterred by the ban, Takriz vowed to "continue to write about what they go through in their daily lives."[41] At the same time, they launched an anti-censorship campaign, which they dubbed "the campaign of the censored against censorship," issuing press releases, contacting media organizations, and writing to embassies of Western countries to urge them to support their cause. Some Takriz members who were based outside the country helped spread the word and draw international press coverage.[42] Takriz also set up a cyber-crisis unit called "Taktik" to instruct users on how to avail themselves of proxies to bypass censorship, enhance the security of communication by using the https protocol, utilize anonymizers to efface traces that could expose users, and avail themselves of the tools of cryptography.[43]

In a heavily policed state like Tunisia, cyber-activism comes with risks. Despite their precautions, Takriz's members found themselves living in constant fear.[44] The vigilance of the authorities, the tightening of Internet control,[45] and the pressure felt by the group led some members to adopt a low profile, discouraged others from writing, and prompted a few to unsubscribe from the forum altogether.[46] Further affecting the group's activism was the fact that a number of its active members left the country to pursue their studies abroad. Although the group continued to interact with one another through Internet Relay Chat, it gradually lost its momentum. Eventually, Takriz fell into a state of hibernation and ceased to be publicly active by 2002.[47] From 2005 to 2009, the movement resumed its cyber-militancy underground, using a secure network to communicate internally. During this period, they also recruited a new generation of cyber-activists who operated mainly in schools and universities, cultivating sources, gathering information, and writing reports. With the wave of censorship and the election of Ben Ali to a fifth term in 2009, the group intensified its cyber-resistance. While continuing to operate anonymously, it reemerged to the wide public, relaunched its website, and increased its activities against the regime.

What is particularly interesting about this early Internet forum is its tacit political dimension. One can outline noteworthy tendencies that will be more pronounced in subsequent cyber-movements: an aspiration to be involved as citizens, a growing awareness of civil rights, and a desire to carve out a space of involvement outside the traditional framework of politics. The group's "cyber civil rights activism" also bespoke an evolving conception of citizenship that appropriated official political discourse about the country's commitment to the principles of democracy. As Célina Braun points out, the kind of discourse Takriz's generation of cyber-activists were introduced to through textbooks was one that celebrated the notion of a modern Tunisia anchored in the principles of human rights, the values of citizenship, and the political institutions of democracy.[48] Interestingly, the country's political environment gave institutionalized movements, in general, and opposition political parties, in particular, little credence or appeal for the young generation. The formal opposition was elitist and perceived as "a product of the same system" that consolidated the rule of Ben Ali.[49] As Braun put it, Takriz stood out for being an "anti-party"[50] that promoted a counter-discourse and advocated "civil disobedience."[51] Although Takriz's charter claims that "it is apolitical" and that "its goal is to form generations of truly free citizens,"[52] the group's proclaimed distance from politics should not obscure its inherently political character. Their inability to identify with formal political institutions or relate to party politics forced them to seek a space of contention that is anchored in what de Certeau calls "tactics" that would take hold with the increase of cyber-activism over the years.[53]

A Catalyst for Cyber-activism

By the time Takriz ceased to be active, other discussion groups had emerged. One was TUNeZINE, established in 2001 by Zouheir Yahyaoui, a thirty-five-year-old pioneering Tunis-based Internet activist who had been active on Takriz.[54] Yahyaoui was an unemployed business graduate who took up a temporary job at a publinet in the suburbs of Tunis, where he negotiated an arrangement with the publinet owner whereby "he worked without pay in the publinet in exchange for having unlimited access to a computer station there."[55] The Internet symbolized freedom for him, and he soon developed an e-interest in politics and opposition movements, only to discover that many of the sites that discussed politics or human rights in Tunisia were blocked.[56] Passion for information and communication technologies and long hours in front of a computer terminal helped him learn about proxies, anonymizers, and mailing lists. As he became savvy with computers, he put his skills to use, setting up a website and a forum (hosted on a server in France) to spread the word about events in the country. Online, he discussed a range of social, cultural, and political issues and did so provocatively and in a captivating style.

Launched in the pre-blogging days, TUNeZINE was a one-man initiative that initially served as a repository for all the material Yahyaoui gathered about sociopolitical issues in the country. It soon evolved into a lively online discussion forum. That the forum had a political orientation was evident in the very name TUNeZINE, an allusion to the Tunisian president's first name. Writing in French and Arabic under the pseudonym *Ettounsi* ("The Tunisian"), Yahyaoui discussed politics via criticism and satire. TUNeZINE also published a newsletter containing newspaper articles, editorials, communiqués from various political actors, letters of support for political prisoners, reports on corruption, and unflattering caricatures of Ben Ali. For Yahyaoui, "access to information could play an important role in shaking off the passivity that plagued the Tunisian population."[57] Compiling articles and distributing them electronically to as wide a readership as possible was geared toward raising an antiestablish-ment political consciousness. Speaking out against the regime of ZABA (the derogatory acronym he used to refer to Zine El Abidine Ben Ali) was a first step toward achieving freedom and Yahyaoui did it with a distinctive style. He wrote about politics within a new communicative context that placed him outside the traditional sphere of political action and distinguished him from conventional political players. His cyber-peers described him as "an ideology-free revolutionary"[58] who "had no political affiliation or allegiance"[59]—someone "who simply stood for freedom and liberty."[60] In the words of those who knew him well, "Yahyaoui, who wrote both in French and Arabic, was a poet and artist; he had a literary sensibility and rare ability to play with words."[61] His use of derision was innovative but was also compelling, showing a bold disposition toward creative dissent.[62] The site's humor and sarcasm were as much a means to fight back the kind of fear instilled by the state as they were a creative tool to ridicule the regime itself and expose its absurdity. As much as it gave the readers of the forum hope by making people laugh at their own misery,[63] Yahyaoui's light touch masked his sadness about the country's reality.[64]

The forum's satirical vein resonated with a number of readers. Many users who were seduced by the talent and insolence of the forum's administrator[65] learned about it through Tunisnews, a widely circulated electronic newsletter that will be discussed in detail later and which occasionally republished some of its material. Among the contributors to TUNeZINE were Tunisian stu-dents abroad who were keen on keeping up with what was happening in their home country. The site's contestatory, analytical, engaging, and open nature favored the exchange of ideas and views among Tunisians at home and abroad. For many of the members who were active on the forum, these debates sig-naled a new spirit, one that Yahyaoui incarnated. To them, he was "a symbol of a youth that was full of talent and that dreamt of a brighter future."[66]

Although TUNeZINE drew a few hundred readers and attracted tens of regular contributors from inside and outside the country, its most revealing dy-namics revolved around a handful of individuals. The nucleus of TUNeZINE was formed over the course of a few months. In addition to Yahyaoui, the inner circle consisted of a group of six who were geographically scattered among Tunisia, Canada, and France.[67] Except for one non-Tunisian member, these individuals adopted pseudonyms that concealed their real identities from their readers and also from one another. Restricting their interaction to email communication, they did not meet in person, call one another over the phone, or probe one another's personal history. Yahyaoui liked to refer to the "anonymous friends" he "came to know thanks to dictatorship" as "incorruptible people who refuse to give in."[68] The forum fostered strong affinities among the members of the group and soon an empowering relationship of trust built up among them.[69]

The way some of these core members came to join TUNeZINE and to be in sync with what was a diverse group is instructive. I present two of their stories to illustrate the process. The first one is a user who migrated to Canada early on in his career and took his name from the acclaimed medieval Persian poet Omar Khayyâam. He came to know about TUNeZINE through Tunisnews. Visiting TUNeZINE gradually became part of his daily routine. In July 2001, he contributed a short piece titled "The Persecution of Words"[70]—a reflective but highly figurative reading on the parallel destiny of words and people in the country. Sensing in this political allegory an answer to his call for people "to shed off their silence and to participate in the edification of a pluralistic Tunisia,"[71] Yahyaoui posted it on the forum. This sign of appreciation encouraged the writer to contribute another piece on the freedom of expression titled "A Deafening Freedom of Expression," a satirical text based on a real-life story.[72] As his writing improved, he became addicted to publishing political fiction online.

The last prominent member to join the group, and whose story is the second one I present, was Sophie Piekarec, a young Frenchwoman in Paris. Sophie was intrigued by the charm of Tunisia, a former French colony, but also perplexed by the irreconcilability of certain trends that she saw on her frequent holidays there. Tunisia was open and progressive, but it was also mired in retrograde practices. With the reelection of Ben Ali in 1999, the French press started to probe the political and human rights situation in Tunisia. The attention the country received in the press resonated with Sophie. After reading Taoufik Ben Brik's book *Such a Soft Dictatorship: Tunisian Chronicles*, a birthday present she received from her mother, Sophie grew curious about the hidden face of the country. As she started to dig for information about Tunisia on the Internet, she came across TUNeZINE and quickly found herself drawn to its debates and discussions. She was intrigued by Yahyaoui's captivating style and his imposing personality. The two quickly developed an intellectual affinity and ultimately a close relationship. The numerous email exchanges between an unconventional figure refusing to accept to live in a country that became "a prison with invisible walls" and an atypical foreigner who refused to be the "dumb tourist" who was content with the sun and the sea the country offered led to a real-life encounter in Tunis in April 2002.[73]

Shortly after her return to Paris following this last visit, Sophie learned that Yahyaoui had been arrested on June 4, 2002. The authorities targeted Yahyaoui in retaliation for what they considered as acts of cyber-defiance.[74] The fact that TUNeZINE crossed a red line—publicly deriding the regime's democratic pretensions—prompted the authorities to censor the site. After a long hunt for the impudent Ettounsi, the Internet police identified his IP address, which led to his arrest in the publinet where he worked.[75] The authorities searched his premises, confiscated his computer, extracted the password for TUNeZINE from him, and destroyed the site, although Sophie diligently worked to resurrect it and managed to keep it active for some time. Yahyaoui was sentenced to two years in prison. One of his offenses was the posting of an open letter to the president in which his uncle, the rebel judge Mokhtar Yahyaoui, called for the independence of the judiciary system.[76] Equally objectionable was his open criticism of the 2002 referendum on the constitutional amendment that eliminated term limits for the presidency and granted the president immunity from prosecution even after leaving office.[77] Resentful of such political stratagems, Yahyaoui conducted a parody-like poll on TUNeZINE, which ridiculed the official referendum and humorously denounced Ben Ali for hijacking the principles of the republic.[78] Officially, Yahyaoui was charged with publishing false news pertaining to speculations about an armed attack on the presidential palace and of fraudulent use of communication.

Whatever the charge, the message was unmistakable. It highlighted "the government's determination to punish criticism and to keep the Internet from becoming a refuge for free expression amidst a heavily censored print press."[79] For the authorities, the case of Yahyaoui was intended as a warning to the Internet community about the risks of cyber-activism. From a legal perspective, this was an unprecedented case involving online criticism of the regime and Yahyaoui was the first Internet activist in the country to be jailed. To protest his mistreatment and his lamentable jail conditions, he went on several hunger strikes. In a show of support, the core group of TUNeZINE sought to publicize his conditions and established an international committee to press for his liberation.[80] Thanks to these efforts, his arrest attracted international attention from many nongovernmental organizations (NGOs) and advocacy groups, leading to his early release in November 2003—a gesture that was meant to improve the country's image ahead of the first 5+5 Summit between the countries of the Western Mediterranean rim, which was held in Tunisia at the end of that year and aimed at enhancing the stability and security of this sub-region.[81] Unfortunately, a few months later, Yahyaoui died of a heart attack at age thirty-seven.[82]

In a symbolic act of defiance, some of the outspoken members on the forum who were emboldened by Yahyaoui's death decided to reveal their real identities for the first time. But the damage had already been done. The death of the chief architect of TUNeZINE was a serious blow to the forum as his style and virtual charisma were a hard act to follow. A sense of sadness and fatigue set in among the core group, but, thanks in large part to Sophie, the forum remained operative. The issue of who would administer the forum added to the confusion. Some were displeased by the fact that the forum was managed by a "foreigner." The desire of others to claim the by-then visible forum created friction. This was evident in the charged language of some contributors, which at times resulted in the truncation of messages that did not abide by the charter of the forum.[83] While some supported the intervention of the administrator to preserve the quality of the discussion, others considered it an attempt to control the debate. Sadly, the forum hardly outlived its zealous initiator. On March 13, 2006, the first anniversary of Yahyaoui's death, Sophie froze the site and posted a quotation from Winston Churchill: "It is not the end; it is not even the beginning of the end. It is the end of the beginning." As it turned out, these words were prophetic. While the forum fell into oblivion, the contentious spirit associated with its founder lived on.

TUNeZINE provided an alternative space of engagement, attracted disparate voices, and encouraged contention thanks to its founder who left an indelible mark. Yahyaoui's personality, drive, humor, resentment of injustice, and yearning for freedom turned him into a "catalyst for a core cyber-dissidence."[84] An obituary published in 2005 on the Tunisian online forum Alternatives Citoyennes powerfully captured Yahyaoui's enduring legacy:

> We recognize in Zouheir Yahyaoui the iconic figure of a trailblazer. Those who expressed their grief over his death, both on authorized and banned forums, had good reason to do so. What they lost was a friend and an alter ego. The insolence of a young man full of irreverence sent shockwaves through the regime. He spoke the language of the rebellious youth, with such an uncalculated audacity and an unyielding spontaneity. He was neither an intellectual of stature nor a complacent man of salons. Nor for that matter could he pass off as a member of the established opposition, which was too archaic for his

sharpness, lucidity and punch. He was a true figure of resistance, using the Internet with the ease of a digital native who saw in new media technologies a unique weapon in the battle for freedom.... Let his young generation embrace the spirit of cyber-dissidence he came to incarnate. Let them make his dream about freedom come true.[85]

Reflection and Information

Some of the active members of TUNeZINE founded a new forum, Reveil Tunisien. Despite its roots, the new site did not adopt TUNeZINE's style. Whereas TUNeZINE was a discussion forum, Reveil Tunisien was more focused on reflection and information. This inclination dates to the controversial 2002 referendum, when TUNeZINE hosted a virtual conference devoted to the future of Tunisia. Among the issues it addressed were the merit of exercising pressure on the regime to improve its human rights record, a campaign to boycott tourism, and the need to reconsider the strategies of online activism. A number of France-based TUNeZINE contributors (all pseudonymous, and introduced to one another online) set up Reveil Tunisien as a vehicle to pursue these issues at a more professional level. Apart from its sober tone, the site was distinguished by the comments section on each post.

As conceived by its founders, Reveil Tunisien was a "space of liberty, information, and free expression."[86] Its core members considered themselves less as "cyber-activists" than as "active citizens."[87] The group's many political colors, views, and allegiances were united by the desire for change. Much like Takriz, Reveil Tunisien did not believe in party politics or identify with traditional forms of contestation. As Hasni, the group's webmaster and prominent contributor, explained to me in an interview,

> In Tunisia, there are two kinds of opposition: the former is the legal opposition which supports Ben Ali and campaigns for his reelection; the latter is the credible and banned opposition which does politics the old-fashioned way—organizations with long-standing figures who adopted a 1970s style political action. Incognizant of the potential of information and communications technologies to revolutionize the way information and ideas circulate, they continue to produce insipid communiqués that hardly anybody reads and hold

public meetings for their limited circle. We wanted to create a "third opposition." For us, the way to go is an Internet-based citizenship whereby people do not claim their rights but exercise them. If there are no journalists, no reporters and no caricaturists, we will—and we did—step in and fill in the void.[88]

This call for cyber-engagement recognizing the need for a committed sense of citizenship was echoed by many group members. For another contributor, political opposition transcended political parties because the Internet allows everyone to take part in political debates: "Being detached from its base, the opposition cannot understand people or live up to their aspirations. We have to take advantage of the Internet. We have to take the matter in our hands and involve the entire society in a debate on the future of the country. Let us capitalize on the Internet to initiate a debate."[89] Given the context of Ben Ali's Tunisia, this kind of involvement necessitated secrecy and anonymity, and the members of Reveil Tunisien, like those of Takriz and TUNeZINE before them, adopted pseudonyms and limited their interaction to the virtual world.

The arrest and sentencing of Zouheir Yahyaoui compelled Reveil Tunisien to go beyond its commitment to free expression and become an advocate for political prisoners. In 2004, it took up the cause of a small group of young Internet users from the southern city of Zarzis. These high school and university students were accused of promoting terrorist attacks because they had downloaded materials from Islamic websites. Reveil Tunisien published their pictures, publicized procedural irregularities in their court hearings, and conducted interviews with their families. Cyber-initiatives such as these helped lend support to the fight for human rights and reinforce the efforts to advocate democracy. However, with the site gaining more readership came the realization that Reveil Tunisien had inadvertently created "an enormous communication machine."[90] For a group comprising amateurs and volunteers, sustaining such work involved a constant and taxing struggle, especially because the site was banned and repeatedly hacked.[91] Lacking resources, the site's momentum ebbed. Over the years, lamented the webmaster of the site, "the strongest wills grew weary and exhausted."[92] Still, initiatives like these by Tunisians both at home and in the diaspora have contributed much to the creation of a contestatory space of interaction that aspired to contribute to the making of a better Tunisia.

Other forums, less popular and mostly based outside of Tunisia, emerged, including Al Khadra (the Green), a forum that had a religious flavor, Nokta

(Joke) a short-lived forum devoted to popular political jokes, and Alternatives Citoyennes (Alternative Female Citizens), a rather elitist forum founded by a Tunis-based independent journalist and a Paris-based researcher. Particularly noteworthy were homegrown pop forums like Dar.net, Marhba.com, Kaftaji.com, and Mac125.com, which attracted thousands of young people who sought to connect to others and communicate with them about a variety of issue and interests. By and large, the topics that were discussed were sociocultural, literary, or common in nature and the contributions were uneven, ranging from the provocative to the controversial to the trivial. Generally, participants in these forums steered clear of political topics, even if some material with political overtones was bound to find its way to these forums.[93] Overall, though restrained politically, this was a lively space that contributed to the formation of an online community and helped connect young people within the country to one another and to the their fellow countrymen in the diaspora.

Reinventing Independent Journalism

Although forums like Takriz, TUNeZINE, and Reveil Tunisien promoted a contestatory culture and adopted a discourse emanating out of the everyday world, other, more overtly political initiatives like Tunisnews attempted to revive an older journalistic experiment. As such, Tunisnews epitomizes the evolutionary disposition and adaptive capabilities of what potentially could have been opposition forces and political actors. It stands out not so much for being an alternative voice, but for designing new tools and adopting different strategies to sustain a political collectivity in the face of hardening authoritarianism.

Tunisnews is an active information repository established in the early days of the Internet but which has endured for over a decade, expanding its readership and increasing its influence. It is a bilingual newsletter created in 1999 by a group of five anonymous Tunisians, most of whom were political refugees from the banned Islamist movement Ennahda. The server was hosted in Sweden, where most of the group's members resided. The project of Tunisnews, as the managers of the site explain, was not planned.[94] It started with a casual exchange of online news and articles about Tunisia among a small group of friends. Initially, the group set up a free mailing list called "Tunispress," renamed "Tunisnews" in 2000. Distinguished by the regular publication of its daily online newsletter since its inception,[95] Tunisnews met with an immense success, especially considering that it was not interactive and did not have debates. Except for a brief interruption in 2006 after a virus attack that disabled the system for a few days, Tunisnews unfailingly published daily posts for its broad and loyal readership. Figuring prominently on their not-so-fancy webpage is a motto in Arabic, French, and English: "Every day, we contribute better information on our country Tunisia." Many users found in Tunisnews a valuable and rich source of credible information, especially as the national press became more controlled and official discourse grew monolithic. Contributing to the receptiveness of this news and information service was the added interest both inside the country and in the diaspora in the real state of affairs in Tunisia.

Tunisnews publishes material related to Tunisia in French and Arabic including newspaper articles, commentaries, open letters, communiqués from activists and NGOs, and occasional translations of material appearing elsewhere in foreign languages. The members of the team invest long hours after work scouring for published material, organizing the material, referencing the source of the information, and then diffusing it via email before posting it on their site. As they see it, their work aims not only at aggregating and publicizing information but also building a repository for material on Tunisia that captured the country's various political, cultural, and intellectual sensibilities.[96] The utter dedication and devotion of the volunteer editorial team sustained them in providing an uninterrupted flow of information for more than a decade.

One of the distinctive features of the forum was its openness to various discourses and orientations. Their commitment to providing all points of view reflected their vision of a better Tunisia. Even though Tunisnews has an obvious Islamist flavor, reflected in the space it gave to Islamic perspectives, it refrained from providing commentary on the material it published or engaging in polemic discussions. Consequently, despite the perceived "Islamist and Islamic preponderance" of its members,[97] Tunisnews is an inclusive forum that is open to various viewpoints and ideological tendencies. Driven by the proclaimed vision of "a Tunisia for all the Tunisians," the site purports to "mirror the political, intellectual, social and associative diversity inside the country."[98] When taken to task for reporting on the launch of a pro-government website, Tunisnews reiterated its editorial policy:

We promote mutual respect and encourage a civilized debate among various perspectives, ideas, figures, tendencies and citizens at home or abroad with the exception of torturers and criminals who have Tunisian blood on their hands. We have always published on the pages of Tunisnews official and non-official material emanating from all currents of the political, cultural and ideological spectrum of the country.[99]

For an Islamic movement like Ennahda that positions itself as moderate, such an inclusive overture can pay dividends. A study of Tunisnews points out how this open forum allows for the regular and prominent articulation of Islamic viewpoints within a broad-based discursive context.[100] For a movement that has been ostracized, engaging the broad public demonstrates the appeal of a subtle and evolving form of political activism that rejected a heavy-handed ideological approach in favor of a commitment to inclusiveness.[101]

Although modest and marginal, Tunisnews had an enduring legacy by providing a sustained platform for a culture of skepticism and vigilance to develop. Over the years, it built a reputation as a militant venue and gave room for all dissenting voices as evinced by the postings of various politically sensitive news items, contributions by independent activists, and critical reports by various associations on lack of freedom, human rights violations, persecution, and corruption in the country. The culture of contention that characterizes Tunisnews extends the short-lived vibrant independent press tradition that animated the early 1980s.[102] Toward the end of Bourguiba's era, a number of privately owned newspapers emerged that included voices from across the political spectrum. Publications like *Errai* (The Opinion), *Democratie* (Democracy), *Le Phare* (The Beacon), *Le Maghreb* (The Maghreb), *Ash-sha'b* (The People), *Al Moustaqbal* (The Future), *Al Fajr* (The Dawn), and *Al Badil* (The Alternative) contributed to the development of an opinionated press that gave an outlet to people's preoccupations.[103] They subsequently became victims of renewed government suspension, harassment, and interference.[104] Under Ben Ali, the press fared no better, and many independent and opposition newspapers were closed down. On the demand side, Tunisnews filled a large gap in independent information and insightful commentary. The fact that the newsletter was diffused through email helped maintain its wide circulation and a loyal readership despite government censorship. Those who feared the consequences of accessing antiestablishment material subscribed to Tunisnews using fake email accounts. The appeal of the newsletter demonstrates the intensity of readers' desire to know more about what was happening in the country.[105] True, the level of interest in the newsletter varied as some politically active individuals read it avidly while others only occasionally consulted it. Nevertheless, "the bulk of the Tunisnews regular public is made up of curious individuals ranging from journalists, to academics, to those in liberal professions, to government officials who typically consult the newsletter at least once a week."[106] For a decade or so, a broad populace was actively interested in and regularly exposed to news and commentaries about what was happening in the country, politically and otherwise, beyond what was covered in the state-sanctioned media. In the words of one Tunisian journalist, "Tunisnews is an experiment that broke the media firewall."[107] Given the censorship and intimidation Tunisnews faced, its unfailing ability to give people open access to information about the country was no mean achievement. It proved important in raising awareness and nurturing a political consciousness. This discrete form of involvement was bound to expand with the heightened penetration of the Internet and the proliferation of online forums.

Although the introduction of search engine services like Google Reader took away from the value of aggregation, Tunisnews kept its reader base. The site's example encouraged others to initiate similar online experiments within the country. In 2000, Sihem Ben Sedrine, a Tunisian human rights activist and journalist, launched an online publication titled Kalima (the Word) after she failed to obtain authorization to issue a paper publication. What defined Kalima was its pursuit of free speech in an environment that was marked by repression. Cofounded and edited by Um Ziad, alias for the veteran journalist and activist Neziha Réjiba, Kalima was a regular monthly publication that featured topics that were typically ignored by the national press. Although Kalima's antiestablishment bent and activist agenda were reminiscent of the foreign-based Tunisnews, the latter's longer experience, resourcefulness, regularity, perseverance, and credibility made it considerably more established and more popular. Additionally, while Kalima centered around its founding figure and was primarily seen as a civil society initiative, in the minds of many users, Tunisnews is widely perceived as being close to the banned religious movement Ennahda, which gave it more weight and authority when it came to political issues. Even though in 2009 Kalima expanded its service to provide a Web radio station, its reach and impact remained limited, partly because of censorship.

The Lure of Cyber-dissidence

Although civil society groups and actors were distinct from political parties, both in the public consciousness and among the online community, they were considered as part of the same institutional politics. This stigma made alternative online ventures of a political import stand out. Such was the case with Nawaat, a dissident portal and a collective blog at the forefront of Tunisian cyber-activism in subsequent years. Nawaat—which, as defined by one of its initiators, signifies a "core" that is bound to become bigger—started as a website and a forum that fostered debate and encouraged citizen involvement.[108] It soon evolved into a blogging platform and a digital activism website concerned with news and politics on Tunisia and strove to give Tunisians the opportunity "to share their daily worries in a public forum."[109] Over the years, this collective blog amassed a wealth of information (mostly critical of the regime) on the country.

Nawaat emerged from forums that developed in the early 2000s. Its founders were active contributors to both Reveil Tunisien and TUNeZINE. They grew gradually disenchanted with the editorial line of the latter forum after Yahyaoui's arrest, which they believed marginalized alternative voices. Sporadic polemics against the adoption of pseudonyms and the calls to "regulate" the use of the forum were symptomatic of internal dissent.[110] It is this dissent that gave rise to Nawaat in 2004. As conceived by its founders, the site's objective was to create a blog that was capable of fostering a free debate in a context marked by the lack of freedoms.[111] From the outset, Nawaat was keen on establishing its independence from any political party, organization, or government.

Nawaat is administered by a close-knit group of four Tunisians operating in the diaspora. Sami Ben Gharbia has been the group's public face because his political refugee status in Europe allows him to avoid anonymity. Born into a family that took an active part in the anti-colonial movement and having grown up in an authoritarian state, Ben Gharbia saw his political fiber hardened when he was pushed into exile. In 1998, he was arrested and interrogated by the police about a trip he made to the Islamic Republic of Iran. When summoned anew by the Ministry of Interior, he went on the run,[112] fleeing Tunisia for sub-Saharan Africa and the Middle East before ending up in Europe.[113] Once settled in the Netherlands, he started to search for information about political prosecution and human rights violations in Tunisia in support of his application for political asylum. He thus became an activist campaigning for freedom of speech and human rights. In 2001, Ben Gharbia teamed up with "Centrist," the pseudonym of a Canada-based IT engineer. The two had grown up together but had lost touch until they met again in 2001 on the TUNeZINE forum. Their identities were initially concealed by their noms de plume, but they soon intuited each other's true identity. A natural team, they were soon joined by Centrist's brother, a France-based law professor who operated online using the name of the famous Carthaginian general Astrubal. The fourth member of the team was Malek Khadraoui, a young business manager who left Tunisia in the mid-1990s to study in Paris and ended up settling there. He joined the site in 2005, publicly revealing only his first name. The group's sense of mission converged around a relationship of trust and friendship that developed in the context of diasporic activism. Nawaat's voice was not monolithic. Its members espoused different views and had various political allegiances. Nevertheless, they always managed to work out their differences in favor of a common cause and a unified strategy.[114]

Nawaat had an overtly political orientation from the start, and this tendency became even more pronounced as a result of the online protest it spearheaded during its second year of existence.[115] The year 2005 was marked by a flurry of cyber-activism that would harden Nawaat. Contributing significantly to this new momentum was a high-profile UN event whose ostensible aim was to shape the future of Internet governance and promote access to information among developing nations. Tunisia's successful bid to host the second phase of the World Summit on the Information Society (WSIS) on November 16–18, 2005, despite its poor Internet and press freedom record, was a disappointment for many because it implicitly legitimized the autocratic practices of Ben Ali's regime. Various civil society and freedom advocacy groups expressed concerns that while Tunisia was ahead of many other developing nations in matters of ICT development, it lagged behind in promoting freedom.[116] The incongruity of the values the UN sought to promote and Tunisia's human rights record prompted a number of activists and organizations, such as the Citizen's Summit on the Information Society, to question the suitability of Tunisia's hosting the summit in a petition to the UN Secretary General, Kofi Annan.[117] A *New York Times* op-ed piece published on the eve of the summit highlighted the irony of having one of the Arab world's most autocratic countries hold a world summit on the global exchange of information and ideas:

> Not only is the choice of Tunisia as host insensitive to the many brave Tunisians who have suffered harsh reprisals from their government for expressing their views, it also signals that repressive governments face little consequence when they systematically curtail basic human rights. Playing host to the WSIS bestows exactly the kind of international legitimacy that dictators like Tunisia's president crave. For years, Ben Ali kept a tight lid on dissent in this often-overlooked North African

police state. He has crushed political opposition, silenced the country's media and shown that criticism of the regime, even on the Internet, can trigger swift retribution.... The government continues to ban access to websites that portray the government in a negative light.... State restrictions go beyond free expression and the Internet. Dissidents, human rights activists and independent civil society groups endure constant harassment from the secret police.[118]

The organizers were not oblivious of these practices. Noting serious concerns about government monopoly over media, restrictions over journalists, and control over the Internet, an international fact-finding mission expressed serious doubts about "the willingness of the Tunisian authorities to meet satisfactorily the international obligations to which Tunisia is party."[119]

Undeterred by the regime's intolerance for dissent but unable to protest physically because of the government's restrictions on assembly, some independent civil society actors, opposition figures, grassroots activists, cyber-dissidents, and bloggers banded together to organize a virtual protest. A blurb on the campaign's website explained: "Since we are physically unable to demonstrate in public spaces, we will use the Internet to organize permanent virtual demonstrations in order to express our total disapproval of the Tunisian dictatorial regime."[120] Activists set up the Tunisian Association for the Promotion and Defense of Cyberspace, created an online freedom of speech protest site,[121] and organized a peaceful Web campaign named "Freedom of Expression in Mourning," which was launched on October 3, 2005, and continued for a fortnight. Drawing attention to the constraints on freedom of expression and information in Tunisia, the group sought to steer the discussion away from the UN's attention on the digital divide to what they called the "democratic gap."[122] "If there is a stake in the World Summit on the Information Society," the group declared in its manifesto, "it should not only be about reducing the digital gap, but it should be about reducing the evil that corrode peace in the world which is the democratic gap."[123]

Motivating this initiative—which echoed social movements like BASTA in Latin America and civic youth movements like OTPOR in Serbia as well as regional precedents like the Kefaya movement in Egypt that opposed the succession of Mubarak's son to the presidency[124]—was a desire to exert pressure on the regime by bringing the restrictions on free speech, civil liberties, and human rights in Tunisia to the world's attention. The operation constituted the first attempt to mount an international Web campaign against Ben Ali, underscoring the contribution of Tunisian Internet activists in the diaspora, particularly their disposition to think beyond local contexts and traditional forms of protest. Cognizant that success required external support and media exposure, a handful of activists who coordinated their efforts through Nawaat set out to internationalize the campaign. Their slogan was "*Yezzi Fock* Ben Ali" (Enough is Enough Ben Ali), a label that also bore the name of the group's campaign and website (www.yezzi.org), which was eventually hacked and destroyed in 2007.[125] The campaign called on users who shared their discontent to take part in the cyber-protest by sending in a picture of themselves—with or without showing their faces—holding a *Yezzi Fock* sign to demand the lifting of restrictions on freedom of expression and to signal their rejection of the regime's authoritarian practices. For some, the online protest

> was a genuine and sincere call from the heart of ordinary citizens who wanted to express to their compatriots how much they long to see progress toward free society and a real democracy. We wanted the world to know that we are out there and that we need their attention and support. We also wanted the regime to understand that it cannot keep intimidating us or indefinitely ignore our will.[126]

Dozens of pictures of anonymous and identifiable netizens posing with the *Yezzi Fock* message were featured on the movement's website, even though fear of reprisal against dissident voices compelled many of the participants in this initiative not to reveal their names or show their faces. Additionally, the group issued an open call for webmasters who were willing to support the cause of democracy to help publicize the protest.[127] A logo was also designed for the occasion consisting of Tunisia's national emblem wrapped in a blue ribbon, which symbolized the state of mourning—a design that was adapted from the San Francisco-based Electronic Frontier Foundation.[128]

What stood out was not only the ability of Tunisian Internet activists, both at home and in the diaspora, to inspire new forms of action and to bring to bear international precedents and alternative traditions but also the conscious attempt to create global resonance for local issues. Several bloggers participated in the *Yezzi Fock* campaign by posting the blue ribbon on their blogs, giving the movement more visibility and inducing other users to endorse their cause and support it.[129] On the eve of the summit, the campaign released a series of video clips aimed at drawing attention to the severity of the freedom of speech situation in the country. To ensure a wide reach, the organizers of the initiative adopted a multi-language communication strategy, issuing press releases in Arabic, French, and English.

Coming at a time when the eyes of the international community were set on the country, the campaign was an embarrassment for the regime. The government blocked the campaign's website the same day it was launched, making it unavailable for users inside the country. Still, three days after the campaign was launched, the site had registered 36,688 hits, and 84,000 by the eve of the summit.[130] Prominent papers like *Le Monde* and *Al Sharq Al Awsat* and international news media organizations like CNN and Al Jazeera reported on the campaign.[131] Finding itself on the defensive and intent on projecting a pro-freedom façade, the government offered unhampered Internet access to the UN delegates. In his address to the Summit, Ben Ali also attempted to placate his critics by reiterating his country's keenness on "building an information society guaranteeing the individual right of access to information and ensuring the free flow of information and knowledge, without restrictions or constraints."[132] Still, the pressure that was generated by the cyber-activists resulted in some missteps on the part of the regime, which further exposed its real face.

Despite providing uncensored access to the Internet on the conference site, the authorities carried on their censorship practices elsewhere. The websites of opposition parties, human rights organizations, and freedom advocacy groups remained inaccessible to the populace. Broadcasts of the summit were also closely monitored and critical remarks on the host country's freedom of speech record were bluntly and unapologetically censored. When the opening WSIS speech by Swiss president Samuel Schmid, which was televised live on the national channel, castigated Tunisia for abridging freedom of speech, the authorities did not hesitate to pull the plug.[133] As it turned out, the hosting of the summit in Tunisia was a double-edged sword, winning the regime acknowledgment and recognition for its efforts to promote an information society while pressuring it to live up to the expectations of the Information Age and the aspirations of the people. In many ways, WSIS was a turning point. The summit was not only set in Tunisia; it became *about* Tunisia. *Yezzi Fock* sparked an interest in cyber-activism that would gain ground over the years with the evolution of the Internet, the advent of Web 2.0, and the emergence of new tools for claiming civil rights in the face of oppression.

Local Grievances, Global Activism

In the post–WSIS era, Nawaat's strategy evolved. In 2006, it started to move away from forums to adopt and promote blogging as a platform for cyber-activism.

Nawaat's blog engaged in grassroots cyber-activism and committed to politicizing the blogosphere. The political instrumentalization of the Internet meant targeting the political legitimacy of the regime: "Benalism thrived on the manipulation of its image, with all the symbolism attached to it, and it is this very image that we targeted.... Shattering the deceptive image of the regime has been the focus of Nawaat's efforts since its inception."[134] Dealing small blows to the regime, chipping away at its image, and creating "points of pressure," as Ben Gharbia calls them,[135] required spreading the word, communicating information, and getting attention.

In order to become a source of alternative information in the country and beyond, Nawaat sought to enhance its communicative abilities through the adoption of a multilingual, multi-platform communication strategy. Using Arabic and French had made the site accessible to a native audience, and expanding into English helped it broaden its reach and communicate with the wider international community. To shield itself and increase its efficacy, Nawaat found it necessary to strengthen its network-building capabilities. The group's cyber-militancy rested on the strong commitment of its core members but also on the external support system it harnessed, particularly its ability to connect to networks of global activists. In 2007, Ben Gharbia became the advocacy director for Global Voices, an organization that seeks to highlight and amplify the voices of people on the blogosphere. The anti-censorship efforts and free speech initiatives he led at Global Voices put him in touch with other activists from throughout the world. It also led him to operate across regions, taking on projects like Threatened Voices, which supported at-risk bloggers and helped create links between blog advocacy efforts around the world. Through Global Voices, he also attempted to cultivate individual and personal contact among the disparate players in the Middle East and North Africa region, getting influential bloggers and Internet activists to meet one another, forge alliances, and support one another. This was particularly evident in the two Arab bloggers meetings he initiated in 2008–9 in Beirut. These were training and networking meetings of young online activists aimed at "supporting an essential tool of expression and activism in the region" and assisting bloggers in raising their voice, organizing online and offline campaigns, and building solidarity networks.[136] The conferences were also meant to give Arab bloggers a chance to exchange experiences, share technical knowledge, and form networks of solidarity.

Nawaat's communication strategy was further enhanced through the creative use of information and communication technologies. One of the innovative initiatives was the Tunisian Prison Map.[137] Using a Google Maps mash-up (mixing composite applications and services available on the Web while adding user-generated content), Ben Gharbia contributed information about some two dozen detention sites in Tunisia.[138] The interactive prison map showed the (sometimes approximate) locations of where political prisoners were held along with pictures and brief information about each prisoner. These descriptions were often connected to external links on the Web or accompanied by online audio and video accounts from the prisoners' families. Digital mapping provided a powerful narrative about the regime's growing authoritarianism. In a country where the government denied the existence of political prisoners and where there was a dearth of information about the penitentiary system, the prison map was a significant achievement.[139]

Nawaat's "maptivism" was also evident in its 2008 Google Earth online initiative.[140] Building on its earlier experiments, Nawaat used geotags to stage a digital sit-in. The initiative consisted of attaching to the presidential palace on Google Maps video testimonies of political prisoners and first-hand accounts about human rights abuses and prison conditions. Visitors of the site could also contribute material and add their own user-generated content. Another noteworthy initiative came from Nawaat's Astrubal. In 2007, he posted a video about the unofficial trips of the presidential airplane. Using plane-spotting databases containing time-stamped photos of aircrafts on runways throughout the world taken by plane-spotting hobbyists, he was able to establish that the presidential jet had been used on several shopping sprees in Europe rather than on official business.[141] For Nawaat, this kind of digital activism was less motivated by a desire for media hype than it was driven by the lack of spaces of engagement within the country's growing authoritarian context.[142] Eventually, the creative and intensive use of communication technologies, the emphasis on multilingual communication, and the exploitation of different platforms meant that Nawaat opted to play in the major leagues. Interestingly, people's exposure to Nawaat within Tunisia was somewhat limited, partly because the blog was censored inside the country and partly because of people's aversion to public political discussion.

Occasionally, the group experienced fatigue, leading some members to doubt if the blog could sustain its momentum.[143] Nevertheless, Nawaat persevered. Its desire for change, political commitment, and group dynamics helped it stay the course. The persistence of the members of the group in light of these hardships can be understood in the context of Nawaat's anti-regime stand and its activism, but is also to be situated within the context of an evolving blogosphere. Significantly, as the following chapter will show, the militant culture of activism Nawaat advocated was out of sync with the general orientation of the Tunisian blogosphere, which was socially oriented and politically averse. For many ordinary bloggers, Nawaat was simply too politicized. Not surprisingly, Nawaat found itself caught up between the skepticism of the cautious ordinary user and the intolerance of a relentless regime that was bent on silencing dissident voices. And it is to the transformative experience of blogging that I now turn.

5

The Politicization of the Blogosphere

When Diarists Become Activists

The technological evolution of the Internet and the advent of a many-to-many system of communication—as contrasted with the legacy media's one-to-many format—brought about significant changes in people's habits and expectations. Previously passive audiences and mass consumers of media products became "active produsers"[1] (i.e., producers and users) who could participate in discussions, share ideas, respond to others, and engage with issues. Web 2.0's shift toward a participatory Internet culture enabled people to share, create, and contribute content and to be more reciprocally involved.[2] As the technical issues became easier to manage, online forums and websites started to lose their appeal and popularity to blogging.

The appeal of blogging in Tunisia needs to be understood within the context of the state's entrenched control over public life. The blogosphere developed as a rich and engaging space of public discourse that was otherwise missing in real life. Blogs encouraged a substantive engagement with a range of issues and promoted a dialogue between different perspectives. Blogs are worthy of attention not only because of their inherent nature and expressive value but also because of their political significance. The blogosphere may be unrepresentative of the society it purports to represent, but it provides a glimpse into the cultural production of contention within an authoritarian context. Of particular interest is the way blogging developed into an act of "transgression"—of crossing a limit the very act of transgression effaces, as Foucault put it[3]—through which bloggers asserted and negotiated political agency. Between 2006 and 2009, blogs were essential to the acquisition of a new form of a political/virtual identity, even if this development appeared inconsequential at the time. The blogosphere was less notable for its effect than it was for its rich dynamics and its contentious spirit. Stated differently, the significance of the blogosphere lay less in its ability to influence the wider public debate or induce political action than in its tendency to carve out a space for participation and shore up the basis for a political consciousness to develop.[4] Considering the often dismissive claims some analysts have made about the "built-in ceiling for the political impact of Arab blogs,"[5] the gradual politicization of the Tunisian blogosphere and its emergence as an incubator of a culture of contention was a significant development.

If I highlight the uniqueness and richness of this experience, it is not to romanticize or eulogize the blogosphere. Certainly, blogging had its limitations: the blogosphere was a somewhat marginal space that attracted relatively few users who operated in a restrictive environment demarcated by fear and caution. Still, the shortcomings that marked this cyber-experience did not have the same hindering effect as real-life experiences given the risks that came with public activism.[6] The originality of this newly carved space of engagement and interaction made it hard not to appreciate the difference the blogosphere made to the question of voice and the issue of political consciousness among bloggers. In this chapter, I follow the evolution of the Tunisian blogosphere in an attempt to shed light on the dynamics of political socialization within a reconfigured space of network-based communication. In the chaos of digital gestation, I argue, a new consciousness of what was politically possible started to take hold.

Blogging Begins to Take Hold

Initially, many of those who were attracted to the blogosphere in Tunisia were content with passive reading. Occasionally, some users contributed their own commentaries, which eventually induced them to set up their own blogs and to shift from being readers to becoming creators of content. The first Tunisian blogs appeared in 2003 and were confined to a small urban circle comprising mainly university students in Tunis.[7] Regionally, the controversial 2003 US-led war on Iraq invited more intense political debate. Many users found in blogging an attractive venue for contributing thoughts, registering reactions, and voicing opposition. The fact that the Iraqi blogger Salam Pax became what Perlmutter calls a "blogthrough"[8] that attracted international media attention during the US invasion of Iraq helped publicize blogging further in the Arab world.[9] Domestically, better and more affordable access to the Internet led to a boom in blogging. The number of blogs grew from some two dozen in 2004 to nearly a hundred in 2005 to several hundred in 2006. The peak came in 2008 when there were more than a thousand aggregated blogs.[10] Although blogging involved only a small segment of society, the size of the blogging community in Tunisia was within the average of the Arab world, which had an estimated thirty-five thousand active blogs in 2009.[11]

Expectedly, the substance of blogs changed as the number of bloggers grew. At the beginning, blogs were personal spaces of exploration that were meant to be shared with others. Bloggers wrote about their daily lives, talked about uneasy relations with their friends, related mundane experiences, gave an outlet to their artistic talent, or simply entertained their personal fantasies. While for some, blogging amounted to little more than "a narcissistic parlor sport,"[12] for others it played a formative role. As a form of self-expression and self-affirmation, blogging propelled the self as a project and a narrative[13]—one that rested on a unique communicative experience and provided anchorage for the virtual self.[14] Merely having the opportunity to express oneself fueled blogging about issues that engaged others. For many bloggers, the interactive nature of blogs made manifest the inclusive and participatory culture of the Internet. As Halavais has argued, "Blogging provided that space of exposition and reflection, and importantly fused it with an ability to interact with others in an assemblage of like-minded individuals. Those who took on blogging balanced the ability to have their voice heard with the ability to easily enter into a drawn out, dispersed conversation."[15] The commentary bloggers received, even if generally thin and inconsistent in terms of substance, provided an added motivation to express specific responses in writing. As one blogger explains, "As soon as people start writing, commenting and responding, the conversation draws you in and you find yourself unable to hold back. Soon enough, you find yourself a faithful reader of and a frequent respondent to other people's postings."[16] In a society used to a hierarchical top-down communication model, finding oneself in the position of a creator and a critic of content rather than a mere passive consumer was particularly attractive. The fact that many bloggers preferred to blog in the Tunisian dialect gave this online discursive space a degree of authenticity that distinguished it from the stilted language that characterized the national media and the moribund press.

Equally appealing were the ways in which blogging unsettled the traditional limits on speaking to and for the public.[17] As "a rare space of free expression,"[18] it allowed open discussions about a range of social issues. The free tone and lively spirit of those exchanges were even more important than restrictions as people learned to air their views without drawing attention to themselves or inviting reprisal. Despite self-censorship, the rich diversity of the blogosphere contrasted sharply with the monolithic discourse promulgated by the national media and the government-controlled press. The kind of socialization this online public experience afforded helped many bloggers come to terms with the reality that "people have different opinions, that one's own views are not necessarily self-evident to all, that one has to find arguments to justify one's beliefs, rationalize them, and accept (if grudgingly) that one will not be able to convince everybody."[19] The realization that one's contribution to the blogosphere mattered was empowering. Blog posts thrust their writers to the fore and drew attention to their views. The less formal "comments" section of blogs—on which readers wrote responses to posts—afforded the ability to influence the debate, even if at times in an uneven and spurious way.

Most significantly, perhaps, blogging brought together people who shared similar interests, experiences, and anxieties. Contributing to the development of the blogosphere was the creation in 2004 of TN-Blogs, a blog aggregator that was administered by the Canada-based Tunisian blogger Houssein Ben Ameur. The aggregator made the community of bloggers readily identifiable, thereby helping to expand and consolidate it by linking bloggers in Tunisia and the diaspora within the same virtual space. The global interconnectivity of bloggers was crucially important in defining the Tunisian blogosphere. In 2005, TN-Blogs initiated a series of blog awards, which further energized the blogosphere and strengthened the bloggers' sense of community.[20] These dynamics also injected the blogosphere with a competitive spirit, which impelled some bloggers to seek virtual fame and prominence and encouraged others to maintain distinctive blogs that earned them a good reputation.[21] It was not unusual for bloggers to install a hit counter on their blogs to track—and publicize—the number of visitors received.[22] It is hard to form an informed characterization of who these people were in terms of age, gender, location, occupation, education, and social class because most bloggers typically opted for anonymity. What can be ascertained is that the blogosphere was a diverse and inclusive body, attracting people with various interests, backgrounds, and profiles. An examination of the blog posts, comments, and exchanges suggests that the blogosphere was not just a space of interaction; it represented the Internet at its best.

While for some bloggers online communication and cyber-interaction were all that mattered, for others the real dimension of the virtual world had a special appeal. As affinities started to be made manifest, strong bonds developed among sub-communities of bloggers, which made blogging a far richer experience. Many bloggers maintained regular contacts with fellow bloggers via Skype, instant messaging, or email. As identifiable groups coalesced, some bloggers felt the desire to extend the relationship beyond the virtual world, leading to real-life interactions enshrined in a relationship of trust. Because of the culture of distrust caused by the country's transformation into a police state, trust became a defining element in the relationship among the bloggers. Whom they revealed their identity to, whom they decided to meet, and whom they could talk to openly and candidly were considerations that mattered.

As early as 2007, there was a meetup in Paris involving a few Tunisian bloggers of the diaspora. In subsequent years, bloggers met one another occasionally in Tunis. These social connections strengthened their sense of community. In the words of the blogger Arabicca, "meet-ups were an opportunity to celebrate knowing each other. They allowed bloggers to better know and appreciate people whose interest they shared and whose writing they appreciated."[23] Naturally, in an environment that favored anonymity, such encounters were tinged with fear because of the risk of unveiling one's true identity. These were calculated risks offset by trust earned through extensive online socialization. Typically, meetups involved a handful of bloggers whose extended online conversations and frequent chats on the margins of the blogosphere helped them acquire an insider's knowledge about one another and better determine their trustworthiness and camaraderie.[24]

The deepening of relationships among bloggers induced various forms of collaboration. In some instances, the kind of intimacy and bonding that developed among bloggers gave birth to collective blogs, organized around themes and interest groups: Les Tunisiens du Monde (Tunisians around the world), a collective blog for Tunisians in the diaspora; The Network of Tunisian Bloggers for Free Blogging, a collective blog advocating Internet freedom; Boudourou (Trashy Tabloid) and TV Bel Malwene (Color TV), two collective blogs targeting the state-run press for its mediocrity; For a Secular Tunisia, a blog advocating secularism; and The Battle Against the Fifth Column, a blog defending Islam against the forces of secularism.[25] In other instances, the "imagined community" encouraged collaborative composition of literary texts online. Such collaboration fostered an enhanced sense of collectivity that was invigorating for an expanding blogging community.

Particularly interesting was a year-long collaborative experiment in radio-blogging—named *Radioun*[26]—which was launched in December 2007 by the blogger Tarek Kahlaoui, who then was a graduate student in the United States. Modeled on the idea of Internet radio, audio-blogging was an innovative experiment that brought together a sub-community of bloggers around debates on a range of issues, events, and developments concerning various aspects of life. The community around which this experiment developed consisted of some twenty bloggers (with each hour-long audio-blogging session involving five or six participants). The topics were varied and ranged from smoking in public places to health care reform and from youth preoccupations to Internet censorship. Because most bloggers preferred to remain anonymous, these sessions were audio-only Skype conversations. Through the experience of radio-blogging, bloggers attempted to counter the government media by giving rein to the free word. Despite never winning a mainstream audience, radio-blogging and its use of sound helped consolidate the community. In an interview, Kahlaoui explained to me that audio-blogging had a special appeal because it amplified the voice of the blogger and gave it weight in ways that were previously unthinkable.[27] Bloggers grew conscious of their voices, not only because they felt that what they had to say mattered to others but also because blogging engulfed them in a different sensory experience. The significance of this experience cannot be underestimated. As Hirschkind reminds us in his analysis of auditory community practices in Egypt, the affects and sensibilities honed though auditory media practices constitute a medium through which forms of self, sociability, and politics that pervade the modern experience are created.[28] In the case of *Radioun*, the element of voice gave an added dimension to the contribution of bloggers and made the experience more intimate, touching on rich modes of reception and response that resonated among the participants. The use of Tunisian dialect gave it an effect that went beyond what the discussion yielded.

The Nawaat Turning Point

Naturally, the blogosphere had limitations. Typically, people avoided politics for the obvious reason of pervasive official repression. In an authoritarian environment, discussing the political sphere—online and offline alike—was a bone fide taboo. Caution and fear usually resulted in acquiescence and self-censorship. The early years of blogging in particular were marked by a notable disinterest in, even disregard for, politics. Overt political discussions occasionally found their way to the blogosphere, but they remained marginal.

As the blogosphere grew, a clear demarcation—even a chasm—emerged between two tendencies: citizen blogs, which dealt with social issues, and dissident blogs, which also delved into politics. The latter were associated with a relatively small group of politically disaffected bloggers who actively used blogging as a tool for opposition and dissent outside the sphere of institutional politics or political opposition. To be sure, cyber-dissidence was a limited phenomenon, and many who indulged in political discussions lived outside the country.[29] A prevailing form of cyber-activism consisted of sharing material critical of Ben Ali's regime. Cyber-activists' very use of the Internet was a factor in the disconnection from the traditional political class, which had nearly no presence on social networks.[30]

Disenchantment with the traditional opposition went beyond the technological. Bloggers and politicians operated in different spheres and represented distinct mentalities. Generally, dissident bloggers and Internet activists looked down on the opposition as archaic and ineffective, blaming them for having "failed to incarnate the future of democracy in the country or bring about real change."[31] The fact that opposition political parties lacked a popular base and were not open to criticism contributed to a growing perception that they were more private clubs than effective political institutions. Indeed, because they revolved around one dominant figure and adopted a top-down approach that marginalized their memberships, their very structure reflected the autocratic ruling party. The generation gap between the members of the opposition and the bloggers accentuated the discrepancy further. Typically, the former were militants, middle-aged or older, who operated within a closed circle; the latter were younger, closer to the sensibility of ordinary people, and generally more open on society.

Still, the tendency of dissident bloggers to be politically engaged was unnerving for citizen bloggers who grew protective of this rare space of relatively free interaction. Even though the advent of the blog aggregator TN-Blogs helped unite the disparate constituents of the blogosphere, blogs that were maintained by dissidents, that had a militant edge, or that were overtly political were not well integrated with other categories of bloggers. Many citizen bloggers feared that if politics seeped in, it would trigger censorship and potentially put bloggers in harm's way. Such an exclusionary approach generated resentment from a number of bloggers. The dissident blog Nawaat in particular was a strong advocate for a politically relevant blogosphere. In December 2005, Nawaat's Ben Gharbia wrote a blog post titled "Tunisian Blogs: Touristic Zones!" in which he castigated TN-Blogs for ostracizing cyber-dissidents and the blogosphere in general for its distinctly apolitical online stance.[32] Lamenting the fact that the bloggers' acquiescence enhanced the regime's efforts to project a deceptive image of the country as a tourist paradise, he called on bloggers to step down from their ivory tower and consider writing about real issues:

> Bloggers write virtually about everything, except the issue of freedom in their own country. They love to wear a Che Guevara T-shirt, but when it comes to matters related to national politics and discussions about the situation at home, they bury their heads in the sand.... The kind of blogs that animate TN-blogs are reminiscent of the country's touristic zones which are designed to conceal any traces of local misery. Such zones have turned Tunisia into a surreal place where poverty, unemployment and lack of freedoms are effaced. Everything is reduced to mere folklore destined for the consumption of tourists who are beguiled by the charm of the blue seas and the golden beach sands. The blogosphere is not all that different. It is as if we—bloggers who do not shy away from politics—belong to a different country; as if the freedom we cherish is not necessarily their freedom![33]

Nawaat's critical post stirred controversy. Politically interested bloggers argued that tolerance for politically charged criticism could not be achieved by disengaging or withdrawing but by exerting increased and constant pressure. This task required that bloggers rid themselves of their fear to engage political questions: "The regime will only be more comforted in its tyranny if we carry on showing our excessive fear," concurred one blogger; "a first subtle step is necessary to overcome the 'politicophobia' plaguing the blogosphere."[34] Many bloggers, though, believed the call to politicize the blogosphere was premature: "It takes considerable courage to blog," exclaimed the blogger Elyssa in her response to Nawaat's blog post. "Merely blogging leaves one exposed, let alone blogging about political issues. We should give the weak time to gather their strength and stand on their feet."[35] While for dissident bloggers it was evident that the de facto strategy of "exclusion for the sake of survival"[36] that TN-Blogs adopted was likely to help the censor and unwittingly aid the regime, for citizen bloggers online political discussions could provoke censorship and jeopardize what TN-Blogs had achieved.[37]

Interestingly, some bloggers argued that the reluctance of citizen bloggers to engage with political matters did not preclude political consciousness. For the blogger Infinity, "The issue was not so much the absence of politics, but the inability to recognize the political in the apolitical."[38] Most citizen bloggers believed they needed not political confrontation but an online culture of active involvement and participation. "It is important that we expand the limits of the 'politically correct,' " one cautious blogger argued, "but we need to do so without provoking polemics or rocking the boat."[39] The Internet held out the promise of a better future and a more inclusive society. This was all the more reason not to jeopardize the survival and continuity of blogging. The value of blogging, as Infinity put it, rested less in its tendency to yield concrete achievements than in its proclivity to promote a new mindset: "We would very much like young people to sit in front of their screens and to start talking; we want them to experience a kind of freedom that is different from the one they are used to on the streets... and the aggregator TN-Blogs is the frame that can bring them together and facilitate their interaction."[40]

Differences over political engagement on the blogosphere remained unresolved, but Nawaat's central message nevertheless had an effect. One of the immediate consequences was that some dissident blogs, which were not previously recognized as members of the blogging community, were subsequently tolerated on TN-Blogs. The fact that the inclusion of a banned blog like Nawaat did not trigger censorship was a relief and encouraged a certain willingness on the part of citizen bloggers to tolerate overt political discussions, even if they continued steering clear of politics on their own blogs. Politics itself ceased to be the same taboo subject it once had been. More significantly, perhaps, there was a recalibration of the general disposition of the blogosphere. The incident was one more step on the way to a more engaged and eventually more politicized blogosphere.

Testing the Waters

By 2006, the blogosphere started to undergo subtle changes. Although blogging continued to favor personal, literary, and social interests, the range of issues that were discussed increased and the circle of interaction widened. TN-Blogs was a factor in the change. While typically bloggers were faithful readers of a handful of blogs, they were not unaware of general tendencies and broader discussions on the blogosphere. Many of them regularly visited TN-Blogs to check the blogosphere's pulse. Exposure to others' writings induced more, and more creative, blogging. What started out as a casual interest evolved into dynamic interactions, engaging reflections and lively conversations about the lived reality. In the words of Mihoub, the blogosphere was a "rich, critical and assertive"[41] arena for virtual encounters. Netizens engaged in public debates about issues that mattered to them and which were also linked to the larger public discourse. On the blogosphere, one enthusiastic observer noted, "You can read about everything and nothing, but the quality of the blogs is guaranteed."[42] Although generally red lines were observed, there was a refreshing degree of openness and unabashedness in expressing one's views away from the watchful eyes of the censor who, up to that point, did not pay much attention to this engaging space of interaction.

One of the kosher topics that generated a lively discussion early on pertained to the prospects of a unified Arab Maghreb. Bloggers needed something to talk about and this was a safe topic to explore—one that could put ordinary Tunisian users in touch with ordinary users from the Maghreb. On May 9, 2007, the blogger Big Trap Boy suggested an e-campaign to promote better cooperation among the countries of the Maghreb. Some bloggers felt that since traditional politics had failed to pool the resources of these countries to promote their development, blogging could help revive the idea of a much-needed unity. On the blogosphere, the idea of a multi-language Web campaign was enthusiastically embraced and the first of June was designated as a day of blogging for a united Maghreb.[43] In order to coordinate efforts, attract support, and promote the debate, a campaign forum was launched.[44] The outcome was an engaging discussion that lasted for a few weeks, as bloggers from throughout North Africa engaged one another over the prospects of overcoming the impediments to an enduring and mutually beneficial unity.[45]

Some dissident bloggers were critical of the unified Maghreb online initiative because they believed it failed to address the root cause of the region's problems. Adopting the counter-slogan "I blog against the blogging day on the Maghreb," a member of the dissident blog Nawaat dismissed the campaign as delusional.[46] From his perspective, nothing much could be expected from governments that lacked legitimacy. Until the individual countries of the Maghreb rid themselves of the legacy of authoritarianism, he argued, one could not realistically aspire to have a free and unified Maghreb. Bloggers should focus their attention on the internal political situation in their countries instead—a bold proposition that, unsurprisingly, did not find much support among a blogging community that was not yet comfortable discussing politics in a public forum.

Although Nawaat's disapproving post was largely shrugged off by citizen bloggers, it helped revive the debate on what blogging should be about. It was hard for many of the participants in this initiative to disagree with Nawaat's diagnosis of the ills of authoritarianism. Where they differed, though, was how to address this endemic problem. For many, Nawaat's radical position was potentially counterproductive. The California-based blogger Samsoum noted that the contribution of the blogosphere was less in what it yielded than in what it nurtured: "Democracy and freedom are key to any solution to the region's problems. Still, it is preferable to raise awareness about this problem than to opt for confrontation. Change may take time, but eventually the power of reason and argumentation will prevail and induce people to contest the current situation."[47] Other respondents advocated moderation, pointing out that a frontal attack was likely to bring the wrath of the authorities and invite censorship, which could further constrain bloggers inside the country and adversely affect a nascent blogosphere.

The debate sensitized some of the participants to the fact that the absence of freedom in the country made discussions about unifying the Maghreb pointless.[48] There was a growing realization that a candid debate on the future of the Maghreb required freedom of speech, which was flagrantly missing.[49] Without guarantees of freedom, the rule of law, and democracy, the idea of an integrated Maghreb was hollow.[50] Yearning for an environment where dissenting voices were engaged rather than censored, Samsoum initiated a call to hold a day for blogging in support of the freedom of expression.[51] Bloggers were urged to liberate themselves of all taboos and to speak their minds freely about what they had always wanted to talk about but never had the courage to do so:

> Organizing a day to blog for the freedom of speech is an opportunity
> for us to express our views, aspirations and thoughts on this issue.
> Write to free yourself and to be yourself; write what comes to your
> mind; write about what you want. What should bring us together is
> the issue of freedom of expression. And if you do not feel like writing,
> do not do it. This is what is great about being free.[52]

And so July 1, 2007, was designated as a day to blog about the freedom of speech. Despite doubts that the proposal would amount to more than rhetoric, many supported it. A logo was designed for the occasion bearing the motto "I blog for the freedom of expression.... Talking is the solution."

Although the organizers of the initiative were keen on preserving the independence of the initiative and to steer it clear of any political association,[53] overt political themes were raised. In a post titled "Do We Need Democracy?" the

US-based blogger Tarek Kahlaoui proposed a day for blogging about the issue of democracy.[54] More significant than the question of whether bloggers should take up political questions was his proposal to entertain a different conception of what it means to write about politics. Keen on not "over-politicizing" the question of the freedom of speech, Kahlaoui advocated a nonconfrontational approach. In his view, "turning the issue of the freedom of speech into an axis of political conflict on the ground can be at the expense of its merit as a value in and of itself."[55] Recognizing the right of the silent majority to eschew polit-ical discussions, the blogger called for a genuine discussion about political is-sues without imposing the category of the political on the discussants. What mattered most was the practice of democracy—the ability to engage and debate, but also the disposition to question and differ:

> Cherishing democracy does not preclude questioning the value of democracy in a society that does not believe yet in its indispensa-bility, nor does it necessarily preclude a rigorous inquiry into the very possibility and means for achieving democracy. There is a tendency to equate pro-democracy advocacy with a confrontational discourse, which leaves little or no room for a reasoned debate about the ques-tion of democracy. It may be that, in some instances, reflecting on democracy is more viable than literally fighting for it.[56]

Kahlaoui concluded that one of the manifestations of the freedom of speech that ought to be protected was "the freedom to think about democracy out-side the political framework guiding the action of democracy activists."[57]

Differences aside, the initiative was noteworthy because getting a group of bloggers to converge on a single issue laid the groundwork for future political engagement and activism. It opened the bloggers' eyes to the possibility of networking among dispersed actors. This entailed taking initiatives, designing logos, coordinating efforts, and engaging in group-activism. The initiative also brought to light and heightened consciousness about the potential of a com-munity of bloggers. Incidentally, that summer, a meetup took place between some of these bloggers who reflected on the development of the blogosphere, discussed constraints on Internet freedom, and assessed the initiatives they have taken.[58] More significantly, the fact that it was possible to "safely" mount such a campaign brought about the realization that discussing politics publicly did not inevitably prove harmful.[59] The blogging community was starting to experience politics at work.

A coda to these initiatives took place in the blogosphere's reaction to how the freedom of speech campaign was covered in the media. In a rare TV program devoted to the event, the foreign-based independent channel Al Hiwar aired a report on July 19, 2007, that offended a segment of the blogging community. They found objectionable a dismissive claim made by a guest speaker on the program—who incidentally was a member of the political opposition—that there was no such thing as a blogging movement and that the Tunisian blogosphere did not concern itself with public affairs but only with literary matters. For the offended bloggers, such a claim pointed to the inability of the political elite to envisage alternative forms of political engagement or to conceive of political action independently of traditional political players and organizational strategies. The lack of imagination the incident revealed, the bloggers claimed, explained why the opposition had become a subordinate actor in a political system dominated by the ruling party.[60]

The Devolution of the Blogosphere

The evolution of the blogosphere did not follow a straight line. While the popularity of blogs fostered a space of relative freedom, it also brought about new challenges and unsettling dynamics. Until 2007, bloggers constituted a rather small and mostly homogeneous community. As blogging became more common, the blogosphere attracted more Internet users, turning the community into a less harmonious society. Although the blogosphere had long teemed with bloggers from various social strata who felt strong affinities with particular intellectual movements and maintained allegiances to political ideologies, these orientations were not articulated. Despite differences in backgrounds and viewpoints, bloggers had been keen on safeguarding the richness and openness of the blogosphere. But this tolerant attitude changed in 2008. What was once valued as a common ground became a battleground.

One of the early manifestations of the declining quality of the discourse was the tension relating to Islam and secularism. Outspoken voices began advocating secularist views, often in a dismissive or antagonistic tone toward religious views.[61] Gradually, an Islamophobic discourse gained currency, with some writings simply expressing criticisms of Islam and others displaying irreverence toward God and the Prophet Mohammed. As more bloggers found themselves dragged into the debate, what had initially appeared as a "digression," as one blogger described it, became a focal issue.[62] The discordance between those who subscribed to secularist views and those who held religious (and pan-Arab) views prompted reactions that made a bad situation worse. The ensuing conflagration helped polarize the partisan camps.[63] Alarmed that the secularists were gaining virtual ground, the rival camp grew defensive. To express their piety, some bloggers designated June 15, 2008, a day for blogging for Islam[64] while others called for a day for blogging devoted to the Prophet. These initiatives provoked an added dose of Islamophobia.

Beneath the tensions was repressed political consciousness. The prevailing atmosphere of political authoritarianism was such that the debate about the duality of Islam and secularism constituted the limit of what could be publicly discussed. For some bloggers, the assault on religious beliefs reflected the inability of the online community to face pressing issues of a social, political, or economic nature in the absence of free speech.[65] The sensitive nature of newly emergent issues like virginity, identity, and normalization of ties with Israel, which became parts of the discussion, exacerbated the tension. Posts contesting such issues were tendentious, abrasive, and often blatantly insulting. The blogger Free Race described the prevailing atmosphere on the blogosphere in grim terms: "The debates were marginal and had no intellectual depth. Cheap shots and tasteless sarcasm on the beliefs of people was the hallmark of a group of bloggers who lost the ability to distinguish between a critique of religious thought and an assault on the spirituality of the people."[66] Anonymity encouraged otherwise timid bloggers to be confrontational. The debasement of the quality of the debate meant necessarily the devolution of the blogosphere from an ideational public sphere into an ideological battleground.[67] The tense atmosphere and the spirit of intolerance that characterized the rejection of the Other turned off many bloggers, leading them to slowly disengage from the blogosphere.[68]

Seen from the perspective of the relationship between the state and the subject, the tension that plagued the blogosphere looked as if it had a divide-and-rule design. Not surprisingly, many bloggers thought that "the authorities had a hand in this unfortunate development since it was in its interest to see the blogosphere mired in quarrels."[69] In this respect, the interest some regime supporters and party activists took in blogging toward the end of 2008 and their improvised immersion in the blogosphere was a noteworthy development. As the ruling party encouraged its youth base to have an active online presence ahead of the 2009 presidential election campaign, pro-ruling party bloggers started to make their presence on the blogosphere known, to the annoyance of both anti-regime and ordinary bloggers. The pro-regime bloggers liked to call themselves "patriotic bloggers," but were largely known instead as the "purple bloggers," a disparaging reference to the color of the ruling party.[70] Although they were a distinct minority, these tenacious regime counter-bloggers infused the blogosphere with a discourse that smacked of propaganda 2.0, which, as the blogger Carpe Diem noted in a critical post, "projected a perfect Tunisia that was sanitized of all problems and devoid of all conflicts."[71]

The tensions, intrusions, and distractions that marked 2008 significantly altered blogging. Trolls, ideological battles, and incivility turned off many bloggers. As the year drew to an end, even more bloggers lost their appetite for blogging. The majority of those who followed the exchanges and read the postings resisted being embroiled in the debate. Many were nostalgic for what appeared, in hindsight, to be the golden days (2006–7). The "last safe haven" for freedom of speech was dying, proclaimed the disheartened blogger Stupeur.[72] As blogging waned, new social media platforms surged in popularity. The year 2009 in particular witnessed a migration to Facebook, which attracted more than eight hundred thousand subscribers.[73] With the blogosphere becoming one of the targets of censorship, bloggers started to shift en masse to Facebook—which will be the focus of chapter 8—rather than maintaining their personal blogs.

A Reanimated Blogosphere

Over time, many of the bloggers who remained active lifted themselves from the quagmire that plagued the blogosphere. Some saw an opportunity for the now-mature blogosphere to learn from its mistakes and to evolve. For the blogger Free Race, the difficulties the blogosphere experienced had a positive outcome: "What happened had the effect of an occasional fever that enhanced the immune system; once the infected body recovered, it gained an added strength."[74] Some pleaded with fellow bloggers not to abandon blogging as that "would leave an intolerable void and invite aberrant voices."[75] In a passionate blog post titled "Is the Tunisian Blogosphere Dying?" the blogger Stupeur lamented the fact that many had unknowingly fallen into the trap they had tried to avoid:

> Isn't the point behind blogging to escape social and political restrictions and to advance different views? Isn't blogging about expressing oneself, giving an outlet to one's views and communicating one's

ideas? Rather than impose our views and suppress those of others, we should welcome ideas and open up the debate. Let there be differences and let the best reasoned and argued opinions prevail.[76]

The tensions, quibbles, and discordances notwithstanding, the blogosphere fostered an enduring bond that brought bloggers closer to one another and led them to identify more closely with issues that affected them directly. The most prominent issue was censorship, which will be discussed in the next chapter. Suffice it here to say that, increasing constraints on Internet freedom made users more aware of the need to protect their right of expression. For the blogger Chanfara, showing tolerance for discourses, positions, or ideologies with which one may not agree helped resist dictatorship: "our society cannot rid itself of despotism if it does not free itself of its authoritarian mentality and respect those who hold different views."[77] There was a growing realization that tolerance toward the other was initially what gave writing an added purpose and pointed meaning. "Writing is my weapon," declared this same blogger;[78] "the free word is the first step toward full freedom."[79] For this zealous blogger and many others, blogging was synonymous with freedom. Giving up—or losing—blogging would be a tremendous setback. Significantly, the renewed interest in blogging was accompanied with noticeable signs of maturity.

The reanimated blogosphere altered the way it discussed issues. While in the past criticism was occasional and timid, it henceforth grew more frequent, more daring, and more tactical. Not only did the increased level of engagement help demonstrate the value of freedom, it did so in concrete ways. Although the discussions and commentary were often not focused on the political reality, in many ways, politics were inescapable. Engaging in public writing favored a cultural and social critique that had political overtones. The overlap between personal interests, social contexts, and political realities was such that even casual conversations acquired elevated significance. In an environment shaped by the official discourse on national cohesion, voicing an opinion becomes a political act. As the blogger Arabicca explained to me when I interviewed her, "In Tunisia almost everything is considered political. A simple comment on crowdedness in the public transportation system could potentially be construed as a political statement. Negative commentary, much like criticism of the system, often stigmatized the commentator as antagonistic to the regime. Not even constructive criticism was tolerated. The expectation was for us to blend in with the crowd—to be among the Yes men."[80] By developing a voice, bloggers broke away from the herd. In an unbounded virtual world, the state was finding it hard to maintain the habits of acquiescence it had so long encouraged.

The loosening demarcation between the real world and the virtual world had an increasingly noticeable effect. The more the people could talk about everyday life issues, the more interested they became in politics: "Whether it is rumors about the president's health, jokes about the ambitions of the first lady, or stories about the abuses of the president's Mafioso in-laws, people were inevitably talking about politics."[81] With the proliferation of these diffuse forms of political expression came the reassurance that "talking about politics did not necessarily stigmatize one as a militant."[82] This kind of engagement not only de-dramatized politics but it also made the political inextricably linked with sociality. As Arabicca explained in a reflective blog post, the lived reality had an inescapable political dimension:

> To want to live freely, to read the newspaper we want, to get together with friends to talk about daily preoccupations, to organize a campaign for a cause, to call for transparency, to create an organization to preserve Andalusian music, to support the victims of a natural disaster, to launch a magazine, to write an article, to attend a political meeting, to elect a member of the parliament, to take part in the management of city life—all these pursuits amount to doing politics. The practice of politics is impelled above all by the love of the idea of freedom, in fact of the country; it is to want the best for our schools, our children, our nature, and our culture—it is to hand in to the next generation a better place so that they continue on the same path.[83]

In this manner, the blogosphere fostered a subtle but growing political affinity. For one blogger, this development was not hard to rationalize: "People were fed up with talking about nothing much; they had it with the mind-numbing mainstream media. There's bound to be a counter-discourse."[84]

Artful Contention

While many bloggers adopted a measured tone that enabled them to test the limits without outwardly transgressing them, some sought to shed their inhibitions altogether through "artful contention."[85] The wealth of artistic, symbolic, and literary expressions that abounded on the blogosphere provided incisive commentary on the writers' lived reality. These ranged from the adoption of literary texts, to the exercise of political life in a fictitious world, to the creative use of language. Such forms of engagement tactfully articulated a hidden message that blurred the lines between conformity and contention, acquiescence and contestation, compliance and defiance. As James Scott reminds us, "Tactful prudence ensures that subordinate groups rarely blurt out their hidden transcript directly."[86] Rather than engage in open defiance, they wittily insinuate contempt for the powerful and the oppressing other.

Kissa Online is an example of a witty blog. Embedded in its avowedly literary orientation was a deep political consciousness that manifested itself through the kind of intertextuality the anonymous blogger strived to foster throughout his or her writings by establishing relationships between texts such that their significance lay not simply in what they invoked but also in the rich allusions that defined the writing. The blog contained powerful distant (both temporally and spatially) passages and quotes that vividly captured the country's lived reality. The site featured some original literary texts but also teemed with elaborate dictionary definitions and excerpts from radical literature: a passionate and revolutionary poem from the acclaimed national poet Abou Al Kacem Chebbi on people's will to live; powerful lines from Pablo Neruda's poem "The Liberators" describing a tree that symbolized people's struggle for freedom; and brilliant selections of prose from Mahmoud Bayrem El Tounsi (the Egyptian poet of Tunisian origin) that aptly described the state of Tunisia under Ben Ali even though they were half a century old.[87] Although unspoken, the kind of critique that was embedded in the act of sharing an excerpt from a literary work was patent. In this manner, a blog consisting of a compelling brief selection of political satire from Gabriel García Márquez's *The Autumn of the Patriarch* (a novel about a fictional dictator) became distinctive for its ability to make a provocative statement about the country's political system while claiming a distance from politics—a form of speech without utterance, as it were.[88]

Blogs were also full of artful contention. The state's intolerance toward freedom of speech unleashed the creative and imaginative potential of many bloggers who adopted a playful style and devised a subversive approach that subjected authority to ridicule. Putting a humorous spin on a desperate situation or being amused by an absurd practice enabled bloggers to pass off their critique as jest. Their medium was new, but the principle was not. In his 1945 essay "Funny, but Not Vulgar," George Orwell profoundly noted: "a thing is funny when—in some way that is not actually offensive or frightening—it upsets the established order. Every joke is a tiny revolution.... You cannot be really funny if your main aim is to flatter the comfortable classes: it means leaving out too much. To be funny, indeed, you have got to be serious."[89] Plays on words, spoonerisms, creative use of language, and discursive swerves empowered bloggers while shielding them from the reaction of the authorities. The appropriation of language, imagery, symbolism, and anecdotes helped creatively invent new forms of expressing oneself freely and of contesting the lived reality. The allusive, the fanciful, and the ludic afforded bloggers the opportunity to tactfully engage a political reality they were keen on being perceived as distant from. In this manner, an entry devoted to a seemingly trivial topic such as the uses of different kinds of "funnels" (*qima'* in the Tunisian dialect) was, in reality, a blog about the Arabic-language homograph *qam'*, signifying "repression" and its various forms.[90] Similarly, a post that provided a casual commentary on the many situations and applications involving simple acts like "folding" and "bending" was really a biting satirical statement about the pliability of the law.[91] In the same vein, the government-controlled media's blackout on the unprecedented social unrest that erupted in the mining region was sarcastically portrayed as a vow of silence and lauded as a form of protest in support of the people's just cause. In all of these instances, the implied message was readily discernible, the sense of humor was brilliant, and the effect was powerful. Through these and other manipulations, which reconfigure the boundaries of the discourse, bloggers subvert dominant practices and narratives even as they engage with them. Tactics such as these, de Certeau reminds us in a different critical register, afford the ability to deflect the power of a system one lacks the means to challenge; they make it possible "to escape a social order without leaving it."[92]

Drawing out the contestatory nature of these discursive moments requires tying them to the imaginary elements and fictive dimensions that underwrite authoritarianism. In her book *The Force of Obedience*, Hibou commented on how the exercise of power in Ben Ali's Tunisia rested on the regime's ability to conceal the obvious through fictions and fabrications.[93] Blatant assertions such as "Tunisia is making democratic progress" or "the national economy has not been affected by the global economic crisis" were presented as indisputable truths. In this manner, the discursive practices and elevated fictions that saturated the public sphere acquired a real effect on institutions and individual behavior. The effectiveness of the fictive element in the exercise of power rested on the ability of the regime—including the ruling party, the national media, and the state bureaucracy—to spin, conceal, appropriate, and reinvent realities. Significantly, it was these categories that witty bloggers sought to undo through the deployment of the same imaginary and fictive dimensions that enabled the deceitfulness of the state-promoted narrative to pass itself off as a consensual reality. Such playfulness is often invested in a grotesque dimension, which as Mikhail Bakhtin explains entails an unsettling of established hierarchies and a "debasement of the higher."[94] The freedom of thought and imagination that underpins the grotesque is potentially subversive insofar as it enables the contestation of one's reality while seemingly accepting it. Thus, a blog post about fictitious waves of illegal Italian immigrants from the shores of Italy to Tunisia with the hope of finding better job opportunities was a derisively literal take on the grossly inflated official figures of the country's economic growth the national press uncritically reported.[95] Read against the surge of illegal immigration among Tunisians to the Italian island of Lampedusa, it was also a powerful statement about the growing desperation among an increasing number of unemployed youth who were willing to risk their lives for a job opportunity elsewhere.

Such satire, which was intimately connected to the national unconsciousness, constituted a defense mechanism that enabled bloggers to engage political topics while maintaining an assuring distance from the formal realm of governance. Cognizant that people resented the fact that they were deprived of a normal political life, one blogger invented a virtual land he named "Normalland"—a light, spirited, yet ingenious allegory about the country and its situation. He endowed his fictional land with a government, installed himself as governor, and created a mock parliament named *majles ezznous* (literally "the chamber of rascals"). He even concocted a coup d'état to infuse it with a dose of sensationalism and verisimilitude. The fact that the blog was comic and satirical encouraged people to make casual commentary, contribute remarks, and crack jokes on political life in this fictive land while insinuating parallels with Ben Ali's Tunisia. Such embedded critique also emboldened the initiator of the blog over time to feature opinion pieces and reflective posts.

Redrawing the Boundaries

Increased contestation meant that more bloggers were willing to shed their ingrained culture of fear and push the red lines. The use of proxies and the adoption of pseudonyms encouraged them to write more confidently, to engage others more openly, and to tackle issues more critically.[96] Bloggers in the diaspora, most notably those living in democratic societies, who enjoyed an unhindered access to the Internet, were better disposed to speak their minds. Toward the end of 2008, the political discourse on blogs started to be more discernible among otherwise non-activist blogs. Increasingly, it became hard to control this aspect or to have a politics-free blogosphere. This necessarily meant that the chasm between the politically engaged and the disaffected started to narrow. Engaging politics though was not simply a blogging effect; it was in many ways part of societal evolution that was reproduced on and reflected in the blogosphere.[97] For some bloggers, the hardening of the blogosphere and its politicization were inevitable. Reflecting on his experience, the blogger Carpe Diem noted: "Considering the regime's intolerance towards any form of dissent, and in the absence of self-criticism, bloggers were bound to claim a space—to contribute alternative points of view, to develop a different discourse, and to speak out on issues."[98] These imperatives became more insistent with the tightening of the regime's authoritarian hold. Three factors in particular mobilized the blogosphere and increased its assertiveness further—the mining protests, the targeting of bloggers, and the restrictions on Internet freedom.

The 2008 riots in the mining region of Gafsa rekindled bloggers' interest in the sociopolitical situation in the country and breathed new energy into the blogosphere. The national media blackout on the events meant that the only available news and images came from the Internet. Some activists passed on video recordings of the protests to foreign media and dissident bloggers abroad. As the word spread about the state's suppression of the labor protests, many bloggers expressed solidarity with the miners by posting a logo on their blogs featuring a protest by a number of local women following the arrest of several male protesters and activists. At the center was a prominent image of an angry old woman in a traditional provincial dress and headscarf with her closed fists raised in protest. The gradations of red that dominated the logo gave it a somber and sinister tone. A motto at the bottom of the picture read: "Tunisian bloggers stand with the people of the mining region." The logo, which came to be known as the "Red Note," was widely adopted, which emboldened a group of bloggers to set up a collective blog devoted to the events in Gafsa.[99] Alarmed by the growing Internet activism and online support of the miners' revolt, the authorities blocked many blogs, prompting an anti-censorship blogging campaign in which bloggers were encouraged to republish posts from censored blogs on their own blogs.[100]

Further accentuating the prevailing atmosphere of intolerance was the authorities' targeting of bloggers themselves. In this respect, the arrest of the blogger Fatma Arabicca on November 2, 2009, was a true test for the blogging community. The authorities (wrongly) suspected that she was connected to an anonymous cartoonist-blogger, known as -Z-, who published satirical and unflattering cartoons of the regime and its icons on his popular antiestablishment blog Débat Tunisie. The authorities first censored her blog,[101] and then formally summoned her a few days later to an interrogation about her online activities. She was released at the end of the day—only to be summoned anew under the pretext of completing administrative formalities necessary to close the file. The authorities often resorted to these tactics to detain people without leaving a paper trail that could be used against them. Arabicca was detained for five days, during which she was subjected to a grueling series of interrogations by alternating teams of interrogators after they seized her laptop. In the meantime, -Z- posted yet another cartoon ridiculing President Ben Ali's post-election public relations campaign.[102] This was followed by a sketch in support of Arabicca, that bore the defiant caption: "I am not Fatma; We are all Fatma."[103] Following a relentless campaign by a group of supporting bloggers, Arabicca was released on November 7; no charges were pressed against her. The case of Arabicca produced considerable online commotion. Many felt that Internet policing had become an arbitrary, indiscriminate witch-hunt. Although bloggers had previously experienced waves of censorship, they thought they had developed a good understanding of the rules the censor played by. The arrest of an ordinary blogger shook their faith in their ability to gauge the authorities' potential reaction about what they wrote.

The perceived victimization of Arabicca unified the blogosphere. The realization that her arrest could lead to a winning battle provoked an unprecedented mobilization and led to a determined campaign. The more vigilant the authorities grew, the more supportive of one another bloggers became. There was a tacit understanding among bloggers that they would stand up for one another should the need arise. When Arabicca received the summoning letter from the police, she alerted some of her fellow bloggers in the hope of getting the word out. She was counting on the Internet community for support, which did not fail to come through. During her detention, a campaign for her release was mounted by a supportive group of bloggers. The campaign was designed to not only secure the freedom of a fellow blogger but also fight for the free word. One of the campaign posters calling for the freedom of Arabicca showed a fountain pen at the center of a page with the following Arabic verse in the background: "If you notice that I am exhausted, my friend, hold my hand; If you see me falling down, take my weapon."[104] "We are all Fatma Arabicca" was more than just a slogan. Bloggers feared that they could also be detained, interrogated, and prosecuted for their blogging activities. The blogger Azwaw wrote: "I am afraid that our fellow blogger is paying for the freedom of expression on the blogosphere which survived a series of crises. The attempts to destabilize the blogosphere were meant to muzzle recalcitrant voices and silence politically incorrect views."[105]

Standing up for Arabicca was an affirmation of the attachment to the freedom of expression and a determination to preserve a space where bloggers could voice their opinions as citizens.[106] To support Arabicca, the blogger Tarek Kahlaoui wrote, was to support the right for blogs to exist.[107] The bloggers' realization that they could create a resistance platform gave them the confidence to act. A Nawaat-led, Skype-based committee was formed with the aim of launching a campaign to free Arabicca. The group worked tirelessly, setting up a campaign blog and a Facebook page,[108] designing logos, composing slogans, spreading the word, and feeding information to the media. They also contacted freedom advocacy groups like Reporters Without Borders and solicited the help of international human rights organizations like the Arabic Network for Human Rights Information. The latter issued press releases denouncing the arrest of Arabicca and the "policy of intimidation of the Tunisian authorities which was aimed to silence any free voice."[109] Tipped by Arabicca's support group, Al Jazeera also featured an article on the blogger's arrest on its much visited website[110] and broadcast the news of Arabicca's arrest along with an interview with her lawyer. The story even made it to the *Los Angeles Times* thanks to the newspaper's contributing writer in Beirut who credited Global Voices—an organization committed to citizen journalism, which included among its leading activists a member of Nawaat.[111]

The campaign managed to exert some pressure on the authorities and made bloggers conscious of what they could achieve. Equally empowering—and frightening—was the realization that the regime's limits were not fixed. The fact that limits could either shrink or expand suggested that power relationships were negotiable even within an authoritarian contest. That realization gave an added meaning and purpose to online group action because it meant that the authorities and the activists alike enjoyed agency. The arrest of Arabicca also gave the fight for Internet freedom a more profound meaning. There was a realization that bloggers were facing the same repressive reality many ordinary people encountered in their daily lives.

Incidentally, one of the outcomes of the campaign to free Arabicca was the creation of the Committee to Protect Tunisian Bloggers.[112] Although this was a token gesture, as it was practically impossible for this body to be officially recognized or to operate, it was still noteworthy because, all along, bloggers had been largely unsupportive of the idea of forming any such union. They favored a more spontaneous and loose blogosphere, lest blogging be turned into a political and ideological battleground where bloggers would wage war against the authorities.[113] What befell Arabicca, though, made it patently clear to the blogging community that, if they were to preserve their virtual freedom, they would need to be proactive and unified.

Conclusion

After years of political development and maturation, the bloggers' reaction to the arrest of Arabicca marked the start of cyber-activism on a relatively large scale. Internet users who thus far had distanced themselves from the sphere of activism were aware of its necessity. In the months that followed the incident, there was a growing willingness to actively use the Internet to assert rights and demand freedoms. The Internet became a tool in the hands of active members of a cyber-generation not simply to disseminate critical information about Tunisia, but also to denounce infringements of users' rights, mobilize bloggers, express concrete demands, and give an outlet to citizen claims. One key issue that would bring bloggers even closer together was censorship. The fight against censorship mobilized bloggers, cultivated their contestatory potential further, and helped blur the line between online and offline activism. And it is to the central issue of censorship and its implication on citizen action and youth mobilization that I now turn.

6

The Battle over Internet Control

From the Web to the Street

The Digital Dilemma

Although cyber-utopians have long celebrated the online domain as a place of freedom, in Tunisia the Internet was, from the outset, a guarded space. In fact, the regime supported Internet development only to the extent that it could control it. The government enthusiastically embraced information and communications technologies (ICT) while at the same time it despised the inconveniences that came with them.[1] The Internet in particular was tolerated as long as the free flow of information did not challenge the regime. As Internet use became more widespread, the prospects for online activism became a source of concern. Freer access to information could conceivably open people's eyes to new realities, alter dispositions, and engender aspirations for greater civil liberty and political freedoms.

For the country's political establishment, the dilemma had always been how to join the information revolution and promote Internet use without eroding the legitimacy of the regime or undermining the structures of the state.[2] In essence, the state was attempting to marry two irreconcilable pursuits: democratizing the means of communication while constraining the free flow of information. Attaining the desired balance between internal security concerns and human rights commitments was not an easy matter. While continuing to expand access to the Internet and advocate the benefits of the information society, the authorities introduced regulations on Internet service providers, subjected Internet use to tight controls, and intensified electronic and human surveillance of users.[3] The state also issued a decree on March 14,

1997, that subjected the production, distribution, and circulation of online information to the country's press code. This Internet decree also compelled Internet service providers to submit each month a list containing the names and IP addresses of their Internet subscribers to the public operator, the state-run Internet Agency. Additionally, the regulation made the service providers unlimitedly liable for the content they carry, burdening them with a regulatory function and necessarily turning them into auxiliary censors for the state. Last but not least, the Internet decree imposed restrictions on the free use of encryption to secure online communication.[4] All domestic and international Internet connections had to go through the Tunisian Internet Agency—the designated quasi-government operator and sole wholesale international Internet access provider that controlled access to the network. Such measures greatly reduced the disruptive potential of the Internet.

Although the legal and administrative structures that were put in place went a long way toward regulating Internet use, the management of micro-practices related to everyday cyber-activities provided the actual control mechanisms for Internet control. In essence, Internet use was policed through a process of normalization reminiscent of the subtle technologies of control described in Foucault's theorization of Panopticism. This "political technology," as Foucault calls it, is "a way of defining power relations in terms of the everyday life of men."[5] It designates modern techniques of power that economically and effectively keep people perpetually under observation, thereby ensuring their acquiescence and subjection. In the case at hand, the primary site of control was publinets. While licensed as business ventures that were owned and operated by private entrepreneurs, they provided an effective control structure. Technically, they fall under the administrative control of the Ministry of Communications, pursuant to a 1998 decree that imposed a form of "standardization"[6] on the usage of Internet-related services designed to increase surveillance. Owners were expected to maintain a database containing the names of their customers and to visibly post information outlining the rules and regulations governing Internet access. The signs usually included a warning about user liability for any infringements of the legal provisions relating to Internet use—particularly access to impermissible content. The publinet owners and managers were expected to actively monitor the activities of their clients, making sure that they did not access prohibited sites or engage in e-activities that went against social mores or were "likely to disturb the public order"—a loosely interpreted phrase in the press code that referred to politically incorrect usage.

Even the publinets' physical arrangements were reminiscent of the architecture of the Panopticon, which ensured the control of the subjects through permanent observation, scrutiny, and knowledge. Typically, computers were arranged in close proximity to one another and in such a way as to have the screens visible to the computer attendant on duty. Individuals could not change the configuration of the computers, which, incidentally, were deprived of disk drives so that USBs, CDs, and disks could not be used. Users who wanted to save documents to a removable disk or print material from the Internet had to go through the manager of the facility. As an occasional publinet user, I could not help feeling the atmosphere of caution such settings prompted. A straightforward, do-it-yourself Internet activity such as online check-in ahead of a flight was a cumbersome process. To print a boarding pass, I had to go through the site manager, explain to him the nature of my transaction, use his terminal to check in with the airline, and then request a printout of the electronic boarding pass—all with the manager standing by my side. For someone who was not used to these restrictive usages, the publinet experience was as unpleasant and intrusive as going through airport security. These restrictions were also operative in semi-public settings and institutional contexts. For example, a university professor explained to me how the same control architecture was operative in institutions of higher education as late as 2005, when the cost of installing a home connection was still prohibitive. In order to access the Internet for research purposes through a dedicated computer terminal at the university, he had to fill out a request form and submit it to his dean's office, outlining the search he intended to undertake and identifying the sites he wished to visit. Such bureaucratic measures provided a perfect surveillance mechanism and an extended control structure that induced self-policing.

In 2009, ahead of the presidential elections, publinets were required to install Publisoft, a program designed to identify users and monitor their online activities.[7] More effective than such technical innovations, though, was the way control mechanisms were internalized, precisely because the livelihood of publinet owners was contingent on user compliance. Keen on protecting their customer base and ensuring the continuity of their business, some publinets had a camera visibly installed in the premises to discourage disapproved user activities, promote self-policing on behalf of Big Brother, and spare themselves police harassment. In some instances, the manager of the publinet would have a private word with users who did not abide by the expected practices. Allowing a readily identifiable activist to use the facility's Internet services would not go unnoticed by the police and would earn the publinet's owner a stern reminder of the consequences of ignoring the rules of the game. In an extreme case, a political dissident from the banned religious party Ennahda was denied access to the community publinets at the behest of the authorities.[8]

This is not to say that the state exerted total control over public Internet spaces and practices. At times, the enforcement of state regulations was loose. For example, the requirement that ordinary users had to produce proper identification cards or register their names before accessing the Internet was not vigorously enforced. Still, the watchful eye of the state was not without a disciplinary effect of the sort Foucault described in his treatise on power. The regime's obsession with monitoring, surveilling, and controlling Internet use shaped users' Internet experience. The techniques that were put in place and the habits users internalized bred fear and acted as deterrents to accessing undesired information, sharing material critical of the regime, or publicly engaging in political discussions.

The 2004 Arabic Network for Human Rights Information report noted the uniqueness of the Tunisian control strategy. While banning critical websites and detaining their creators are "normal strategies" used in the Arab region, in Tunisia merely visiting a website could be cause for detention.[9] One user who was interviewed in the course of this research recalled how, back in 2005, he would think twice before consulting aljazeera.net, because its critical stance on Tunisia made it a liability. In many ways, the culture that marked the cyberworld was an extension of the public culture that shaped real-world experiences. The user's hesitation to consult Al Jazeera's website reflected a deep consciousness of what was expected from citizens, both on- and offline. These expectations are ingenuously captured in a cartoon that circulated among Tunisian Internet users showing a man anxious to lock the door, shutter windows, and let his dog out in the garden. Asked by his wife if he was afraid of burglars, the husband explained that he was getting ready to watch Al Jazeera's political talk show *The Opposite Direction*. The reigning "net of fear"[10] that marked people's real-life experience operated in some degree on the Internet.

The technical effectiveness of Internet regulation and control rested in great part on the engendered psychological effect and behavioral impact. As Wacker explains in the instance of China, which recalls Internet practices in Tunisia:

> The physical ability of the state to surveil and punish is not necessarily the most important factor when it comes to maintaining "security" in the realm of information technology.... The concept of security

in this field must be understood in terms of the "objective security" that is derived from the reliability of social and technical functions, and the "subjective security" that arises from the state of consciousness that is determined by individual perception and social communication.... The introduction of regulations is only really necessary to complement this strategy by increasing the deterrence effect of feeling that one's actions just might be under observation and by making examples of high-profile cases in the courts.[11]

Examples of these practices abound. In 2002, Zouheir Yahyaoui, the administrator of the online forum TUNeZINE, was sentenced to two years in prison for posting satirical material on the country's staged presidential elections. In 2006, five young students from the southern town of Zarzis were jailed for accessing material deemed to be subversive. In 2006, the outspoken lawyer Mohamed Abbou was jailed for publishing an article on the Internet that criticized the head of state. Similarly, in 2009, the human rights activist Zouheir Makhlouf served a three-month prison term for posting a video exposing polluted sites and depicting environmental problems in his town. Incidents like these heightened the users' awareness of the risks that came with certain online activities. The targeting of cyber-activists was a constant reminder of prescribed red lines. The proclivity of the state to monitor cyber-activities and its ability to access online communication and turn the "subject in communication" into an "object of information,"[12] to use Foucault's terms, eroded trust in the medium and therefore reduced the likelihood of it being embraced by people for any form of political engagement. Suspicion of being continuously under observation became a strong deterrent that induced voluntary self-control and self-censorship.

Looming Challenges

Over the years, the growing popularity and widening appeal of the Internet proved to be a source of challenge. The state's attempt to ensure the manageability of Internet use by holding the number of licensed publinets at about three hundred despite increased demand was hard to implement. In practice, the number of public Internet access points was considerably higher because of the proliferation of unlicensed quasi-publinets and communication centers. These loosely regulated spaces of communication deserve attention in part because they reveal evolving societal dynamics, particularly among the middle and lower classes. Families that had access to the Internet would make available one or two computers in their garage for use by friends and neighbors. Such relatively safe and small operations obeyed a supply-and-demand logic. On the providers' end, it enabled the initiators of these quasi-publinets to have a much-needed supplementary income; on the receiving end, it provided the neighborhood with ready, cheap, and uncontrolled access to the Internet. These trends and spaces, which were often tied to marginalized or underprivileged urban subjects, are also significant in another way. As underground activities that recalled the widespread phenomenon of illegal trade, which was lucrative for the networks of traders and smugglers and convenient for a population with a declining purchasing power, they elucidate evolving dynamics of resistance and change punctuating everyday life. Both the users and suppliers were bound by a shared sentiment of entitlement to better economic opportunities and to connected spaces of communication. Studying engagement in public communication spaces in contexts and ways other than those dictated by the state reveals contentious practices through which individuals attempted to renegotiate boundaries delineated by the state. The appropriation of these uncontrolled activities underpins the culture of contention this book maps out.

The same logic animates the dynamics through which private individuals altered and reclaimed the usage of spaces of communication the state defined. For example, most Internet-wired entertainment and videogame centers that were officially designed for the use of children and teens operated as de facto publinets for users irrespective of age or activity. To the state, these centers were illegal, a status that made them vulnerable and therefore controllable. For the owners and managers of these centers, they were a source of income but also a heterogeneous public space that reflected the complexities of society and reproduced the challenges of shared spaces of interaction. For the users, such public space constituted a new form of agora where all parts of the community met—from the high school student who needed to research school projects on the Internet, to children who frequently visited these facilities to play videogames, to adults who sought to access their email accounts or surf the Web.

Since 2006, growing demand on Internet services, reduced economic barriers to Internet access, and improved ICT infrastructure capabilities—coupled with tight control over publinets and the weight of the watchful eye of the authorities—encouraged more middle-class users to install home Internet connections that offered them permanent access, convenience, and privacy. Consolidating this withdrawal from the public to the private space[13] was the demise of the café as people became increasingly reluctant to interact freely and share their views publicly with the culture of fear taking hold. As a space that invited "fluidity in identity,"[14] the Internet afforded an assuring distance, which allowed people to interact with others without having to engage fully or directly with them. The retreat of Internet users to the privacy of the home was also convenient for a regime that faced the easy and affordable access to the Internet with exerting more control over the flow of information and the exchange of ideas on cyberspace. It enhanced the authorities' surveillance capabilities by making it possible to track the IP addresses of the users who accessed undesired material, shared political content, or engaged in cyber-activism. It was also lucrative for the Internet providers who were either controlled or owned by Ben Ali's family and inner circle.

The state also employed direct censorship. Sites that contained political and human rights content or criticism of the regime, such as Reporters Without Borders, the Committee to Protect Journalists, Amnesty International, and Human Rights Watch were systematically and permanently blocked, as were organizations like the Tunisian League for Human Rights, legal opposition parties like the Progressive Democratic Party, unrecognized political parties like the Congress for the Republic, banned movements like Ennahda, and online news services like Tunisnews. The 9/11 attacks on the United States provided the Tunisian regime with a pretext to increase its monitoring of online activities and censorship of critical content. The counter-terrorism law of December 2003 was less a measure to curb incitement to hatred, violence, and terrorism than an opportunity to increase censorship of online information and control over cyber-activism. As one report noted, "The pattern of Tunisia's online censorship suggests that its policy has been guided less by a fear of terrorism or incitement to violence than by a fear of peaceful internal dissent."[15] The security instinct of the regime impelled it to monitor online correspondence, close down undesired blogs, interfere with email accounts, and deny Internet services to blacklisted individuals.[16]

Naturally, such surveillance activities necessitated deploying an army of cyber-police, investing in acquiring monitoring technology, and installing electronic filtering programs. The consolidation of these structures of control made the system more intolerable. Overall, the authorities were determined to control the use of the Internet as a tool of contestation and a platform for activism. Cracking down on critical Internet users to discourage outspokenness and prosecuting those who "transgress[ed] the unidentified line between that which is permitted and that which is prohibited"[17] was not uncommon. In fact, those who dared publish material that was critical of the regime knew they could have ended up in jail.[18] The constraints on Internet freedom were so egregious that many international freedom advocacy groups ranked the country at the forefront of cyber-repression.

Interestingly, in spite of the security challenges the regime perceived, which prompted the need for devising control mechanisms capable of curbing the ability of the Internet to empower people, the state saw the Internet as more of an opportunity than a threat. For one thing, the commercial applications of and investments in the Internet apparently outweighed its political risks. Additionally, considering the growing culture of connectivity, the ability to acquire Internet data and to use it for repressive purposes enhanced the control capabilities of the state over its subjects and made it potentially more powerful. Whatever risks existed, they were largely deemed manageable.

New Dispositions

Internet control did not go unchallenged. Over the years, sporadic grumbling about cyber-control and calls for Internet freedom started to percolate online. On the blogosphere, such reactions manifested themselves in the form of symbolic virtual actions and modest perennial online freedom advocacy campaigns. Eventually, the regime's determination to restrict access to the Internet led to an inevitable tension with aspiring users enchanted with what the Internet had to offer. Over time, the fight against censorship became a rallying cause for many young people. While Web 2.0 users were still vulnerable and could suffer consequences for online activities the authorities frowned upon, they did not seem to internalize punishment the way Web 1.0 users did. The shift in technology, increased access to the Internet, and the change in user habits helped alter dispositions. The evolving experience of the Internet from the surveilled publinet to the privacy of the home to the convenience of the portable smartphone would prove to be empowering.

As Internet censorship grew more widespread, sophisticated, and systematic, so too did forms of contention. A fierce battle over Internet control ensued, mobilizing users in unprecedented ways, consolidating grassroots activism, and giving rise to a loose Internet freedom youth movement that coalesced around a number of demands, expectations, and actions. This was not merely an outlet to frustration and resentment. The kind of networks the anti-censorship movement enabled, the community of resistance it garnered, and the collective action it spurred were evidence of a simmering tension in the relationship between the state and its subjects. Studying the evolution of that relationship can help inform our understanding of the nature of Internet-based activism and collective cyber-action within an authoritarian context. It also sheds light on dynamics that developed at the intersection of the real and virtual world.

Closely connected to the issue of censorship were evolving conceptions of what it meant to be a citizen in the digital age. The battle for Internet freedom was indicative of a growing desire among a predominantly young and networked society to renegotiate a more meaningful form of citizenship—one that lived up to the democratic pretensions of the regime and was attuned to the global discourse on human rights. Censorship helped to turn the Internet into a crucible in which netizens sought to reaffirm their rights in a country where citizenship was being suspended. Even though the anti-censorship movement involved only a few hundred people and yielded few tangible results, the movement provides insights into the evolving nature of cyber-activism among the youth.

The issue of censorship deserves close attention also because it provides insights into the evolving nature of political action in the digital age. Four themes stand out, which will be the focus of this chapter: the illusion of controllability, the potential for resistance, the expandability of the fight against censorship, and the real dimension of virtual contention. To start with, the battle over Internet control points to the challenge Internet control poses for an autocratic regime that projects an image of openness and modernization. The regime's desire to appear liberal and open to new information and communication technologies contrasts sharply with its instinct for controlling the means of communication and stifling free speech. The acuteness of this dilemma can be pointed out in the state's inconsistent policy and erratic approach toward the Internet and the reaction of the users to what they perceived as arbitrary censorship. For the regime, the negative publicity generated by censorship was an embarrassment; for the users, it brought the online community together.

Second, the issue of censorship illustrates the ways in which Internet control in an era characterized by global openness invites resistance. Although Internet freedom activists were a small, even marginal, group of young people, they were strikingly innovative in their claims, tactics, and strategies, particularly given the constraints on organized action, critical voices, and public dissent.

Embracing the creative possibilities the Internet afforded, they were able to raise public awareness of censorship and to mobilize popular support against the censors.

The battle over Internet control also highlights the intricate interconnectedness between the online and offline worlds. Although initially the Internet provided an interactive space free from the constraints people experienced in reality, increasingly the regime sought to bring it under control. Reclaiming Internet freedom called for online initiatives but it also triggered action on the ground. The increasingly blurred demarcation between the real and the virtual in the Internet freedom movement also points to the evolving relationship between the realm of everyday life and the sphere of politics. The battle against censorship did not merely induce added political engagement; it reconfigured the nature of political action.

Finally, the anti-censorship movement reshaped the issue of censorship and broadened its significance, making it inextricably linked to the larger question of freedoms under authoritarianism. Over time, resistance to Internet censorship and to constraints on free speech developed into claims for broader citizenship rights. The anti-censorship movement reconfigured the problem of censorship from a technical problem of Internet access to an issue of citizen rights. In a state that touted its commitment to democracy, its respect for human rights, and its belief in the potential of the young generation, the youth-led anti-censorship movement exposed its hypocrisy to a wider audience. Doing so in turn helped empower users and open their eyes to the possibilities of political action away from the trappings of formal politics.

Counter-Strategies and Maneuvers

Corresponding to the spread and popularity of the Internet was a decline in online freedom. Wary of the potential of the Internet to challenge official control over the information environment, the authorities tightened their control over cyberspace and stepped up their monitoring of cyber-activism. Political matters and sensitive social topics were typically censored. Websites run by the opposition and those critical of the regime were banned. The sites of various human rights and freedom advocacy groups like Human Rights Watch, Reporters Without Borders, and Amnesty International were invariably inaccessible, as were popular news sites like Aljazeera.net. In addition to such blatant censorship, the authorities instilled a culture of fear that encouraged

self-censorship. Those who adopted critical positions or expressed independent views on the Internet faced serious repercussions. A counterculture developed in reaction to these measures. Determined users learned to dodge
censors by developing a proxy culture and hiding behind anonymity. No less
important was their development of a contestatory spirit that manifested itself
in subtle forms. Adopting cautious positions, using tactful language, and
resorting to playful creativity enabled many Internet users and bloggers to flirt
with red lines without crossing them outright. These strategies and tactics deserve close attention.

Technical solutions to the problem of censorship were easy to find. The
most popular were proxies, intermediary servers that permit users to access
blocked sites by tagging to a foreign IP address. The exponential increase in
domestic Internet subscriptions, coupled with extended hours in front of
computer terminals, raised the level of sophistication among Internet users.
Although recourse to proxies was initially the domain of tech-savvy users and
determined activists, over time ordinary Internet users adopted them as well.
Young users, in particular, became skillful, working around government filters
and breaking firewalls. Overcoming censorship and surveillance became an
art in the hands of numerous users.[19] The use of proxies gave users unmoni-
tored access to the Internet, permitting them to acquire restricted information, take part in forums, and post videos without having to disclose their true
identities, reveal their IP addresses, or leave a trace. Keen on communicating
with their readers and getting their message across, both home-based forums
and foreign-based sites that were censored promoted the use of proxies. The
fact that the government started to actively block popular proxy servers fueled
an even bigger demand for proxies and more activists, both inside and outside
the country, offered tips on how to bypass government bans. Over time, using
anti-blocking software and advanced methods of circumvention started to become more generalized among users, many of whom grew up as "digital natives."
These tactics became part of an everyday Internet culture of contestation.

The use of proxies also entailed technical complications and engendered
risks. Proxies slowed the network considerably, affecting the quality of the
users' experience. Additionally, as proxies changed, became ineffective, or were
censored, users found themselves constantly scouring for alternative routes to
gain access to certain websites. Furthermore, although proxies helped users
get around censorship, they did not exonerate them from accessing banned
sites. Under a regime that invested heavily in Internet surveillance, such practices could have undesired consequences. Generally, though, people grew less

risk averse regarding unauthorized techniques or accessing proscribed sites, and were more willing to overlook the nuisances or risks that came with the use of proxies so long as they had control over their Internet experience and enjoyed unhindered access to what they wanted.

Proxies were more than a technical fix. The development of a proxy culture enabled users to negotiate a strategy for assertion, which may be described as peripheral positionality. While helping escape the watchful eyes of the authorities, the use of proxies also permitted Internet users to claim the virtual sphere as their own. Although new in its manifestation, this positioning extends a long-standing disposition to assert claims to the media sphere. Proxy culture was part of a rooted culture of defiant media appropriation and consumption, including TV signal capturing, pay channel card decoding, mobile phone unlocking, and copyright infringement, which were often met with regulations that proved hard to implement. Growing official concern over unhindered access to ICT prompted more control measures. Yet even as ICT underwent profound changes and induced new user habits, the tactics the state resorted to remained rudimentary and blunt. The heavy-handed approach clearly showed the government's inability to adapt to an evolving media environment. Facing challenges associated with twenty-first-century communication, the regime employed the traditional approaches designed for controlling print and broadcast media.

Only a decade earlier, a similar battle had been fought over open access to satellite television. The regime sought to regulate the use of satellite dishes to limit people's access to political programs on the myriad satellite channels that cropped up, and especially political talk shows on the maverick Qatari channel Al Jazeera. Its attempts were futile.[20] The regime could claim control over what people talked about publicly but not what they watched privately. The attempt to regulate the Internet was an extension of the same battle. Despite the authorities' upgraded monitoring capabilities, the Internet community managed to remain ahead of the censorship police. The ensuing tug of war meant that the battle over Internet control followed a spiral progression model: the more powerful the surveillance systems grew, the more sophisticated users' circumvention tools became. Over time, the country's authoritarian context made contention a necessary corollary to Internet use, at least among the more seasoned and experienced users.

Users' preference for anonymity online complemented their use of proxies. Since the inception of Tunisian online activism, anonymity had been the rule. Most of those who participated in or subscribed to popular forums or information sites used pseudonyms. With the advent of blogging, many active Internet users and bloggers also preferred to hide their real identities. Anonymity provided a form of protection but it also made it easy for the police to infiltrate online discussion groups, monitor discussions on the blogosphere, and circulate competing pro-regime narratives. The removal of inhibitions also coarsened the quality of the discussion as contributors could hide behind their fictive identities. Interestingly, the anonymity of Internet users did not simply engender effacement. While enabling a segment of those who were active on the Internet to hide their civil identities from the authorities, it also helped them develop digital identities, build a reputation, and establish themselves as important players on cyberspace.[21] These disguises helped redraw the boundary between the private and the public realm, enshrining a public dimension to the private space of interaction the Internet afforded. Within this act of transgression lay a latent inscription of politics, which would become more pronounced over the years.

Not only the users' identities but their messages were also veiled.[22] Users understood the rules of the game and adjusted to the reality of censorship. They recognized red lines and avoided writing overtly about political or sensitive topics so as not to give the authorities an excuse to censor their blogs. Typically, direct and personalized critiques, much like criticism of the government, were not common among citizen bloggers and lay Internet users. As one blogger explains, censorship did not muzzle people as much as it made them more creative and more adaptive: "We understood early on the rules of the game and the risks that come with Internet use. The cyber-activist Zouheir Yahyaoui spoke his mind and ended up in jail. We share the same consciousness and fight the same battle but we use different tools and strategies. We learned to express ourselves differently and subtly—and we are not the only ones to do so."[23] Users sought to foil filters by avoiding the use of conspicuous names and other obvious references that would draw attention from the censors. In this context, references to Tunisia were substituted for distant and dissimilar African countries like Congo, while the head of state was never mentioned by name. In other instances, users resorted to a variation of "leetspeak"—a symbolic form of writing that uses alpha-numeric combinations to represent standard language ("leet" itself comes from the English "l33t," a corruption of "elite"). In leetspeak, the French word *censure* (i.e., censorship) became "ce.s.re" and "Tunisie" became "Tun1s1e," a deliberately inaccurate spelling that made such words undetectable to content filters. Resorting to figurative language, allusion, and euphemism were also common communication strategies that stretched the amount of freedom that was available on the Internet. The most active bloggers in particular learned to be evasive and subtle, often adopting a coded language that made some of the blog posts appear simple and ordinary despite their rich and suggestive content.

The Facebook Clash

Unsurprisingly, "the diminished online experience" ensuing from state restrictions on content bred resentment among users.[24] While learning to work around Internet censorship, many users attempted to resist it head-on. To protest the limits on Internet freedom, a group of bloggers organized in 2006 what came to be known as the White Note Campaign, designating December 25 as "a day without blogging" to protest government restrictions on Internet freedom.[25] The initiative was daring but constituted "the limits of the thinkable."[26] Censorship was contested through its own logic: withholding the word. The event promoted a feeling of solidarity. As articulated in the initiative's collective blog, the purpose of the action was "to unite all those who defend the freedom of expression and wish to see the contraction of censorship over the Internet."[27] The linkage between bloggers within the country and outside the country helped raise consciousness about censorship and motivate more users to take a stand against it. Thanks to the aggregator TN-blogs, the action received wide publicity and drew many participants. So compelling was the issue of Internet freedom that the action became annual, repeated yearly in 2006 through 2009.

Online calls to lift censorship and protect freedom of speech fell on deaf ears. In 2007, the bloggers' decision to organize the anti-censorship virtual action "I Blog for the Freedom of Expression" was met with even greater official resistance. While continuing to block access to dissident websites and sites run by antiestablishment voices both at home and abroad, the authorities extended Internet censorship to include emerging social media platforms and multimedia-sharing websites. Web 2.0 video sharing sites like YouTube and Daily Motion were blocked for hosting content the government did not want its citizens to access. Some of the sites that were targeted hosted videos that documented human rights abuse in the country, contained critical messages, and featured segments of programs originally aired on foreign television stations and other material that constituted bad publicity for the regime, but also political satire, probing reports, and alternative newscasts on the ruling family and their entourage.

Although censorship was already rife, it reached new proportions in the summer of 2008. In the words of one blogger, the Web was hit by "a tsunami of censorship."[28] So precarious was the situation of Internet freedom that it invited comparisons with China, notorious for its tight Internet regulations. The circulation of information about the riots in the mining region contributed to this new wave of censorship.[29] With the country preparing for the presidential and legislative elections, even if their outcome was largely foregone, information control became more systematic.[30] As a consequence, several blogs were censored, including Samsoum, Free Race, Ennaqued, Mochagheb, Radioun, and For Gafsa, along with the websites of a number of political parties, opposition figures and news services.[31] More alarmingly for Internet users, on August 18, 2008, the authorities closed down access to the social networking site Facebook. A new threshold had been breached and a new consciousness emerged in response.

While puzzling, the move to censor Facebook was expected. Only a few months before this popular social media site was taken out, the blogger Zizou posted a sarcastic open letter alerting the censor to the potential of Facebook to erode state control over the Internet and expressing surprise at the censor's tolerance for such a free space of interaction:

> Isn't it high time Facebook was censored? Tunisian Facebook users can now access just about everything. They can see videos (including videos you censored on YouTube), have access to undesired information, read the blogs of *non grata* individuals, follow what is happening in the rest of the world, and watch all sorts of shows. Additionally, Facebook makes it easy for non-authorized associations to exist and for citizens to express their views.... I would like to think that this unhindered freedom is only an oversight on your part, and that you will see to it that it is rectified at your earliest convenience.[32]

The inability to access this popular social networking site went a long way toward alerting casual Internet users to the reality of censorship. While in the past censorship went largely unnoticed, as it was mostly felt by a minority of affected users, active bloggers, and avid information seekers, it suddenly became an imposing reality and an annoying inconvenience that directly affected the daily routines of an estimated twenty-eight thousand Facebook users. Many felt robbed of their right to use their favorite site.[33]

Facebook's ban prompted mobilization. There was a strong urge to hold on to a relatively insulated space in what became a "sprawling surveillance state."[34]

A reaction was inevitable. Only a few months earlier, one blogger warned: "We will continue to suffer the consequences of censorship if we remain passive and do not demand our rights."[35] Users were increasingly unwilling to tolerate restriction on Internet access and information circulation. Unblocking Facebook became a rallying cry with strong calls to be united against the issue of censorship. A number of Facebook groups were formed, ranging from "United against the Blocking of Facebook"[36] to "If they do not Restore Facebook, I will Emigrate to the Republic of Niger" to "Together against the Internet Agency's Ban of the Internet."[37] Never before had the Internet mobilized people in this manner. A battle over Internet control was shaping up. Faced with the resentful reaction of Internet users, the authorities attempted to influence public opinion. It was not hard to detect echoes of a counter-campaign against Facebook in the printed press, which published articles portraying Facebook as a threat to social values and associating it with perversion and identity theft.[38]

Interestingly, the authorities' attempt to discredit the medium made users more determined and more assertive. Three major groups mobilized their efforts to put pressure on the censor to restore access to Facebook. The first group wanted to petition the government, but was not able to muster much support. The second group proposed staging a protest, but was dissuaded by the intolerance of the security forces. The third and most popular group took a different approach, targeting the economic stakeholders rather than the political decision-makers. Resentful of the fact that they paid hefty Internet subscription fees but received mediocre service in return, this group vowed to boycott the Internet providers if Facebook continued to be inaccessible. In support of this initiative, a Facebook page was set up bearing the name "If they Block my Facebook, I will Cancel my Contract with my Internet Provider."[39] On the wall of the campaign's Facebook page, the protesters articulated the nature of their action: "We urge you to act in order to restore access to Facebook. We have opted for a peaceful, legal and inoffensive act that may prove effective. We opted for action where others preferred polemics."[40]

Surprisingly, before the action fully materialized, the local newspapers started to write about the Facebook situation with a somewhat conciliatory tone, which suggested to the users that the online mobilization was noted by the authorities. Some suspected that their intended action could adversely affect the financial interests of members of the president's family who owned the largest Internet service providers, PlaNet and TopNet.[41] In early September 2008, an article appeared in the daily newspaper *Le Temps* reconsidering the wisdom of the ban. The piece speculated that blocking Facebook could possibly be a measure aimed at depriving extremists of appropriating this tool, but then went on to enumerate its many benign and valuable uses for young people.[42] The fact that the article took notice of the proposed e-petition suggested that even traditional media was attuned to what was happening in the online world. Shortly thereafter, access to the site was restored as a result of Ben Ali's personal intervention.[43] The pro-government papers were quick to massage the news. An article in the daily *Assabah* dwelt on the potential dangers of emerging information and communication technologies and called for a legal framework for regulating Internet control in a way that safeguarded the interests of the country, protected its image, and pulled the rug from underneath those who sought to misuse it while hiding behind anonymity—a move that bloggers perceived as a campaign to institutionalize control and legalize censorship.[44] Not surprisingly, in the months that followed, there were signs of a campaign against Internet use, with articles highlighting its undesired effects and warning parents of the potential dangers of the Net—all of which pointed to the need for tighter state regulation and control.[45]

The unexpected decision to rescind the widely resented ban after it had been in effect for a fortnight (August 18–September 2, 2008) was a significant development. What had always been a shadowy practice was revealed as a state-sanctioned operation that was supported by an elaborate control apparatus. Technically, as the blogger Arabasta put it, "Ben Ali's ordering the reinstatement of Facebook was a *de facto* acknowledgment, even a sanctioning of censorship since the president could not officially block a non-official decision."[46] For many users, lifting the ban on Facebook constituted a precious symbolic victory. Interestingly, the ban went a long way toward publicizing Facebook, helping to increase its use from some one hundred thousand at the end of 2008 to nearly two million in early 2011. The widespread use of Facebook would constitute a unique context for youth socialization and communication and would also help intensify cyber-activism.

The Tortuous Politics of Censorship

Although access to Facebook returned, the issue of censorship refused to go away. There was a widely held perception among disaffected Internet users that government censorship was absurd. The blogger Werewolf exclaimed, "What good is censorship if it can be readily bypassed!"[47] Another blogger,

Carpe Diem, doubted that "it is ever possible to censor a rapid technology that has an unmatched ability for regeneration."[48] The strong appeal and high penetration of the Internet made it hard to restrict access to information. What was particularly unique about the case of Tunisia, as this blogger put it, was the practice of censoring censorship.[49] The problem was not just the exercise of censorship, but the fact that the authorities were adamant in their refusal to admit that censorship even existed. The official state position insisted that only culturally insensitive material and sites that encouraged terrorism were targeted. Similarly, the National Internet Agency rejected claims that it was behind existing censorship practices. By officially proclaiming censorship nonexistent while actively doing it, the state also made the censor evanescent.[50]

Users called the mysterious censor "Ammar 404" (or "Ammar Scissorhands"), which became the subject of numerous jokes, stories, and anecdotes.[51] "Ammar," as one blogger explains, is a generic name that is associated in popular culture with two characters in two classic comedies; it is also the name of one of Ben Ali's close advisers who is believed to be a pioneer of Internet censorship.[52] The designation "404" was a pun on the error message that appeared on censored websites. When users tried to access banned sites, they got the message "error 403" in lieu of "error 404: page not found."[53] The National Internet Agency displayed a fake error message indicating that the searched page could not be found, which suggested that there was a technical glitch when in reality the page was blocked.

The hidden identity of the censor was deeply problematic for users concerned with censorship. The blogger Free Race sarcastically noted: "What if the employee who is in charge of censorship made a judgment error as to the ceiling of freedom that is permitted? What if he abuses his powers? Who is this censor anyway? The designation 'Ammar' makes us cling to a fictive character when in fact the censor is a real person. Ammar is one of us, and we ought to be able to identify him. He owes us answers."[54] The blog post reflected a sentiment shared among many users. There were increasingly more pronounced demands that the censor cease to hide behind a cryptic and dismissive error message. Revealing the identity of the censor was an important initial step for dealing with the issue of Internet control.

Many Internet users resented the tactless manner in which the Internet was censored. So obscure and nonsensical was censorship that it became a source of anxiety.[55] For many users, the problem was not censorship itself, as it was not difficult to bypass from a technical standpoint, but the disregard for users who were becoming increasingly more technically savvy and globally connected.[56]

As citizens, they expected the right to access the Internet; as customers, they expected good services; as youth, they expected an understanding of their needs and their sensibilities. In the eyes of some users, the authorities' silence on censorship was a sign of contempt for its citizens.[57] For a liberal country that claimed respect for human rights and adherence to the rule of law, this was an embarrassment.

For the blogger Antikor, the issue was not Internet control but the exercise of control: "Even though censorship is practiced in democratic countries, it is usually undertaken within a legal framework."[58] Initially, some bloggers expressed their readiness to help the state develop more appropriate forms of information control and determine how to best regulate the Internet. As one blogger explains:

> Considering that most democracies exercise some form of censorship, the question is not whether or not to censor, but how to practice censorship. If censorship is deemed necessary, it has to be exercised in a consensual, legal, and transparent way.... The authorities need to reconsider the way they go about censorship. It behooves them to form a working group to assess what is really being achieved by the current censorship practices. We are willing and ready to take part in this endeavor, submit proposals and contribute ideas.[59]

For some, then, the issue was not censorship in itself but the arbitrary way it was carried out. Many sought to attenuate the effect of censorship through the expressed willingness to work within the system. Significantly, such reaction was a de facto call for the formulation of a state policy to ensure that censorship met "the bare minimum level of transparency and institutionalism."[60]

For the blogging community, arbitrary censorship was aggravating precisely because it was not sanctioned by the law or determined by a judicial body. Consequently, its victims had no way to appeal the censor's decisions. The absence of legal and institutional guarantees was not simply an indication of the increasingly exclusionary nature of the state but pointed to a growing disjunction between the state and its subjects: "If the rationale for censorship, as practiced, is to safeguard the interests of the state, the latter cannot be defined independently of the ability of the institutions of the state to represent the interests of the people and to honor the social contract with the people."[61] The lack of legal foundation for censorship highlighted the state's violation of the terms of the social contract.

Recourse to the law and to litigation became the hallmark of a new phase in the struggle against censorship that would have a broader appeal. There was a rising consensus among a number of proactive bloggers that the censor could not act incognito and with impunity. Their ultimate goal was to force the state to officially acknowledge that it exercises censorship and to take responsibility for its actions. These demands were particularly salient in the case of Zied El Heni, a journalist and blogger who filed a lawsuit against the National Internet Agency for restricting access to Facebook.[62] This was the first court case to be filed against the agency since its launch in 1996. Although El Heni lost his case, his action proved to be significant in a number of ways. Intrigued by his initiative, a group of Internet users, Internet freedom activists, and bloggers rallied around him and sought to capitalize on this case to advance the campaign against censorship. The group launched a coordinated campaign to expose the censorship practices the Internet Agency exercised. Declaring November 4—the date of the court hearing—a national day for the freedom of blogging, they designed a logo for the event and set up a collective blog that attracted hundreds of Internet users.[63] Several bloggers accompanied El Heni to court, took minutes of the proceedings, uploaded pictures and videos of the event, blogged about the case, and issued press releases. They reached out to people beyond the blogosphere using a variety of media outlets to publicize the case and mediatize the campaign. A strong team spirit developed among those who were involved in this anti-censorship initiative, impelled by the shared belief that censorship was everybody's problem. The ensuing momentum speaks of the ability of a core group to instigate action and to turn this small incident into a focal point of activism.

Although the group knew that their action could not end censorship, they were hopeful that applying pressure would pay off and get the message through to the powers that be. At least the bloggers could aspire for a moral victory: an acknowledgment of the continued practice of censorship. Emboldening the group was their earlier victory of restoring access to Facebook. As the blogger Astrubal put it, the real value of such action lay not in the immediate outcome of the case but in the reformulation of the problem of censorship from a technical issue to an issue of citizen rights.[64] If the constitution provided for fundamental human rights like freedom of speech, and if the regime promulgated a rhetoric that upheld its commitment to the rule of law, it fell on the citizens to reaffirm their rights:

> In the short term, such litigations are unlikely to yield concrete results. What matters are the public debates these initiatives spur and

the kind of awareness they raise about the intolerable nature of these violations. Safeguarding the rule of law cannot rest on hollow slogans; it comes from the ability to nurture a popular culture that rejects infringements on people's rights. We need to express our adamant rejection of the transgression of the law. The judicial system can play an effective role only if the will of the social body provides a counterweight to political pressure.[65]

The added momentum of the anti-censorship movement revealed a significant development. Whereas in the past, users and bloggers had been content with outperforming and bypassing the censors to gain free access to the Internet, they became focused on the root cause of the problem. The principle of censorship itself was now called into question.[66] People had come to realize that acquiring the technical ability to bypass censorship afforded little more than a quick fix to a more complex problem. A new mindset started to crystallize, leading more people to coalesce around the issue of freedom of speech. The fight against censorship would help integrate blogs more tightly with the public sphere.

Orwellian Schemes

The raising of consciousness among Internet users was met with more intolerance from the authorities. While censorship is a regional reality, Tunisia's case was unique in terms of scope and depth. Over the years, the surveillance power of the state, its control over information flows, and its technical capabilities for tracing and filtering had increased noticeably. Overall, censorship relied on four techniques or layers: selective URL blocking, DNS blocking, IP filtering, and keyword filtering.[67] The fact that all data flew through the National Internet Agency facilitated Internet control. The regime expended a considerable amount of resources to build a technological architecture of control. It invested in a sophisticated array of technologies to block websites that were deemed antagonistic, to the point that the country became a testing ground for Western suppliers of monitoring technology.[68] It purchased sophisticated Internet monitoring systems, high-tech surveillance equipment, and powerful interception gear including Smart Filter to block sites, ETI systems for identifying users who consulted particular websites and tracking logs of email correspondences, and deep-packet inspection for filtering content and intercepting emails. So intrusive was the surveillance system Tunisia adopted that some Western suppliers of interception gear grew uncomfortable supplying the government, as their association with a country that had one of the worst Internet freedom records could tarnish their reputation.[69]

Equipped with a state-of-the-art censorship apparatus, the authorities were at the forefront of cyber-repression. The year 2010 in particular witnessed an unprecedented wave of censorship. While in the past censorship had targeted the pages of political activists and human rights organizations and websites that delved into sensitive subjects or featured political content, repression became more pervasive and more indiscriminate. Tight control over political content developed into a near-total intolerance of critical opinions. Any site with nonconformist views or social criticism was a target for censors. French information sites like Rue98.com, ReadWriteWeb, and *Le Nouvel Observateur* were banned, as were Blib.tv, Metacafe, and Flicker. The censor also pursued selective filtering of Facebook, targeting certain profiles and taking out pages. Even Twitter, not yet widely used, reported that some of its feeds were being filtered.[70]

The blogosphere was probably hit the hardest. On what came to be known as Black Tuesday, April 27, 2010, more than one hundred blogs were censored. Among these were some of the most respected blogs by some of the finest bloggers, including Big Trap Boy, Carpe Diem, Antikor, Stupeur, Bent Aayla, and Nocturnal Thoughts. Some bloggers called it "a massacre on the Web";[71] others decried it as "an intellectual genocide" that recalled "book-burning by the medieval church."[72] Merely flirting with political topics of sorts or approaching red lines now provoked censorship, regardless of how the topic was treated and irrespective of whether the approach was critical, analytical, or merely informational.[73] Even reposting articles or relaying information that had been previously published elsewhere and that was available through a simple Google search could bring down the wrath of the authorities. So pervasive was censorship that Tunisia was deemed by the Committee to Protect Journalists to be among the most dangerous places to be a blogger.[74] Excessive censorship was a preemptive strike to discourage users from voicing their opinions, criticizing the system, or tackling political issues. And many bloggers saw censorship in just that light: to exclude all those who displayed the slightest signs of independent thinking.[75]

What had once been targeted and selective censorship increasingly became more widespread and more irrational. Even cultural and culinary sites were not immune from censorship. Puzzled by the blocking of the website of the chocolate spread Nutella, one blogger sarcastically exclaimed: "Could it be that the prefix 'nu' in 'Nu-tella' was confused with the French word 'nu' [meaning 'nude']?"[76] Incredulous at what happened on Black Tuesday, the anonymous blogger-cartoonist -Z- posted a cartoon on his blog Débat Tunisie ridiculing Internet censorship practices. Titled "Indigestion with an Eggroll at Carthage," the cartoon showed a fuming Ben Ali, pounding on the table during a cabinet meeting and yelling at his submissive ministers. He demanded that culinary websites be blocked, supposedly because the West seemed to be more attracted to the popular Tunisian eggrolls than with Ben Ali's vision and achievements. The caption stated: "Our sovereign has ordered the censorship of all blogs and websites that do not go well with his regime"—punning on the original French word *regime*, which means both "diet" and "political regime."[77] With censorship devolving into "indiscriminate shelling," as one activist put it,[78] the country became notorious for cyber-control. A 2010 Reporters Without Borders report classified the country among the top ten violators of freedom of expression in the world in its list of enemies of the Internet.[79]

The Irksomeness of Censorship

Censorship became a source of immense frustration. There was an obvious disjuncture between the retrograde political culture of the regime and the kind of acquiescence it expected, on the one hand, and the liberating culture of inquisitiveness and engagement that marked an aspiring generation increasingly attuned to global discourses on empowerment and citizen rights, on the other. Ben Ali's repeated claims that youth were the means of achieving Tunisia's aspirations and that the state would spare no effort to promote the new generation did not reflect the reality many young people experienced. Not only did censorship make the democratic pretensions of the regime embarrassingly hollow, it was also out of sync with the country's liberal orientation. As a modern country, Geisser notes, Tunisia was mired in a patent paradox: "while the regime remains politically archaic, a vestige of the past so to speak, society has largely evolved in its attitude, behavior and mentality."[80] In the context of a networked society, the regime's tendency to simultaneously embrace ICT while controlling it, to open access to the Internet while restricting its usage, made this incongruence more deeply felt. The youth were not unaware of the incongruity of the state's proclaimed modernity: "We have been lectured about the virtues of civil liberties and human rights from elementary school all the way to college, but we know full well that what figured in the textbooks and what we learned at school have nothing to do with our lived reality."[81]

The fact that these contradictions were also operative at the micro-societal level gave Internet control a broader significance. Socially, there was disparity between the way the state treated people and the way the modern nuclear family brought up their children. The government adopted a repressive instinct that made people, in general, and the young generation, in particular, internalize the culture of fear in the public arena even as they were nurtured at home by parents who tried to cultivate their talents, foster their sense of self-worth, and put them on the path to success. To the extent that the state's authoritarian political culture started to collide with the upbringing and mindset of the younger generation, it gave a new dimension to the reigning culture of censorship. The practice of censorship assumed that citizens were not free-thinking individuals capable of governing themselves. As the blogger Arabasta put it, "The Internet Agency treats people as minors—as individuals who are incapable of distinguishing between the good and the bad. This is not only an insult to the people, but a sulfurous denunciation and a virulent critique of the entire educational system which has turned out citizens who can easily be channeled and manipulated."[82]

A witty and cultivated blog, Kissa Online, observed that "censorship is an institution created by an authority, presumably a state authority, to examine the content of different forms of expression or information before publication, representation or distribution. 'Censorship is my literary enemy,' Victor Hugo once wrote; 'It is my political enemy. I accuse censorship.' "[83] The blog post's emphasis on the confluence between the literary and the political dimensions gave censorship an added significance. More than ever before, there was a pointed awareness of what censorship meant, and many bloggers saw it for what it was—an assault not just on their freedom of expression, but on their being. Quoting Flaubert, the above-mentioned blogger further noted, "Irrespective of the form censorship takes, it is a monstrosity, something worse than homicide; any attempt against thought is a 'crime of lese-majeste'—an affront to the soul, so to speak."[84] Censorship weighed heavily on Internet users because it came to epitomize repression: "When citizens are deprived of the right of expression in public, when their blogs are censored, and when they cannot access the Internet—that's repression."[85] For an aspiring young generation that was not unaware of the increasingly globalized discourse on freedoms, access to information was a fundamental human right. As one militant blogger put it, "The censorship of my Facebook account is an assault on my right to exchange information and to express my views on matters of public interest. The vigilant censor who violates our natural right to free expression and to blogging and who assaults our 'virtual imagination' cannot but be born out of the womb of repression."[86]

The battle against Internet censorship developed into a battle against constraints on free speech, which in turn became inextricably linked with the broader issue of freedom. As one dissident blogger wrote, "The efficacy of state censorship notwithstanding, the battle for the freedom of expression remains cardinal. The stakes are high. If we let go of it, we lose everything. It is not simply a battle against the regime, it is in essence a battle against obscurantism."[87] For many, the price of giving up free speech was costlier than ever before: "The battle against censorship is the engine for a bigger, more fundamental and more lasting fight. For a young generation that suffers from social and political deprivation, there is nothing left except to take a peek at the wide world through the small openings the Internet affords. If it gets more suffocating, they will not have anything to lose."[88] This feeling was echoed by yet another blogger, who warned, "The children who are punished without knowing what they did wrong could become dangerous when they come of age. Maybe the censor should consider what this means for the future."[89] A common feeling prevailed that citizens "deserve better."[90] The growing popular resentment toward the intensification of censorship marked the point of no return.

More bloggers were determined to resist. The slogan "I blog therefore I am" became a form of resistance. Blogs that were censored were quickly resurrected. One of the targeted blogs, Journalist Tunisien, was relaunched no fewer than 110 times. A strong sense of bonding developed.[91] Many bloggers hosted "cyber-refugees" on their own blogs, giving them the right to post their own blog entries and administer their blogs. The logic, as one blogger put it, is one of numbers: "the censor could target some politicized blogs and censor them, but cannot silence all bloggers or prevent them from blogging on sensitive topics—unless they decide to enact a blackout on the entire blogosphere."[92] As the following blog post by Arabasta suggests, some bloggers did not shy away from publicly expressing such a defiant attitude:

> Because I am convinced of the futility of censorship, because I do not blog about illegal matters or post false news, because I respect the intelligence of my fellow citizens, because there is nothing that can stand in the face of freedom, because writing is what unites us all, I continue to blog on a new address while maintaining my original

blog. I will not give up until the censor shows respect for our intelligence and grants us back the right to surf the Net—just like the rest of the world.[93]

An Electronic Uprising

The way opposition to censorship gained ground is instructive. For a few years, there were a number of modest online initiatives. These protests, confined to proactive bloggers and digital activists, did not have an impact on the offline world or garner the support of the young masses. Spring 2010 was a significant turning point, giving rise to a popular anti-censorship movement. Increased censorship was not met with acquiescence but with a more pointed contestatory spirit and a steady growth in activism. There were more people who were either active on the Internet or who supported cyber-activism, and their efforts resonated among users, the overwhelming majority of whom preferred to be either passive or minimally involved.[94] One initiative helped to popularize the movement and draw a broad swath of the online community to it. Dismayed and frustrated with the intensification of government censorship, a group of Internet users launched an anti-censorship campaign against Ammar the censor, which they named "Sayyeb Salah," a slang expression in the Tunisian dialect that literally means "enough...leave me alone." The campaign was a creative mixture of jest and sincerity. It attracted a great many users who resented censorship but did not feel comfortable condemning it publicly or speaking out against the censor. The campaign encouraged users to overcome their fear and to upload pictures that displayed signs bearing the Sayyeb Salah slogan. Action started unintentionally and developed organically. As one of the participants recounts, the action was one of several attempts to express his views on the Internet regarding a range of issues.[95] Sometime in April 2010, he learned of a planned strike by the employees of the National Internet Agency to protest their work conditions. In a pseudo-gesture of support, he took a picture of himself in front of the agency building holding a placard on which he jotted down the words "Give them what they want; Let go of the Internet" and uploaded it on the Net. The gesture was sarcastic, since in the minds of many users the Internet Agency was part of the censorship machine. Someone came across the sign and decided to modify the message from "Sayyeb l'Internet" (let go of the Internet) to "Sayyeb Salah" (let go, that's enough), a reference to censorship.

The slogan "*Sayyeb Salah*" went viral. Several Internet users posed with the campaign sign, typically with their faces not showing, and uploaded the pictures on their blogs or Facebook pages. Some of the protesters were courageous enough to either reveal their faces or use their real names when posting material. A group of Internet freedom activists created the site Ammar 404 to host the numerous pictures that started to circulate featuring *Sayyeb Salah* slogans and to manage the reactions the initiative generated.[96] In a matter of days, the site attracted thousands of supporters who posted their photos with anti-censorship slogans, uploaded videos, or drew cartoons ridiculing Ammar. One observer noted that "the silent crowd is not so silent anymore."[97] Many of those who joined the campaign were neither bloggers nor activists but young Internet and social media users who were frustrated by Internet censorship. A number of artists and singers were also keen on supporting the campaign, circulating songs on the Internet that were composed specifically to mock Ammar.[98] This unprecedented mobilization against censorship led some to describe the campaign as an "electronic uprising."[99] So compelling was the *Sayyeb Salah* initiative that Al Jazeera devoted an episode of its weekly program *The Altar of Al Jazeera* to discuss censorship in Tunisia, in particular, and in the Arab world, in general.[100]

The *Sayyeb Salah* initiative demonstrates how the battle against censorship evolved from individual action to group initiative to a broad-based youth movement. Reflecting on this transmogrification, the blogger Kahlaoui wrote: "Stepping up censorship helped push the struggle beyond individual or elite protests and occasional condemnations by a small circle of cyber-activists. A new phase has been inaugurated which seeks to involve all Internet users and to get them to mobilize around a set of demands which concern everybody regardless of whether they are 'politicized' or not."[101] The campaign became a rolling protest movement, calling for the end of censorship, the lifting of all forms of Internet control, and respect for freedom of speech. There was a sense of righteousness anchored in a pointed awareness that this was a just cause. This assertiveness translated into the adoption of a legal discourse about human rights and civil rights. It also took the form of concrete initiatives, some of which deserve more than cursory attention.

The UN Year of Youth

The year 2010 registered an increase in protests, ranging from calls to start blogs[102] to online campaigns to street protests. In April 2010, a number of anti-censorship activists proposed an online petition stating that Internet censorship was "a violation of the freedom of thought and freedom of expression and a violation of the country's laws and international conventions."[103] It also called on the authorities to determine the party that was responsible for enforcing censorship and to spell out well-defined criteria for censorship. The motto for the group's Facebook page reflected their ideals: "I am a citizen; I am not a minor; I say No to censorship."[104] In a matter of days, the petition drew thousands of Facebook fans, many of whom signed using their real names. Support for the petition emboldened other Internet users and bloggers to come up with more creative initiatives, including protest letters addressed to prominent political figures in the country. The line between the political and the nonpolitical, and that between the real and the virtual was more blurred than ever.

On May 3, 2010, which marked the International Day for Press Freedom, a group of Internet users published an open letter to President Ben Ali expressing the disappointment and frustration Internet censorship caused the young generation during the United Nations "year of youth." The letter, which was titled "Censorship Harms the Image of the Country," also urged the president to take the necessary measures to ensure that censorship was not enacted outside a legal framework capable of safeguarding the exercise of constitutional rights.[105] For some, this was a bold step; for others, it was too timid. For one blogger, the issue came down to demanding a right: "We should demand and not plea. We are the ones who vote. It is we, the people, who rule. This is what the constitution stipulates. It is our right to demand the lifting of censorship."[106] A similar view was voiced by the rebel judge Mokhtar Yahyaoui in his blog. In an open letter addressed to his fellow bloggers, he advocated a firm approach:

> Tunisia is a dictatorship that feeds on an authoritarian system which rests on propaganda and censorship. Freedom of expression simply does not exist...and it would be delusional to believe that one can graciously regain freedom of expression by pleading directly with a dictator. Even if we imagine, in our wildest dreams, that the dictator grants this liberty, it can only be in the image of the slave whose master permits him to eat on his table, as narrated in Frantz Fanon's *The Wretched of the Earth*.[107]

There was also a call to flood the private mail of the representatives in the House of Parliament with letters of protest to pressure them to assume their responsibility as representatives of the people. In June 2010, a number of anti-censorship activists sent letters via registered mail to members of the Parliament demanding that the issue of Internet censorship be included as a discussion item on the legislature's agenda.[108] The campaign drew modest participation[109] and elicited hardly any responses from the members of the Parliament.[110] Nevertheless, the initiative was significant because it helped further sensitize Internet users and activists to the need for sustaining the momentum of the anti-censorship campaign by keeping up the pressure on the authorities. It also emboldened companies whose businesses were adversely affected by censorship to consider filing a class-action lawsuit against those who were responsible for the practice.[111] Making the fight against censorship everybody's battle turned it from a question of whether an individual could access a particular website to that of the people's entitlement to exercise their rights as citizens and the state's duty to act in accordance with the law. As it evolved, the anti-censorship movement started to question the terms under which the state-society relationship was conceived in a country that spared no effort to flaunt its democratic pretentions.

A Real Protest for Virtual Freedom

The more Internet users encountered the reality of censorship, the more they doubted the efficacy of virtual action. Some of them held onto their constitutional right to express themselves openly but started to reconsider the best ways to secure that right. There was a feeling among this group that the proliferation of e-campaigns drained the struggle against censorship of its efficacy and resulted in an added feeling of frustration.[112] One blogger noted that "supporting the Internet freedom cause with a click of a mouse is a convenient form of activism that amounted to nothing much."[113] Up to that point, the sphere of action had been limited to cyberspace. Cyber-activism was appealing precisely because real-world activism was risky and everybody recognized the street as belonging to the regime. Over time, though, what was once unthinkable turned out to be inevitable. A small number of bloggers and Internet users were willing to go beyond the confines of the virtual. The *Sayyeb Salah* campaign played an important role in rallying people around the cause of Internet freedom, broadening the popular base of the movement, and awakening the political consciousness of young users, and now a bolder protest action would be crucial in moving the battle from the virtual domain to the real world.

Although a significant development, closing the gap between the virtual and the real spheres did not happen immediately. On the blogosphere, one could detect alternative discourses on the best way to counter censorship, including calls to take direct action. The reaction of the blogger Antikor to the arbitrariness of censorship reveals a noticeable willingness to take the battle to the street: "In democratic countries, there is an enormous pressure against censorship. People disapprove of it, speak out against it, and denounce it. They protest to say 'No' to censorship."[114] There was a growing consciousness that the fight against censorship was a real fight: "It is my hope," noted passionately the same blogger, "that our young people understand that, in much the same way this country needed our grandfathers to liberate itself of foreign invaders and colonizers, it needs every one of us so that this freedom can flourish."[115] In May 2010, and as an offshoot of the *Sayyeb Salah* campaign, the idea of a concrete action circulated on the blogosphere. This loose initiative started as part of a Skype discussion among a few bloggers and online activists both at home and abroad. An invitation-only Google group was then formed to plan a peaceful protest that would take place on May 22, 2010, in front of the Ministry of Communication and Technology to demand an end to all forms of Internet censorship. The action was named *Nhar ala Ammar*—a vernacular expression meaning "a miserable day for Ammar." The campaign attracted a number of Internet users who thought that such action would expose the country's censorship practices, embarrass the government, and exert more pressure on the censor to ease its control over the Internet. The aim of the protest, a dedicated Facebook page noted, was to defend Article 7 of the Constitution, namely that "citizens exercise the plenitude of their rights in the forms and conditions provided for by the law."[116]

The legal provisions for organizing a protest in Tunisia stipulated that the authorities must be informed in order to take the necessary security measures. To prove the legality of the protest, applicants needed a receipt of acknowledgment from the Ministry of Interior. Sometime in May 2010, the group attempted to inform the authorities of their planned demonstration by depositing a notification letter with the ministry. Having repeatedly failed in their endeavors to submit their application and secure a written acknowledgment, they redrafted their protest notification using appropriate legal jargon and sent it to the Minister of Interior via registered mail. Simultaneously, they issued a communiqué to this effect to the press to advertise their action. The group also made it a point to video-record all the steps they took, along with the participants' commentary on all the hurdles they encountered, and to upload the videos to the Web, giving the operation a tragicomic flavor. No less comic was the organizers' attempt to commission the printing of anti-censorship slogans on white T-shirts. Feeling uncomfortable with the order that was placed, the manufacturer decided to check with a contact he had in the security services, who in turn informed him that designing such T-shirts required authorization from the Ministry of Interior. Thus, the T-shirts for the anti-censorship campaign ended up being censored by the authorities.[117]

Such setbacks were discouraging, to say the least. With so much uncertainty, the organizers of the protest started to contemplate canceling the operation altogether. Before they could make a decision, the initiative was thwarted by the authorities. Initially, the police had perceived an anti-censorship protest by a handful of bloggers as eccentric, but they soon became alarmed. On the eve of the protest, two of the organizers of the event were detained and were coerced into posting a video announcing that the planned protest had been called off to allow for better organization. To further ensure that the initiative was effectively squelched, security forces were deployed in front of the Ministry of Communication and Technology, where the protest was supposed to take place. The show of force did not dissuade some bloggers and Internet freedom activists from executing plan B: Operation White T-shirt.[118] The idea was for the protesters to wear customized white outfits bearing anti-censorship slogans and to converge in the capital's main thoroughfare, which also housed the Ministry of Interior, the symbol of state repression. Although only a handful of people showed up, their daring to protest was enough to prompt the authorities to react by driving out anyone wearing a white outfit, effectively putting an end to the protest.

Even though the *Nhar ala Ammar* protest fizzled out, it was a significant development because it endowed the anti-censorship campaign with a broader significance. For many participants and supporters, it was evident that the protesters were law-abiding while Ammar was above the law. For one blogger, the message was resounding: "The action of the two young activists of the 22 May protest is a brave initiative, which—contrary to censorship—is anchored in the rule of law. This is the beginning of a new era where citizens demand the respect of their rights as guaranteed by the constitution. This initiative is a peaceful citizen response to the arbitrary and anti-constitutional exercise of censorship."[119] If nothing else, *Nhar ala Ammar* constituted a moral victory that cemented the culture of contesting censorship.

Henceforth the battlefield would not be confined to cyberspace but gradually moved to the street, which was significant because of the political risks associated with street activities. Such protests marked a departure from the early anti-censorship initiatives. Although previously some bloggers had accepted the authorities' need to regulate and were willing to contemplate ways of helping the authorities rationalize and manage censorship, bloggers henceforth called for a quasi-confrontational approach with the regime. The state's censorship approach had hardened the attitude and approach of bloggers, eventually leading to a rolling campaign that was as much real as it was virtual. What made this transition possible was people's new predisposition to take action and their energized willingness to claim their rights.

Chagrined by the authorities' security approach to the Internet, their tabs on free speech, and their restrictions on access to the Internet, but buoyed by the *Nhar ala Ammar* initiative, a small group of activist bloggers proposed the idea of a flash mob to further protest censorship.[120] This was a first in Tunisia. Participants were to show up in the suburb of Sidi Bou Saïd on August 4, 2010, wearing a white outfit. The flash mobbers would then enact a swift choreography and observe one minute of silence before dissipating. The scene would be recorded and uploaded on the Internet. Although this restrained action drew only a handful of participants, it triggered an official reaction. On the day of the event, and despite the organizers' discretion, the secret police intercepted the small group of participants, and instructed them to board the train back to where they came from.

The authorities' zero tolerance policy toward any form of protest, including the flash mob, drew negative publicity. Al Jazeera picked up the story, airing a critical report on innovative and creative forms of protest in North Africa, followed by a live phone interview with one of the flash mob participants. The report aired segments from an older video recording capturing a group of young people enacting what looked like a flash mob in the midst of a bustling thoroughfare in Sidi Bou Saïd, leading the audience to believe that the flash mob had in fact taken place. The report thereby turned what was otherwise a limited and rather symbolic protest involving a small group of young bloggers into a movement throughout North Africa. At the same time, the reporter took pains to distinguish this initiative from traditional political action, reiterating that the initiative was undertaken by young people who did not have a political affiliation or association.

The interview drew mixed reactions from the team that organized the protest. Although convinced about the need to take the battle against censorship to the street, some members were wary of the risks of what they perceived as the politicization of the protest; for them, as for many others, Al Jazeera was synonymous with traditional politics, which they distrusted. Throughout the campaign, activists were keen on distancing themselves from political parties and organizations. There was a pointed resistance to any attempt to politicize the campaign partly because there was a deep-seated fear of the consequences if such action came to be perceived as overtly political. There were also concerns that the authorities would react vindictively by stepping up censorship. Insisting that their action was "a non-politicized citizen movement,"[121] the organizers called on all interested individuals and potential protesters not to hold signs, use banners, or chant slogans that might give the demonstration a political dimension.[122] Precisely because of its apolitical claim, the campaign against censorship attracted a good number of young people with varied orientations and diverse backgrounds.

Although the "symbolic" street protests against censorship were aborted, the outcome was noteworthy. People showed that their sensibility was not dead and that they had expectations they were keen on voicing publicly. Daring to protest against the government in the streets under Ben Ali's rule in order to assert citizen rights was a firmly inscribed red line; but this had now changed: "With the 22 May action, the anti-censorship protest movement has reached a new threshold. Cyber-activism is giving way to real, on the ground action. It is no longer sufficient to express one's discontent or to show one's solidarity on one's blog or on Facebook. What is henceforth claimed is a constitutional right—hailing the government and peacefully expressing one's anger in the street."[123] The protest brought about a realization that the margin for action could be expanded. As one of the activists explains, "What we wanted to achieve is to get rid of the fear of acting in public and of staging a peaceful street protest."[124] For another participant, the encounter with the authorities unraveled an important insight about the malleability of the system and the prospects for collective action: "the limits are not where we think they were. It is only when we push the limits that we come to this realization. The state could be more willful. The agents of the state have a margin which allows them to maneuver, but they either do not make use of it or are simply not conscious of it."[125] With a degree of audacity, activists could defend their rights and claim a space. The activists also realized that the authorities were as afraid of cyber-activists as the activists were of the authorities.

Reimagining Citizenship

The strategies the youth activists employed were as different from traditional channels as the mindset of the young activists was to the paradigm of the older organizers. The structure and characteristics of digital networks facilitate the creation of organized action and account for much of the movement's success. The nature of the Internet has favored new modalities for communicating and networking, organizing, and mobilizing that bypass the confines of physical space.[126] New media in particular foster what Clay Shirky terms a sense of "everybodyness" or "togetherness" that is amenable to collective action.[127] The form of engagement social networks favor, though, is peculiar. Signaling one's support by clicking on the "I like" button on Facebook requires no formal organization or planning. Neither the anti-censorship campaign nor the May 22 protest was organized in the conventional sense of the term. Using a Google mailing list, activists and bloggers threw in ideas that induced a stream of emails and Skype conversations. Marking these initiatives were both creativity and independence. The loose sense of organization the Internet affords gave activists an edge over the bureaucracy-ridden security service. Unlike the classical hierarchical pyramid-like mode of operation, the decentralized mode of operation is conducive to a more diffuse and more effective form of activism. As one media critic notes, citizen activism online thrives on amorphous dynamics: "the most influential and widely publicized online protests tend to take spontaneous forms, with large numbers of Internet users participating simultaneously but without coordination."[128]

These dynamics necessarily redefine political action. Action is anchored in a discreet form of participation that does not so much rely on broad-based and well-organized collectivity as it rests on an "ambient voluntarism"[129] such that the circumscribed action of a few individuals can have a wide appeal and a high impact. Loosely organized individual action could have echoes and undulations on cyberspace to gather momentum and spur action. Social networks are such that a simple statement or a position is energized by being subject to replication and extension by otherwise discreet individuals whose collectivity remains virtual. In such a setting, movements are created spontaneously and develop through peculiar dynamics, which leads them to acquire a life of their own.

What is particularly significant about the increased disposition to contest censorship through digital activism and street protests is the way it rekindled a desire to renegotiate what it means to be a citizen. The increase in online activism was indicative of a pronounced state-society disconnect. There was a deep awareness that censorship was carried on without the consent of the governed—indeed, against the will of the people. For years, users had been content with the kind of "digital citizenship"[130] the Internet afforded but the regime's repression, which increasingly impinged on the online world, increased users' need for the reassertion of citizenship. In this regard, the anticensorship movement reflects an attempt not only to regain access to the Internet but also to reinvigorate the very sense of citizenship. For one blogger, censorship was "an assault on one's basic rights as a citizen, which has been a hollow category so far."[131] For another blogger, censoring a blog—that is, making it inaccessible to readers inside the country—necessarily meant banishing it and its writer: "Censorship is no longer a technical or bureaucratic decision which prevents Internet users from accessing certain websites. Whether intended or not, the decision to censor a particular blog is a decision to rob the blog of its citizenship.... Forcing a blog into exile necessarily means condemning the blogger into exile."[132] Increasingly, the fight against censorship highlighted an awareness of citizen rights and the meaning of citizenship as such. A quote from Alfred Sauvy on an anti-censorship Facebook page reads: "Well informed, people are citizens; ill informed, they become subjects."[133] The movement against censorship became inseparable from the demand for recognition as citizens with actual rights.

Conclusion

Censorship was thus a double-edged sword for the regime. Partly because of the lack of free spaces of engagement and partly because of the crackdown on freedoms, the Internet early on became a refuge for writers and intellectuals. Easy and affordable access increased its popularity, making it a much-sought-after alternative space not just for the youth, the techies, and the activists but also the broader public. This generalization constituted an important development as it altered user habits, making censorship and Internet control anachronistic. The nature of the Internet makes such a disjuncture untenable. As Internet use became inextricably linked to ordinary practices and daily pursuits, censorship became more widely felt and users grew more resentful of it. While initially censorship targeted cyber-activism, it gradually started to impinge on everyday life and to affect online communities. The delineation between what had been a bounded free space and the real, lived experience started to be thinner. The fight for Internet freedom thus became a fight for freedom in general. Apprehensive of repressive tendencies that interfere with daily routines but also cognizant of global discourses about human rights, citizen rights, and information rights, more people grew intolerant of Internet control and inclined to resist it. Eventually, the battle against censorship became a battle to have a voice, to defend one's rights, and to reclaim one's citizenship.

To the extent that the battle over Internet freedom was a battle to reclaim citizenship, it was also necessarily a political battle. Censorship turned the Internet into an arena of political struggle and political contention for an increasingly broad segment of the population. It blurred the line between the political sphere and the nonpolitical sphere. The battle against censorship was not manifestly political, but in the aggregate it became a political statement. Cracking down on individual liberty not only spurred cyber-dissidents to fight censorship but also prompted the public to enlist in their cause. Reflecting on her experience with the anti-censorship movement, the blogger Liliopatra noted: "I did not mean to be a cyber-activist. That word was never in my active vocabulary. All I wanted was to access information and pass it on to others. I realized that being deprived of information was like being deprived of oxygen— worse, like being in a state of coma. The circulation of information in the brain of the social body was the only thing that could bring one back to life."[134]

Initially, many cyber-dissidents and political activists did not identify with the more restrained engagement most users adopted in their fight against censorship. The new users' efforts seemed banal and amateurish, not to say apolitical. The government's obsessive control and indiscriminate censorship went a long way toward bridging the gap between the two camps. Their positions eventually met halfway; while ordinary bloggers started to harden their position and to cultivate political inclinations, the strident bloggers moderated their stance. The demand for freedom of speech impelled activists and users alike to go back to basics. For citizen bloggers, Internet freedom constituted an unalienable right; for dissident bloggers, freedom of speech was the sine qua non for democracy. Interestingly, even the political opposition started to realize that the battle against censorship was crucial. In 2010, the editor of the opposition paper *Al Mawqif* published a letter on the banned online news service Tunisnews titled "Censorship Paralyzes My Work" that, interestingly enough, couched the argument in pure professional rather than political terms:

> Supposedly a liberating tool, the Internet has fallen under the control of the authorities. For a journalist like me, free access to the Internet is of vital importance. Censorship has unjustifiably paralyzed my work. I hold government officials responsible for this blatant attack on the freedom to access information and infringement on the right to exercise the profession of journalism. Allowing the cyber-police to

control the Internet helped make Tunisia one of the most repressive countries in terms of Internet and press freedom.[135]

The nature of the medium contributed to these effects. The anti-censorship movement reflects a bottom-up activism that would be made more expandable through social media platforms like Facebook, which gradually became a de facto tool for activism. Although fighting censorship honed the skills of many users and cyber-activists, it would be imprecise to say that the predominantly urban and relatively small anti-censorship movement was a training ground for a media-savvy youth. What can be ascertained, though, is that the regime's unyielding control unwittingly unleashed the creative capabilities of Internet users and attracted more publics to digital contention that will also come into play during the popular uprising that ended Ben Ali's rule.

7

Mediatizing the Revolution

The Appeal of Social Networks

In 2008, an Internet user initiated a call on Facebook for the establishment of a virtual parliament where users could exchange their views and opinions and deliberate on issues relevant to the country. The context of this online initiative was the predetermined parliamentary and presidential elections of 2009. The virtual parliament—which adopted the motto "standing up to despotism"—was meant as a protest of the country's rigged elections. The idea quickly gained momentum, bringing together a number of Tunisians living inside the country and abroad. The participants were keen on showing that Tunisia could, in fact, produce an effective and participatory democracy. Dozens of candidates with various backgrounds entered the race for the election of twenty-five members to this newly envisaged online entity. Over the following few months, the Tunisian virtual parliament generated enthusiasm on Facebook and promoted online engagement as evinced by the various active online committees that were established and the different causes it took up.[1] Although the parliament drew in primarily users who were politicized, it was also attractive for many ordinary users who welcomed the experiment in e-democracy.[2] Interestingly, the first president of the Tunisian virtual parliament was a Tunisian producer with Al Jazeera. Having left the country following the crackdown on the Islamists in the 1990s, he embarked on a journalism career that led him to work with a UK-based news agency before joining the Al Jazeera channel in Doha shortly after its launch. As a member of the diaspora, he maintained ties with his country through the Internet—initially through email and online forums and then through Facebook, which provided him with a surrogate community, satisfied his need to reconnect with the homeland,

and enabled him to engage in measured forms of activism. When the protests broke out in Sidi Bouzid, he was well positioned to take part in the events. During the four-week-long revolution, the line between his status as a member of the diaspora who used Facebook avidly to connect to his online community of friends and his role as an Al Jazeera producer who relied heavily on social media for his coverage of the uprising became blurred.

Stories like this help elucidate the significance of media convergence for activism. While old and new media are still delineated spheres of communication, the distinction between the two is increasingly dissolving. In a controlled society like Tunisia, media convergence was particularly empowering. The revolution unfolded within "a hybrid media system"[3] marked by the confluence of logics from old and new communication practices. The fact that media services are available on mobile devices has even further blurred the line between old and new media; the fact that content flows across different platforms has redefined actors and reshaped audiences.[4] Pointing out these interrelations between new and old media sheds light on digital communication practices that are increasingly redefining the category of the political.

In this chapter, I explore the emergence of social media as a mass phenomenon, focusing on the rapidly growing online service Facebook and how the new culture of sharing everyday events, stories, and preoccupations online nurtured a nascent political consciousness. I then examine the media dynamics that developed during the 2010–11 uprising. The focus throughout is not on the role of media in the revolution but on their workings and dynamics. In the last part, I turn to the relationship between this new media phenomenon and the old media, focusing primarily on the prominent television network Al Jazeera. I argue that although new media like Facebook and old media like television are often portrayed as adversaries, Al Jazeera's involvement with new media during the Tunisian revolt shows instead a complex, symbiotic, and evolving relationship between the two that has implications for contention.

Connective Digital Networks

In an authoritarian environment like Ben Ali's Tunisia, new media had a special appeal. By tightening Internet control and stepping up censorship, the regime inadvertently encouraged the use of social media and contributed to its growth and popularization. The mass adoption of Facebook in particular created new dynamics. The number of Tunisian users with a Facebook account rose exponentially from a mere 16,000 in 2008 to 1.82 million at the close of 2010. On the eve of the revolution, one-third of Tunisia's 10.6 million inhabitants had access to the Internet, and nearly half of those had Facebook accounts.[5]

Facebook was popular because it encapsulated the more social, more interactive, and more personalized nature of Web 2.0 media. As an intimate communication space, Facebook sheltered users from the wilder parts of the Web while enriching their social experience. By encouraging users to share aspects of their personal lives with a designated group of friends, Facebook promoted the self as the center of an extensive network of friends.[6] Increasingly, this connectivity revolved around what users liked or produced in their daily lives, from sharing pictures of family and friends to posting their favorite music videos and entertainment programs. As a "clever mixture of private life and voyeurism,"[7] Facebook enabled users to reconstitute the boundaries between the public and the private. For some observers, compared to the rich content produced by blogging, Facebook represented the "banalization of online presence" with superficial communication, mundane pursuits, trivial conversations, and compulsive sharing of material.[8]

What makes Facebook particularly appealing is its ability to fulfill social and relational functions. Motivated by the need for self-expression and self-exteriorization but also the desire for communication and socialization, it favors the exchange of information while allowing for the consolidation of existing ties and the building of new relationships.[9] While all media are inherently social, social networks are distinctly more so because relationships constitute the "social capital" at the heart of the users' motivation.[10] Being connected to Facebook meant being immersed in public life. Facebook's distinctive connective function gives users the ability to publicly network with others in a quasi-private setting. As a public but admission-based network where users have control over their privacy settings, Facebook not only blurs the distinction between the public and the private but also allows for the coexistence of online and offline relationships. It connects people who know one another in real life, while facilitating virtual linkages to related networks of people and fostering relations with new friends either directly or indirectly. Much of this connection is articulated through the social task of "liking," whereby users express their instant approval of the digital material that circulates through the click of a mouse.

Facebook constitutes a space that is both tightly connected to the real world and distinct from it. By taking refuge in a virtual space that affords the possibility to connect with one another, young people insulated themselves, even if for a few hours a day, from the oppressive atmosphere of the real world. In a social, cultural, and political context characterized by stifling constraints on the freedom of speech, social media like Facebook concretely epitomized the liberating appeal of the Internet.[11] Within the prevailing culture of surveillance, control, and censorship, Facebook stood out as a unique space of engagement, offering a freer and more dynamic sphere of social interaction. As such, the ability to claim authority over and ownership of one's life on cyberspace was empowering. The participatory nature of social media nourished a sense of self-worth and a consciousness that one's voice mattered—and that others shared one's views. It also fostered a sense of commonality, conviviality, and community.[12] Even if at times this sense of immersion turned cyberspace into a form of refuge, the experience was empowering.

Digital Discontent

In Tunisia, Facebook was free and safe only to the extent that its users maintained their distance from politics. While initially suspicious of the environment of online sociality, the regime came to view this popular social networking site as perhaps conveniently contributing to the depoliticization of the young generation. From time to time, though, glimmers of the site's potential for mobilization appeared. On a number of occasions, some active social media users set up dedicated Facebook pages to mount campaigns, publish information, share pictures, or show support for others, as was the case with the protests of the mining region in 2008 or the floods that ravaged several towns in 2009. Despite such initiatives, Facebook did not have a pronounced political flavor, nor was it readily associable with politics. It was more the epitome of a lifestyle for a predominantly young population than a tool for political activism.

Ironically, Facebook acquired a political valence not through activism but through its users' incorporation of the site into their everyday lives. These dynamics gave a special relevance to what may be termed, after Henri Lefebvre, the political underpinnings of everyday life. The ordinariness of everyday life encompasses that which is permissible and that which is not; within the lived reality of the quotidian, the social and the political are intricately connected, such that social practices and pursuits are often tinged with a political investment. The regime's obsession with control and its aversion to criticism encroached on daily interactions such that discussions about common issues could become political. Constraints on freedom, the policing of society, and control over public life rendered everyday topics of discussion an encroachment on the political sphere. Significantly, many people were able to reconfigure their relationship to the lived reality by learning to obey and oppose at the same time, to work within the system while defying it.[13] This double bind also figured on social media. While providing an alternative arena for engagement, social media platforms like Facebook gave rise to an undefined space of contestation. If that trend was not readily discernible, it was because the use of the Internet was increasingly indistinguishable from the daily routines and everyday practices of average citizens. In today's environment, Mark Poster notes, "Media transforms place and space in such a way that what had been regarded as the locus of the everyday can no longer be distinguished as separate from its opposite."[14] The fact that Facebook usage was enmeshed in the everyday lived reality of young people turned it into a subculture that was relatively free from the restrictions, inhibitions, and controls that became the hallmark of the dominant culture.

Political activism was not wanting but it remained confined to a limited circle of individuals, both in the homeland and in the diaspora. Generally, activists tended to emerge either from a family with a history of activism or from experience with the authoritarian state that had hardened them. The forms of cyber-activism these players engaged in had a dramatic effect over time not only because the technology had a distinctive ability to amplify the information but also because these political forms of engagement were themselves formulated around an intensive communicative culture that increased people's awareness of what was happening around them. An illustrative example of these evolving cyber-dynamics is the case of Faouzi Mahbouli. In 2008, this young entrepreneur begrudgingly left Tunisia after the president's in-laws, who laid their hands on nearly every lucrative business in the country, had attempted to extort him following his planned acquisition of the dealership of the French home improvement store Bricorama. Forced to become a dissident and empowered by his political refugee status in France, he initially set out to denounce the corruption of Ben Ali's entourage and then started to expose the regime online. Having been initiated to Facebook in 2007, he turned it into an afflictive tool against Ben Ali's authoritarian regime. Equipped with the Facebook group Real Tunisia News, he would spend hours every day after work searching for information and posting articles about the corruption and abuses of the Ben Ali regime.[15]

Facebook thrust these and other issues in the public sphere. The regime's repressive tendencies led to an added interest in the country's state of affairs.

More people dared to seek out political information, even visiting banned sites. Social media made the exchange of such information relatively safer, more effective, and more widespread. As information circulated more quickly and rumors traveled more widely, people's distaste for the regime and its practices grew. Stories about human rights violations, corruption, economic profiteerism, shady deals, and palace intrigues became a constant aspect of the public sphere. To many, these suggested that the country was undergoing a disheartening deterioration. Users grappled with an unsettling experience of their country, which preached modernization, respect for the rule of law, and the valorization of youth but which was also marked by the lack of respect for citizens, infringement on civil rights, and restrictions on freedoms.

The Silent Opposition

Over time, the Internet nurtured a silent opposition—a segment of society that resented the reality they experienced but were disinclined to publicly express their dissatisfaction or openly give an outlet to their disenchantment. In this context, manifest passivity and apparent disengagement were less indicative of an acceptance of one's reality than suggestive of a willingness to adapt to constraints. Within a restrictive context that does not permit public protest, silence became "a weapon of the weak," to borrow James Scott's terminology.[16] Acquiescence and unresponsiveness became a form of subversion. Facebook was simultaneously a space of complacency and an arena of contestation. Everyday life offered a peculiar space of engagement whereby people publicly disconnected from politics only to informally and serendipitously encounter it independent of the sphere of formal politics. The widespread use of social media further distanced youth in particular from institutional politics. The young generation found itself incapable of identifying with the country's political culture or relating to political actors. For swaths of youth, the opposition was simply unable to relate to their situation, understand their realities, or represent their needs.[17] Increasingly, the digital culture that took hold became indicative of a "generational shift."[18] The new generation was marked by a growing consciousness about issues of civil liberty, social justice, human rights, and citizen participation.[19] Established political actors who took up these issues were older and less open to the opportunities that information and communications technologies afforded for political activism. For the most part, opposition parties operated offline, within the framework of traditional political organizations. Their idea of expressing opposition to Ben Ali and advocating reform meant making statements in foreign newspapers, issuing communiqués, organizing hunger strikes, and calling for repression to stop. Social media introduced different forms of engagement. The average young Internet user became a "passive contributor" who was not only receptive to information but also willing to share it. A growing mass of bloggers and Facebookers constituted "a multitude of subjectivities that expressed a rejection of the prevailing social, political and cultural system."[20] It is from this perspective that one can understand the gradual transformation of Facebook from a favorite pastime to a space that gave rise to a culture of contestation. With the 2010 anti-censorship campaign, which drew a few thousand Internet users, the use of Facebook as a tool for mobilization and an arena for contestation gained more ground among youth circles.

A small incident pertaining to the closing down of a mosque can help exemplify these dynamics. In early September 2010, Zouheir Makhlouf—a human rights activist and a former political prisoner—posted a ten-minute YouTube clip on the independent news website Assabil Online featuring an abandoned and dilapidated mosque in Al Manar, a socially upscale suburb of Tunis.[21] Located in a densely populated area near a large university campus with a rich history of student movement activism, the mosque, which had a distinct architecture and attracted a sizable congregation, was ordered closed on July 21, 2002, officially for maintenance purposes. But work on the building never started, and for nearly a decade the mosque was left to deteriorate, eventually falling into sacrilegious use by those seeking a hideout for debauchery. Many speculated about the real motive for closing what had been a well-frequented place of worship.

The carefully produced video clip, which had the features of a documentary, was designed to elicit a strong emotional response. The narrator's deep voice took the viewer on a virtual tour as the camera zoomed in on artistic inscriptions and architectural features that made the mosque a cultural monument and a historical site. Against this background of grandeur and holiness, the clip revealed a decrepit and deserted building. Human waste was visible everywhere, worn out and dust-clad copies of the Koran were scattered throughout the premises, and empty alcohol cans were strewn around. To dramatize the decaying condition and the purposeful neglect of the mosque, the clip used a voice-over drawn from a documentary titled "The Mosques that Israel Destroyed" that had previously aired on Al Jazeera. Makhlouf's adoption of features of Al Jazeera's critical program in the video clip was meant to suggest that Ben Ali's attitude toward Islam was no different from the Israeli practices in Palestine. Emphasizing the special place mosques have in the Muslim world, the clip called for mobilization to protect the Al Manar mosque, ending with a verse from the Koran condemning those who prevent the invocation of the name of God in places of worship.

The YouTube clip circulated widely, sparking a controversy among the Facebook community about the veracity of the posted material. Before long, Al Jazeera aired a report on it.[22] The report started with the invocation of another site, the Zeitouna mosque as a revered cultural monument with a long and rich history, noting that the government has often used the stature and eminence of this historic mosque, which attracted many worshipers and visitors, to promote an image of commitment to the preservation of Tunisia's Islamic heritage. The report then presented the state of Al Manar mosque as a counterexample. Al Jazeera placed the issue squarely within a political context, pointing out that the mosque had probably been closed because it was near a university campus that was a fertile ground for student activism and because students had started to frequent it. The program was the subject of heated discussion on Facebook. Some people were shocked, while others expressed skepticism about the program's claims. Many users rejected the claim that the mosque was in Tunisia and suggested it was in Palestine instead. In reaction, one Facebook user named Hamadi Kaloutcha decided to visit the mosque to verify the information.[23] He took pictures of the interior of the mosque along with a glimpse of that day's local newspaper, which he used to prove that the footage shown was not of an earlier time and to ascertain that the abandoned mosque featured in the video clip was in fact in Tunisia. Finding itself under pressure from traditional and new media, the government promised in December to reopen the mosque, although the latter did not become operative until after the revolution.

The case is significant in a number of ways. It sheds light on the subtle dynamics that social media helped unleash, in particular how social media served as an interface between those who were active and those who were not. The generation of news by social media users, the telling of compelling stories by bloggers, and the examination of claims through evidence collected by determined cyber-activists point to the incipient role of citizen journalism in breaking the state media's monopoly over discourse. Equally interesting is the two-way link between traditional and new media, namely the way online material was picked up by mainstream media to give each a bigger impact. TV reports on social media discourses found their way back to the social Web, fueling even more discussion. These micro-spaces of engagement nurtured a political con-sciousness, affecting even users who did not typically have a predilection for political action or favor overt political involvement. Dynamics such as these will come to play an even more important role as the country found itself caught in a revolutionary fervor. The resonance of the cause, the receptiveness to the message, and the commotion that enveloped the case—all these point to an altered sensibility that developed at the intersection between everyday experiences and virtual spaces of engagement.

Into the Storm

These dynamics also suggest that social media was poised to play a mobiliza-tional role under certain conditions. During the December 2010 protest move-ments, digital media was intensely used. Initially, media fulfilled an urgent need among the community to communicate about the tragedy of Mohamed Bouazizi's self-immolation. The news circulated instantly through mobile phones. Soon, family, friends, townspeople, and local activists began to show their sup-port and vent their anger at the authorities by gathering in front of the regional government office where Bouazizi had set himself on fire. The spontaneous outburst of popular rage was captured on mobile phones and soon images of angry protesters found their way to the Internet, which quickly made it a matter of interest to the broader public.

What was interesting was not simply the speed with which the story spread but the determined effort on the part of local activists to capitalize on it. Particularly noteworthy was the ingenious mediatization of Bouazizi, who be-came the icon of the revolution. Along with the news about the tragic incident that circulated on the social Web, there was a gripping picture of a hardly dis-cernible individual ablaze. This iconic image became a crucially important mobi-lizing factor—even though the incident itself was not captured on camera.[24] According to Bouazizi's cousin, the picture, which depicted South Korean cults, was downloaded from the Internet by local cyber-activists to capture people's attention, evoke considerable sympathy, and generate publicity for the situation in Sidi Bouzid.[25] The Bouazizi picture and its accompanying nar-rative were the result of cyber-activism calculated to elicit maximum effect.

Similarly, the profile of Bouazizi that was propagated online was deliber-ately engineered to resemble the profile of many young graduates who had seen their hopes for a better future dashed by scarce job opportunities, especially in the inner cities and the provinces. For several weeks, the Bouazizi biography that prevailed on the Internet maintained that he was a poor unemployed college graduate whose dire social conditions compelled him to become a street vendor and who struggled to support his family only to see his vegetable cart confiscated by the authorities. During the altercation with the female municipal police officer, Bouazizi was reportedly insulted and the combination of injustice and dishonor led him to his dramatic protest. Like the photo, the story was deliberately manipulated for maximum effect. In reality, Bouazizi was a high school dropout. The much-publicized story of the slap he allegedly received from the officer appeared to be groundless as a court subsequently acquitted her of wrongdoing. Regardless of its veracity or falsehood, the constructed narrative, which appealed to many young people across the country, made Bouazizi a powerful icon.

The relationship between constructed narratives and activism has to be understood in relation to government control over the media sector. The troubling events were met with a media blackout. To break the official silence and tell their stories, activists turned to social media, making Facebook the principal source of information about the events. The scarcity of news reports and restrictions on journalists as the town of Sidi Bouzid came under siege gave new media a larger impact. With peaceful protests quickly devolving into violent clashes with armed anti-riot police forces who did not hesitate to use tear gas and to resort to force, local activists recorded scenes of the confrontations with their mobile phone cameras and uploaded them on social media networks, capturing the attention of sympathetic audiences.[26] Such uses of social media helped construct what Gerbaudo described as "an emotional space within which collective action can unfold."[27] The fact that the number of people who initially engaged cyber-activism was limited did not matter much. Only a few brokers needed to use social tools to keep others up to date and facilitate action.[28] As the news started to spread about Bouazizi's self-immolation and the ensuing violence in Sidi Bouzid, some of these activists were contacted by regional satellite TV channels like Al Jazeera and France 24 for video segments, eyewitness accounts, and commentary. The appropriation of Facebook material by these transnational Arabic news channels to report on the story gave a special weight to Internet activism and presented the people's stories to a much wider audience. For a number of activists, protesters, and spectators, capturing the intensity of the moment and sharing those moments on the Internet became a common pursuit, expanding the scope of citizen journalism. Increasingly, cyberspace teemed with communication practices emanating from participants outside traditional media institutions impelled by a deepening consciousness about what it meant to be a citizen.

Central to the information dynamics that evolved was mobile technology, which offered portable and affordable connectivity. Mobile phones were ubiquitous. In the years before the revolution, the use of smart phones had risen sharply, giving ordinary people increased capability to stream data at high speed. Using cell phone cameras, people actively witnessed the events, filming protests, recording riots, and capturing police brutality. The video-sharing feature of Facebook made publishing such user-generated material technically simple. Equipped with mobiles, those on the street became increasingly aware of the importance of being a "self-documenting public."[29] In a police state, the citizens' instinctive use of cell phone video recorders and other digital tools to record practices, witness events, and disseminate information stood out as a form of inverted surveillance—that is, a self-empowering "sousveillance" premised on observing the observer and surveilling the surveiller—that went a long way toward challenging authority and undermining narrative control.[30]

Much of the momentum that animated the Internet was driven by mobile footage from local militants, politicized youth, and cyber-activists. On the receiving end, the layman's involvement was largely passive. Most people would read about the protests, follow what was happening, and watch posted YouTube clips. Occasionally, they would click the "like" button or write commentaries on what they had watched and then share those links. Soon, self-propelling information dynamics involving different types of actors started to take hold and many citizens started to partake in content creation and news production. Over the next few days, there was a notable increase in the use of Facebook, initially to find out about new developments. As more people started to use social networks to keep up with the spreading protests, more user-generated content became available on the Internet and more Facebookers were willing to share it. With the swelling of street protests, there was an unprecedented boldness and a clear attitude of defiance on Facebook, with more users accessing user-generated content, sharing material about the protests, and expressing their "likes" and "dislikes." Initially, sharing was not so much underpinned by overt cyber-activism as it was impelled by the urge to communicate about events that were hard to ignore. Gradually, though, people came to realize that mere "sharing" of information and images could break the official information blockade, raise consciousness about the reality of what was happening, expose the practices of the regime, lend support to the protesters, and mobilize people further. Online accounts and digital images offered a counter-narrative that undermined the official story promulgated on national media that the social unrest was the work of looters and criminal gangs. That amateurish footage published on Facebook was picked up by broadcast media on widely watched transnational satellite television channels only fueled interest in social media further and increased its relevance.

Social media did more than feed content to users. By relaying images of how others became involved—how they participated in protests, chanted slogans, spoke against the regime, asserted their rights, and contributed material— social media raised expectations about protesting and taught people new techniques to protest effectively. With more people taking to the street—a turf the regime has always been keen on controlling—the Internet became a more overt space of contention. More protest participants, townspeople, and eyewitnesses started to record scenes of the protests on their mobiles and to diffuse them on social media networks. A number of seasoned cyber-activists and established bloggers also reproduced press articles, relayed video scenes, and posted YouTube segments of foreign TV programs about the situation on their Facebook pages. By drawing people to and immersing them into the events, social media stimulated their desire for a more active form of communication. The most empowering implication of the increase in the use of social media by ordinary people was not simply the ability to contribute and share user-generated content during critical times but the proclivity to turn witnesses into activists.[31] What had initially been a social media site for communicating and sharing information evolved into a space that held together disparate networks of laypeople, activists, protesters, citizen journalists, and media professionals.

The mediatization of the unrest also helped connect the local setting to the broader national context. As more material became available, people started to relate more closely with the protesters and identify with their cause. The images of violence and police brutality were a stark reminder of the ruthlessness of the regime. By amplifying the events, social media helped create a widely shared awareness of the extent of people's frustration and the widening nature of dissent among a broad section of the population across regions but also among the various social strata. These dynamics also entailed a distantiation from authority by openly rejecting a situation that was no longer deemed tenable. Online, people were ashamed of accessing entertainment or sharing music during these sensitive and hard times. Even forums that were dedicated to sports dropped coverage of soccer to engage in discussions about the deteriorating situation in the country.[32] To display solidarity with the protesters, many Facebookers changed their profile photos, visibly and prominently displaying a logo featuring a Tunisian flag that was either bloodstained or refigured in black and white as a sign of mourning. Others adopted an image of a choreographed movement featuring the flag encircled with and embraced by a string of tightly held hands representing solidarity. By adopting and adapting the nation's flag, users momentarily gave up their personal identities as individuals for a collective identity as citizens.

The disjointed groups, various activists, connected individuals, and active users across social classes were henceforth united. The precise form of the alliances among these players varied. While some groups worked together in a coordinated action and mounted collective information campaigns, others acted individually and spontaneously. The weakness of ties among Internet users helped facilitate the flow of information and the coalescence of the movement, as Mark Granovetter had predicted decades earlier. Strong ties may block organization within a social network because factors like friendship and (dis)trust prevent enthusiasm from spreading beyond a given social group. Individuals linked by weak ties were predisposed to act as local bridges to enhance transmission probabilities. In other words, although strong ties breed local cohesion and overall fragmentation, weak ties generate more linkages among communities and facilitate societal cohesiveness. The implication is that "the personal experience of individuals is closely bound up with larger-scale aspects of social structure, well beyond the purview or control of individuals."[33] The loose and leaderless nature of the online movement proved to be a source of strength in the authoritarian context. Although the regime was skilled at co-opting opposition political parties, repressing opponents who would not be co-opted, and crippling independent civil society organizations, it was not well prepared to deal with broad-based discontent, fast-spreading rage, and a swelling protest movement led by loosely coordinated publics. The same weak ties that enabled massive online and offline mobilization also disarmed the regime.

The resilience of the regime depended in great part on its ability to control information. The authorities treated new media the way they had always approached traditional media. But the new technologies of the Web were far more difficult to control. Shutting down social networking sites was more problematic than shutting down an opposition newspaper, because closing Facebook would inconvenience a considerable part of society and thereby encourage more activism. Such a blunt measure would also invite further criticism from abroad, weakening the foreign support the regime needed. While reluctantly tolerating the use of Facebook, the authorities sought to minimize its effect, hinder the flow of information, and limit cyber-activism by increasing Internet filtering, blocking websites, breaking into private email accounts, erasing content, meddling with Facebook accounts, and deleting pictures of protests.[34] To further undermine the ability of savvy Internet users to bypass government control, the authorities disabled the secure protocol https that allowed encrypted information to be sent to Facebook without the government's ability to monitor it or identify its source.[35] When stepping up control over the Web failed to reduce antiestablishment cyber-activism, the authorities took direct action offline and arrested three cyber-activists.

Increased censorship and systematic crackdown by the regime's cyber-police did not go unanswered. The medium and the message had never been so interlaced. As one cyber-activist put it, "The regime wanted to strike a blow to Facebook and we were determined not to let that happen. We needed to provide accurate, verified and credible information. The war that was being waged on Facebook was all about credibility."[36] Curious about the situation in Tunisia and outraged at the government's censor, Anonymous—a loosely knit group of global Web activists—lent a hand to Tunisian Web activists, vowing to help the people fight against oppression in their country. In support of the cause of Internet users in Tunisia, they carried multiple attacks on government and administrative websites, taking out some while defacing others, including those of the president, a number of ministries, and the stock exchange. Their distributed denial-of-service attacks generated false traffic that led Web servers to believe thousands of computer users were accessing a site simultaneously, overwhelming its server and causing it to crash. The organized action—which Anonymous dubbed Operation Payback—was a denunciation of the government's censorship of the Internet.[37] The interventions by Anonymous helped publicize the events in Tunisia and garner attention from the international media. Pressure on the government to remove censorship and allow for Internet freedom increased. The rash of hacking attacks and the targeting of cyber-activists impelled the US State Department to express concern over Tunisia's crackdown on social media and to call for the lifting of restrictions on Internet access.[38] Although these declarations were shrugged off by the Tunisian government, the United States' rare criticism of what it considered an ally showed how deep was the quagmire the regime found itself in.

On the ground, the raging social movement became entwined with an intense information battle. Data streaming and the use of nontraditional media defied government control. Continued cyber-activism and growing citizen journalism meant that the government could no longer cover up the reality of what was happening. If anything, government tactics led to what has been dubbed the Streisand effect: the more the government censored the Internet and controlled the information, the wider and more intensely the videos of the protests circulated.[39] The number of active Facebook users multiplied and their support for the evolving social movement grew considerably to an extent that it became virtually impossible for the government to either monitor it or control it. Increasingly, the popular social networking site looked like an unstoppable tide.[40]

With a ceaseless stream of news, videos, and updates about the upheavals, there was a shift in online communication; it grew more overtly political and acquired a mobilizing dimension. By the time the authorities became alarmed at the mobilizing potential of social media, Internet dynamics took on a life of their own. With the escalation of events, the fear of government reprisal started to dissipate. As more people shed their inhibitions and overcame their fears by demonstrating in public spaces, cyber-activism increased dramatically. The notable increase of online support and the rise in social media activism gave the protesters who were already out in the streets the impression that the people were behind them. By amplifying people's voices and accentuating their power, new—and traditional—media helped shake off the ingrained culture of fear. This added consciousness became a lubricant for more intense online involvement and more transnational TV coverage. The dissipation of fear among the people loosened the clearly delineated demarcation between the real and the virtual. All along, the regime reaffirmed its authority over the realm of the street, while Internet users claimed the virtual space. Internet activism helped redefine the parameters of the public sphere and reconfigure the space of engagement. These dynamics went a long way toward blurring the distinction between populism and elitism, between those who were politicized and those who were not politicized, between the laymen and the activists. The remapping of hierarchies and the convergence of voices contributed to the nurturing of an assertive collectivity and emboldened people to take collective action.

There was an unprecedented mobilization on the Internet, much of which was the result of "a spontaneous coordinated effort."[41] Dedicated Facebook pages like "Mr. President, Tunisians Are Setting Themselves on Fire" and "Ma Tunisie" became popular platforms for diffusing video footage and sharing information. Online support groups cropped up, citizen journalism networks emerged, social media campaigns proliferated, and cyber-initiatives multiplied.

The underground cyber-group Takriz formed a crisis group to break the media blackout by helping collect and diffuse information, pictures, videos, and eyewitness accounts on the events.[42] A few initiatives approximating conventional journalism started to emerge. A group of Tunisian activist bloggers and journalists set up the News Agency of the Movement of the Tunisian Street. This Facebook-based operation was meant to mimic a real newsroom, adopting professional editorial standards with rigorous fact-checking efforts. Within two days of its launch, the page had more than twenty thousand members, leading the authorities to censor it.[43] Driving this "counterpositioning of citizen journalists"[44] was not only a desire to support the protesters and expose the practices of the regime but also a determination to assert the authority of cyberspace as a source of information.

That an initiative like the News Agency of the Movement of the Tunisian Street was coordinated in large part by Tunisians living outside the country underscores the role of the diaspora in supporting the protesters and getting the word out to the broader international community. These groups and individuals played a significant role in part because they were unconstrained by the kind of limits on the freedom of speech the average citizen faced at home. Many members of the Tunisian community in Europe helped mobilize support, which contributed to a surge in Internet activism. A number of foreign-based Tunisian Facebook pages and blogs were dedicated to the protest movement. Many Tunisians with roots in the provinces where the protests were raging actively supported the protesters, relaying information and exposing the authorities' repressive response to peaceful protests and nonviolent activism.

Facebook had technical and linguistic limitations. Being a closed platform accessible only to those admitted as "friends," relying on the "share" and "like" features for the circulation of information, and using primarily Tunisian Arabic and French limited the audience. For the Facebook information and images to find their way to the open Web and to gain a wide circulation, the intervention of a curator was necessary. Activists in the diaspora filled this role. Particularly noteworthy was the strategic approach to activism taken by Nawaat. During the revolution, Nawaat's activists worked around the clock to aggregate, curate, and promote protest videos first posted on Facebook. They also translated and contextualized the information, adding tags to the material to make it searchable, before re-diffusing it on multiple platforms using the blogging platform Posterous. Nawaat also sought to amplify the information using their international links to advocacy groups and their contacts with the international media. This entailed feeding images to widely viewed satellite channels like Al Jazeera and tweeting valuable updates in the hope that foreign journalists would report on the events.[45]

Compared to Facebook, which had more than two million users, the use of the microblogging site Twitter was limited to a few hundred Internet-savvy urbanites.[46] With no visual features and messages limited to 140 characters, Twitter had less appeal to social media users. Still, Twitter was attractive because, unlike the friends-and-family social structure of Facebook, tweeting is public and more immediate. On a few occasions, Twitter may have served as a useful tool for coordinating action and responding rapidly to changes in the situation. When the violence intensified and the protests started to edge toward the capital, Twitter feeds increased noticeably. The hashtag #sidibouzid connected activists to the outside world and allowed many people to follow what was happening. Several Tunisians in the diaspora and foreign activists used Twitter to provide updates about the situation on the ground.[47] Writing in multiple languages, they shared news they gained from activists and information they extracted from Facebook, thus increasing their reach and prompting an information cascade.[48] For such updates, Twitter was especially important in making information available to the international media.[49] Increasingly, foreign journalists became dependent on tweets for their reporting.[50]

Cherchez Al Jazeera

The prominence of social media should not obscure the role of traditional broadcast media. Although more and more younger viewers turned to the Internet, television remained the dominant medium. According to the 2010 Arab Youth Report, television was the most popular source of news for Arabs.[51] Tunisia was no exception. Initially, state TV ignored Bouazizi's self-immolation. It was not until four days after the event that the national media reported on the protests, and then it was only to condemn them. As the protests started to escalate, making it impossible to ignore the gravity of what was happening, the semi-independent television channel Nesma aired a discussion program about the riots. Owned in part by the Tunisian film producer Tarak Ben Ammar and the Italian media mogul Silvio Berlusconi, this relatively popular entertainment TV channel, launched in 2007 with a focus on the Maghreb, had a slightly bigger margin of maneuverability than the state channels. When the content of the program turned out to be too frank for the regime, the latter banned its rerun.

The international press was disinterested. Social protests in a not-so-significant North African country did not seem newsworthy. Nor was the regional media eager to report. Typically, state media in the Arab world refrain from probing the affairs of other Arab countries. It was especially unlikely that they would cover sporadic local protests in the inner provinces of an Arab country everybody saw as stable and uneventful. There were exceptions, though: Al Jazeera made the budding protests a news item on primetime news, and the Paris-based (but Arabic-language) France 24 also took note. The extensive and distinctive coverage of Al Jazeera and France 24 prompted the competing Dubai-based news channel Al Arabiya to start reporting on the protests, even if it did so only intermittently during the movement's early stages. Over the span of four weeks, these news channels contributed to shedding light on what was happening for both the Tunisian public and a broader Arab audience.

Al Jazeera deserves close attention not only because it has been closely involved with social movements in Tunisia but also because of the innovative nature and political significance of its reporting. Relying extensively on user-generated information circulated on the social Web, Al Jazeera latched onto the events in Tunisia, positioning itself as a leading source of news. That the Tunisian revolution was played out in real time on the airwaves of the channel should come as no surprise. With a leading role, a sizable audience, and an increasingly felt influence, Al Jazeera has been at the forefront of the development of a vibrant Arab mediascape that contrasts with the more restrained state media, often seen as a tool or even a lackey of authoritarian regimes, pioneering a new kind of journalism in a region where journalists have been weaned on self-censorship. Since the network's inception, it has adopted a freewheeling journalistic style and pioneered political debate programs that rankled Arab regimes. For years, its journalists and producers have tested the limits of what is permissible in their reporting on the problems of the Arab world. While helping develop a common narrative of Arab grievances and revive pan-Arab feelings across the Arab world through its agenda-setting power and its framing ability, the network has also contributed considerably to the rise of political consciousness in the region. By positioning itself as an advocate for democracy, Al Jazeera helped instill a culture of accountability that is all but unknown to the political culture of the Arab world. Particularly distinctive is Al Jazeera's ability to foreground "a narrative of regional discontent with authoritarian rule which tied together dissent and protest across the Arab world."[52] Its probing journalism, its privileging of a culture of argumentation and debate, and its tendency "to swim against the current" have made it a rare contestatory force in the region.[53]

Faced with the wide reach of Al Jazeera and wary of its growing political influence, the Ben Ali regime started to insulate itself from the network's maverick reporting through a dual strategy of information blockade and media disengagement. Tunisia was one of the very few Arab countries, possibly the only one, that refused to accredit Al Jazeera's reporters or authorize the network to open a bureau in its territory. Nevertheless, determined to keep an eye on all Arab states, Al Jazeera managed to establish a connection to the Tunisian scene.[54] Beginning in 2005, it unofficially maintained a correspondent in Tunis, even if his activities were restricted. Although Tunisia seldom figured as the subject of discussion on Al Jazeera's current affairs program, the regime chided the channel for serving as an outlet for Tunisian dissidents and the network became a target of a smear campaign.[55] On more than one occasion, Al Jazeera's probing of Tunisia's affairs, weak as such efforts were, and its invitation of Tunisian dissidents in exile to come on air, even if such appearances were rare, led to diplomatic tiffs with Qatar. As a result, the country remained undercovered compared to other Arab states.

In more recent years, Al Jazeera's desire to be truly pan-Arab impelled it to provide a more substantial coverage of North Africa. Accordingly, Al Jazeera established a Maghreb desk in its news division and introduced an evening news program section of its main news bulletin focusing exclusively on the Arab Maghreb titled "The Maghreb Harvest." In the summer of 2010, the network recruited Rachid Khechana, a veteran Tunisian journalist who had served for years as the editor of the opposition newspaper *Al Mawqif*. Having been immersed in the sociopolitical scene in Tunisia, Khechana brought a deep current understanding of the state of affairs in the country and an intimate knowledge of the dispositions of political activists, unionists, and militants, thus enhancing the resourcefulness of the channel and its ability to tap into local commentators for its reporting. When the events broke out in Sidi Bouzid, Al Jazeera was well positioned to cover them. While the network did not get any scoops, it realized early on the potential significance of the news. Having followed the protests closely since their outbreak, Al Jazeera had a keen eye on the pulse of the street.[56] Over four weeks, the network managed to draw on a rather broad network of militants, trade unionists, human rights activists, lawyers, active members of the opposition, and dissidents in exile who helped articulate the nature of the grievances and embarrass the regime. By and large, Al Jazeera became a platform for critical voices—who previously lacked access to media—to weigh in on the events, assert the right of the pro-testers to demonstrate peacefully, denounce police brutality, and call for the end of state violence.

In covering the protests, the network confronted the challenge of incorpo-rating unconventional sources into traditional journalistic practices. Barred from sending journalists to areas of unrest, Al Jazeera relied almost exclusively on sources from the social Web, most notably Facebook. The network has al-ways been open to alternative reporting, receptive to new information and communication technologies, and adept at keeping up with changing media consumption habits. Because Al Jazeera's antiestablishment orientation made it subject to boycotts, bans, and signal jams, it established a strong online pres-ence with the aim of increasing its regional and international reach. The net-work had also been quick to integrate new platforms for disseminating content, encouraging its staff, producers, and anchors to enhance and support existing programs with features of emergent media like Facebook and Twitter. Despite such Internet literacy, Al Jazeera's use of nontraditional news-gathering tech-niques and its reliance on social media posed both technical and editorial is-sues. Initially, there was some hesitation, even apprehension, about using Facebook material because of questions about its authenticity and reliability. High professional expectations also compelled Al Jazeera to adhere to high production standards.[57] However, in the business of twenty-four-hour news, considerations of quality are often sacrificed for immediacy. In the case of Tunisia, the wealth of material about the protests that circulated on the Inter-net invited an in-depth coverage that made many people who were eager to know more about what was happening in the country riveted to Al Jazeera, giving it reason to rely even further on user-generated content for its reporting. Tunisia henceforth became a headline story on Al Jazeera's primetime news. Three weeks into the protests, the succession of fast-breaking newsworthy events encouraged the network to drop its regular programing and opt for an open news cycle, airing unedited footage, providing raw images, and broad-casting news as reports came in.[58]

In addition to its infrastructure and resources, Al Jazeera's indigenous char-acter and its rich experience when it comes to crisis reporting in the region would also prove to be a valuable asset. Unlike most Arab media, Al Jazeera enjoys more editorial independence and a wide margin of freedom. Import-antly, Al Jazeera favored what it calls "the growing periphery in the Arab world" over the unrepresentative political center. These factors helped consol-idate its agenda-setting power and its political influence. Working for a media institution that enjoys a wide margin of freedom and adopts an unspoken reformist agenda was empowering for the network staff, many of whom had grown up in an Arab authoritarian context. Some research on Arab media suggests that there is a self-perception among some Arab journalists of being drivers of social and political change in the region.[59] Certainly, some of Al Jazeera's staff were determined to make the most out of the popular protests in Tunisia, politically and otherwise. Further fueling the interest of the network was the fact that it employs a number of Tunisian journalists, producers, and editors. Their native knowledge of the country proved to be valuable for the rest of the newsroom. Being in the diaspora while maintaining their links to their country, many of them were active social media users, regular Web surfers, and savvy information seekers. Some Al Jazeera staff had pronounced political and ideological affinities and, over the years, they had found the uncensored Internet to be a valuable space of engagement and, at times, an area for cyber-activism.[60] Aspiring to see change in their own country, several Al Jazeera staff members identified closely with the cause of the Tunisian people. When the protest broke out in the provincial town of Sidi Bouzid, those who were most familiar with the country volunteered their time when off duty and took a leading role in the newsroom. As the significance of the events became evident, there was a total mobilization by the network's staff.

Al Jazeera's reporting amplified the voices of the protesters. For many, the network's extensive coverage made patent the severity of the situation and the degree of popular anger. By garnering sympathy for the protesters and stoking anger at the authorities, Al Jazeera added momentum to the protests while making itself indispensable for covering the unrest. It did so by "allowing a large number of people to see themselves as activists because they were creating content; [in fact,] transforming them from observers of activism to activists themselves."[61] Fast unfolding developments and the abundance of online material compelled Al Jazeera to increase its reporting. While ample attention was given to the events on the network's English channel and its website, the coverage on the Arabic channel, which was arguably more ideological, had a distinctive momentum, drive, and immediacy. The persistence of the protests and the recurrent confrontations with the security forces made the coverage of the story hard to ignore and gave it a sense of urgency that warranted even more intense coverage in subsequent days. Therein lies the peculiarity of the network. The demand for more media coverage was perpetuated by the spread and intensification of the protests that Al Jazeera's reporting helped energize in the first place. In a boomerang effect, Al Jazeera's mediatization of the events helped propel the protest movement, which in turn called for more media engagement with the story.

Conclusion

While social media captured the unfolding of events and provided a constant stream of images, videos, reactions, and statements, transnational media like Al Jazeera wove the material into a powerful and compelling narrative that brought together people's voices, activists' accounts, political commentary, and civil society perspectives. If Facebook facilitated information flows and made the events public, Al Jazeera helped politicize them; if Facebook turned local forms of dissent and dispersed protests into a nationwide movement that was sustained by a collective consciousness, Al Jazeera confirmed that the protests constituted a serious challenge to the regime. Significantly, Al Jazeera's reporting did more than break the media blackout; it made the protests an agenda item on primetime news and framed the events to draw out and accentuate their political thrust. The network thus bestowed a political narrative on the initially disparate regional events in neglected towns in a way that helped them evolve into a social movement. Neither Al Jazeera's staff nor its audiences are oblivious to the power of the network. Asked what was the point in time when he started to realize the political significance of the situation, a Tunisian producer with the network responded: "That's irrelevant. The moment it is on Al Jazeera, it is political."[62]

The fact that Al Jazeera operates in a hybrid media environment enhanced its influence. The imbrication of old and new media is such that the user-generated content that was diffused through social media was picked up by Al Jazeera. Al Jazeera reports that fed off Facebook footage were posted online and then shared on Facebook. That feedback loop energized the protesters. While allowing many Internet users and Facebook account holders to follow the unfolding of the events through the posted links and videos, the broadcasts of scenes of protests also emboldened more people to voice their discontent and take a proactive stance in the protests. The interpenetration between citizen journalism and traditional, mainstream journalism had never been stronger. Broadcast media like Al Jazeera helped merge online and offline action. It is these dynamics that were unleashed by this broader media ecology, rather than the particularity of any single media platform, that gave the Tunisian revolution its theoretical relevance and its historical significance.

8

Post-Revolutionary Dynamics

Changes and Challenges

Rough Edges and Uncharted Paths

The revolution irreversibly altered both Tunisia's official politics and the politics of Tunisians' everyday lives. The day after Ben Ali fled the country, Foued Mebazaa, the Speaker of the Parliament, was sworn in as acting president in accordance with the constitution, while Prime Minister Mohamed Ghannouchi moved to constitute a transitional government. Ghannouchi wanted to work with established structures and existing players to abate the threat of political instability. Such half-measures poorly meshed with the country's revolutionary momentum. On January 23, thousands of young protesters and activists occupied Al Kasbah Square in front of the seat of government to demand the expulsion of cabinet members associated with the Ben Ali regime. A second sit-in followed on February 25, this one demanding the departure of Ghannouchi and his government, the suspension of the legislative assembly, the banning of the ruling party, the dismantling of Ben Ali's security apparatus, and the electing of a new legislature to write a new constitution. On February 27, Ghannouchi bowed to the pressure and resigned. He was succeeded by a new interim government headed by Beji Caïd Essebsi, a former minister under Habib Bourguiba. In March 2011, the previously established High Commission for Political Reform merged with the Revolutionary Committee for the Safeguarding of the Revolution to form a more credible transitional legislative body: the High Commission for the Protection of the Objectives of the Revolution, Political Reform, and Democratic Transition. During this eventful period, the political police was also dissolved, the ruling party was dismantled, and more than one hundred political parties were legalized, including the once-banned moderate Islamist party Ennahda. Most significantly, the government gave in to the pressure to elect a Constituent Assembly to draft a new constitution and hold elections within a year. Tunisia moved toward establishing a democracy in which politics would no longer be the prerogative of a particular class.

The country's first democratic elections on October 23, 2011, which ended the interim phase of the transitional period, brought Ennahda to power. Short of an outright majority, Ennahda formed a ruling coalition with two secular parties (the Congress for the Republic and the Democratic Front for Labor and Liberty); their alliance soon became known as the ruling Troika. Hamadi Jebali, then Ennahda's secretary general, was sworn in as prime minister; the dissident human rights activist Moncef Marzouki was elected as president; and Mustafa Ben Jafaar became the Speaker of the Constituent Assembly. With the Ennahda-led government, Tunisia entered a new post-revolution phase that differed sharply from the harmony of the first months after Ben Ali. In fact, political partisanship increased and ideological splits intensified. The rise of Ennahda sparked the formation of the political party Nidaa Tunis under the leadership of Beji Caïd Essebsi. Widely perceived as the successor to the former ruling party, Nidaa Tunis soon became a key political player, with significant media clout even though it lacked members in the Constituent Assembly.

The transitional period was marred by political tensions, social instability, economic difficulty, and security challenges. Gradually, the sense of euphoria that had followed the fall of Ben Ali dissipated and impatience mounted. From a socioeconomic perspective, people's lives had changed little, and so the social anger that had fed the revolution remained largely unappeased. In 2013, a wave of political violence increased political tensions and threatened the transition toward democracy. The assassination on February 6 of Chokri Beleid, a secular opposition member of the Constituent Assembly, marked the beginning of a period of political instability that put the Troika government in a difficult position. The opposition blamed Ennahda for the deterioration of the situation in the country and called for a broad-based political participation in the transitional process. Prime Minister Hamadi Jebali resigned after failing to form a new cabinet of technocrats. He was succeeded by Minister of Interior Ali Larayedh, a prominent member of Ennahda. The assassination of a second opposition figure, Mohamed Brahmi, five months later, weakened Ennahda's position further. Rachid Al Ghannouchi's party was also taken to task for adopting a lax attitude toward the hardline Islamist movement and the ultra-religious conservatives who advocated Islamic rule. A series of deadly clashes in 2013–14 between jihadist groups and security forces further united the opposition.

Outraged by the government, protesters took to the street and demanded that the Ennahda government resign, the Constituent Assembly be dissolved, and a government of national salvation be formed. Many members of the opposition boycotted the Constituent Assembly and joined the protests. These tensions coincided with the ousting of the democratically elected Egyptian president, Mohamed Morsi, and the ostracizing of the Muslim Brotherhood from Egypt's political scene. In response, Ennahda adopted a more strategic approach and eventually sought a political agreement with the opposition. A national dialogue, brokered by four key professional and civil society organizations led by the Labor Union, put an end to the stalemate after several rounds of failed negotiations. In December 2013, the ruling Ennahda government agreed to step down, making way for a transitional government of technocrats headed by Mehdi Jomaa. The adoption of a political roadmap within the framework of a national dialogue and the ratification of a modern and progressive constitution paved the way for the much-awaited legislative and presidential elections in 2014. These favored the rise of Nidaa Tunis as a secular political counterweight to the still-preponderant Ennahda. In early 2015, Beji Caïd Essebsi was sworn in as president and a unity government, headed by Prime Minister Habib Essid, won the approval of the parliament. Four years after the revolution, Tunisia could look forward to the end of the transitional period and the materialization of real democratic change at a time when other countries in the region have been struggling with the effects of the 2011 uprisings.

In spite of these achievements, daunting challenges remained. A number of political, social, and economic difficulties persisted, including the fragility of the political scene, schisms between the country's political players, the slow pace of reform, deepening economic difficulties, the unrealized aspirations of the youth, and unfulfilled development in the inner regions. No less significant were the security challenges the country faced. The armed assault on the Bardo Museum, which claimed the lives of twenty-three people, mostly European tourists, and the deadly attacks in and around Mount Chaanbi on the western border with Algeria made concrete the risk of terrorism and highlighted the threat of armed groups, weapons trafficking, radical Islamism, growing jihadi violence, and the permeability of the country's borders which were made all the more precarious with neighboring Libya descending into chaos. Together, these problems made a delicate situation during a crucial phase in the history of the country even more complicated.

The shifting dynamics that marked the post-revolutionary phase bear strongly on the evolution of contention. Even though the country became freer and more open, the widely held perception that this was an unfinished revolution meant that various forms of contention persisted. A number of questions deserve attention when considering the evolution of the revolution: How have the politics of everyday life been proceeding in these uncertain times? How have the voices of contention been affected by the revolution and by the country's reconfigured media landscape? What happened to digital activism in the new environment? What forms of resistance emerged and how were they articulated? What new modalities of activism have youth resorted to? How has the relationship between online and offline activism been redefined after the revolution? While the fast unfolding changes Tunisia experienced during the transition period make it difficult to gain the necessary distance to reflect on the broad significance of emerging trends and draw out their theoretical implications, a few observations can be ventured.

An Altered Media Landscape

After the revolution, a newfound freedom of expression transformed the national media scene. For the first time, journalists could cover stories freely and citizens could speak without fear of reprisals. Anxious to safeguard these gains, many voices pressed the government to reform the regulatory framework for media. This resulted in institutional attempts to put in place a system of communication that is more attuned to the needs and realities of the new Tunisia and to revise existing laws to fit the requirements and expectations of the transitional period. Three decrees issued in 2011 helped meet those demands. Decree 41 enhances official transparency by giving journalists and the public the right to access administrative documents. Decree 115 guarantees the freedom of expression and the freedom to disseminate information, limits the interference of the security office in the industry, and, with the exception of a limited number of offenses, eliminates prison sentences for reporters. Decree 116 lays the groundwork for the creation of a regulatory body for regulating the audiovisual sphere, formally called the Independent High Authority for Audiovisual Communications (HAICA), to reform the media sector and formulate guidelines for licensing media ventures. The new constitution similarly enshrines freedom of expression, guarantees the right to access information, and bans censorship.

These developments were complicated as the media gradually became enmeshed in the country's political struggles. As the gap widened between Ennahda and its political opponents, particularly after the 2011 elections, the partisan nature of the media became more obvious. Consequently, the media's new freedom remains fragile, and skepticism that the media can help democracy is widespread. The legacy of the Ben Ali era and the historical role of the country's loyalist press cannot be underestimated. Hampered by the lack of a strong tradition of independent journalism, the media have been slow to exploit the freedoms the new laws allegedly guarantee them. In effect, the maintenance of old broadcasting structures, questionable appointments, and insufficient protection for journalists meant that the old, closed system remained dominant.[1] Not surprisingly, mistrust persists between journalists and the government. Journalists criticize officials for their reluctance to uphold press freedom and their attempt to exert new controls over the media, while officials criticize journalists for failing to practice objective, professional, and nonpartisan journalism.[2]

The problems and limitations of traditional media gave new media an added relevance. After the revolution, official Internet censorship practically ceased, giving free rein to online communication. Facebook particularly benefited, especially given "the platform's acceptance into so many people's everyday routines."[3] According to the Arab Social Media Report, in 2014 the number of Facebook users reached 4.6 million, nearly half of the Tunisian population.[4] Citizens who were not previously users became avid consumers of Facebook, sharing information, discussing issues, and voicing criticism. With more people clamoring to have their voices heard, the Tunisian cyberspace became unrivaled in its popularity. Many of those who were not satisfied with the way the traditional media reported events embraced citizen journalism to voice their opinions and tell their stories. Political players and interest groups also sought to establish a strong presence on the Internet. For the many publics who took a keen interest in the country's sociopolitical scene, Facebook became the new agora where public opinion is shaped and people are continuously implicated in the *res publica*.

If social media became such a dynamic space of engagement, it has also at times been mired in excess. With Facebook gaining more popularity, troubling tendencies also emerged. The social networking site helped create a dynamic space of engagement but also favored misinformation and rumors. Sometimes those were spontaneous; sometimes they were the product of attempts to influence public opinion. The fact that Facebook has been used as a means for political partisanship contributed to the country's political, social, and religious polarization. Online media and news sites generally fed this divisiveness, as new, more ideological outlets took extreme political stands. Even though most of these outlets have small core readerships, their articles are usually recirculated on Facebook and other social networks, greatly increasing their influence over time. As it developed, Facebook, and online media generally, became powerful communication tools for some but repugnant tools to others.

Old Voices, New Roles

The youth most movingly articulated the country's gradual loss of faith in politics. "The only thing we got out of the revolution," noted one young Internet activist I interviewed, "is the freedom of expression. Practically, though, such freedom amounted to nothing much."[5] For this activist, as for the great many young Tunisians who were active during the revolution, the protracted transitional period was disorienting, resulting in a mixed feeling of enthusiasm and fatigue, of optimism and disillusionment. Sporadic street protests continued, but were officially deemed disruptive. As street activism died down, the youth were pushed to the margins. Attempts to involve young people in political life amounted to little more than token appointments. This is the case, for instance, with the Internet freedom activist Slim Amamou, who served as Minister for Sports and Youth for a few months before becoming disenchanted with the transitional process and quitting. Increasingly, there was a realization that effecting change from within was not a realistic expectation.[6] In the absence of political strategies and concrete programs beyond the desire to contest the status quo, traditional political players were bound to prevail. The positioning by various political forces circumscribed the sphere of political action and limited it to professional politics and political parties. Being either locked out of the political game or feeling themselves with no stakes and buy-ins, many young people who did not identify with the new political landscape chose to distance themselves from formal politics and operate outside traditional political structures. For them, the Internet continued to be an espace vital—but one that acquired a different dimension.

The presumed role social media played during the 2010–11 uprising put bloggers (who henceforth moved to Facebook) and Internet activists under the spotlight. Gradually, though, they ceased to be distinctive as a category after Ben Ali's fall. For Hamadi Kaloutcha, an Internet activist who was arrested during the revolution, "the problem is not with the bloggers, but the expectations that were put on them. Their role during the uprising was exaggerated. In many ways, they were a media creation....After all, they make a good story."[7] Bloggers were never unified except by a common enemy—Ben Ali's authoritarianism. When that vanished, they dispersed. "As an Internet activist," the above-mentioned blogger explained to me, "I wanted to expose the regime. I wanted people to know what was happening around them. I was filling a void; but that void is not there anymore. After the revolution, people tend to be better informed. Everything and everybody is out there on Facebook."[8]

In the post–Ben Ali Tunisia, online activist groups lost their raison d'être. For example, the once widely read oppositional news site Tunisnews became irrelevant with the free circulation of information. Part of its strength had come from its loose association with the Islamists who were persecuted under Ben Ali. With the ascension of Ennahda to power in 2011, the contestatory dimension of Tunisnews lost its significance. Other online activist groups that failed to adapt to the country's changing reality succumbed to the same fate. A case in point is the pioneer group Takriz, which continued its cyber-activism after the fall of Ben Ali. Disenchanted with what it considered an unfinished and vulnerable revolution, Takriz continued to be a voice of contention, refusing to come out of obscurity or reveal the identity of its members. As one member of Takriz explained during an interview, the group held on to anonymity as a bulwark against attempts to silence dissenting voices.[9] The fact that Takriz was one of the very few sites that was censored by a military tribune after the revolution made the group more radical. It continued to rely on the same tools and techniques it adopted a decade earlier: anonymity, provocative language, and uncompromising positions. Ironically, what has always been an element of strength for Takriz became a source of weakness in the new Tunisia. In spite of its continuous activism, Takriz, now reduced to a handful of members, stood out less for its effectiveness and more for its legacy of a "spirit of contestation."[10]

Some vigilant bloggers and Internet activists sought to reinvigorate that spirit by acting as watchdogs. A case in point is Olfa Riahi, a blogger who in 2002 published on her blog documents relating to a suspected misappropriation of public funds by the then Minister of Foreign Affairs from Ennahda party.[11] Riahi subsequently revealed information about an unpublicized large grant from the Chinese government this same minister received in his personal account. These revelations circulated widely on the social Web and received considerable media attention; the resultant scandal eventually led to the launch of an official investigation. Even though contestatory actions such as these obeyed loose dynamics, they cannot be dissociated from the political and ideological tensions that emerged in the post-revolution context. Chagrined with these trends, a few bloggers created the Association of Tunisian Bloggers, which charged itself with monitoring political misinformation on the Internet—a task that proved overly ambitious.[12] Another example of the type of digital activism the country's new reality induced are the efforts of hacker groups like Sawaed (Muscles) and Fallega (Fighters).[13] The latter comprises a core group of some thirty anonymous young activists but claims to have two thousand members.[14] Launched in 2011, the Fallega hacker team initially set out to defend the Muslim world and support the Palestinian cause, but gradually became focused on Tunisia's internal political affairs. They hack websites, pirate email and Facebook accounts, and publish classified documents that expose remnants of the old regime. On its Facebook page and e-forum,[15] Fallega defends its actions as an attempt to prevent the revolution from being hijacked. In the eyes of its critics, though, the group's widely shared frustration with the transitional process does not legitimize its means or justify taking the law in its own hands.

Although these forms of contention created a buzz, they were not representative of dominant trends that took hold after the revolution. For some of those who were put off or disenchanted by the world of formal politics, journalism became attractive. Further reinforcing this trend is the fact that, after the revolution, a number of television channels and radio stations recruited bloggers and Internet activists to keep up with what was happening online, invigorate their programs with new talent, and court young audiences. Entering the world of professional journalism, though, proved to be a mixed experience. While the opportunity to work with television channels and radio stations meant having access to a wider audience, it also entailed working within institutional frameworks and following editorial guidelines that were deemed limiting for bloggers and internet activists who were used to the unedited word and who were more at ease with an unstructured online environment. Most bloggers and Internet activists continued to operate outside mainstream media. Many of those who embraced citizen journalism were courted by the various international media assistance groups that took interest

in the country in the few months following the revolution and set out to cultivate the citizen journalism potential of the youth through training programs
and workshops on digital media and online journalism. Overall, though, citizen journalism was marked by unevenness and lack of credibility, particularly
as the country started to experience intense political polarization.

Some bloggers attempted to go beyond citizen journalism. They saw
Tunisia as entering a new phase in its history and thought that playing a role
in that transition required a more professional ethos than blogging or Face-
booking afforded. Experimenting with news and opinion sites that adopted
professional journalistic standards became particularly appealing. In March
2011, a group of bloggers joined activists that were involved with the News
Agency of the Movement of the Tunisian Street (a citizen journalist initiative
established a few months before to relay information about the protests) to
create a news website named Al Machhad Ettounsi (the Tunisian Scene).[16]
Distancing themselves from social and national media, they set out to support
the revolution by providing "free opinions and accurate news" to help people
remain vigilant about the risks of a counter-revolution. Despite the team's enthusiasm and commitment, they lacked financial resources, and the devotion
and contributions of its members could only sustain the initiative for two years.
Several other sites and online initiatives with various backgrounds, agendas,
and allegiances emerged, but most of these either succumbed to partisanship
or did not have a notable impact.[17]

One exception to this general pattern is Nawaat. After the revolution, Nawaat
quickly realized that it needed to adapt to play a role in the new Tunisia.
Accordingly, it transformed itself from a diasporic collective blog to a Tunis-
based professional online journalism venture. Realizing that such work required a larger and more fully devoted team, Nawaat recruited a dozen young
journalists and secured funding from international organizations like the
Open Society Foundation. While continuing to serve as a platform for diverse
views and opinions, it was also keen on keeping its activist edge.[18] More than
merely reporting on the sociopolitical affairs of the country during the democratic transition, Nawaat attempted to actively bring about change. Its recruitment strategy reflected this goal. The site assembled a young team with an
activist profile instead of hiring seasoned journalists with professional training.
The collective's experimentation with investigative journalism manifested
these trends as well. Whether it is the freedom of the judiciary and the rule of
law or the victims of the revolution and the economic choices the governments adopted, Nawaat has been relentless in denouncing the deficiencies

and abuses of the system while at the same time attempting to stay above the political fray.

Nawaat's attention to investigative reporting sprang from the realization that digital activism is important but insufficient to cause reform. The most effective and most enduring initiatives are those that combined online and offline activism. One noteworthy initiative is an innovative civil society organization spearheaded by Amira Yahyaoui, a young Internet activist who comes from a family that experienced repression first-hand under the Ben Ali regime. Her father is the rebel judge who wrote an open letter to President Ben Ali that cost him his career; her cousin is Zouheir Yahyaoui, the emblematic figure of cyber-dissidence who died shortly after he was released from prison. After unsuccessfully standing as an independent candidate for the Constituent Assembly in the 2011 elections, she channeled her energy into civil-society activism. Along with a small and young team, she set up Bawsala (Compass), a nongovernmental organization (NGO) that seeks to support democratization, promote citizen empowerment, foster political awareness, enhance political participation, and establish practices that are amenable to open government and good governance. In 2002, and in collaboration with the Berlin-based NGO Media in Cooperation and Transition and the German Parliament Watch, Bawsala launched Marsad, an electronic monitoring site that provides free and open online access to the activities of the Constituent Assembly.

The first issue Marsad took up was the controversial dismissal of the head of the Central Bank. Marsad not only made public guarded information about the vote on a successor but also revealed that several deputies neither attended the deliberative session nor took part in the vote. After that, the deputies' irregular attendance of the assembly's sessions, which frequently resulted in the absence of a quorum, became a prominent issue. By posting information and providing statistics about how few deputies were present during votes, Marsad raised serious concerns about the assembly's representativeness and accountability. The desire to instill a culture of openness and to defend the right to access information became a driving impetus for Bawsala. Even in the new and open environment, this was hard. Although censorship ceased after the revolution, transparency remained an insistent issue. Having operated for years under a repressive environment that was fraught with risks, the various political parties and political players had internalized a culture of secrecy and opacity as part of a survival strategy. While a few members of the Constituent Assembly were appreciative of the kind of work Bawsala was doing, many more found the idea of being scrutinized by a group of young activists to be unwelcome.

The setbacks the group faced made them more determined to be a force of contention. Establishing a permanent presence on the journalists' bench under the Constituent Assembly's dome, Bawsala set out to monitor the work of the deputies around the clock, with one foot in the real world and the other foot in the digital world. One of their early contributions was reporting on voting in the assembly in the absence of public information about the process, the deliberations, and the positions of the representatives of the people. Equipped with mobile phones, some of Bawsala's team members diligently took photos of the overhead scoreboard that tallied the assembly's votes while others photographed the deputies present at the time of the vote. They thus figured out how each deputy voted and, in some instances, even detected irregularities in the vote count. Social networking tools like Twitter and Facebook have been instrumental in their effort to inform, educate, expose, and pressure. Their networks of followers regularly retweet and share their stories and calls to action. But not all of their tactics involved technology. Bawsala also worked through the system to promote shared governance. Having repeatedly failed to persuade the leadership in the Constituent Assembly to make public information relating to the work of the assembly, Bawsala took advantage of the newly ratified Decree 41, which allows access to documents of public institutions, and successfully sued the Constituent Assembly in 2012 to make available to the public the minutes of assembly meetings, committee reports, and other relevant information.

The coverage of the assembly's deliberations on the new draft constitution thrust Al Marsad to the nation's attention and gave it an added momentum. The new constitution was the single most important document in determining the country's future, and Bawsala was not ready to see the fate of the country determined by a handful of deputies behind closed doors. Raising awareness about the work of the Constituent Assembly was an important first step to enhance the role of citizens in political affairs and to reposition them at the core of political action. Bawsala's keenness on providing independent information enhanced their credibility. Growing public impatience with politicians and the general perception that the members of the Constituent Assembly cared more about themselves than the needs of the people stimulated interest in the work of Bawsala. The fact that the national media relied on Marsad's insights in their coverage of the activities of the Constituent Assembly increased their visibility and gave them an added weight. In March 2013, Bawsala was even invited to testify in front of the assembly's Internal Affairs Committee. Noticeably, the political process started to improve: information became more accessible, the speaker of the assembly more cooperative, and members of the assembly more tolerant of Bawsala's watchdog function. These gains prompted Bawsala to expand its outreach and activities to include the monitoring of local and municipal councils, where the stakes are arguably higher and the impact of these institutions on the daily lives of citizens is more directly felt.

Conclusion

Although elections and a new constitution may have put Tunisia on the path toward a durable democracy, the challenges and setbacks of the transitional period suggest that the revolution is not over. Interestingly, the youth who played an important role during the revolution found themselves marginalized by traditional political players who reclaimed their role in political life. Although the Internet continued to offer a space of engagement and an arena of contestation for the youth, the newfound freedom and the altered media environment introduced new dynamics. In the post-revolutionary context, the proclivity of voices of contention to influence public discourse became contingent on their willingness to adapt and to evolve, but also on their ability to act in both the real and virtual world.

What does the complexity of Tunisia's post-revolutionary transition reveal about change? We should learn, first, to distrust overly broad generalizations. Exciting narratives about noble activists and heroic technologies make for good Twitter updates, but they are no substitute for careful analysis about how ordinary people interact with structures of oppression or how shifts in quotidian practices affect the constant negotiation of what is permissible for state and subject alike. Second, we should be reminded that even dramatic events like the fall of a dictator do not upset social structures overnight. During the peak of the revolution, the youth appeared to be on the verge of seizing the power they had been denied for so long, but their passionate voices were stilled by the internecine partisan bickering that followed Ben Ali's ouster. The extraordinary passions of the revolution were themselves tamed and channeled by the ordinary actions of politicians and powerbrokers. Finally, the ways in which some activists were able to adapt and to thrive in the new, uncertain, uncharted Tunisian political landscape shows that the same processes that had eroded the Ben Ali regime could be transformed to meet new circumstances.

What will prove critical is whether these newly claimed freedoms can become habitual. If the practices of contestation, inquiry, and activism that emerged from the publinets and blogs of the Ben Ali era can mature, then they will nurture the public sphere that only a few Tunisian public activists once dreamed of. But if instead the activists distance themselves from the public and see their work as isolated from and higher than the concerns of ordinary people, then they will not only fail to see their immediate policy agendas enacted but will also see the habits of democracy wither away.

List of Interviews

Interview with Ahmed Moeed, Doha, March 13, 2011.

Interview with Aicha Teib Korchid, Doha, April 19, 2011.

Interview with Ali Bouazizi, Sidi Bouzid, July 3, 2011.

Interview with Ali Larayedh, Doha, May 26, 2014.

Interview with Astrubal (Riadh Gurefali), Tunis, June 27, 2011.

Interview with Barbach (Mohamed Mtaallah), Nabeul, July 7, 2011.

Interview with Bassam Bounenni, Doha, March 12, 2011.

Interview with Bilal Ahmed Banderee, Doha, January 19, 2011.

Interview with Carpe Diem (Selim Kharrat), July 19, 2011, and March 16, 2014.

Interview with Centrist (Sofiene Guerfali), Doha, March 13, 2011.

Interview with Decepticus (Foued Bouzaouèche), Tunis, October 14, 2011.

Interview with Ezzeddine Abdelmoula, Doha, April 19, 2011.

Interview with Fatma Arabicca (Fatma Riahi), Tunis, June 30, 2011.

Interview with Fœtus, Tunis, May 21, 2011 (via Skype).

Interview with Ghassen Ben Khelifa, Tunis, July 30, 2011, and March 18, 2014.

Interview with Habib Gheribi, Doha, April 20, 2011.

Interview with Hamadi Kaloutcha (Sofiene Bel Haj), Tunis, April 23, 2011, and March 4, 2014.

Interview with Hasni, May 31, 2011 (via email).

Interview with Haythem El Mekki, Tunis, April 24, 2014.

Interview with Houeida Anouar, Tunis, April 8, 2014.

Interview with Houssein Ben Ameur, Montreal, June 19, 2011 (via Skype).

Interview with Imed Daimi, Doha, March 12, 2011.

Interview with Ismail Dbara, Tunis, July 4, 2011.

Interview with Kerim Bouzouita, Tunis, June 30, 2011.

Interview with Lamine Bouazizi, Doha, April 19, 2011.

Interview with Larbi Chouikha, Tunis, April 22, 2011.

Interview with Le Gouverneur de Normalland (Wessam Tlili), Djerba, July 4, 2011.

Interview with Liliopatra (Lilia Weslaty), Tunis, June 25, 2012.

Interview with Lina Ben Mhenni, Doha, March 13, 2011.

Interview with M'hamed Krichene, Doha, March 13, 2011.

Interview with Malek Khadraoui, Doha, March 14, 2011, and Tunis June 27, 2011.

Interview with Mehdi Horchani, Sidi Bouzid, July 3, 2011.

Interview with Mokhtar Yahyaoui, Tunis, July 31, 2011.

Interview with Moncef Marzouki, Doha, March 11, 2011.

Interview with Mongi Mabrouki, Doha, March 13, 2011.

Interview with Mustafa Souag, Al Jazeera Network, Doha, May 1, 2011.

Interview with Nabil Rihani, Al Jazeera, Doha, June 21, 2011.

Interview with Nader Hamdouni, Sidi Bouzid, July 3, 2011.

Interview with Noureddine Al Ouididi, Doha, April 19, 2011.

Interview with Omar Kayyâam (Mohamed Bouriga), Sousse, July 28, 2011.

Interview with Rached Ghanouchi, Doha, March 11, 2011.

Interview with Rachid Khechana, Doha, February 28, 2011.

Interview with Ramzi Betteibi, Tunis, March 18, 2014.

Interview with Riyaad Minty, Doha, January 19, 2011.

Interview with Salem Labiyadh, Doha, April 21, 2011.

Interview with Sami Ben Gharbia, Tunis, June 27, 2011, and January 27, 2012.

Interview with Sarra Grira, France 24, Paris, October 14, 2012 (via Skype).

Interview with Selim Boukhit, Tunis, April 22, 2011.

Interview with Slimane Rouissi, Sidi Bouzid, July 3, 2011.

Interview with Sophie Piekarec, Paris, October 14, 2011 (via phone).

Interview with Tarek Kahlaoui, Tunis, July 13, 2011.

Interview with Thameur El Mekki, Tunis, April 22, 2011.

Interview with Walid Haddouk, Doha, March 12, 2011.

Interview with Waterman, Tunis, March 23, 2014 (via Skype).

Interview with Yassine Baccouri, Tunis, April 22, 2011.

Interview with Zied El Heni, Tunis, July 26, 2011.

Interview with Zouheir Makhlouf, Tunis, April 25, 2011, and July 3, 2011.

Notes

Chapter 1

1. Manuel Castells, *Networks of Outrage and Hope: Social Movements in the Internet Age* (Cambridge: Polity, 2012), 81.

2. See Marc Lynch, *Voices of the New Arab Public: Iraq, Al Jazeera, and Middle East Politics Today* (New York: Columbia University Press, 2006); Muhammad Ayish, *The New Arab Public Sphere* (Berlin: Frank & Timme, 2008); Dale F. Eickelman and Armando Salvatore, *The Public Sphere and Muslim Identities* (Bloomington: Indiana University Press, 2003); Richard August Norton, "The New Media, Civil Pluralism and the Struggle for Political Reform," in *New Media in the Muslim World: The Emerging Public Sphere*, ed. Dale F. Eickelman and Jon W. Anderson (Bloomington: Indiana University Press, 2003), 19–32. For a critical engagement with the notion of an Arab public sphere, see Mohamed Zayani, "The Challenges and Limits of Universalist Concepts: Problematizing Public Opinion and a Mediated Arab Public Sphere," *The Middle East Journal of Communication and Culture* 1, no. 1 (2008): 60–79.

3. See, for instance, Kai Hafez, "Arab Satellite Broadcasting: Democracy without Political Parties," *Transnational Broadcasting Studies* 15 (Fall 2005), http://www.tbsjournal.com/Archives/Fall05/Hafez.html; Laurence Pintak, "Satellite TV and Arab Democracy," *Journalism Practice* 2, no. 1 (2008): 15–26; Philip Seib, *The Al Jazeera Effect: How the New Global Media Are Reshaping World Politics* (Washington, D.C.: Potomac, 2008); Mamoun Fandy, *(Un)Civil War of Words: Media and Politics in the Arab World* (Westport, Conn.: Praeger, 2007); Mohammed El Oifi, "Faire de la Politique par les Médias Arabes," *Maghreb-Machrek* 193 (2007): 81–108.

4. A number of book-length studies focus on the pre-Arab spring digital culture of the MENA region. One of the early works on the topic is Jon W. Anderson's *Arabizing the Internet*, which situates the development of the Internet in the Arab world between local exigencies and global processes. Grey E. Burkhart and Susan Older's *The Information Revolution in the Middle East and North Africa* (Washington, D.C.: Rand, 2003) argues that the spread of information technologies did not necessarily lead to political change or alter the nature of governance in the Middle East and North Africa region. Shanthi Kalathil and Baylor C. Boas's *Open Networks, Closed Regimes: The Impact of the Internet on Authoritarian Rule* (Washington, D.C.: Carnegie Endowment for the International Peace, 2003) argues that, in spite of its disruptive potential, the Internet has not been a threat to authoritarian regimes, including Middle Eastern states. J. Roberts's *How the*

Internet Is Changing the Practice of Politics in the Middle East: Political Protest, New Social Movements, and Electronic Zamizdat (Lewiston: Edwin Mellon, 2009) focuses on the role of convergent media, specifically the Internet, in social movements. Last, Philip N. Howard's *The Digital Origins of Dictatorship and Democracy: Information Technology and Political Islam* (Oxford: Oxford University Press, 2010) studies the political impact of the Internet on the political culture of the Middle East, focusing on the relationship between technology diffusion and democratization processes.

5. Marwan Kraidy and Joe Khalil, "Youth, Media and Culture in the Arab World," in *International Handbook of Children, Media and Culture*, ed. Kristen Drotner and Sonia Livingstone (London: Sage, 2008), 331.

6. Annabelle Sreberny, "Television, Gender and Democratization in the Middle East," in *De-Westernizing Media Studies*, ed. James Curran and Myung-Jin Park, 66.

7. Barry Mirkin, "Population Levels, Trends and Policies in the Arab Region: Challenges and Opportunities," UNDP Research Paper Series, 2010, http://www.arab-hdr.org (accessed September 22, 2012), 11.

8. Samir Khalaf and Roseanne Saad Khalaf, eds., *Arab Youth: Social Mobilization in Times of Risk* (London: Saqi, 2011), 9.

9. Dale F. Eickelman, "New Media in the Arab Middle East and the Emergence of Open Societies," in *Remaking Muslim Politics: Pluralism, Contestation, Democratization*, ed. Robert W. Hefner (Princeton: Princeton University Press, 2005), 37–59.

10. Ibid., 45–46.

11. Marwan Kraidy and Joe Khalil, *Arab Television Industries* (London: Palgrave Macmillan, 2009), 9–32.

12. Kalathil and Boas, *Open Networks, Closed Regimes*, 2.

13. Barrie Axford, "Talk about a Revolution: Social Media and the MENA Uprisings," *Globalizations* 8, no. 5 (2011), 683.

14. See Deborah L. Wheeler, *The Internet in the Middle East: Global Expectations and Local Imaginations in Kuwait* (Albany: State University of New York Press, 2006) and David Faris, *Dissent and Revolution in a Digital Age: Social Media, Blogging and Activism in Egypt* (London: I. B. Tauris, 2012), which focus on Kuwait and Egypt, respectively. See also Marwan Kraidy, *Reality Television and Arab Politics: Contention in Public Life* (Cambridge: Cambridge University Press, 2009), which focuses on the hybrid media space within the context of the Middle East, in particular the Levant and the Gulf region.

15. See Samia Mihoub, *Internet dans le Monde Arabe: Complexité d'une Adoption* (Paris: L'Hamattan, 2005).

16. See, for instance, Castells, *Networks of Outrage and Hope*; Philip N. Howard and Muzammil M. Hussain, *Democracy's Fourth Wave? Digital Media and the Arab Spring* (Oxford: Oxford University Press, 2013); Charles Kurzman, "The Arab Spring Uncoiled," *Mobilization: An International Journal* 17, no. 4 (2012): 377–90; Paolo Gerbaudo, *Tweets and the Streets: Social Media and Contemporary Activism* (London: Pluto, 2012); Zeynep Tufekci and Christopher Wilson, "Social Media and the Decision to Participate in Political Protest: Observations from Tahrir Square," *Journal of Communication* 62 (2012): 363–79.

17. See, for instance, Elizabeth Dickinson, "The First WikiLeaks Revolution?" *Foreign Policy* (January 13, 2013), http://wikileaks.foreignpolicy.com/posts/2011/01/13/wikileaks_and_the_tunisia_protests (accessed October 12, 2012); Andrew Sullivan, "Tunisia's WikiLeaks Revolution," *The Atlantic* (January 14, 2011), http://www.theatlantic.com/daily-dish/archive/2011/01/tunisias-wikileaks-revolution/177242/ (accessed October 12, 2011); Mike Giglio, "Tunisia Protests: The Facebook Revolution," *The Daily Beast* (January 15, 2011), http://www.thedailybeast.com/articles/2011/01/15/tunisa-protests-the-facebook-revolution.html (accessed January 31, 2014).

18. Daniel Lerner, *The Passing of Traditional Society* (Glencoe, Ill.: Free Press, 1958).

19. Clay Shirky, "Reply to Malcolm Gladwell's 'From Innovation to Revolution: Do Social Media Make Protesters Possible,'" *Foreign Affairs* 90, no. 2 (March/April 2011), http://www.foreignaffairs.com/articles/67325/malcolm-gladwell-and-clay-shirky/from-innovation-to-revolution (accessed December 15, 2012).

20. Annabelle Sreberny and Ali Mohammadi, *Small Media, Big Revolution: Communication, Culture, and the Iranian Revolution* (Minneapolis: University of Minnesota Press, 1994).

21. See Yahya Kamalipour, ed., *Media, Power and Politics in the Digital Age: The 2009 Presidential Election Uprising in Iran* (Lanham: Rowman & Littlefield, 2010).

22. Clay Shirky, "The Twitter Revolution: More than Just a Slogan," *Prospect* (January 6, 2010), http://www.prospectmagazine.co.uk/magazine/the-twitter-revolution-more-than-just-a-slogan/ (accessed December 18, 2012).

23. Ibid.

24. Clay Shirky, "The Net Advantage," *Prospect* (December 11, 2009), http://www.prospectmagazine.co.uk/magazine/the-net-advantage (accessed June 12, 2013).

25. Navid Hassanpour, "Media Disruption and Revolutionary Unrest: Evidence from Mubarak's Quasi-Experiment," *Political Communication* 31, no. 1 (2014): 1–24.

26. Malcolm Gladwell, "Small Change: Why the Revolution Will Not Be Tweeted," *The New Yorker* (October 4, 2010), http://www.newyorker.com/reporting/2010/10/04/101004 fa_fact_gladwell (accessed June 12, 2013).

27. Malcolm Gladwell, "Does Egypt Need Twitter?" *New Yorker* (February 2, 2011), http://www.newyorker.com/online/blogs/newsdesk/2011/02/does-egypt-need-twitter.html#ixzz1CqneJJOu (accessed June 12, 2013).

28. Evgeny Morozov, "Freedom.gov: Why Washington's Support for Online Democracy Is the Worst Thing Ever to Happen to the Internet," *Foreign Policy* 34 (February 2011): 34.

29. Evgeny Morozov, *Net Delusion: The Dark Side of Internet Freedom* (New York: Public Affairs, 2011).

30. Evgeny Morozov, "Why the Internet Is Failing Iranian Activists," *Prospect* (January 5, 2010), http://www.prospectmagazine.co.uk/magazine/why-the-internet-is-failing-irans-activists/ (accessed December 18, 2012).

31. See Marc Lynch, "Globalization and Arab Security," in *Globalization and National Security*, ed. Jonathan Kirshner (New York: Routledge, 2006), 184; Rasha Abdulla, *Policing the Internet in the Arab World* (Abu Dhabi: ECSSR, 2009).

32. Clay Shirky, "Reply to Malcolm Gladwell's 'From Innovation to Revolution: Do Social Media Make Protesters Possible,'" *Foreign Affairs* 90, no. 2 (March/April 2011).

33. David Faris and Patrick Meier, "Digital Activism in Authoritarian Countries," in *The Participatory Cultures Handbook*, ed. Aaron Delwiche and Jennifer Jacobs Henderson (London: Routledge, 2013), 203.

34. Geoffrey L. Herrera, "New Media for a New World: Information Technology and Threats to National Security," in *Globalization and National Security*, ed. Jonathan Kirshner (New York: Routledge, 2006), 97.

35. Maha Taki, "Beyond Utopias and Dystopias: Internet in the Arab World," in *The Middle East in the Media: Conflicts, Censorship and Public Opinion*, ed. Arnim Heinemann, Olfa Lamloum, and Anne Françoise Weber (London: Saki, 2009), 185.

36. Manuel Castells, *Communication Power* (Oxford: Oxford University Press, 2009), 9.

37. Generally, the case of Tunisia is more usually analyzed from a political science perspective that privileges the political and economic lenses. The handful of available book-length studies on Ben Ali's Tunisia tend to either focus on regime durability and authoritarian robustness or dwell on the disjuncture between the country's economic and political spheres—more specifically the way the regime's commitment to liberal economic reforms did not engender political liberalization or lead to genuine democratization but further entrenched authoritarianism as the ruling elite came to coopt the economic elite. Among the works that appeared in the decade or so preceding the revolution,

the following are noteworthy: Emma Murphy's *Economic and Political Change in Tunisia* (London: Palgrave Macmillan, 1999); Olfa Lamloum and Bernard Ravenel's *La Tunisie de Ben Ali: La Société Contre le Régime* (Paris: L'Harmattan, 2002); Stephen King's *Liberalization against Democracy: The Local Politics of Economic Reform in Tunisia* (Bloomington: Indiana University Press, 2003); Michel Camau and Vincent Geisser's *Le Syndrome Autoritaire: Politique en Tunisie de Bourguiba à Ben Ali* (Paris: Presses de Sciences Po, 2003); Kenneth Perkins's *A History of Modern Tunisia* (Cambridge: Cambridge University Press, 2004); Brieg Powel and Larbi Sadiki's *The EU and Tunisia: A Study of Democratization via Association* (London: Routledge, 2009); and Christopher Alexander's *Tunisia: Stability and Reform in the Modern Maghreb* (London: Routledge, 2010). Along with a handful of scholarly articles—including insightful work by Larbi Sadiki, Larbi Chouika, Eric Gobe, John Entelis, and Francesco Cavatorta—the aforementioned studies shed light on formal state politics during the Ben Ali era but leave unaddressed subtle developments, underlying currents, and evolving dynamics within society.

38. Béatrice Hibou, *The Force of Obedience: The Political Economy of Repression in Tunisia*, trans. Andrew Brown (Cambridge: Polity, 2011), 12.
39. Ibid., 16.
40. Ibid., 9.
41. Ibid., 12.
42. Michel Foucault, "The Subject and Power," *Critical Inquiry* 8 (1982): 786–88.
43. Hibou, *The Force of Obedience*, 14.
44. Ibid., 2.
45. Ibid., xvii–xviii.
46. Foucault, "The Subject and Power," 794.
47. Michel de Certeau, *The Practice of Every Life*, trans. Steven Rendall (Berkeley: University of California Press, 1984), xiv.
48. Ibid., xv.
49. Ibid., 37; James C. Scott, *Domination and the Arts of Resistance: Hidden Transcripts* (New Haven: Yale University Press, 1990).
50. Ibid., xvii.
51. Asef Bayat, *Life as Politics: How Ordinary People Change the Middle East* (Stanford: Stanford University Press, 2009), 3.
52. Asef Bayat, "Muslim Youth and the Claim of Youthfulness," in *Being Young and Muslim: New Cultural Politics in the Global South and North*, ed. Linda Herrera and Asef Bayat (Oxford: Oxford University Press, 2010), 45–46.
53. Bayat, *Life as Politics: How Ordinary People Change the Middle East* (Stanford: Stanford University Press, 2009), 11.
54. Ibid., 14.
55. Ibid.
56. Ibid., 22.
57. Henri Lefebvre, *Everyday Life in the Modern World* (London: Allen Lane, 1971), 45.
58. Charles Kurzman, "The Arab Spring Uncoiled," *Mobilization: An International Journal* 17, no. 4 (2012): 377–78.
59. Annabelle Sreberny and Ali Mohammadi, *Small Media, Big Revolution: Communication, Culture, and the Iranian Revolution* (Minneapolis: University of Minnesota Press, 1994), 20.
60. Michael Warner, "Publics and Counterpublics," *Public Culture* 14, no. 1 (2002): 49–90.
61. Sreberny and Mohammadi, *Small Media, Big Revolution*, 3–4.
62. Ibid., 25.
63. Kay Richardson, Katy Parry, and John Corner, *Political Culture and Media Genre: Beyond News* (London: Palgrave Macmillan, 2013), 4.
64. Mieke Bal, *Narratology: An Introduction to the Theory of Narrative* (Toronto: University of Toronto Press: 2009), 145.

65. See Michael Herzfeld, "Anthropology and the Politics of Significance," *Etnográfica* 4, no. 1 (2000): 5–36.
66. Gregory F. Gause, "Why Middle East Studies Missed the Arab Spring," *Foreign Affairs* (July–August 2011), http://www.foreignaffairs.com/articles/67932/f-gregory-gause-iii/why-middle-east-studies-missed-the-arab-spring (accessed November 8, 2012).

Chapter 2

1. Zine El Abidine Ben Ali, "Statement from the President of the Republic of Tunisia at the World Summit on the Information Society," November 16, 2005, www.itu.int/wsis/tunis/statements/docs/g-tunisia-opening/1.doc (accessed February 11, 2012).
2. Taoufik Ben Brik, "Ben Ali y est et y Restera," TF1 (January 15, 2001), http://lci.tf1.fr/monde/2001-01/ben-ali-est-restera-4899973.html (accessed February 11, 2012).
3. See Sayed Hamdi, "The Opposition Figure Moncef Marzouki Calls for a Popular Uprising," Al Jazeera.net (April 11, 2006), http://www.aljazeera.net/news/pages/f617e417-331f-4647-9e01-0295e30c1ea1 (accessed July 7, 2012); Moncef Marzouki, "Isn't It Time to Change the Discourse?" (January 24, 2008), http://moncefmarzouki.com/spip.php?article179 (accessed July 7, 2012); Faisal Al Kassim, "The Future of Arab Regimes," *The Opposite Direction Program*, Al Jazeera Arabic Channel (April 27, 2010), http://www.aljazeera.net/programs/pages/0672b8a3-6002-4824-80bd-829ac52860b5 (accessed July 7, 2012).
4. Sihem Ben Sedrine, "Monsieur le Président, Partez: Une Tribune Contre Ben Ali," *L'Obs*, December 11, 2009, http://tempsreel.nouvelobs.com/opinions/20091210.OBS0281/monsieur-le-president-partez-une-tribune-contre-ben-ali.html (accessed October 12, 2011).
5. John P. Entelis, "Republic of Tunisia," in *The Government and Politics of the Middle East and North Africa*, ed. David E. Long, Bernard Reich, and Mark Gasiorowski (Boulder: Westview, 2011), 522.
6. Ibid.
7. Mounira Charrad, *States and Women's Rights: The Making of Postcolonial Tunisia, Algeria and Morocco* (Berkeley: University of California Press, 2001), 233–41.
8. Clement Henry, "Tunisia's Sweet Little Regime," in *Worst of the Worst: Dealing with Repressive and Rogue Nations*, ed. Robert Rotberg (Washington, D.C.: Brookings Institution Press, 2007), 301.
9. Entelis, "Republic of Tunisia," 525.
10. Jennifer Noyon, *Islam, Politics and Pluralism: Theory and Practice in Turkey, Jordan, Tunisia and Algeria* (Washington, D.C.: The Royal Institute of International Affairs, 2003), 96.
11. Kenneth Perkins, *A History of Modern Tunisia* (Cambridge: Cambridge University Press, 2004), 167–77.
12. Michele Penner Angrist, "Parties, Parliament and Political Dissent in Tunisia," *The Journal of North African Studies* 4, no. 4 (1999): 93; Lisa Anderson, "Political Pacts, Liberalism and Democracy: The Tunisian National Pact of 1988," *Government and Opposition* 26, no. 2 (1991): 244–60.
13. Francesco Cavatorta, "Geopolitical Challenges to the Success of Democracy in North Africa: Algeria, Tunisia and Morocco," *Democratization* 8, no. 4 (2001): 183.
14. The failure to embrace genuine democratic reform in spite of democratic discourses and announced elections has been well noted. See, for instance, Michel Camau and Vincent Geisser, *Le Syndrome Autoritaire: Politique en Tunisie de Bourguiba à Ben Ali* (Paris: Presses de Sciences Po, 2003); Éric Gobe and Larbi Chouikha, "Tunisie: Des Élections pour Quoi Faire?" SciencesPo-CERI (February 2010), http://www.sciencespo.fr/ceri/en/content/tunisie-des-elections-pour-quoi-faire-signification-et-portee-des-scrutins-presidentiel-et-l (accessed October 24, 2012).

15. Larbi Sadiki, "Ben Ali Baba Tunisia's Last Bey," Aljazeera.net (September 27, 2010), http://english.aljazeera.net/indepth/opinion/2010/09/20109238338660692.html (accessed March 25, 2011), 63.

16. Emma C. Murphy, "The Tunisian *Mise à Niveau* Programme and the Political Economy of Reform," *New Political Economy* 11, no. 4 (2006): 519–40.

17. Azmi Bishara, *Tunisia: The Diary of a Resplendent Revolution in the Making* (Doha: Arab Center for Research and Policy Studies, 2012), 164.

18. International Crisis Group, "Popular Protest in North Africa and the Middle East: Tunisia's Way," Middle East/North Africa Report No. 106 (April 28, 2011): 1, http://www.crisisgroup.org/en/regions/middle-east-north-africa/north-africa/tunisia/106-popular-protests-in-north-africa-and-the-middle-east-iv-tunisias-way.aspx (accessed June 30, 2012).

19. John P. Entelis, "The Democratic Imperative vs the Authoritarian Impulse: The Maghrib State Between Transition and Terrorism," *Middle Eastern Journal* 59, no. 4 (2005): 550. On the containment and appropriation of the opposition, see also Amin Allal and Florian Kohstall, "Opposition within the State: Governance in Egypt, Morocco and Tunisia," in *Contentious Opposition in the Middle East: Political Opposition under Authoritarianism*, ed. Holger Albrecht (Gainesville: University Press of Florida, 2010), 181–204.

20. Bishara, *Tunisia*, 155.

21. Ahmed Nejib Chebbi's Progressive Democratic Party was founded in 1983 and legalized in 1988. Mostapha Ben Jaafar's Democratic Front for Labor and Liberties came to being in 1994 but was not legalized until 2002. Moncef Marzouki's Congress for the Republic was founded in 2001.

22. Angrist, "Parties, Parliament and Political Dissent in Tunisia," 90.

23. Ibid., 97–99.

24. Camau and Geisser, *Le Syndrome Autoritaire*, 359.

25. Perkins, *A History of Modern Tunisia*, 166.

26. Entelis, "Republic of Tunisia," 525.

27. Christopher Alexander, *Tunisia: Stability and Reform in the Modern Maghreb* (London: Routledge, 2010), 50.

28. David S. Sorenson, *An Introduction to the Modern Middle East: History, Religion, Political Economy, Politics* (Boulder: Westview, 2008), 364.

29. Perkins, *A History of Modern Tunisia*, 189–90.

30. Noyon, *Islam, Politics and Pluralism*, 103.

31. Ibid.

32. Larbi Sadiki, "Political Liberalization in Ben Ali's Tunisia: Façade Democracy," *Democratization* 9, no. 4 (2002): 125.

33. Perkins, *A History of Modern Tunisia*, 190.

34. Noyon, *Islam, Politics and Pluralism*, 105.

35. Sadiki, "Political Liberalization," 130–32.

36. Perkins, *A History of Modern Tunisia*, 166–67.

37. Alexander, *Tunisia*, 79.

38. Perkins, *A History of Modern Tunisia*, 202–3.

39. *Tunisia's Global Integration: A Second Generation of Reforms to Boost Growth and Employment* (Washington, D.C.: World Bank Publications, 2006), 1.

40. "Tunisia's Global Integration: A Second Generation of Reforms to Boost Growth and Employment," World Bank Social and Economic Development Sector Unit for the Middle East and North Africa Region (May 2008): viii, http://siteresources.world bank.org/INTTUNISIA/Resources/Global-Integration-ReportSept08.pdf (accessed February 12, 2012).

41. Georgie Anne Geyer, *Tunisia: A Journey through a Country that Works* (London: Stacey International, 2003), 27–28.

42. Ibid., 34.
43. For an overview of Tunisia's economic situation, see Alexander, *Tunisia*, 68–88.
44. Entelis, "The Democratic Imperative," 549.
45. Stephen J. King, *Liberalization against Democracy: The Local Politics of Economic Reform in Tunisia* (Bloomington: Indiana University Press, 2003), 138.
46. Béatrice Hibou, "Tunisie: Économie Politique et Morale d'un Movement Social," *Politique Africaine* 121 (2011): 6.
47. Jean-François Daguzan, "De la Crise Économique à la Revolution Politique?" *Maghreb-Machrek* 206 (2010–11): 13.
48. Sadiki, "Tunisia: The Battle of Sidi Bouzid," Aljazeera.net (December 27, 2010), http://www.aljazeera.com/indepth/opinion/2010/12/20101227142811755739.html (accessed May 10, 2012).
49. See King, *Liberalization against Democracy*, 28, 34, 139.
50. Sadiki, "Political Liberalization in Ben Ali's Tunisia," 127.
51. Alexander, *Tunisia*, 88.
52. On the centrality of patrimonial and corporatist ties to the MENA region's political systems, see Mehran Kamrava, *The Modern Middle East* (Berkeley: University of California Press, 2013), 272–81.
53. Alexander, *Tunisia*, 203.
54. Raoul Saïdi, "La Pauvreté en Tunisie: Présentation Critique," in *La Tunisie de Ben Ali: La Société Contre le Régime*, ed. Olfa Lamloum and Bernard Ravenel (Paris: L'Harmattan, 2002), 26.
55. Sadiki, "Ben Ali Baba Tunisia's Last Bey," 69; Perkins, *A History of Modern Tunisia*, 196.
56. Habib Ayeb, "Social and Political Geography of the Tunisian Revolution: The Alfa Grass Revolution," *Review of African Political Economy* 38, no. 129 (2011): 469.
57. Béatrice Hibou, *The Force of Obedience: The Political Economy of Repression in Tunisia*, trans. Andrew Brown (Cambridge: Polity, 2011), 87.
58. Angrist, "Parties, Parliament and Political Dissent in Tunisia," 102.
59. Significantly, the official rate of poverty that was released shortly after the revolution was 24.7 percent. See "Rate of Poverty Estimated at 24.7%," Tunisian Press Agency (May 28, 2011), http://www.tap.info.tn/en/en/society/2749-rate-of-poverty-estimated-at-247.html (accessed May 29, 2011).
60. Ayeb, "Social and Political Geography of the Tunisian Revolution," 471.
61. Michaël Béchir Ayari, Vincent Geisser, and Abir Krefa, "Chronique d'une Révolution Presque Annoncée," *L'Année du Maghreb* 7 (2011): 361.
62. Hajer Bettaïeb, "Les Nouveaux Défis du Secteur Textile en Tunisie," *L'Année du Maghreb* 2 (2005–6): 419–25.
63. Gonzalo Escribano and Alejandro V. Lorca, "Economic Reform in the Maghreb: From Stabilization to Modernization," in *North Africa: Politics, Religion and the Limits of Transformation*, ed. Yahya H. Zoubir and Haizam Amirah-Fernández (London: Routledge, 2008), 138; Philippa Dee and Ndiamé Diop, "The Economy-wide Effects of Further Trade Reforms in Tunisia's Service Sectors," *World Bank Policy Research Working Paper* No. 5341 (June 2010), http://www-wds.worldbank.org/servlet/WDSContentServer/WDSP/IB/2010/06/21/000158349_20100621084841/Rendered/PDF/WPS5341.pdf (accessed July 12, 2012).
64. See Jane Harrigan, "Did Food Prices Plant the Seeds of the Arab Spring?" SOAS Inaugural Lecture Series, School of Oriental and African Studies, University of London (April 28, 2011), http://www.soas.ac.uk/about/events/inaugurals/28apr2011-did-food-prices-plant-the-seeds-of-the-arab-spring.html (accessed May 4, 2012).
65. The inability to suppress food prices had economic and political implications as it made the bread pact increasingly untenable. Significantly, in his last speech to the people, Ben Ali promised to reduce prices on basic food items.

66. Murphy, "The Tunisian *Mise à Niveau* Programme and the Political Economy of Reform," 523.
67. "Tunisia: Integrity Indicators Scorecard," Global Integrity (2008), https://www.globalintegrity.org/global/the-global-integrity-report-2008/tunisia/ (accessed February 11, 2012).
68. Lahcen Achy, "Substituer des Emplois Précaires à un Chômage Élevé: Les Défis de l'Emploi au Maghreb," Carnegie Middle East Center Paper No. 23 (November 2010), http://carnegieendowment.org/files/TEXTE2%2Epdf (accessed January 30, 2012), 11.
69. Mohamed Haddar, "L'Économie Tunisenne: État des Lieux," *Maghreb-Mashrek* 206 (Winter 2010–11): 66. See also Paul Rivlin, "The Constraints on Economic Development in Morocco and Tunisia," in *The Maghreb in the New Century: Identity, Religion and Politics*, ed. Bruce Maddy-Weitzman and Daniel Zisenwine (Gainesville: University of Florida Press, 2007), 208–10.
70. "Arab Despots Should Heed Events in Tunisia," *The Guardian*, January 16, 2011, http://www.guardian.co.uk/commentisfree/2011/jan/16/observer-editorial-tunisia-support-arabs (accessed January 16, 2011).
71. Hassine Dimasi, "The Social and Political Significance of the Middle Class in Tunisia," in *The Tunisian Revolution: Causes, Contexts and Challenges* (Doha: Arab Center for Research and Policy Studies, 2012), 149–50.
72. Hamza Meddeb, "L'Ambivalence de la Course à *el Khobza*: Obéir et se Révolter en Tunisie," *Politique Africaine* 121 (March 2011): 35–51.
73. Jean-Pierre Séréni, "Le Réveil Tunisien," *Le Monde Diplomatique* (January 6, 2011), http://www.monde-diplomatique.fr/carnet/2011-01-06-Tunisie (accessed January 30, 2012).
74. Baccar Gherib, "Les Classes Moyennes Tunisiennes entre Mythe et Réalité," *L'Année du Maghreb* 7 (2011): 419–35.
75. Asef Bayat, "A New Arab Street in Post Islamist Times," *Foreign Policy* (January 26, 2011), http://mideast.foreignpolicy.com/posts/2011/01/26/a_new_arab_street (accessed July 7, 2012).
76. *Tunisia: Understanding Successful Socio-Economic Development: A Joint World Bank-Islamic Development Bank Evaluation of Assistance* (Washington, D.C.: The World Bank, 2005), 24.
77. Olivier Piot, "De l'Indignation à la Révolution," *Le Monde Diplomatique* (February 2011), http://www.monde-diplomatique.fr/2011/02/PIOT/20114 (accessed January 30, 2012).
78. For more on the devolution of the country's educational system, see Dimasi, "The Social and Political Significance of the Middle Class in Tunisia," 154–57.
79. *United Nations Arab Human Development Report* (New York: UNDP, 2009), http://www.arab-hdr.org/publications/other/ahdr/ahdr2009e.pdf (accessed January 23, 2011), 3.
80. "Tunisia: Basic Demographic Indicators," World Bank, http://web.worldbank.org/WBSITE/EXTERNAL/TOPICS/EXTGENDER/EXTANATOOLS/EXTSTATINDDATA/EXTGENDERSTATS/0,,contentMDK:21438838~menuPK:4080892~pagePK:64168445~piPK:64168309~theSitePK:3237336,00.html (accessed January 23, 2011); "World Population Prospects," World Bank, http://web.worldbank.org/WBSITE/EXTERNAL/TOPICS/EXTGENDER/EXTANATOOLS/EXTSTATINDDATA/EXTGENDERSTATS/0,,contentMDK:21438838~menuPK:4080892~pagePK:64168445~piPK:64168309~theSitePK:3237336,00.html (accessed January 23, 2011).
81. *United Nations Arab Human Development Report*, 111.
82. Michele Dunne, "What Tunisia Proved and Disproved about Political Change in the Arab World," *Arab Reform Bulletin* (January 18, 2011), http://www.carnegieendowment.org/arb/?fa=downloadArticlePDF&article=42320 (accessed February 5, 2012).

83. "Tunisia's Global Integration: A Second Generation of Reforms to Boost Growth and Employment." World Bank Social and Economic Development Sector Unit for the Middle East and North Africa Region (May 2008), 4, http://siteresources.worldbank .org/INTTUNISIA/Resources/Global-Integration-ReportSept08.pdf (accessed February 12, 2012).
84. Achy, "Substituer des Emplois Précaires à un Chômage Élevé," 11.
85. Ibid.
86. "Human Rights Watch, World Report 2011: Tunisia," United Nations Human Rights Commission for Refugees (January 24, 2011), www.unhcr.org/refworld/docid/4d3e80261a .html (accessed March 16, 2011).
87. Lise Garon, *Dangerous Alliances: Civil Society, The Media and Democratic Transition in North Africa* (London: Zed Books, 2003); Marine Desmères, "La Société Civile Tunisienne en Otage?" December 2000, http://www.ceri-sciencespo.com/archive/ Dec00/desmeres.pdf (accessed November 29, 2011).
88. "Independent Voices Stifled in Tunisia," Amnesty International (July 13, 2010), www .amnesty.org/en/library/info/MDE30/008/2010 (accessed June 1, 2011).
89. Larbi Chouikha, "Tunisie: Les Chimères Liberals," *La Pensée de Midi* 19 (2006): 29–37, http://www.cairn.info/resume.php?ID_ARTICLE=LPM_019_0029 (accessed May 28, 2012).
90. "Independent Voices Stifled in Tunisia"; Bassam Bounenni, "Dictatorship: Tunisia's Undeserved Fate," *The Daily Star*, May 18, 2009, http://www.dailystar.com.lb/Opinion/ Commentary/May/18/Dictatorship-Tunisias-undeserved-fate.ashx (accessed March 4, 2012).
91. "Tunisia's Media Landscape," *International Media Support* (June 2002), http://www .i-m-s.dk/wp-content/uploads/2012/11/ims-tunisia-assessment-2002.pdf (accessed July 7, 2012).
92. Charrad, *States and Women's Rights*, 233–41.
93. Noyon, *Islam, Politics and Pluralism*, 106; Hibou, *The Force of Obedience*, 3–9.
94. Lotfi Hajji, "The 18 October Coalition for Rights and Freedoms in Tunisia," *Arab Reform Initiative Brief*, October 13, 2006, http://www.arab-reform.net/18-october-coalition- rights-and-freedoms-tunisia (accessed June 6, 2011), 2.
95. Entelis, "Republic of Tunisia," 526.
96. "Rapport Annuel 2008, Moyen-Orient et Afrique du Nord: Tunisie," Reporters Without Borders (2008), 182, http://archives.rsf.org/article.php3?id_article=25310 (accessed March 13, 2012).
97. Hibou, *The Force of Obedience*, 9.
98. Ibid., 88.
99. Walid Haddouk, "The Tunisian Revolution: An Exploration of the Socio-economic Background," in *The Tunisian Revolution: Causes, Contexts and Challenges* (Doha: Arab Center for Research and Policy Studies, 2012), 94.
100. Cavatorta, "Geopolitical Challenges to the Success of Democracy in North Africa," 181.
101. "Deadly Attack Keeps World on Alert," *The Guardian*, September 4, 2002, http://www .guardian.co.uk/world/2002/sep/04/september11.usa (accessed December 30, 2011).
102. Christina Wood, "French Foreign Policy and Tunisia: Do Human Rights Matter?" *Middle East Policy* 9, no. 2 (2002): 92–110.
103. Cavatorta, "Geopolitical Challenges to the Success of Democracy in North Africa," 183–84.
104. See, for instance, Commission Européenne, "Rapport de Suivi Tunisie" (May 12, 2010), http://ec.europa.eu/world/enp/pdf/progress2010/sec10_514_fr.pdf (accessed June 11, 2011); European Commissioner, "Tunisia and the European Union," March 25, 2010, http://ec.europa.eu/commission_2010-2014/fule/docs/articles/article_tunisia_ 10-03-25_en.pdf (accessed June 11, 2011).

105. See "PES against Tunisia Receiving Advanced Status from the EU," European Forum (November 18, 2009), http://www.europeanforum.net/news/775/pes_against_tunisia_receiving_advanced_status_from_the_eu (accessed June 11, 2011).
106. Kristina Kausch, "Tunisia: EU Incentives Contributing to New Repression," FRIDE (September 9, 2010), http://www.fride.org/publication/807/tunisia:-eu-incentives-contributing-to-new-repression (accessed May 7, 2012).

Chapter 3

1. Adnan Mansar, "The Tunisian General Labor Union: Socio-Political Dialectics," in *The Tunisian Revolution: Causes, Contexts and Challenges* (Doha: Arab Center for Research and Policy Studies, 2012), 280–82.
2. Ibid., 285–87.
3. Stephen J. King, *Liberalization against Democracy: The Local Politics of Economic Reform in Tunisia* (Bloomington: Indiana University Press, 2003), 5.
4. Khalil Zamiti, "La Question Syndicale: Contradictions Sociales et Manipulations Politiques," in *Tunisie au Présent: Une Modernité au dessus de tout Soupçon?* ed. Michel Camau (Paris: CNRS, 1978), 287–96.
5. Michaël Béchir Ayari et al., "Chronique d'une Révolution Presque Annoncée," *L'Année du Maghreb* 7 (2011): 377.
6. Ibid., 374.
7. Ibid., 376.
8. For a detailed discussion of the relationship between the lawyers and the regime, see Éric Gobe and Michaël Béchir Ayari, "Les Avocats dans la Tunisie de Ben Ali: Une Profession Politisée?" *L'Année du Maghreb* 3 (2007): 105–32; Éric Gobe, "The Tunisian Bar to the Test of Authoritarianism: Professional and Political Movements in Ben Ali's Tunisia (1990–2007)," *The Journal of North African Studies* 15, no. 3 (2010): 333–47.
9. The editors of the opposition newspapers *Al Mawqif, Attariq Al Jadid* and *Mouwatinoun* were Rachid Khechana, Hichem Skik, and Abdel Latif Abid/Mostapha Ben Jaafar, respectively.
10. Quoted in Maud Hand, "Il Fait Bon Vivre en Tunisie?" Association for Progressive Communication (April 1, 2005), http://www.apc.org/en/news/access/world/il-fait-bon-vivre-en-tunisie-state-human-rights-tu (accessed December 15, 2012).
11. Hanène Chaâbane, "La Presse d'Opposition en Tunisie entre Liberté, Censure et Autocensure: Le Cas d'*Attatiq Al Jadid*," *Horizons Maghrebins* 62 (2010): 32.
12. Interview with Rachid Khechana, Doha, February 28, 2011.
13. Lotfi Hajji, "The 18 October Coalition for Rights and Freedoms in Tunisia," *Arab Reform Initiative Brief* (October 13, 2006), http://www.arab-reform.net/18-october-coalition-rights-and-freedoms-tunisia (accessed June 6, 2011).
14. "Parties, Associations and Unions Support the 18 October Movement," *Al Badil* (November 14, 2005), http://albadil.org/spip.php?article595 (accessed November 21, 2012).
15. Farah Samti, "Eight Years Ago, When Leftists and Islamists Got Along," *Tunisalive* (October 18, 2013), http://www.tunisia-live.net/2013/10/18/eight-years-ago-today-when-leftists-and-islamists-got-along/ (accessed November 18, 2013).
16. Azmi Bishara, *Tunisia: The Diary of a Resplendent Revolution in the Making* (Doha: Arab Center for Research and Policy Studies, 2012), 181.
17. Hajji, "The 18 October Coalition for Rights and Freedoms in Tunisia"; Vincent Geisser and Éric Gobe, "La Question de L'Authenticité Tunisienne: Valeur Refuge d'un Régime à Bout de Soufflé," *L'Année du Maghreb* 3 (2007): 378–81; Nejib A. Chebbi, "On the Rapprochement between the Islamists and the Secularists: The 18 October Experiment in Tunisia," *Adab* 11–12 (2010), www.adabmag.com/node/353 (accessed June 12, 2012).
18. Florence Beaugé, "Le Combat Perdu du Président Ben Ali," *Le Monde*, July 21, 2001.

19. Jocelyne Dakhlia, *Tunisie: Le Pays sans Bruit* (Paris: Actes Sud, 2011).

20. Nicolas Beau and Jean-Pierre Tuquoi, *Notre Ami Ben Ali: L'Envers du Miracle Tunisien* (Paris: La Decouverte, 2002).

21. Carlotta Gall, "Buffeted by Tumult, Jewish Population in Tunisia Dwindles," *New York Times*, June 26, 2014, A6.

22. Garçon José, "Tunisie: Des Jihadistes Contre Ben Ali," *Libération* (January 10, 2007), http://www.liberation.fr/monde/2007/01/10/tunisie-des-jihadistes-contre-ben-ali_81526 (accessed February 2, 2012).

23. Samy Ghorbal, "Comment les Salafistes ont été Neutralizés," *Jeune Afrique* (January 7, 2007), http://www.jeuneafrique.com/Article/LIN06018commessilar0/actualite-afrique comment-les-salafistes-ont-ete-neutralises.html (accessed August 26, 2012).

24. José, "Tunisie: Des Jihadistes Contre Ben Ali."

25. Comité pour le Respect des Libertés et des Droits de l'Homme en Tunisie, "Les Derniers Événements en Tunisie: Le Devoir d'Informer, le Droit à la Vérité" (January 9, 2007), http://tunisie.over-blog.org/article-5211786.html (accessed October 5, 2011).

26. Éric Gobe, "The Gafsa Mining Basin between Riots and a Social Movement: Meaning and Significance of a Protest Movement in Ben Ali's Tunisia," HAL-SHA (2010), http://hal.archives-ouvertes.fr/docs/00/55/78/26/PDF/Tunisia_The_Gafsa_mining_basin_between_Riots_and_Social_Movement.pdf (accessed February 13, 2012).

27. Karine Gantin and Omeyya Seddik, "Révolte du Peuple des Mines en Tunisie," *Le Monde Diplomatique* (July 2008), 11, http://www.monde-diplomatique.fr/2008/07/GANTIN/16061 (accessed June 12, 2011).

28. Ibid.

29. Amnesty International, "Behind Tunisia's Economic Miracle: Inequality and Criminalization of Protest," (June 17, 2009), http://www.amnesty.org/en/library/info/MDE30/003/2009 (accessed August 30, 2012); Karine Gantin, "Tunisie: Des Luttes Renouvellées pour des Droits Inextinguibles," Centre Tricontinental (December 15, 2010), http://www.cetri.be/spip.php?article1469&lang=fr (accessed August 29, 2012).

30. Larbi Chouikha and Éric Gobe, "La Tunisie entre la Révolte du Bassin Minier de Gafsa et l'Echéance Electorale de 2009," *L'Année du Maghreb* 5 (2009): 13.

31. Because of his coverage of the popular protests, he was arrested. He was handed a four-year prison term for the propagation of false information that was deemed harmful to the social order. His real offense was reporting on the events in Gafsa. See "Le Journaliste Tunisien Fahem Boukadous Condamné à 4 Ans de Prison Ferme," *Libération* (July 7, 2010), http://www.liberation.fr/monde/0101645674-le-journaliste-tunisien-fahem-boukadous-condamne-a-4-ans-de-prison-ferme (accessed June 12, 2011); "Paris Préoccupé par l'Arrestation du Journaliste Tunisien Fahem Boukadous," *Jeune Afrique* (July 16, 2010), www.jeuneafrique.com/actu/20100716T141602Z20100716T141558Z (accessed January 15, 2012); "Journalist Faces Imprisonment for Covering Gafsa Unrest," Amnesty International (June 20, 2010), http://www.amnesty.org/en/library/info/MDE30/006/2010/en (accessed January 15, 2012).

32. Chouikha and Gobe, "La Tunisie entre la Révolte du Bassin Minier de Gafsa et l'Echéance Electorale de 2009," 19.

33. Amin Allal, "Ici Ça Bouge Pas, Ça n'Avance Pas!" in *L'État Face aux Débordements du Social au Maghreb*, ed. Myriam Catusse, Blandine Destremau, and Eric Verdier (Paris: Karthala, 2009), 181.

34. Interview with Zouheir Makhlouf, Tunis, July 3, 2011.

35. Sofiene Chourabi, "Violences dans le Sud Tunisien Suite à la Fermeture d'un Poste-Frontière entre la Tunisie et la Libye," France24 (August 24, 2010), http://observers.france24.com/fr/content/20100820-violences-sud-tunisien-suite-fermeture-frontieres-entre-tunisie-libye (accessed January 7, 2011).

36. Ali Saidi, "Interview with BBC Arabic," (August 20, 2010), http://www.youtube.com/watch?feature=endscreen&v=UrD-1nkM6Mg&NR=1 (accessed January 8, 2011).

37. Comité pour le Respect des Libertés et des Droits de l'Homme en Tunisie, "Après Gafsa, la Répression Sauvage du Régime Tunisien s'Abat sur Ben Guerdane," *Tunisnews* 3739 (August 18, 2010), http://tunisnews.net/archive/18Out10f.htm (accessed March 1, 2012).

38. Chourabi, "Violences dans le Sud Tunisien"; "Tunisie: Violents Affrontements entre Habitants et Forces de l'Ordre," *Le Nouvel Observateur* (August 15, 2010), http://temps-reel.nouvelobs.com/monde/20100815.OBS8521/tunisie-violents-affrontements-entre-habitants-et-forces-de-l-ordre.html (accessed January 6, 2011).

39. "Le Mouvement de Protestation s'Étend à Ben Gardane, en Dépit de la Férocité de la Répression et des Promesses du Pouvoir," *Tunisnews* 3739 (August 18, 2010).

40. Ayari et al., "Chronique d'une Révolution Presque Annoncée," 365.

41. Slimane Rouissi, "Les Agriculteurs Tunisiens Manifestent pour Conserver leurs Terres," France 24.com (July 16, 2010), http://observers.france24.com/fr/content/20100716-agriculteurs-tunisiens-manifestent-conserver-leurs-terres (accessed January 3, 2012).

42. Béatrice Hibou, *The Force of Obedience: The Political Economy of Repression in Tunisia*, trans. Andrew Brown (Cambridge: Polity, 2011), 27–51.

43. Ibid., 182.

44. Hassine Dimasi, "The Social and Political Significance of the Middle Class in Tunisia," in *The Tunisian Revolution: Causes, Contexts and Challenges* (Doha: Arab Center for Research and Policy Studies, 2012), 151–52.

45. Walid Haddouk, "The Tunisian Revolution: An Exploration of the Socio-economic Background," in *The Tunisian Revolution: Causes, Contexts and Challenges* (Doha: Arab Center for Research and Policy Studies, 2012), 97.

46. Tawfik Ayechi, "Accusations of Fraud in the Name of the Law," *Attatiq Al Jadid* 188 (July 10, 2010), 5, http://attariq.org/IMG/jpg/Page_05-73.jpg (accessed February 17, 2012); Mehdi Horchani, "The Policy of Impoverishment and Land Seizure in Regueb," The Tunisian Cyber Parliament, Forum for Rights and Freedoms (July 14, 2010), http://24sur24.posterous.com/23252863 (accessed January 3, 2012); Rouissi, "Les Agriculteurs Tunisiens Manifestent pour Conserver leurs Terres."

47. Habib Ayeb, "Social and Political Geography of the Tunisian Revolution: The Alfa Grass Revolution," *Review of African Political Economy* 38, no. 129 (2011): 472.

48. Rouissi, "Les Agriculteurs Tunisiens Manifestent pour Conserver leurs Terres."

49. Ayechi, "Accusations of Fraud in the Name of the Law."

50. Interview with Lamine Bouazizi, Doha, April 19, 2011. See also Sarra Grira and Julien Pain, "Connaissez-vous Slimane Rouissi: L'Homme qui a Lancé la Révolution Tunisienne?" France24 (October 25, 2011), http://tunisie.france24.com/2011/10/25/connaissez-vous-slimane-rouissi-l%E2%80%99homme-qui-a-lance-la-revolution-tunisienne/ (accessed January 9, 2011).

51. Hibou, *The Force of Obedience*, 63.

52. Interview with Slimane Rouissi, Sidi Bouzid, July 3, 2011.

53. Ibid.

54. Bishara, *Tunisia*, 193.

55. Ibid., 134–35.

56. Interview with Lamine Bouazizi, Doha, April 19, 2011.

57. Ibid.

58. Ibid.

59. Ibid.

60. Interview with Mehdi Horchani, Sidi Bouzid, July 3, 2011.

61. Interview with Hamadi Kaloutcha, Tunis, April 23, 2011.

62. Aicha Teib, "The Socio-Economic Context of the Tunisian Revolution: A Sociological Reading," in *The Tunisian Revolution: Causes, Contexts and Challenges* (Doha: Arab Center for Research and Policy Studies, 2012).

63. Larbi Sadiki, "Ben Ali Baba Tunisia's Last Bey," Aljazeera.net (September 27, 2010), http://english.aljazeera.net/indepth/opinion/2010/09/20109238338660692.html (accessed March 25, 2011).

64. "Tunisie: On Assiste à une Cyber-Révolution," (January 12, 2011), http://www.youphil .com/fr/article/03370-tunisie-on-assiste-a-une-cyber-revolte-emeute-facebook? ypcli=ano (accessed January 26, 2012).

65. Mehdi Mabrouk, "A Revolution for Dignity and Freedom: Preliminary Observations on the Social and Cultural Background to the Tunisian Revolution," *Journal of North African Studies* 16, no. 4 (2011): 628.

66. Michel Camau and Vincent Geisser, *Le Syndrome Autoritaire: Politique en Tunisie de Bourguiba à Ben Ali* (Paris: Presses de Sciences Po, 2003), 207–11.

67. James L. Gelvin, *The Arab Uprisings: What Everyone Needs to Know* (Oxford: Oxford University Press, 2012), 61.

68. The number of lawyers in Tunisia is estimated to be around eight thousand. See Jean-Pierre Séréni, "En Tunisie, les Soubresauts de la Revolution," *Le Monde Diplomatique* (May 2011), http://www.monde-diplomatique.fr/2011/05/SERENI/20484 (accessed January 30, 2012).

69. Ayari et al., "Chronique d'une Révolution Presque Annoncée," 377.

70. Ibid., 372.

71. Interview with Slimane Rouissi, Sidi Bouzid, July 3, 2011.

72. Interview with Larbi Chouikha, Tunis, April 22, 2011.

Chapter 4

1. Jean-Philippe Bras, "Ordre Public, Politiques Publiques et Internet en Tunisie," in *Mondialisation et Nouveaux Médias dans L'Espace Arabe*, ed. Franck Mermier (Paris: Maisonneuve et Larose, 2003), 247.

2. Ibid., 248.

3. Farouk Kamoun, Jamil Chaabouni, Sami Tabbane and Asma Ben Letaifa, "Tunisia ICT Sector Performance Review, 2009–10: Towards Evidence-Based ICT Policy and Regulation," Policy Paper No. 12, Research ICT Africa, 2010, 6, http://researchictafrica .net/publications.php (accessed June 10, 2011).

4. Tunisian Internet Agency, "Internet in Tunisia," http://www.ati.tn/en/index .php?id=68&rub=26 (accessed February 5, 2012).

5. Bras, "Ordre Public, Politiques Publiques et Internet en Tunisie," 251; Samia Mihoub, "Particularités de l'Appropriation du Réseau Internet en Tunisie," Archive Ouverte en Sciences de l'Information et de la Communication (November 17, 2003), http:// archivesic.ccsd.cnrs.fr/sic_00000804 (accessed June 1, 2011), 3; Sihem Ben Sedrine, "Tunisie Internet: La Navigation sous Haute Surveillance," *Kalima Tunisie*, October 3, 2001," www.kalima-tunisie.info/magazine/mum1/index3.htm (accessed June 1, 2011).

6. Samia Ben Sassi, "Les Publinets de Tunis: Une Analyse Micro-Économique," *Netsuds* 2 (2004): 107–22, http://www.gdri-netsuds.org/IMG/pdf/Samider.pdf (accessed December 8, 2012).

7. Tunisian Internet Agency, "Internet in Tunisia," http://www.ati.tn/en/index.php?id= 68&rub=26 (accessed February 5, 2012).

8. Samia Mihoub, *Internet dans le Monde Arabe: Complexité d'une Adoption* (Paris: L'Hamattan, 2005), 13.

9. Tunisian Internet Agency, "Internet in Tunisia," http://www.ati.tn/en/index.php?id= 68&rub=26 (accessed February 5, 2012).

10. Kamoun et al., "Tunisia ICT Sector Performance Review, 2009–10," 18.

11. Tunisian Internet Agency, "Statistiques du Mois de Janvier 2011 sur l'Internet en Tunisie," http://www.ati.tn/en/index.php?id=90&rub=27 (accessed June 10, 2011).

12. Interview with Mokhtar Yahyaoui, Tunis, July 31, 2011.

13. Albrecht Hofheinz, "The Internet in the Arab World: Playground for Political Liberalization," *Internationale Politik und Gesellschaft* 3 (March 2005): 93.

14. Teresa Graziano, "The Tunisian Diaspora: Between Digital Riots and Web Activism," Fondation Sciences de L'Homme (April 2012), http://www.e-diasporas.fr/working-papers/Graziano-Tunisians-EN.pdf (accessed April 14, 2012).

15. Interview with Fœtus, Tunis, May 21, 2011.

16. Ibid.

17. Ibid.

18. Florence Beaugé, "Les Cyber-Résistants Tunisiens Donnent Naissance à une Nouvelle Forme de Contestation," *Le Monde*, September 22, 2000.

19. Interview with Waterman, Tunis, March 23, 2014.

20. Ibid.

21. Hanene Zbiss, "Qui est Derrière Takriz," *Réalités* (May 19, 2011).

22. Armaud Gonzague, "Takriz Donne de l'Urticaire au Régime Tunisien" (February 1, 2011), http://www.transfert.net/Takriz-donne-de-l-urticaire-au (accessed May 12, 2011).

23. Géraldine Faes, "www.Takriz.org," *Le Monde*, September 13, 2000.

24. Fœtus, "L'Essence de Takriz" (January 2010), http://takriz.com/emag/article/essence-de-takriz (accessed June 10, 2011).

25. Fœtus, "Takriz en 2010," http://foetus.me/blog/2010 (accessed May 24, 2011).

26. "De Takriz à la France et l'Europe," www.takriz.com/emag/article.takriz-a-la-france-europe" (accessed April 27, 2011).

27. Fœtus, "L'Essence de Takriz."

28. Célina Braun, "À Quoi Servent les Parties Tunisiens? Sens et Contre-Sens d'une Libéralisation Politique," *Revue des Mondes Musulmans et de la Méditerranée* 111–12 (March 2006): 54.

29. Faes, "www.Takriz.org."

30. "Yahoo! Still First Portal Call," *BBC News* (June 5, 1998), http://news.bbc.co.uk/2/hi/business/107667.stm (accessed December 15, 2012).

31. Rami Brahem, "La Tunisie, Première Cyber-Révolution: Interview avec Fœtus," (January 20, 2011), http://www.michelcollon.info/La-Tunisie-premiere-cyber.html (accessed May 23, 2011); Beaugé, "Les Cyber-Résistants Tunisiens Donnent Naissance à une Nouvelle Forme de Contestation."

32. Fœtus, quoted in Faes, "www. Takriz.org."

33. Gonzague, "Takriz Donne de l'Urticaire au Régime Tunisien."

34. Seif Soudani, "Takriz: Quand les Hooligans Font de la Politique," *Le Labo Politique* (March 12, 2011), http://www.edupartage.com/web/labopolitique/magazine/-/asset_publisher/J9Zk/content/1641587 (accessed May 23, 2011).

35. Interview with Fœtus, Tunis, May 21, 2011.

36. Maryam Mnaouar, "Takriz: La Violence était Légitime Face à une Dictature Meurtrière et Barbare," *Afrik* (June 2, 2011), http://www.afrik.com/article22996.html (accessed June 7, 2011).

37. Interview with Fœtus, Tunis, May 21, 2011.

38. Ibid.

39. Brahem, "La Tunisie, Première Cyber-Révolution."

40. Fœtus, "Quand ils ont Peur ils Censurent: Campagne des Censuré Contre Censure," *Takriz E-mag* 2, no. 3 (2000), http://takriz.com/gdim/archives/n2vol3.html (accessed May 23, 2011).

41. "Ce Site a été Censuré par le Gouvernement Tunisien," *Takriz E-mag* 2, no. 3 (2000), http://takriz.tunezine.tn/archives/n2vol3.html (accessed May 23, 2011).

42. Stéphane Arteta, "Des Souris Contre Ben Ali," *Le Nouvel Observateur*, August 21, 2011, http://tempsreel.nouvelobs.com/actualite/monde/20010821.OBS7638/des-souris-contre-ben-ali.html (accessed May 22, 2011).

43. Braun, "À Quoi Servent les Parties Tunisiens," 54.

44. Arteta, "Des Souris Contre Ben Ali."

45. Eric Mugneret, "Le Web Censuré, à la Mode Tunisienne," (January 18, 2001), http://www.transfert.net/Le-Web-censure-a-la-mode (accessed May 22, 2011).

46. Interview with Fœtus, Tunis, May 21, 2011.

47. Brahem, "La Tunisie, Première Cyber-Révolution."

48. Braun, "À Quoi Servent les Parties Tunisiens," 54.

49. Meryem Marzouki, "Pendant les Travaux, le Gâchis Continue," Alternatives Citoyennes (November 24, 2005), http://www.alternatives-citoyennes.sgdg.org/num17/dos-bilan-w.html (accessed May 25, 2011).

50. Braun, "À Quoi Servent les Parties Tunisiens," 54.

51. Fœtus, "L'Essence de Takriz." See also Samia Mihoub, "Le Cyberactivism à l'Heure de la Révolution Tunisenne," *Archivio Anthropologico Mediterraneo* 12, no. 2 (2011): 18.

52. Fœtus, "L'Essence de Takriz."

53. Michel de Certeau, *The Practice of Everyday Life*, trans. Steven Rendall (Berkeley: University of California Press, 1984), 36–38.

54. Brahem, "La Tunisie, Première Cyber-Révolution."

55. "False Freedom: Online Censorship in the Middle East and North Africa," Human Rights Watch, November 15, 2005, http://www.hrw.org/reports/2005/11/14/false-freedom (accessed February 14, 2012).

56. "Emprisonné pour Avoir Critiqué: Zouheir Yahyaoui," Reveil Tunisien (March 16, 2005), www.reveiltunisien.org/spip.php?article1707 (accessed June 10, 2011).

57. "Conférence de TUNeZINE: Synthèse des Travaux sur la Logistique," Reveil Tunisien, (June 12, 2002), http://www.reveiltunisien.org/spip.php?article35 (accessed June 5, 2011).

58. Interview with Decepticus, Tunis, October 14, 2011.

59. "Intervenez pour Libérer Zouheir Yahyaoui," Reveil Tunisien (June 16, 2002), http://www.reveiltunisien.org/spip.php?article78 (accessed June 8, 2011).

60. Interview with Sophie Piekarec, October 14, 2011.

61. Interview with Omar Khayyâam, Sousse, July 28, 2011.

62. Ibid.

63. Lilia Weslaty, "Entretien avec Sophie Piekarec," Nawaat (March 14, 2012), http://nawaat.org/portail/2012/03/14/entretien-avec-sophie-piekarec-la-fiancee-de-zouheir-yahyaoui/ (accessed March 12, 2013).

64. Omar Khayyâam, "À la Recherche d'une Espèce Perdue: Les TUNeZINiEns," *Tunisia Watch* (February 10, 2010), http://tunisnews.net/112010 (accessed October 14, 2011).

65. Florence Beaugé, "Zouheir Yahyaoui, le Pionnier des Cyberdissidents," *Le Monde*, January 19, 2011.

66. "Intervenez pour Libérer Zouheir Yahyaoui," Reveil Tunisien (June 16, 2002), http://www.reveiltunisien.org/spip.php?article78 (accessed June 8, 2011).

67. The nucleus of the group included Ettounsi, Sophie Piekarec, Omar Khayyâam, Lecteur Assidu, Decepticus, and Hsouna.

68. Ettounsi de TUNeZINE, "Merci Monsieur le Précédent," January 2002, http://omarkhayyam.blogsome.com/2007/05/14 (accessed October 15, 2011).

69. Interview with Mokhtar Yahyaoui, Tunis, July 31, 2011.

70. Omar Khayyâam, "Les Maux de Tout les Mots," TUNeZINE 8 (July 8, 2001), www.tunezine.com/tunezine08.htm (accessed October 24, 2011).

71. Ibid.

72. Interview with Omar Khayyâam, Sousse, July 28, 2011.
73. Interview with Sophie Piekarec, October 14, 2011.
74. Beaugé, "Zouheir Yahyaoui, le Pionnier des Cyberdissidents."
75. Lilia Weslaty, "Les Cyberdissidents Tunisiens Rendent Homage à Zouheir Yahyaoui" (March 8, 2011), http://www.tunivisions.net/les-cyberdissidents-tunisiens-rendent-hommage-a-zouheir-yahyaoui,11604.html (accessed June 11, 2011).
76. Mokhtar Yahyaoui, "Open Letter to the President of the Republic," TUNeZINE (July 6, 2001), www.tunezine.comtunezine07.htm (accessed October 24, 2011); "Tunisian Web Journalist Jailed," BBC News (June 20, 2002), http://news.bbc.co.uk/2/hi/middle_east/2050453.stm (accessed May 22, 2011).
77. Kamel Labidi, "No Place to Talk about Internet Freedom," *Internal Herald Tribune*, November 11, 2005, http://www.nytimes.com/2005/11/15/opinion/15iht-edlabidi.html (accessed March 23, 2011).
78. Florence Beaugé, "En Tunisie, Police et Justice Contre le plus Célèbre des Cyber-Résistants," *Le Monde*, June 13, 2002.
79. "Tunisia: Release Urged for Online Magazine Editor," Human Rights Watch (June 6, 2002), http://www.hrw.org/en/news/2002/06/05/tunisia-release-urged-online-magazine-editor (accessed February 14, 2012).
80. Alexandre Piquard, "Zouheir Yahyaoui Libre, les Cyberdissidents Tunisiens Restent Harcelés par le Régime," Transfert.net (November 20, 2003), http://www.transfert.net/Zouhair-Yahyaoui-libre-les (accessed October 15, 2011); Angelica, "Communiqué N°4: Participation du Comité National pour la Libération de Zouheir Yahyaoui," Reveil Tunisien, (February 8, 2003), http://www.reveiltunisien.org/spip.php?article419 (accessed October 24, 2011).
81. Arab Network for Human Rights Information, "The Internet in the Arab World: A New Space of Repression" (2004), http://www.anhri.net/en/reports/net2004/ (accessed October 9, 2011).
82. Committee to Protect Journalists, "Without a Net," (June 2004), http://cpj.org/reports/2004/10/yahyaoui.php (accessed May 18, 2011); "False Freedom: Online Censorship in the Middle East and North Africa," Human Rights Watch (November 15, 2005), http://www.hrw.org/reports/2005/11/14/false-freedom (accessed February 14, 2012).
83. Tsar Boris, "A Propos de la Charte." TUNeZINE 100 (October 10, 2002), http://www.tunezine.com/tunezine100.htm (accessed February 8, 2012).
84. "Tunisie: Hommage au Cyber-Militant Zouheir Yahyaoui." *Tekiano* (March 11, 2011), http://www.tekiano.com/net/7-web-2-0/3451-tunisie-hommage-au-cyber-militant-zouhair-yahyaoui.html (accessed May 19, 2011).
85. Nadia Omrane and Meryem Marzouki, "Zouheir Yahyaoui, la Figure de L'Éclaireur," Alternatives Citoyennes (March 14, 2005), http://www.alternatives-citoyennes.sgdg.org/zouhair.html (accessed May 25, 2011).
86. "Reveil Tunisien après 10 Ans." Reveil Tunisien (May 18, 2011), http://www.reveiltunisien.org/spip.php?breve4018 (accessed June 6, 2011).
87. Interview with Hasni, May 31, 2011.
88. Ibid.
89. T.I.Z., "Opposant: Un Métier à Temps Plein!" Reveil Tunisien (May 21, 2003), http://www.reveiltunisien.org/spip.php?article607 (accessed June 6, 2011).
90. Interview with Hasni, May 31, 2011.
91. Ibid.
92. Ibid.
93. Interview with Ghassen Ben Khelifa, Tunis, July 30, 2011; and interview with Haythem El Mekki, Tunis, April 24, 2014.
94. Olfa Lamloum, "Entretien avec Tunisnews," in *La Tunisie de Ben Ali: La Société Contre le Régime*, ed. Olfa Lamloum and Bernard Ravenel (Paris: L'Harmattan, 2002), 249.

95. Ibid., 250.
96. Larbi Chouikha, "Un Cyberespace Autonome dans un Espace Autoritaire: Le Cas de Tunisnews," in *Les Médias en Méditerranée: Le Pouvoir de Penser les Relations Internationals*, ed. Khadija Mohsen-Finan (Paris: Actes Sud, 2009), 217–35.
97. Ibid.
98. Lamloum, "Entretien avec Tunisnews," 250.
99. Chouikha, "Un Cyberespace Autonome dans un Espace Autoritaire," 217–35.
100. Ibid.
101. Ibid.
102. Larbi Chouikha, "Pluralisme Politique et Presse d'Opposition sous Bourguiba," in *Habib Bourguiba: La Trace et L'Héritage*, ed. Michel Camau and Vincent Geisser (Paris: Karthala, 2004), 341–55.
103. Aly Zmerli, *Ben Ali le Ripou* (2011), http://kapitalis.com/fokus/62-national/2522-tunisie-ben-ali-les-annees-bonheur-les-annees-labeur.html (accessed June 1, 2011), 51.
104. Rachid Khechana, "Les Médias Tunisiens Face à la Prépondérance de l'État Partisan," *Confluences Méditerranée* 69 (2009), 99–105.
105. Chouikha, "Un Cyberespace Autonome dans un Espace Autoritaire," 217–35.
106. Ibid.
107. Interview with Ismail Dbara, Tunis, July 4, 2011.
108. Interview with Sami Ben Gharbia, Tunis, June 27, 2011.
109. Angela Charlton, "Tunisian Bloggers Win Online Media Award," *Washington Post*, March 11, 2011, http://www.washingtonpost.com/wp-dyn/content/article/2011/03/11/AR2011031102643.html (accessed March 7, 2011).
110. Interview with Sami Ben Gharbia, Tunis, January 27, 2012.
111. Hélène Puel, "Astrubal: La Revolution en Tunisie aurait eu Lieu sans Internet," *La Sentinelle de Tunisie* (March 11, 2011), http://www.01net.com/editorial/529946/astrubal-la-revolution-en-tunisie-aurait-eu-lieu-sans-internet/ (accessed February 9, 2012).
112. Sami Ben Gharbia, "Digital Activism: Arabs Can Do It Themselves," in *Perspectives II: People's Power—The Arab World in Revolt*, ed. Layla Al-Zubaidi et al. (Beirut: Heinrich Böll Stiftung, 2011), 86, http://www.boell.de/downloads/Perspectives_02-13_Interview_with_Sami_Ben_Gharbia.pdf (accessed March 12, 2012).
113. Sami Ben Gharbia, *Borj Erroumi*, http://samibengharbia.com/borj-erroumi-xl (accessed November 15, 2011).
114. Interview with Astrubal, Tunis, June 27, 2011.
115. "The Keyboard Revolution," Nawaat (August 30, 2005), http://nawaat.org/portail/2005/08/30/the-keyboard-revolution/ (accessed March 3, 2011).
116. Meryem Marzouki and Rikke Frank Jørgensen, "Human Rights: The Missing Link," in *Visions in Process II: The World Summit on the Information Society*, edited by Olga Drossou and Heike Jensen, 17-23. Berlin: Heinrich Böll Stiftung, 2005; Meryem Marzouki, "WSIS in Tunisia: The Reign of the Arbitrary," *Third World Resurgence Magazine* no. 184 (December 2005), http://www.twn.my/title2/twr184.htm (accessed June 8, 2011).
117. "Open Letter to Kofi Annan," (October 1, 2005), http://www.worldsummit2003.de/en/web/21.htm (accessed March 23, 2011).
118. Labidi, "No Place to Talk about Internet Freedom."
119. "International Fact-Finding Mission: Tunisia and the World Summit on Information Society," FIDH, OMCT & ICHRDD Report No. 418.2 (May 2005), http://www.fidh.org/IMG/pdf/tn418a.pdf (accessed January 31, 2012).
120. "Launching the 'Freedom of Expression in Mourning' Campaign," (October 3, 2005), http://tounis.blogspot.com (accessed October 27, 2011).
121. See www.yezzi.org and http://www.tounis.blogspot.com (accessed February 6, 2012).
122. "Launching the 'Freedom of Expression in Mourning' Campaign."

123. Ibid.
124. Interview with Sami Ben Gharbia, Tunis, June 27, 2011.
125. See http://tounis.blogspot.com/2005/10/freedom-of-expression-in-mourning-la_03 .html (accessed March 17, 2011); Rebecca Mackinnon, "Tunisian Online Protest Blocked," Global Voices (October 4, 2005), http://globalvoicesonline.org/2005/10/04/tunisian-online-protest-blocked/ (accessed March 17, 2011).
126. Neila Charchour Hachicha, "Yezzi...Fock," Nawaat (October 3, 2005), http://nawaat .org/portail/2005/10/03/yezzi-fock-nch (accessed October 28 2011).
127. "Communiqué du 1er Novembre 2005," http://www.tounis.blogspot.com (accessed October 27, 2011).
128. Interview with Sami Ben Gharbia, Tunis, January 27, 2012.
129. "Launching the 'Freedom of Expression in Mourning' Campaign."
130. "Seuls les Résultas Comptent," Nawaat (December 20, 2005), http://nawaat.org/portail/2005/12/20/seuls-les-resultats-comptent/ (accessed March 19, 2011).
131. "Tunisians Demonstrate Online Instead of Taking to the Streets," CNN (October 6, 2005), http://nawaat.org/portail/2005/10/06/tunisiens-manifestent-sur-internet/ (accessed May 17, 2011); Faisal Al Kassim, "The Internet as a Safety Valve," *Behind the News Program*, Al Jazeera Arabic Channel (October 14, 2005), http://www.aljazeera .net/NR/exeres/EB218269-F269-4B15-A1D2-0D71F34A8256.htm (accessed March 17, 2011); Fahmi Houeidi, "The Crisis of Freedom in the Arab World: Tunisia as a Model," *Al Sharq Al Awsat*, November 23, 2005, http://www.aawsat.com/leader.asp?section=3&article=334808&issueno=9857 (accessed March 22, 2012).
132. Zine El Abidine Ben Ali, "Statement from the President of the Republic of Tunisia at the World Summit on the Information Society" (November 16, 2005), www.itu.int/wsis/tunis/statements/docs/g-tunisia-opening/1.doc (accessed February 11, 2012).
133. "General Disappointment in WSIS-Host Tunisia," Digital Civil Rights in Europe (November 21, 2005), http://www.edri.org/edrigram/number3.23/Tunisia (accessed March 23, 2011).
134. Malek Khadraoui, "Interview avec Malek Khadraoui: Un Blogeur-Militant" (December 6, 2011), http://capharnaum-tremens.blogspot.com/2011/12/malek-khadraoui-blogueur-militant-la.html (accessed February 9, 2012).
135. Interview with Sami Ben Gharbia, Tunis, January 27, 2012.
136. Sami Ben Gharbia, "Second Arab Bloggers Meeting," *Global Voices*, December 5, 2009, http://advocacy.globalvoicesonline.org/2009/12/05/2nd-arab-bloggers-meeting/ (accessed December 16, 2012).
137. See http://nawaat.org/tunisianprisonersmap/ (accessed November 25, 2011).
138. Sami Ben Gharbia, "Tunisian Prison Map" (September 29, 2006), http://ifikra.wordpress.com/2006/09/29/en-tunisian-prisons-map/ (accessed November 24, 2011).
139. Sameer Padania, "Tunisia: Opening Prisons to the World," Global Voices (September 27, 2006), http://globalvoicesonline.org/2006/09/27/tunisia-opening-prisons-to-the-world/ (accessed July 2, 2011).
140. Brannon Cullum, "Maptivism: Mapping Information for Advocacy and Activism," (September 29, 2009), http://www.movements.org/blog/entry/maptivism-mapping-for-advocacy-and-activism/ (accessed December 16, 2012).
141. See http://www.dailymotion.com/video/x2uv4a_tunisie-avion-presidentiel-a-quoi-e_news (accessed April 6, 2012); Astrubal, "Tunisie: Qui Utilise l'Avion de la Présidence de la République Tunisienne?" (August 29, 2007), http://www.dailymotion.com/video/x2uv4a_tunisie-avion-presidentiel-a-quoi-e_news (accessed May 4, 2012); "Caught in the Net: Tunisia's First Lady," *Foreign Policy* (December 13, 2007), http://www.foreignpolicy.com/articles/2007/12/13/caught_in_the_net_tunisias_first_lady (accessed May 4, 2012).

142. Sami Ben Gharbia, "The Internet Freedom Fallacy and the Arab Digital Activism," Nawaat (September 17, 2010), http://nawaat.org/portail/2010/09/17/the-internet-freedom-fallacy-and-the-arab-digital-activism/ (accessed April 4, 2011).
143. Interview with Astrubal, Tunis, June 27, 2011.

Chapter 5

1. Alex Bruns and Joanne Jacobs, eds., *Uses of Blogs* (New York: Peter Lang, 2006), 6.
2. Davis Beer, "Power through the Algorithm: Participatory Web Cultures and the Technological Unconscious," *New Media and Society* 11, no. 6 (2009): 986.
3. Michel Foucault, "A Preface to Transgression," in *Language, Counter-Memory, Practice: Selected Essays and Interviews*, ed. Donald F. Bouchard (Ithaca: Cornell University Press, 1980), 34–36.
4. Samia Mihoub, "Internet en Tunisie: Régulation, Usages et Conflits Émergents," *Horizons Maghrebins* 62 (2010): 109.
5. Marc Lynch, "Blogging the New Arab Public," *Arab Media and Society* 1 (2007), http://www.marclynch.com/wp-content/uploads/2011/03/20070312155027_AMS1_Marc_Lynch.pdf (accessed October 6, 2010).
6. Melissa Y. Lerner, "Connecting the Actual with the Virtual: The Internet and Social Movement Theory in the Muslim World," *Journal of Muslim Minority Affairs* 30, no. 4 (2010): 555–74.
7. Interview with Houssein Ben Ameur, June 19, 2011.
8. David D. Perlmutter, *Blogwars* (Oxford: Oxford University Press, 2008), 66.
9. Tourya Guaaybess, *Les Médias Arabes: Confluences Médiatiques et Dynamique Sociale* (Paris: CNRS Éditions, 2011), 189.
10. Interview with Houssein Ben Ameur, June 19, 2011.
11. Bruce Etling et al., "Mapping the Arabic Blogosphere: Politics, Culture and Dissent," Berkman Center Research Publication No. 2009–6 (June 2009), http://cyber.law.harvard.edu/sites/cyber.law.harvard.edu/files/Mapping_the_Arabic_Blogosphere_0.pdf (accessed March 21, 2011), 3; Jeffrey Ghannam, "Social Media in the Arab World: Leading up to the Uprisings of 2011" (February 3, 2011), http://cima.ned.org/publications/social-media-arab-world-leading-uprisings-2011- 0 (accessed February 26, 2012).
12. "Bloggers May Be the Real Opposition: How the Authorities Are Being Nettled," *The Economist* (April 12, 2007), http://www.economist.com/node/9010890 (accessed June 17, 2012).
13. Mihoub, "Internet en Tunisie," 108.
14. Rym Chebbi, "Communité en Ligne et Nouvelles Formes de Liens Sociaux: Étude de Cas de la Blogosphere Tunisienne," in *Les Nouvelles Sociabilités du Net en Méditerranée* (Paris: Karthala, 2012), 63–74.
15. Alexander Halavais, "Blogging as a Free Frame of Reference," in *The Participatory Cultures Handbook*, ed. Aaron Delwiche and Jennifer Jacobs Henderson (London: Routledge, 2013), 115.
16. Interview with Houssein Ben Ameur, June 19, 2011.
17. Albrecht Hofheinz, "The Internet in the Arab World: Playground for Political Liberalization," *Internationale Politik und Gesellschaft* (March 2005): 93.
18. Hédi Ben Ismail, "Massacre sur la Toile," *Attariq Al Jadid*, August 21, 2010, http://blogamiattariq.blogspot.com/2011/10/massacre-sur-la-toile.html (accessed February 8, 2012).
19. Albrecht Hofheinz, "Arab Internet User: Popular Trends and Public Impact," in *Arab Media and Political Renewal: Community, Legitimacy and Public Life*, ed. Naomi Sakr (London: IB Tauris, 2007), 78.

20. Interview with Houssein Ben Ameur, June 19, 2011.
21. Afraa Ahmed Albabtain, "Downloading Democracy: Bloggers in the Gulf," *Arab Insight* 2, no. 2 (Summer 2008): 55.
22. Among the more visible blogs and active bloggers one could note, for instance, Antikor, Arabasta, Arabicca, Astrubal, Aswat wa Soubol, Azwaw, Barbach, Bent Ayla, Big Trap Boy, Brastos, Carpe Diem, Chanfara, Clandestino, Cosmauxpolis, Débat Tunisie, Eddouaaji, Extravaganza, Fikra, Free Thought, Free Race, HouHou Blog, Khil ou Lil, Kissa Online, L'As Number One, Le Gouverneur de Normalland, Lina Ben Mhenni, Mayadeen, Mon Massir, Nocturnal Thoughts, Nofrage, Sami Ben Gharbia, Samsoum, Sofiene Chourabi, Stupeur, Taht El Yessmina Fil Lil, Tarek Cheniti, Tarek Kahlaoui, Titof, Tunisia Watch, Tunisian Girl, Wallada, Werewolf, Zizou from Djerba, and -Z-.
23. Interview with Fatma Arabicca, Tunis, June 30, 2011.
24. Interview with Barbach, Nabeul, July 7, 2011. See also Barbach, "The Story of a Blogger... Three Years On" (November 22, 2010), http://tbarbich.blogspot.com/2010/11/blog-post.html (accessed June 13, 2011).
25. See http://yatounes.blogspot.com/2010/02/blog-post_23.html, http://www.tunisiens-dumonde.com/, http://talfza-bel-malwene.blogspot.com/, http://boudourou.blogspot.com/, http://laicstunisiens.blogspot.com/, and http://anti-tabour-5.blogspot.com (accessed May 20, 2011).
26. See http://radyountounes.blogspot.com/ (accessed May 20, 2011).
27. Interview with Tarek Kahlaoui, Tunis, July 13, 2011.
28. Charles Hirschkind, *The Ethical Soundscape: Cassette Sermons and Islamic Counter Publics* (New York: Columbia University Press, 2006).
29. Samia Mihoub, "Le Cyberactivism à l'Heure de la Révolution Tunisenne," *Archivio Anthropologico Mediterraneo* 12, no. 2 (2011): 18–19; Arab Network for Human Rights Information, "The Internet in the Arab World: A New Space of Repression" (2004), http://www.anhri.net/en/reports/net2004/ (accessed October 9, 2011).
30. Astrubal, "Tunisie: Retour sur les Échanges Zied El Heni," *Nawaat* (September 25, 2008), http://astrubal.nawaat.org/2008/09/25/tunisie-retour-sur-les-echanges-zied-el-heniaymen-rezgui-sur-canal-du-dialogue-tunisien/ (accessed June 16, 2011).
31. Ibid.
32. Sami Ben Gharbia, "Blogs Tunisiens: Des Zones Touristiques!" (December 21, 2005), http://samibengharbia.com/2005/12/20/blogs-tunisiens-des-zones-touristiques/ (accessed November 2, 2011).
33. Ibid.
34. Nasnousa, quoted in Sami Ben Gharbia, "Blogging Tunisia: Whisper!" *Global Voices*, October 5, 2006, http://globalvoicesonline.org/2006/10/05/blogging-tunisia-whisper/ (accessed February 3, 2012).
35. Elyssa, "Comment on Sami Ben Gharbia's 'Blogs Tunisiens'" (December 21, 2005), http://samibengharbia.com/2005/12/20/blogs-tunisiens-des-zones-touristiques/ (accessed November 2, 2011).
36. Al Ansari, "Comment on Sami Ben Gharbia's 'Blogs Tunisiens'" (December 24, 2005), http://samibengharbia.com/2005/12/20/blogs-tunisiens-des-zones-touristiques/ (accessed November 2, 2011).
37. See, for instance, Djbouzz, "Comment on Sami Ben Gharbia's 'Blogs Tunisiens'" (December 23, 2005), http://samibengharbia.com/2005/12/20/blogs-tunisiens-des-zones-touristiques/ (accessed November 2, 2011); Just an Illusion, "Comment on Sami Ben Gharbia's 'Blogs Tunisiens'" (December 23, 2005), http://samibengharbia.com/2005/12/20/blogs-tunisiens-des-zones-touristiques/ (accessed November 2, 2011).
38. Infinity, "Comment on Sami Ben Gharbia's 'Blogs Tunisiens'" (December 21, 2005), http://samibengharbia.com/2005/12/20/blogs-tunisiens-des-zones-touristiques/ (accessed November 2, 2011).

39. Big Trap Boy, "The Tunisian Blogosphere and the Unspoken" (October 1, 2006), http://trapboy.blogspot.com/2006/10/la-blogosphre-tunisienne-et-ceux-dont.html (accessed June 11, 2011).

40. Infinity, "Comment on Sami Ben Gharbia's 'Blogs Tunisiens.'"

41. Mihoub, "Internet en Tunisie," 108.

42. Rose de Sable, "Comments" (August 21, 2008), http://www.marhba.com/forums/actualites-3/que-pensez-vous-blogs-tunisiens-32642.html (accessed June 14, 2011).

43. Big Trap Boy, "Action Speaks Louder than Words" (May 9, 2007), http://trapboy.blogspot.com/2007/05/blog-post_09.html (accessed November 17, 2011); Big Trap Boy, "Le 1er Juin: Je Blogue pour un Maghreb Uni" (May 9, 2007), http://trapboy.blogspot.com/2007/05/le-1er-juin-je-blogue-pour-le-maghreb.html (accessed November 17, 2011).

44. See http://maghreb.coolbb.net (accessed November 17, 2011).

45. Big Trap Boy, "Maghreb Blogging Day: Liste des Participants" (June 5, 2007), http://trapboy.blogspot.com/2007/06/maghreb-blogging-day-liste-des.html (accessed November 17, 2011).

46. Sami Ben Gharbia, "I Blog for Tunisia, against the Maghreb" (June 1, 2007), http://samibengharbia.com/tag/blogsphere/page/2/ (accessed November 17, 2011).

47. Samsoum, "Comment on Sami Ben Gharbia's 'I Blog for Tunisia, against the Maghreb'" (June 7, 2007), http://samibengharbia.com/tag/blogsphere/page/2/ (accessed November 17, 2011).

48. Mazen, "Comment on Sami Ben Gharbia's 'I Blog for Tunisia.'"

49. Interview with Carpe Diem, July 19, 2011.

50. Tarek Kahlaoui, "The Prospects of Democracy in the Arab World: A Historical Perspective," *Middle East Online* (September 27, 2007), http://www.middle-east-online.com/?id=52912 (accessed December 19, 2011).

51. Samsoum, "Je Blogue pour la Liberté de la Parole" (July 9, 2007), http://samsoum-us.blogspot.com/2007/06/je-blogue-pour-la-libert-de-la-parole.html (accessed December 17, 2011); Samsoum, "First of July: I Blog for the Freedom of Expression" (June 12, 2007), http://samsoum-us.blogspot.com/2007/06/le-1er-juillet-je-blogue-pour-la-libert.html (July 12, 2007) (accessed May 28, 2011).

52. Samsoum, "Liberté d'Expression" (June 10, 2007), http://samsoum-us.blogspot.com/2007/06/libert-dexpression.html (accessed May 26, 2011).

53. Tarek Kahlaoui, "Comments on Al Hiwar TV's Report on Tunisian Bloggers" (July 20, 2007), http://tareknightlife.blogspot.com/2007/10/1.html (accessed May 26, 2011).

54. Tarek Kahlaoui, "Do We Need Democracy?" (July 9, 2007), http://tareknightlife.blogspot.com/2007/06/blog-post_09.html (accessed December 17, 2011); See also Tarek Kahlaoui, "The Prospects of Democracy in the Arab World: A Historical Perspective," *Middle East Online* (September 27, 2007), http://www.middle-east-online.com/?id=52912 (accessed December 19, 2011).

55. Tarek Kahlaoui, "Political Freedom of Expression and the Politicization of the Freedom of Speech" (June 11, 2007), http://tareknightlife.blogspot.com/2007/06/blog-post_2973.html (accessed December 17, 2011).

56. Tarek Kahlaoui, "Reflecting on Democracy and Fighting for It" (June 17, 2011), http://tareknightlife.blogspot.com/2007/06/blog-post_9196.html (accessed December 18, 2011).

57. Kahlaoui, "Political Freedom of Expression and the Politicization of the Freedom of Speech."

58. Tarek Kahlaoui, "Summer Reflections" (July 27, 2007), http://tareknightlife.blogspot.com/2007/07/blog-post.html (accessed December 18, 2011).

59. Interview with Tarek Kahlaoui, Tunis, July 13, 2011.

60. Tarek Kahlaoui, "Comments on Al Hiwar TV's Report on Tunisian Bloggers" (July 20, 2007), http://tareknightlife.blogspot.com/2007/10/1.html (accessed May 26, 2011).

61. Free Race, "On That Which Makes You Laugh" (July 23, 2008), http://www.free-race
.blogspot.ca/2008/07/blog-post_23.html (accessed June 13, 2011).
62. Tarek Kahlaoui, "The Tunisian Blogosphere: A New Horizon" (November 11, 2009),
http://tareknightlife.blogspot.com/2009/11/blog-post_7663.html (accessed March 6,
2012).
63. For reactions to these exchanges, see Tarek Kahlaoui, "Who Is Islamophobic?" (June 6, 2008),
http://tareknightlife.blogspot.com/2009/06/blog-post_06.html (accessed December
18, 2012); Chanfara, "To Achour Al Neji" (June 12, 2008), http://chanfara.blogspot
.com/2008/06/blog-post_12.html (accessed December 18, 2012).
64. See, for instance, "Je Blog pour l'Islam: L'Islam et Moi" (June 15, 2008), http://toreach-
thegoal.blogspot.com/2008/06/je-blog-pour-lislam-lislam-et-moi.html (accessed June
17, 2011).
65. Free Race, "On That Which Makes You Laugh."
66. Free Race, "The Blogosphere Is Fevered" (June 22, 2008), http://www.free-race
.blogspot.com/2008_06_01_archive.html (accessed June 13, 2011).
67. Tarek Kahlaoui, "How Tunisian Bloggers Reacted to the Arrest of Fatma Arabicca"
Magharebia (November 17, 2009), http://www.magharebia.com/cocoon/awi/
xhtml1/ar/features/awi/blog/2009/11/17/feature-05 (accessed March 19, 2011);
Tarek Kahlaoui, "When the Debate Digresses" (March 11, 2008), http://tareknightlife.
blogspot.com/2008/03/blog-post_11.html (accessed December 19, 2011).
68. For a revealing post that discusses Islamophobia and the problems of argumentation on
the blogosphere, see Tarek Kahlaoui, "Who Is Islamophobic?" (June 6, 2008), http://
tareknightlife.blogspot.com/2009/06/blog-post_06.html (accessed December 18,
2012).
69. Kahlaoui, "How Tunisian Bloggers Reacted to the Arrest of Fatma Arabicca."
70. Interview with Fatma Arabicca, Tunis, June 30, 2011.
71. Carpe Diem, "Propagande 2.0" (December 20, 2008), http://carpediem-selim.blogspot
.com/2008/12/propagande-20.html (accessed June 19, 2011).
72. Stupeur, "Is the Tunisian Blogosphere Dying?" (June 5, 2009), http://blog.kochlef
.com/2009/06/05/dying-blogosphere/ (accessed June 19, 2011); Tarek Kahlaoui, "To
the Blogger Ehmida" (November 15, 2009), http://tareknightlife.blogspot.com/2009/
11/blog-post_15.html (accessed January 3, 2012).
73. M.B.H., "Tunisie: Facebook Bat de Nouveaux Records," *Tekiano* (October 13, 2009),
http://www.tekiano.com/net/web20/2-70-1196/tunisie-facebook-bat-de-nouveaux-
records.html (accessed March 12, 2011).
74. Free Race, "The Blogosphere Is Fevered."
75. Ibid.
76. Stupeur, "Is the Tunisian Blogosphere Dying?"
77. Chanfara, "On Religion and Other Related Matters" (June 17, 2008), http://chanfara
.blogspot.com/2008/06/blog-post_17.html (accessed June 13, 2011).
78. Chanfara, "Freedom" (July 2, 2008), http://chanfara.blogspot.com/2008/07/blog-
post.html (accessed June 13, 2011).
79. Chanfara, "To Ammar" (October 28, 2008), http://chanfara.blogspot.com/2008/10/
blog-post_195.html (accessed June 13, 2011).
80. Interview with Fatma Arabicca, Tunis, June 30, 2011.
81. Interview with Carpe Diem, July 19, 2011.
82. Ibid.
83. Fatma Arabicca, "Dommage" (November 6, 2009), http://fatmaarabicca.blogspot
.com/2010/06/dommage.html (accessed February 8, 2012).
84. Interview with Carpe Diem, July 19, 2011.
85. Guobin Yang, *The Power of the Internet in China: Citizen Activism Online* (New York:
Columbia University Press, 2011), 58.

86. James C. Scott, *Domination and the Arts of Resistance: Hidden Transcripts* (New Haven: Yale University Press, 1990), 15.

87. See Kissa Online, "The Centenary of Abou Al Kacen Chebbi" (February 23, 2009), http://kissa-online.blogspot.com/2009/02/blog-post_23.html (accessed May 12, 2011); Kissa Online, "The Tree" (September 18, 2009), http://kissa-online.blogspot.com/2009/09/pablo-neruda-larbre.html (accessed May 12, 2011); and "For the Youth to Laugh" (September 3, 2009), http://kissa-online.blogspot.com/2009/09/blog-post.html (accessed May 12, 2011).

88. Tarek Kahlaoui, "Selections from Gabriel García Márquez's *The Autumn of the Patriarch*" (December 14, 2007), http://tarek-kahlaoui404.blogspot.com/2007/12/blog-post_9183.html (accessed May 12, 2012).

89. George Orwell, "Funny, but Not Vulgar," http://orwell.ru/library/articles/funny/english/e_funny (accessed December 20, 2012).

90. Free Race, "On the Culture of Funnels" (June 13, 2007), http://free-race.blogspot.com/2007/06/la-culture-de-lentonnoir.html (accessed May 30, 2012).

91. Free Race, "On the Question of Law Enforcement" (June 7, 2007), http://free-race.blogspot.com/2007/06/blog-post_07.html (accessed June 30, 2012).

92. Michel de Certeau, *The Practice of Everyday Life*, trans. Steven Rendall (Berkeley: University of California Press, 1984), xiii.

93. Béatrice Hibou, *The Force of Obedience: The Political Economy of Repression in Tunisia*, trans. Andrew Brown (Cambridge: Polity, 2011), 14–16.

94. Mikhail Bakhtin, *Rabelais and His World*, trans. Hélène Iswolsky (Bloomington: Indiana University Press, 1984), 21.

95. Free Race, "Non-Urgent News" (June 3, 2007), http://free-race.blogspot.com/2007/06/blog-post_03.html (accessed June 30, 2012).

96. Afraa Ahmed Albabtain, "Downloading Democracy: Bloggers in the Gulf," *Arab Insight* 2, no. 2 (Summer 2008): 62.

97. Interview with Carpe Diem, July 19, 2011.

98. Ibid.

99. See http://pourgafsa5.blogspot.com/ (accessed May 30, 2013).

100. Ben Gharbia, "Silencing Online Free Speech"; "Digital Battle between Authorities and Bloggers."

101. Fatma Arabicca's blog is http://fatma-arabicca.blogspot.com (accessed March 16, 2011).

102. -Z-, "Jacques Doucinaud Sauve la Tunisie," Débat Tunisie (November 6, 2009), http://www.debatunisie.com/archives/2009/11/06/15699298.html (accessed February 7, 2012).

103. -Z-, "Nous Sommes Tous Fatma!" Débat Tunisie (November 6, 2009), http://www.debatunisie.com/archives/2009/11/06/15709603.html (accessed February 7, 2012).

104. See "Freedom to Fatma Arabicca," http://www.facebook.com/photo.php?fbid=103806709635814&set=o.171535170769&type=1&theater (accessed November 24, 2011).

105. Azwaw, "Fatma Arabicca: Une Femme Libre Hors du Commun, mais qui Derange" (November 6, 2009), http://azwaw.net/2009/11/06/fatma-arabicca-une-femme-libre-hors-du-commun-mais-qui-derange/ (accessed February 6, 2012).

106. Ibid.

107. Tarek Kahlaoui, "Arabicca and -Z-" (November 5, 2009), http://tareknightlife.blogspot.com/2009/11/blog-post_4092.html (accessed January 2, 2012).

108. See http://freearabicca.wordpress.com, http://freearabicca.wordpress.com/ils-en-parlent/, and http://www.facebook.com/group.php?gid=171535170769&v=info (accessed November 10, 2012).

109. "Tunisian Authorities Continue to Suppress Bloggers," The Arabic Network for Human Rights Information (November 9, 2009), http://old.openarab.net/en/node/1548 (accessed November 24, 2011).

110. "Tunisian Blogger Detained," Aljazeera.net (November 7, 2009), http://www.aljazeera.com/news/africa/2009/11/2009117751273306.html (accessed December 11, 2012).

111. Meris Lutz, "Tunisia: Online Activist Rally to Free Fellow Blogger," *Los Angeles Times*, November 6, 2009, http://latimesblogs.latimes.com/babylonbeyond/2009/11/tunisia-blogger-fatma-riahi-arrested-held-incommunicado.html (accessed December 11, 2012).

112. Lina Ben Mhenni, "Comité de Protection des Blogueurs Tunisiens" (October 14, 2010), http://atunisiangirl.blogspot.com/2010/10/le-comite-de-protection-des-blogeurs.html (accessed January 17, 2012).

113. Ismail Dbara, "The Arrest of Fatma Arabicca Preoccupies Tunisian Bloggers on Their National Day," *Al Hayat* (November 23, 2009), http://international.daralhayat.com/internationalarticle/79189 (accessed November 24, 2011).

Chapter 6

1. Sihem Ben Sedrine, "Tunisie Internet: La Navigation sous Haute Surveillance," *Kalima Tunisie*, October 3, 2001, www.kalima-tunisie.info/magazine/mum1/index3.htm (accessed June 1, 2011).

2. Samia Mihoub, "Internet en Tunisie: Régulation, Usages et Conflits Émergents," *Horizons Maghrebins* 62 (2010): 33.

3. Jean-Philippe Bras, "Internet au Maroc et en Tunisie: Entre Réglementation et Régulation," in *Le Maghreb dans L'Économie Numérique* (Paris: Maisonneuve, 2007), 163–80.

4. "False Freedom: Online Censorship in the Middle East and North Africa," Human Rights Watch (November 15, 2005), http://www.hrw.org/reports/2005/11/14/false-freedom (accessed February 14, 2012), 98.

5. Michel Foucault, *Discipline and Punish: The Birth of the Prison* (New York: Vintage, 1979), 205. See also James Boyle, "Foucault in Cyberspace: Surveillance, Sovereignty and Hardwired Censors," *University of Cincinnati Law Review* 66 (1997): 177–205.

6. Samia Mihoub, "La Question de l'Internet Arabe ou Quand les États se Trompent de Cible," *Africultures* (April 10, 2008), http://www.africultures.com/php/?nav=article&no=7494 (accessed February 10, 2012).

7. "Enemies of the Internet: Countries under Surveillance," Reporters Without Borders (March 12, 2010), 30, en.rsf.org/IMG/pdf/Internet_enemies.pdf (accessed 23 May 2012).

8. "Tunisia: Internal Exile Used to Silence Dissent," Human Rights Watch (February 1, 2005), http://www.hrw.org/en/news/2005/01/31/tunisia-internal-exile-used-silence-dissident (accessed June 30, 2012).

9. Arab Network for Human Rights Information, "The Internet in the Arab World: A New Space of Repression" (2004), http://www.anhri.net/en/reports/net2004/ (accessed October 9, 2011).

10. Béatrice Hibou, *The Force of Obedience: The Political Economy of Repression in Tunisia*, trans. Andrew Brown (Cambridge: Polity, 2011), 81.

11. Gurdrun Wacker, "The Internet and Censorship in China," in *China and the Internet: Politics of the Digital Leap Forward*, ed. Christopher R. Hughes and Gudrun Wacker (London: Routledge, 2003), 67–73.

12. Foucault, *Discipline and Punish*, 200.

13. Jean-Pierre Filiu, *The Arab Revolution: Ten Lessons from the Democratic Uprising* (London: Hurst & Company, 2011), 46.

14. Tim Jordan, *Internet, Society and Culture: Communicative Practices Before and After the Internet* (New York: Bloomsbury, 2013), 88.

15. "False Freedom," 107.

16. Mihoub, "La Question de L'Internet Arabe ou Quand les États se Trompent de Cible."

17. The Arab Network for Human Rights Information, "The Internet in the Arab World: A New Space of Repression" (2004), http://www.anhri.net/en/reports/net2004/ (accessed October 9, 2011).

18. In a few cases, the authorities detained individuals for accessing certain Internet sites. See "False Freedom"; Zouheir Makhlouf, "Cyberspace under the Thumb of the Police," in *Tunisian Journalists Standing up to Dictatorship* (Tunis: Tunis Center for Press Freedom, 2013), 123–49.

19. Loubna Hanna Skalli, "Youth, Media and the Art of Protest in North Africa," in *Mediating the Arab Uprisings*, ed. Adel Iskandar and Bassam Haddad (Washington, D.C.: Tadween, 2013), 55.

20. Larbi Chouikha, "Autoritarisme Étatique et Débrouillardise Individuelle," in *La Tunisie de Ben Ali: La Société Contre le Régime*, ed. Olfa Lamloum and Bernard Ravenel (Paris: L'Harmattan, 2002).

21. Romain Lecomte, "L'Amonymat Comme Art de Résistance: Le Cas du Cyberespace Tunisien," *Terminal* 105 (2010): 64–66.

22. Ibid., 66.

23. Interview with Kerim Bouzouita, Tunis, June 20, 2011.

24. Walid Al Saqaf, "Circumventing Internet Censorship in the Arab World," in *Liberation Technology: Social Media and the Struggle for Democracy*, ed. Larry Diamond and Marc Plattner (Baltimore: The Johns Hopkins University Press, 2012), 134.

25. Lina Ben Mhenni, "The White Note Campaign against Cyber Censorship," Global Voices (December 30, 2009), http://globalvoicesonline.org/2009/12/30/tunisia-the-white-note-campaign-against-cyber-censorship/ (accessed March 19, 2011); Sofiene Chourabi, "Tunisian Bloggers to Hold a Non-Blogging Day" (December 21, 2007), http://www.aafaq.org/news.aspx?id_news=3528 (accessed March 3, 2011).

26. Interview with Tarek Kahlaoui, Tunis, July 13, 2011.

27. On Action Blank Post, see http://www.facebook.com/group.php?gid=37588326723 (accessed November 16, 2011).

28. Carpe Diem, "Censure" (August 26, 2008), http://blogs.mediapart.fr/blog/carpe-diem/260808/censure (accessed February 11, 2012).

29. Sami Ben Gharbia, "Silencing Online Free Speech in Tunisia," Nawaat (August 18, 2008), http://nawaat.org/portail/2008/08/20/silencing-online-speech-in-tunisia/ (accessed March 19, 2011); see also "Digital Battle between Authorities and Bloggers in Tunisia," Aljazeera.net (August 9, 2008), http://www.aljazeera.net/news/archive/archive?ArchiveId=1096460 (accessed March 19, 2011).

30. Jamel Arfewi, "Facebook Users Launch a New Campaign against Censorship," Magharebia (July 8, 2009), http://www.magharebia.com/cocoon/awi/xhtml1/ar/features/awi/blog/2009/07/08/feature-03 (accessed November 10, 2011).

31. Ismail Dbara, "Internet Censorship in Tunisia Reaps the Wrath of Journalists and Users," Nawaat (June 4, 2008), http://nawaat.org/portail/2008/06/04/online-censorship-angers-journalists-and-users/ (accessed May 16, 2011).

32. Zizou from Djerba, "Il est Temps de Censurer Facebook en Tunisie" (June 2, 2008), http://www.zizoufromdjerba.com/2008/06/il-est-temps-de-censurer-facebook-en.html (accessed December 19, 2011).

33. In 2008, Facebook attracted an estimated 28,000 users. See Jamei Al Gasimi, "Ben Ali Rescues Facebook from Censorship," *Middle East Online* (September 3, 2008), http://www.middle-east-online.com/english/?id=27687 (accessed December 17, 2012).

34. Vernon Silver, "Post-Revolt Tunisia Can Alter E-mail with 'Big Brother' Software," Bloomberg (December 13, 2011), http://www.bloomberg.com/news/2011-12-12/tunisia-after-revolt-can-alter-e-mails-with-big-brother-software.html (accessed February 11, 2012).

35. The Man Who Sold the World, "Comment on Free Race's 'It is a Matter of Reputation.'"

36. "Tous Solidaires: Non à la Fermeture de Facebook en Tunisie," http://facebook.com/group.php?gid=32550875030 (accessed November 11, 2012).

37. Djeneba Manfila, "Facebook Censuré en Tunisie," *Afrik* (August 28, 2008), http://www.afrik.com/article15084.html (accessed June 11, 2012).

38. Asma El Bakkouch, "Is Facebook Innocent?" *Al Hadath*, January 28, 2009; Tarek El Boughanmi, "How Facebook Invaded Every Circle ... and What Tunisians Use It For," *Al Bayan*, January 29, 2009, 3; Samir El Wafi, "The Facebook Virus," *Assarih*, January 31, 2009.

39. See "Si on me Coupe Facebook je Résilie mon Contrat avec mon Fournisseur Internet," http://fr-fr.facebook.com/events/27877300142/ (accessed February 6, 2012).

40. Ibid.

41. Ibid.

42. Khalil Khalsi, "'Error 404 Not Found: 28 Mille Facebookers Tunisiens Privés d'Accès à leur Site Préféré," *Le Temps* (September 1, 2008), http://anticensuretounes.blogspot.com/2008/09/28-mille-facebookers-tunisiens-privs.html (accessed May 27, 2011).

43. "Facebook: Intervention du Président de la République," *Le Temps*, September 3, 2008, http://www.letemps.com.tn/article.php?ID_art=19890 (accessed February 7, 2012).

44. Borhen Bsayess, "The Other Dimension: On Monitoring the Internet," *Assabah* (September 25, 2008), http://www.assabah.com.tn/article-14204.html (accessed August 21, 2012). For a reaction to this article, see Carpe Diem, "(Mis)Using the Law to Manage the Internet?" (September 28, 2008), http://carpediem-selim.blogspot.com/2008/09/une-loi-pour-encadrer-la-toile.html (accessed July 17, 2012).

45. Kawther Agrebi, "On Facebook, Groups for Mass Suicide and Devil Worship," *Assabah* (December 24, 2009), http://www.assabah.com.tn/recherche_details-27671.html; Saida Bouhlal, "The Phobia of the Net in Tunisia," *Assabah* (June 12, 2009), http://www.assabah.com.tn/recherche_details-21811.html (accessed August 22, 2012).

46. Arabasta, "My Story with Censorship," (January 17, 2010), http://arabasta1.blogspot.com/2010/01/mon-histoire-avec-la-censure.html (accessed June 13, 2011).

47. Werewolf, "Comment on Tarek Kahlaoui's 'Ammar Censors the Blog Nocturnal Thoughts'" (February 5, 2010), http://tareknightlife.blogspot.com/2010/02/blog-post_05.html (accessed December 17, 2011).

48. Carpe Diem, "Censure."

49. Tarek Kahlaoui, "Internet Control: Censoring Censorship," Nawaat (October 28, 2010), http://nawaat.org/portail/2010/10/28/ (accessed August 23, 2011).

50. So obscure and secretive was censorship that it recalled the Portuguese dictatorship years, when the existence of the office that was responsible for censorship—which became instrumental to António Salaza's rule—could not be mentioned or hinted at. See John D.H. Downing, *Radical Media: The Political Experience of Alternative Media Communication* (Boston: South End, 1984), 171.

51. See, for instance, Bechir, "The Censor Consults a Psychiatrist" (June 21, 2008), http://anticensuretounes.blogspot.com/2008/06/blog-post_6903.html (accessed April 11, 2013).

52. "Notre Article sur la Censure Censuré en Tunisie," France24.com (May 12, 2010), http://observers.france24.com/fr/20100505-404-not-found-message-courant-internet-tunisie-censure-blogs-protestation-pacifique-ammar (accessed January 25, 2012).

53. Astrubal, "Tunisie: Le Scandale de la 403 Maquillée en 404," Nawaat (June 12, 2006), http://nawaat.org/portail/2006/06/13/tunisie-le-scandale-de-la-403-maquillee-en-404/ (accessed March 4, 2011).

54. Free Race, "When the Censor Is Held Accountable" (March 9, 2010), http://www.free-race.blogspot.com/2010/03/blog-post.html (accessed May 29, 2011).

55. Antikor, "Do Speak Ammar" (March 9, 2010), http://antikor.blogspot.com/search/labael/404YonAmmar (accessed February 8, 2012).

56. The Man Who Sold the World, "Comment on Free Race's 'A Foreign Body'" (December 5, 2007), http://free-race.blogspot.com/2007/12/blog-post_02.html?showComment =1196844780000#c2326898256664877731 (accessed June 13, 2011).

57. Baccar Gherib, "Censure sur Internet: Qui est Ammar?" Les Amis d'Attariq (May 14, 2010), http://ahbebattariq.blogspot.com/2010/05/censure-sur-internet-qui-est-ammar .html (accessed June 12, 2011).

58. Antikor, "La 404 YonAmmar" (March 9, 2010), http://antikor.blogspot.com/search/ label/404%20YonAmmar (accessed February 26, 2012).

59. Tarek Kahlaoui, "A Vocal Blog on the Occasion of the National Day for the Freedom of Blogging" (October 12, 2008), http://radyountounes.blogspot.com/2008_10_01_ archive.html (accessed September 18, 2011); Antikor, "La 404 YonAmmar."

60. Kahlaoui, "Internet Control: Censoring Censorship."

61. Ibid.

62. Zied El Heni, "Court Dismisses Case against Internet Agency" (November 27, 2008), http:// journaliste-tunisien-29.blogspot.com/2008/11/blog-post_27.html (accessed November 10, 2011).

63. "Tunisia: Bloggers and Censorship... Mocking Ammar 404, Re-Launching Blogs and Fighting Legal Battles," Magharebia.com (November 5, 2008), http://www.magharebia .com/cocoon/awi/xhtml1/ar/features/awi/features/2008/11/05/feature-01 (accessed November 10, 2011).

64. Astrubal, "Censure, Hypocrisie et Etat de Droit," Nawaat (May 9, 2010), http://nawaat.org/ portail/2010/05/09/censure-hypocrisie-et-etat-de-droit-lettre-ouverte-aux-malentendants/ (accessed February 27, 2011).

65. Ibid.

66. Baccar Gherib, "Mobilisation Contre la Censure sur Internet: De l'Officiel, du Virtuel et du Réel," Nawaat (May 29, 2010), http://nawaat.org/portail/2010/05/29/mobilisation-contre-la-censure-sur-internet-de-l'officiel-du-virtuel-et-du-reel/ (accessed February 8, 2012).

67. Sami Ben Gharbia and Astrubal, "A Glimpse at Internet Filtering in Tunisia," Nawaat (August 18, 2010), http://nawaat.org/portail/2010/08/19/a-first-glimpse-at-the-internet-filtering-in-tunisia/ (accessed June 21, 2011).

68. Helmi Noman and Jillian C. York, "West Censoring East: The Use of Western Technologies by Middle East Censors, 2010–2011," OpenNet Initiative (March 2011), http://opennet.net/west-censoring-east-the-use-western-technologies-middle-east-censors-2010-2011 (accessed December 12, 2012); "Internet Filtering in Tunisia," OpenNet Initiative (November 2005), www. opennet.net/studies/tunisia (accessed March 1, 2011).

69. Vernon Silver, "Post-Revolt Tunisia Can Alter E-mail with 'Big Brother' Software," Bloomberg (December 13, 2011), http://www.bloomberg.com/news/2011-12-12/tuni sia-after-revolt-can-alter-e-mails-with-big-brother-software.html (accessed February 11, 2012).

70. "Tunisian Government Severely Restricts Media Freedoms," Open Source Center (March 4, 2010), http://publicintelligence.net/ufouo-open-source-center-tunisian-government-severely-restricts-media-freedoms/ (accessed June 10, 2011), 5.

71. Hédi Ben Ismail, "Massacre sur la Toile," Attariq Al Jadid, August 21, 2010, http:// blogamiattariq.blogspot.com/2011/10/massacre-sur-la-toile.html (accessed February 8, 2012).

72. Free Thoughts, "An Intellectual Genocide" (April 28, 2008), http://freethoughts-antiguerre.blogspot.com/2010/04/blog-post_28.html (accessed December 17, 2012).

73. Sarra Grira, "Les Cyber Réfugiés en Tunisie: Un Contre-Poids à la Censure de Ammar sur Internet," (February 25, 2010), http://courantalternatif.blogspot.com/2010/02/ les-cyber-refugies-en-tunisie-un-contre.html (accessed June 15, 2011).

74. "Ten Worst Countries to Be a Blogger," Committee to Protect Journalists (2009), http://cpj.org/reports/2009/04/10-worst-countries-to-be-a-blogger.php (accessed May 1, 2012).

75. Arabasta, "Back to Basics" (May 28, 2010), http://arabasta1.blogspot.com/2010/05/back-to-basics-bribes-propos-de-la.html (accessed June 13, 2011).

76. Tarek Kahlaoui, "Ammar Censors the Blog Nocturnal Thoughts" (February 5, 2010), http://tareknightlife.blogspot.com/2010/02/blog-post_05.html (accessed December 18, 2012).

77. -Z-, "Indigestion de Brick au Thon à Carthage," Débat Tunisie (April 29, 2010), http://www.debatunisie.com/archives/2010/04/29/17724823.html (accessed December 23, 2012).

78. Ismail Dbara, "Ammar 404: Indiscriminate Shelling," *Elaph*, February 7, 2010, http://www.elaph.com/Web/opinion/2010/2/531784.html (accessed May 16, 2011).

79. "Enemies of the Internet: Countries under Surveillance," Reporters Without Borders (March 12, 2010), en.rsf.org/IMG/pdf/Internet_enemies.pdf, 29–31.

80. Vincent Geisser, "Les Blagues Tunisiennes: Analyse Socio-Politique," Forum Nokta (October 28, 2001), www.facebook.com/group.php?gid=61012075361, and reproduced on http://cosmauxpolis.com/2007/06/19/humour-satire-et-ironie-l'art-tunisien/ (accessed June 15, 2012).

81. Nasnousa, quoted in Sami Ben Gharbia, "Blogging Tunisia: Whisper!" *Global Voices* (October 5, 2006), http://globalvoicesonline.org/2006/10/05/blogging-tunisia-whisper/ (accessed February 3, 2012).

82. Arabasta, "My Story with Censorship" (January 17, 2010), http://arabasta1.blogspot.com/2010/01/mon-histoire-avec-la-censure.html (accessed June 13, 2011).

83. Kissa Online, "Censorship" (February 9, 2010), http://kissa-online.blogspot.com/2010/02/dico-15.html (accessed June 15, 2011).

84. Kissa Online, "An Attempt against Thought" (May 2, 2010), http://kissa-online.blogspot.com/2010/05/un-attentat-contre-la-pensee.html (accessed June 15, 2011).

85. Kissa Online, "Whenever You See It…You Know There Is Repression" (July 1, 2008), http://kissa-online.blogspot.com/2008/07/blog-post.html (accessed June 15, 2011).

86. Belgacem Ben Abdallah, "Censorship: Another Face of Repression," *Al Badil* (March 3, 2010), http://www.albadil.org/spip.php?article2767 (accessed September 2, 2012).

87. Mokhtar Yahyaoui, quoted in "Tunisie: Le Courage d'Informer." Reporters Without Borders (February 2009), http://fr.rsf.org/tunisie-tunisie-le-courage-d-informer-11-02-2009,30271.html (accessed March 1, 2012).

88. Kahlaoui, "Internet Control: Censoring Censorship."

89. Olfa Youssef, "Lettre Très Objective à Ammar" (May 22, 2010), http://olfayoussef.blogspot.com/2010/05/lettre-tres-objective-ammar.html (accessed May 12, 2011).

90. Gouverneur de Normalland, "The Blogging Movement Says No to Ammar" (December 27, 2010), http://normalland.blogspot.com/2010/12/blog-post_27.html (accessed June 13, 2011).

91. Lina Ben Mhenni, "Mon Expérience avec la Censure et le Blogging" (November 9, 2010), http://atunisiangirl.blogspot.com/2010/11/mon-experience-avec-la-censure-et-le.html (accessed February 2, 2012).

92. Grira, "Les Cyber Réfugiés en Tunisie."

93. Arabasta, "I Will Not Give Up" (April 28, 2010), http://arabasta1.blogspot.com/2010/04/blog-post_28.html (accessed April 11, 2012).

94. Interview with Tarek Kahlaoui, Tunis, July 13, 2011.

95. Maryam Mnaouar, "Internet: L'Inextinguible Soif de Liberté des Jeunes Tunisiens—Interview de Slim Amamou," Afrik (October 10, 2010), http://www.afrik.com/article20977.html (accessed March 21, 2011).

96. For the campaign's sites, see http://ammar404-tumblr.com, http://ammar405.tumblr.com/, https://www.facebook.com/pages/Sayeb-salah/172435742855017, http://www.facebook.com/ammar404?v=wall&ref=ts, and https://twitter.com/SayebSala7 (accessed February 6, 2012).

97. Nadia, "Tunisian Internet Citizens Protest against Censorship," *MidEast Youth* (May 20, 2010), http://www.mideastyouth.com/2010/05/20/7527/ (accessed May 8, 2012).

98. Mona Karim, "Singing against Censorship," *Alrai*, February 8, 2011, http://www.alraimedia.com/Alrai/Article.aspx?id=255281&date=08022011 (accessed March 18, 2011).

99. Ismail Dbara, "The Ministry of Interior Bans an Anti-Censorship Youth Protest," *Elaph*, May 22, 2011, http://www.elaph.com/Web/news/2010/5/563606.html (accessed May 15, 2011).

100. Mona Suleiman, "Internet Censorship," *The Altar of Al Jazeera*, Al Jazeera Arabic Channel (May 22, 2010), http://www.aljazeera.net/NR/exeres/DC620C2A-9274-4C04-9D00-806DF9A986A3.htm (accessed February 8, 2012).

101. Tarek Kahlaoui, "Tunisia Censors Dozens of Sites in a Single Week…and Invites Ridicule of the Censor Ammar 404" (May 10, 2010), www.traidnt.net/vb/showthread.php?t=1557352 (accessed May 16, 2011).

102. On the initiative "7ell blog" (literally "start a blog"), see Amy Aisen Kallander, "From TUNeZINE to Nhar Ala Ammar: A Reconsideration of the Role of Bloggers in Tunisia's Revolution," *Arab Media and Society* 17 (2013), http://www.arabmediasociety.com/articles/downloads/20130221104651_Kallander_Amy.pdf (accessed May 11, 2013).

103. "The 10,000 Signature Petition against Internet Control and Censorship," https://www.facebook.com/Tunisie.libre.1714?v=wall&ref=ts (accessed January 25, 2012).

104. Ibid.

105. See Dbara, "The Ministry of Interior Bans an Anti-Censorship Youth Protest."

106. Antikor, "We Must Break the Shackles" (August 12, 2009), http://antikor.blogspot.com/search/label/404%20YonAmmar (accessed February 26, 2012).

107. Mokhtar Yahyaoui, "La Dictature Nuit à l'Image de Notre Pays: Letter Ouverte aux Blogeurs Tunisiens" (May 4, 2010), http://nawaat.org/portail/2010/05/04/la-dictature-nuit-a-limage-de-notre-pays-lettre-ouverte-aux-blogeurs-tunisiens/ (accessed February 9, 2012).

108. Ismail Dbara, "Tunisian Internet Users Embarrass MPs with Anti-Censorship Letters," Alhiwar (July 22, 2010), http://www.alhiwar.net/ShowNews.php?Tnd=8510 (accessed May 15, 2011).

109. According to one source, some fifty individuals participated. See Mnaouar, "Internet: L'Inextinguible Soif de Liberté des Jeunes Tunisiens—Interview de Slim Amamou," Afrik (October 10, 2010), http://www.afrik.com/article20977.html (accessed March 21, 2011).

110. Mnaouar, "Internet: L'Inextinguible Soif de Liberté des Jeunes Tunisiens."

111. Chourabi, quoted in Dbara, "Tunisian Internet Users Embarrass MPs."

112. Barbach, "The Story of a Blogger…Three Years On" (November 22, 2010), http://tbar-bich.blogspot.com/2010/11/blog-post.html (accessed June 13, 2011).

113. Free Race, "No More Fear after Today" (July 6, 2009), http://www.free-race.blogspot.com/2009/07/blog-post_06.html (accessed May 29, 2011).

114. Antikor, "La 404 YonAmmar" (March 9, 2010), http://antikor.blogspot.com/search/label/404%20YonAmmar (accessed February 26, 2012).

115. Ibid.

116. See http://fr-fr.facebook.com/nhar3la3ammar (accessed February 11, 2012).

117. "Organiser une Manifestation en Tunisie" (May 23, 2010), http://larbieh.blogs.france24.com/article/2010/05/23/organiser-une-manifestation-en-tunisie-0 (accessed January 15, 2012).

118. Gherib, "Mobilisation Contre la Censure sur Internet."

119. Mokhtar Yahyaoui, "Tunisie: Interpellation des Deux Jeunes Initiateurs d'un Rassemblement Contre le Blocage d'Internet à Tunis," Tunisia Watch (May 21, 2010), http://www.tunisiawatch.com/?p=2413 (accessed February 1, 2012).

120. Lina Ben Mhenni, "Flashmob Contre la Censure" (August 5, 2010), http://atunisiangirl.blogspot.com/2010/08/comme-tous-les-combats-qui-ont-fait.html (accessed June 13, 2011).

121. Khmais Ben Brik, "Tight Security around Bloggers in Tunisia," Aljazeera.net (May 27, 2010), http://www.aljazeera.net/NR/exeres/6AEB24DE-4B48-4E99-8032-A78F7C8F0380.htm (accessed March 19, 2011).

122. "Tunisia Aborts a Demonstration by Bloggers," Aljazeera.net (May 23, 2010), http://www.aljazeera.net/NR/exeres/8C5BB7B5-2663-44DA-B044-137F6BFAF617.htm (accessed March 21, 2011).

123. "Manifestation Contre la Censure sur Internet: Ça Bouge sur le Front de la Citoyenneté!" *Attariq Al Jadid* 181 (May 22, 2011), http://ahbebattariq.blogspot.com/2010/05/manifestation-contre-la-censure-sur.html (accessed February 8, 2012); see also Arabasta, "Back to Basics."

124. Interview with Ismail Dbara, Tunis, July 4, 2011.

125. Mnaouar, "Internet: L'Inextinguible Soif de Liberté des Jeunes Tunisiens."

126. See Howard Rheingold, *Smart Mobs* (Cambridge: Perseus, 2002).

127. See Clay Shirky, *Here Comes Everybody: The Power of Organizing without Organizations* (New York: Penguin, 2008).

128. Guobin Yang, *The Power of the Internet in China: Citizen Activism Online* (New York: Columbia University Press), 2011, 32.

129. Mnaouar, "Internet: L'Inextinguible Soif de Liberté des Jeunes Tunisiens."

130. Karen Mossberger, "Toward Digital Citizenship: Addressing Inequality in the Information Age," in *The Routledge Handbook of Internet Politics*, ed. Andrew Chadwick and Philip N. Howard (London: Routledge, 2009), 173–85.

131. Belgacem Ben Abdallah, "Ammar 404 the Enemy of Freedom," *Al Badil*, May 11, 2010, http://www.albadil.org/spip.php?article2946 (accessed February 8, 2012).

132. Tarek Kahlaoui, "Dotting the i's and Crossing the t's: On Exiled Blogs" (February 9, 2010), http://tkharbich.blogspot.com/2010/02/blog-post_09.html (accessed April 13, 2013).

133. See http://www.facebook.com/pages/All-Against-the-Dictatorship-of-Ben-Ali-in-Tunisia/156421814410770?sk=info (accessed June 10, 2012).

134. Interview with Liliopatra, Tunis, June 25, 2012.

135. Rachid Khechana, "La Censure Paralyse mon Travail," *Tunisnews* 3739 (August 18, 2010), http://tunisnews.net/archive/18Out10f.htm (accessed March 1, 2012).

Chapter 7

1. See http://fr-fr.facebook.com/pages/Parlement-virtuel-tunisien/186487538042284, and http://parlement.virtuel.tunisien.over-blog.com/article-55685897.html (accessed February 12, 2013).

2. "Pluralism in Tunisia's Virtual Parliament," Aljazeera.net (November 16, 2009), http://www.aljazeera.net/NR/exeres/7CA1232D-65AE-4C49-A1FA-191E6384A328.htm (accessed February 11, 2012).

3. Andrew Chadwick, *The Hybrid Media System: Politics and Power* (Oxford: Oxford University Press, 2013), 4.

4. Henry Jenkins, *Convergence Culture: Where Old and New Media Collide* (New York: NYU Press, 2006), 6.

5. For statistics on Internet usage and population growth in Tunisia, see "Tunisia: Internet Usage and Marketing Report," http://www.internetworldstats.com/af/tn.htm (accessed March 23, 2011); and www.socialbakers.com (accessed March 23, 2011).

6. José Van Dijck, *The Culture of Connectivity: A Critical History of Social Media* (Oxford: Oxford University Press, 2013), 51.

7. Philippe Rivère, "Facebook: The Magic Mirror," *Le Monde Diplomatique* (January 16, 2011), http://mondediplo.com/2011/01/16facebook (accessed February 21, 2011).

8. Josiane Jouët, "Des Usages de la Télématique aux Internet Studies," in *Communiquer à l'Ère Numérique: Regards Croisés sur la Sociologie des Usages*, ed. J. Denouël and F. Granjon (Paris: Presses des Mines, 2011), 61.

9. Samia Mihoub, "Internet en Tunisie: Régulation, Usages et Conflits Émergents," *Horizons Maghrebins* 62 (2010): 108.

10. Van Dijck, *The Culture of Connectivity*, 47.

11. Mihoub, "Internet en Tunisie," 108; Linda Herrera, "Egypt's Revolution 2.0: The Facebook Factor," in *Mediating the Arab Uprisings*, ed. Adel Iskandar and Bassam Haddad (Washington, D.C.: Tadween, 2013), 48.

12. Rasha Abdulla, "The Federal Democratic Republic of Facebook," *Al Ahram Democracy Review* 34 (April 2009), http://democracy.ahram.org.eg/eng/ (accessed September 24, 2012).

13. Hamza Meddeb, "L'Ambivalence de la Course à *el Khobza: Obéir et se Révolter en Tunisie*," *Politique Africaine* 121 (March 2011): 35–51; Béatrice Hibou, *The Force of Obedience: The Political Economy of Repression in Tunisia*, trans. Andrew Brown (Cambridge: Polity, 2011).

14. Mark Poster, "Everyday (Virtual) Life," *New Literary History* 33, no. 4 (2002): 743.

15. See https://www.facebook.com/pages/Faouzi-Mahbouli/156635871013223 (accessed December 22, 2012); and https://fr-fr.facebook.com/pages/Real-Tunisia-News/157227300996531 (accessed December 22, 2012).

16. James C. Scott, "Everyday Forms of Resistance," *Copenhagen Papers* 4 (1989): 42.

17. Emma C. Murphy, "Problematizing Arab Youth: Generational Narratives of Systemic Failure," *Mediterranean Politics* 17, no. 1 (2012): 11.

18. Interview with Larbi Chouikha, Tunis, April 22, 2011.

19. See Samir Khalaf and Roseanne Saad Khalaf, eds., *Arab Youth: Social Mobilization in Times of Risk* (London: Saqi, 2011), 9; Linda Herrera and Asef Bayat, eds., *Being Young and Muslim: New Cultural Politics in the Global South and North* (Oxford: Oxford University Press, 2010), 11.

20. Samia Mihoub, "Internet en Tunisie," 108.

21. Interview with Zouheir Makhlouf, Tunis, April 25, 2011.

22. "The Maghreb Harvest Program," Al Jazeera Channel (September 19, 2010), www.aljazeera.net/NR/exeres/F7AD880B-6860-461C-A035-5BB15E1756F1.htm (accessed November 16, 2012).

23. Interview with Hamadi Kaloutcha, Tunis, April 23, 2011.

24. Lina Khatib, *Image Politics in the Middle East East: The Role of the Visual in Political Struggle* (London: IB Tauris, 2012), 11.

25. Interview with Lamine Bouazizi, Doha, April 19, 2011.

26. Interview with Ali Bouazizi, Sidi Bouzid, July 3, 2011.

27. Paolo Gerbaudo, *Tweets and the Streets: Social Media and Contemporary Activism* (London: Pluto, 2012), 5.

28. Philip N. Howard, *The Digital Origins of Dictatorship and Democracy: Information Technology and Political Islam* (Oxford: Oxford University Press, 2010), 11.

29. Clay Shirky, "The Twitter Revolution: More than Just a Slogan," *Prospect* (January 6, 2010), http://www.prospectmagazine.co.uk/magazine/the-twitter-revolution-more-than-just-a-slogan/ (accessed December 18, 2012).

30. David Faris and Patrick Meier, "Digital Activism in Authoritarian Countries," in *The Participatory Cultures Handbook*, ed. Aaron Delwiche and Jennifer Jacobs Henderson (London: Routledge: 2013), 203; Vian Bakir, *Sousveillance: Media and Strategic Political Communication: Iraq, USA, UK* (New York: Continuum, 2010).

31. Jon B. Alterman, "The Revolution Will Not Be Tweeted," *The Washington Quarterly* 34, no. 4 (2011): 111–12.

32. Romain Lecomte, "Révolution Tunisenne et Internet: Le Rôle des Médias Sociaux," *L'Année du Maghreb* 7 (2011): 400–402.

33. Mark Granovetter, "The Strength of Weak Ties," *The American Journal of Sociology* 78, no. 6 (1973): 1377.

34. Fabrice Epelboin, "Le Gouvernement Tunisien Passe à l'Offensive," Fhimt, May 22, 2010, http://www.fhimt.com/2010/05/22/le-gouvernement-tunisien-passe-a-l'offensive (accessed February 24, 2012); Danny O'Brien, "Tunisia Invades, Censors Facebook, Other Accounts," Committee to Protect Journalists (January 5, 2011), http://cpj.org/internet/2011/01/tunisia-invades-censors-facebook-other-accounts.php (accessed January 22, 2011); Neal Ungerleider, "Tunisian Government Allegedly Hacking Facebook," *Fast Company* (January 10, 2011), http://www.fastcompany.com/1715575/tunisian-government-hacking-facebook-gmail-anonymous (accessed January 22, 2011).

35. Alexis C. Madrigal, "The Inside Story of How Facebook Responded to Tunisian Hacks," *The Atlantic* (January 24, 2011), www.theatlantic.com/technology/archive/2011/01/the-inside-story-of-how-facebook-responded-to-tunisian-hacks/70044/ (accessed August 3, 2012).

36. Interview with Tarek Kahlaoui, Tunis, July 13, 2011.

37. Arnaud Vaulerin, "Opération Tunisia: La Cyberattaque d'Anonymous aux Côtés des Manifestants," *Libération* (January 12, 2011), http://www.liberation.fr/monde/2011/01/12/operation-tunisia-la-cyberattaque-d-anonymous-aux-cotes-des-manifestants_706827 (accessed January 23, 2011).

38. Philip J. Crowley, "Statement on Protests and Website Hacking in Tunisia" (January 7, 2011), http://iipdigital.usembassy.gov/st/english/texttrans/2011/01/20110108193659su0.5481488.html#axzz3VKDVAJ8K (accessed December 2, 2013).

39. The name comes from an incident in which the American singer Barbra Streisand tried to censor photos of her home on a public website, which attracted far greater attention to the images than they otherwise would have received.

40. Boris Manenti, "Sidi Bouzid ou la Révolte Tunisienne Organisée sur Facebook," *Le Nouvel Observateur* (January 4, 2011), http://tempsreel.nouvelobs.com/actualite/vu-sur-le-web/20110104.OBS5680/sidi-bouzid-ou-la-revolte-tunisienne-organisee-sur-facebook.html (accessed January 23, 2011).

41. Tarek Kahlaoui, "A Brief Account of the Tunisian Revolution's Media Branch" (January 20, 2011), http://open.salon.com/blog/tkahlaoui/2011/01/20/a_brief_account_from_my_perspective_of_the_tunisian_revolu (accessed September 24, 2011).

42. Rami Brahem, "La Tunisie, Première Cyber-Révolution: Interview avec Fœtus" (January 20, 2011), http://www.michelcollon.info/La-Tunisie-premiere-cyber.html (accessed May 23, 2011).

43. Tarek Kahlaoui, "A Brief Account of the Tunisian Revolution's Media Branch"; Tarek Kahlaoui, "The Powers of Social Media," in *The Making of the Tunisian Revolution: Contexts, Architects, Prospects*, ed. Nouri Gana (Edinburgh: Edinburgh University Press, 2013), 154.

44. Guy Berger, "Empowering the Youth as Citizen Journalists: A South African Experience," *Journalism* 12, no. 6 (2011): 714.

45. Interview with Sami Ben Gharbia, Tunis, June 27, 2011.

46. Peter Beaumont, "The Truth about Twitter, Facebook and the Uprisings in the Arab World," *The Guardian*, February 25, 2011, http://www.guardian.co.uk/world/2011/feb/25/twitter-facebook-uprisings-arab-libya (accessed October 4, 2011).

47. Zouha Dahmen-Jarrin, "Les Aléas de la Libre Circulation de l'Information dans les Nouveaux Médias en Tunisie," *ESSACHESS: Journal of Communication Studies* 5, no. 1 (2012): 131–32; Tarek Kahlaoui, "The Powers of Social Media," in *The Making of the*

Tunisian Revolution: Contexts, Architects, Prospects, ed. Nouri Gana (Edinburgh: Edinburgh University Press, 2013), 154.

48. Lotan, Gilad, Erhardt Graeff, Mike Ananny, Devin Gaffney, Ian Pearce, and Danah Boyd, "The Revolutions Were Tweeted: Information Flows during the 2011 and Egyptian Revolution," *International Journal of Communication* 5 (2011): 1380.

49. Dhiraj Murthy, *Twitter: Social Communication in the Twitter Age* (Cambridge: Polity, 2013), 106.

50. Thomas Poell and Kaouthar Darmoni, "Twitter as a Multilingual Space: The Articulation of the Tunisian Revolution through #sidibouzid," *European Journal of Media Studies* 1, no. 1 (2012): 7, http://ssrn.com/abstract=2154288 (accessed September 4, 2013). For a skeptical perspective, see Eli'Coopter, "Quelle Twitter Revolution en Tunisie," Nawaat (January 19, 2011), http://nawaat.org/portail/2011/01/19/quelle-twitter-revolution-en-tunisie/ (accessed February 19, 2012).

51. "Third Annual ASDA'A Burson-Marsteller Arab Youth Survey" (2010), 22–23, http://arabyouthsurvey.com/wp-content/themes/arabyouth-english/downloads/2010-2011/ays-whitepaper-2010.pdf (accessed October 3, 2012).

52. Marc Lynch, "Political Science and the New Arab Public Sphere," *Foreign Policy* (June 12, 2012), http://lynch.foreignpolicy.com/posts/2012/06/12/political_science_and_the_new_arab_public_sphere (accessed August 30, 2012).

53. Waddah Khanfar, "At Al Jazeera, We Saw the Arab Revolutions Coming. Why Didn't the West?" *Washington Post*, February 25, 2005, http://www.washingtonpost.com/wp-dyn/content/article/2011/02/25/AR2011022503177.html (accessed September 25, 2012).

54. Interview with M'hamed Krichene, Doha, March 13, 2011.

55. On the tension between Tunisia and Al Jazeera, see Hedi Brik, "Mercenary Tunisian Media Lash out at Al Jazeera," *Arab News*, November 3, 2005, www.alarabnews.com/alshaab/2005/11-03-2005/a13.htm (accessed January 24, 2011).

56. Aref Hijjawi, "The Role of Al Jazeera (Arabic) in the Arab Revolts of 2011," in *Perspectives II: People's Power: The Arab World in Revolt*, ed. Layla Al-Zubaidi and Paul Joachim (Beirut: Heinrich Böll Stiftung, 2011), http://www.boell.de/publications/publications-perspectives-2-mai-2011-11961.html (accessed March 12, 2012), 69.

57. Interview with Nabil Rihani, Doha, June 21, 2011.

58. Hijjawi, "The Role of Al Jazeera," 69.

59. Laurence Pintak and Jeremy Ginges, "The Mission of Arab Journalism: Creating Change in a Time of Turmoil," *The International Journal of Press/Politics* 13, no. 3 (2008): 193–227.

60. Taoufik Ben Brik, "En Tunisie, le Règne sans Partage d'Al Jazeera," *Slate*, January 19, 2011, http://www.slate.fr/story/32871/al-jazeera-tunisie-television-islamisme-desinformation (accessed March 4, 2012).

61. Alterman, "The Revolution Will Not Be Tweeted," 104.

62. Interview with Noureddine Ouididi, Doha, April 19, 2011.

Chapter 8

1. Kamel Labidi, "Letter of Resignation as Head of Tunisia's INRIC," World Press Freedom Committee (August 14, 2012), http://www.wpfc.org/?q=node/485 (accessed April 5, 2014).

2. Fatma El Issawi, "Tunisian Media in Transition," Carnegie Endowment for International Peace (July 10, 2012), http://carnegieendowment.org/2012/07/10/tunisian-media-in-transition (accessed September 5, 2012).

3. José Van Dijck, *The Culture of Connectivity: A Critical History of Social Media* (Oxford: Oxford University Press, 2013), 65.

4. Arab Social Media Report, "Citizen Engagement and Public Services in the Arab World: The Potential of Social Media" (June 28, 2014), http://www.mbrsg.ae/getattachment/e9ea2ac8-13dd-4cd7-9104-b8f1f405cab3/Citizen-Engagement-and-Public-Services-in-the-Arab.aspx (accessed July 8, 2014).

5. Interview with Hamadi Kaloutcha, Tunis, March 4, 2014.

6. Alcinda Honwana, *Youth and Revolution in Tunisia* (New York: Zed, 2013), 105.

7. Interview with Hamadi Kaloutcha, Tunis, March 4, 2014.

8. Ibid.

9. Interview with Waterman, Tunis, March 23, 2014.

10. Ibid.

11. Olfa Riahi, "Fortes Présomptions de Malversation et d'Affaire de Mœurs—Urgence d'une Enquête Officielle" (December 26, 2012), http://tobegoodagain.wordpress.com/2012/12/26/rafik-abdessalem-bouchleka-fortes-presomptions-de-malversation-et-daffaire-de-moeurs-urgence-dune-enquete-officielle/ (accessed on April 21, 2012); Rached Cherif, "Tunisie: Un Sheratongate pour le Ministre des Affaires Étrangères," Nawaat (December 27, 2012), http://nawaat.org/portail/2012/12/27/tunisie-un-sheratongate-pour-le-ministre-des-affaires-etrangeres-rafik-abdessalem/ (accessed April 21, 2014).

12. See https://www.facebook.com/blogueurstunisiens?hc_location=timeline and http://associationdeblogueurstunisiens.blogspot.com (accessed June 2, 2012).

13. See http://www.fallega.tn (accessed July 5, 2013).

14. "The Fellaga and the Information Revolution," Al Mutawassit TV Channel (September 27, 2013), www.youtube.com/watch?v=mbCN0ITZ9wc (accessed March 31, 2014).

15. See https://www.facebook.com/Fallega.tn and http://www.fallega.tn (accessed June 2, 2013).

16. See http://www.machhad.com (accessed July 20, 2012).

17. See, for instance, Achahed, www.achahed.com (accessed February 3, 2014); and Al Sada, www.al-sada.net (accessed February 3, 2014).

18. Ana Luz Muñoz, "Le Rôle des Médias Comme Nawaat est d'Essayer de Changer les Choses," EMI (June 10, 2013), http://emi-cfd.com/echanges-partenariats/?p=2023 (accessed April 19, 2014).

References

Abdelmoula, Ezzeddine. *Al Jazeera and Democratization: The Rise of the Arab Public Sphere.* London: Routledge, 2015.

Abdulla, Rasha. "The Federal Democratic Republic of Facebook." *Al Ahram Democracy Review* 34 (April 2009). http://democracy.ahram.org.eg/eng/, accessed September 24, 2012.

Abdulla, Rasha. *Policing the Internet in the Arab World.* Abu Dhabi: ECSSR, 2009.

Achy, Lahcen. "Substituer des Emplois Précaires à un Chômage Élevé: Les Défis de l'Emploi au Maghreb." Carnegie Middle East Center Paper No. 23 (November 2010). http://carnegieendowment.org/files/TEXTE2%2Epdf (accessed January 30, 2012).

Aday, Sean, et al. *Blogs and Bullets: New Media in Contentious Politics.* Washington, D.C.: United States Institute of Peace, 2012.

Agrebi, Kawther. "On Facebook, Groups for Mass Suicide and Devil Worship." *Assabah* (December 24, 2009). http://www.assabah.com.tn/recherche_details-27671.html (accessed August 22, 2012).

Al Ansari. "Comment on Sami Ben Gharbia's 'Blogs Tunisiens'" (December 24, 2005). https://ifikra.wordpress.com/2005/12/20/blogs-tunisiens-des-zones-touristiques (accessed November 2, 2011).

Albabtain, Afraa Ahmed. "Downloading Democracy: Bloggers in the Gulf." *Arab Insight* 2, no. 2 (Summer 2008): 53–65.

Alexander, Christopher. *Tunisia: Stability and Reform in the Modern Maghreb.* London: Routledge, 2010.

Al Gasimi, Jamei. "Ben Ali Rescues Facebook from Censorship." *Middle East Online* (September 3, 2008). http://www.middle-east-online.com/english/?id=27687 (accessed December 17, 2012).

Al Kassim, Faisal. "The Future of Arab Regimes." *The Opposite Direction Program*, Al Jazeera Arabic Channel (April 27, 2010). http://www.aljazeera.net/programs/pages/0672b8a3-6002-4824-80bd-829ac52860b5 (accessed July 7, 2012).

Al Kassim, Faisal. "The Internet as a Safety Valve." *Behind the News Program*, Al Jazeera Arabic Channel (October 14, 2005). http://www.aljazeera.net/NR/exeres/EB218269-F269-4B15-A1D2-0D71F34A8256.htm (accessed March 17, 2011).

Allal, Amin. "Ici Ça Bouge Pas, Ça n'Avance Pas!" In *L'État Face aux Débordements du Social au Maghreb*, ed. Myriam Catusse, Blandine Destremau, and Eric Verdier, 175–86. Paris: Karthala, 2009.

Allal, Amin, and Florian Kohstall. "Opposition within the State: Governance in Egypt, Morocco and Tunisia." In *Contentious Opposition in the Middle East: Political Opposition under Authoritarianism*, ed. Holger Albrecht, 181–204. Gainesville: University Press of Florida, 2010.

Alonso, Andoni, and Pedro J. Oiarzabal. *Diasporas in the New Media Age: Identity, Politics, and Community*. Reno: University of Nevada Press, 2010.

Al Saqaf, Walid. "Circumventing Internet Censorship in the Arab World." In *Liberation Technology: Social Media and the Struggle for Democracy*, ed. Larry Diamond and Marc Plattner, 124–38. Baltimore: The Johns Hopkins University Press, 2012.

Alterman, Jon B. "The Revolution Will Not Be Tweeted." *The Washington Quarterly* 34, no. 4 (2011): 103–16.

Amnesty International. "Behind Tunisia's Economic Miracle: Inequality and Criminalization of Protest" (June 17, 2009). http://www.amnesty.org/en/library/info/MDE30/003/2009 (accessed August 30, 2012).

Anderson, Jon W. *Arabizing the Internet*. Abu Dhabi: ECSSR, 1998.

Anderson, Jon W. "Between Freedom and Coercion: Inside Internet Implantation in the Middle East." In *The New Arab Media: Technology, Image and Perception*, ed. Mahjoob Zweiri and Emma C. Murphy, 19–30. Reading: Ithaca Press, 2010.

Anderson, Lisa. "Political Pacts, Liberalism and Democracy: The Tunisian National Pact of 1988." *Government and Opposition* 26, no. 2 (1991): 244–60.

Angelica. "Communiqué N°4: Participation du Comité National pour la Libération de Zouheir Yahyaoui." Reveil Tunisien (February 8, 2003). http://www.reveiltunisien.org/spip.php?article419 (accessed October 24, 2011).

Angrist, Michele Penner. "Parties, Parliament and Political Dissent in Tunisia." *The Journal of North African Studies* 4, no. 4 (1999): 89–104.

Antikor. "Do Speak Ammar" (March 9, 2010). http://antikor.blogspot.com/search/labael/404YonAmmar (accessed February 8, 2012).

Antikor. "La 404 YonAmmar" (March 9, 2010). http://antikor.blogspot.com/search/label/404%20YonAmmar (accessed February 26, 2012).

Antikor. "We Must Break the Shackles" (August 12, 2009). http://antikor.blogspot.com/search/label/404%20YonAmmar (accessed February 26, 2012).

Arabasta. "Back to Basics" (May 28, 2010). http://arabasta1.blogspot.com/2010/05/back-to-basics-bribes-propos-de-la.html (accessed June 13, 2011).

Arabasta. "I Will Not Give Up" (April 28, 2010). http://arabasta1.blogspot.com/2010/04/blog-post_28.html (accessed April 11, 2012).

Arabasta. "My Story with Censorship" (January 17, 2010). http://arabasta1.blogspot.com/2010/01/mon-histoire-avec-la-censure.html (accessed June 13, 2011).

Arabicca, Fatma. "Dommage" (November 6, 2009). http://fatmaarabicca.blogspot.com/2010/06/dommage.html (accessed February 8, 2012).

"Arab Despots Should Heed Events in Tunisia." *The Guardian*, January 16, 2011. http://www.guardian.co.uk/commentisfree/2011/jan/16/observer-editorial-tunisia-support-arabs (accessed January 16, 2011).

Arab Network for Human Rights Information. "The Internet in the Arab World: A New Space of Repression" (2004). http://www.anhri.net/en/reports/net2004/ (accessed October 9, 2011).

Arab Social Media Report, "Citizen Engagement and Public Services in the Arab World: The Potential of Social Media" (June 28, 2014). http://www.mbrsg.ae/getattachment/e9ea2ac8-13dd-4cd7-9104-b8f1f405cab3/Citizen-Engagement-and-Public-Services-in-the-Arab.aspx (accessed July 8, 2014).

Arfewi, Jamel. "Facebook Users Launch a Campaign against Censorship." Magharebia (July 8, 2009). http://www.magharebia.com/cocoon/awi/xhtml1/ar/features/awi/blog/2009/07/08/feature-03 (accessed November 10, 2011).

Armbrust, Walter. "A History of New Media in the Arab Middle East." *Journal for Cultural Research* 16, nos. 2–3 (2012): 155–74.

Arteta, Stéphane. "Des Souris Contre Ben Ali." *Le Nouvel Observateur*, August 21, 2011. http://tempsreel.nouvelobs.com/actualite/monde/20010821.OBS7638/des-souris-contre-ben-ali.html (accessed May 22, 2011).

Asen, Robert. "A Discourse Theory of Citizenship." *Quarterly Journal of Speech* 90, no. 2 (2004): 189–211.

Astrubal. "Censure, Hypocrisie et Etat de Droit." Nawaat (May 9, 2010). http://nawaat.org/portail/2010/05/09/censure-hypocrisie-et-etat-de-droit-lettre-ouverte-aux-malentendants/ (accessed February 27, 2011).

Astrubal. "Tunisie: Le Scandale de la 403 Maquillée en 404." Nawaat (June 12, 2006). http://nawaat.org/portail/2006/06/13/tunisie-le-scandale-de-la-403-maquillee-en-404/ (accessed March 4, 2011).

Astrubal. "Tunisie: Qui Utilise l'Avion de la Présidence de la République Tunisienne?" (August 29, 2007). http://www.dailymotion.com/video/x2uv4a_tunisie-avion-presidentiel-a-quoi-e_news (accessed May 4, 2012).

Astrubal. "Tunisie: Retour sur les Échanges Zied El Heni." Nawaat (September 25, 2008). http://astrubal.nawaat.org/2008/09/25/tunisie-retour-sur-les-echanges-zied-el-heniaymen-rezgui-sur-canal-du-dialogue-tunisien/ (accessed June 16, 2011).

Atkinson, Joshua D. *Alternative Media and Politics of Resistance.* New York: Peter Lang, 2010.

Axford, Barrie. "Talk about a Revolution: Social Media and the MENA Uprisings." *Globalizations* 8, no. 5 (2011): 681–86.

Ayari, Michaël Béchir, Vincent Geisser, and Abir Krefa. "Chronique d'une Révolution Presque Annoncée." *L'Année du Maghreb* 7 (2011): 359–87.

Ayeb, Habib. "Social and Political Geography of the Tunisian Revolution: The Alfa Grass Revolution." *Review of African Political Economy* 38, no. 129 (2011): 467–79.

Ayechi, Tawfik. "Accusations of Fraud in the Name of the Law." *Attatiq Al Jadid* 188 (July 10, 2010). http://attariq.org/IMG/jpg/Page_05-73.jpg (accessed February 17, 2012).

Ayish, Muhammad. *The New Arab Public Sphere.* Berlin: Frank & Timme, 2008.

Azwaw. "Fatma Arabicca: Une Femme Libre Hors du Commun, mais qui Dérange" (November 6, 2009). http://azwaw.net/2009/11/06/fatma-arabicca-une-femme-libre-hors-du-commun-mais-qui-derange/ (accessed February 6, 2012).

Bakhtin, Michail. *Rabelais and His World.* Translated by Hélène Iswolsky. Bloomington: Indiana University Press, 1984.

Bakir, Vian. *Sousveillance: Media and Strategic Political Communication: Iraq, USA, UK.* New York: Continuum, 2010.

Bal, Mieke. *Narratology: An Introduction to the Theory of Narrative.* Toronto: University of Toronto Press: 2009.

Barbach. "The Story of a Blogger…Three Years On" (November 22, 2010). http://tbarbich.blogspot.com/2010/11/blog-post.html (accessed June 13, 2011).

Barbero, Martin J. *Communication, Culture and Hegemony.* London: Sage Publications, 1993.

Bayat, Asef. *Life as Politics: How Ordinary People Change the Middle East.* Stanford: Stanford University Press, 2009.

Bayat, Asef. "Muslim Youth and the Claim of Youthfulness." In *Being Young and Muslim: New Cultural Politics in the Global South and North,* ed. Linda Herrera and Asef Bayat, 27–47. Oxford: Oxford University Press, 2010.

Bayat, Asef. "A New Arab Street in Post Islamist Times." *Foreign Policy* (January 26, 2011). http://mideast.foreignpolicy.com/posts/2011/01/26/a_new_arab_street (accessed July 7, 2012).

Beau, Nicolas, and Jean-Pierre Tuquoi. *Notre Ami Ben Ali: L'Envers du Miracle Tunisien.* Paris: La Decouverte, 2002.

Beaugé, Florence. "En Tunisie, Police et Justice Contre le plus Célèbre des Cyber-Résistants." *Le Monde,* June 13, 2002.

Beaugé, Florence. "Le Combat Perdu du Président Ben Ali." *Le Monde,* July 21, 2001.

Beaugé, Florence. "Les Cyber-Résistants Tunisiens Donnent Naissance à une Nouvelle Forme de Contestation." *Le Monde,* September 22, 2000.

Beaugé, Florence. "Zouheir Yahyaoui, le Pionnier des Cyberdissidents." *Le Monde,* January 19, 2011.

Beaumont, Peter. "The Truth about Twitter, Facebook and the Uprisings in the Arab World." *The Guardian*, February 25, 2011. http://www.guardian.co.uk/world/2011/feb/25/twitter-facebook-uprisings-arab-libya (accessed October 4, 2011).

Bechir. "The Censor Consults a Psychiatrist" (June 21, 2008). http://anticensuretounes .blogspot.com/2008/06/blog-post_6903.html (accessed April 11, 2013).

Beer, Davis. "Power through the Algorithm: Participatory Web Cultures and the Technological Unconscious." *New Media and Society* 11, no. 6 (2009): 985–1002.

Ben Abdallah, Belgacem. "Ammar 404 the Enemy of Freedom." *Al Badil*, May 11, 2010. http://www.albadil.org/spip.php?article2946 (accessed February 8, 2012).

Ben Abdallah, Belgacem. "Censorship: Another Face of Repression." *Al Badil* (March 3, 2010). http://www.albadil.org/spip.php?article2767 (accessed September 2, 2012).

Ben Abdallah, Chirine. "L'Engagement Politique des Intranautes Tunisiens au Lendemain de la Révolution." In *Le Cyberactivisme au Maghreb et dans le Monde Arab*, 125–40. Paris: Karthala, 2013.

Ben Ali, Zine El Abidine. "Statement from the President of the Republic of Tunisia at the World Summit on the Information Society" (November 16, 2005). www.itu.int/wsis/tunis/statements/docs/g-tunisia-opening/1.doc (accessed February 11, 2012).

Ben Brik, Khmais. "Tight Security around Bloggers in Tunisia." Aljazeera.net (May 27, 2010). http://www.aljazeera.net/NR/exeres/6AEB24DE-4B48-4E99-8032-A78F7C8F0380 .htm (accessed March 19, 2011).

Ben Brik, Taoufik. "Ben Ali y est et y Restera." TF1 (January 15, 2001). http://lci.tf1.fr/monde/2001-01/ben-ali-est-restera-4899973.html (accessed February 11, 2012).

Ben Brik, Taoufik. "En Tunisie, le Règne sans Partage d'Al Jazeera." *Slate*, January 19, 2011. http://www.slate.fr/story/32871/al-jazeera-tunisie-television-islamisme-desinformation (accessed March 4, 2012).

Ben Gharbia, Sami. "Blogging Tunisia: Whisper!" *Global Voices*, October 5, 2006. http://global-voicesonline.org/2006/10/05/blogging-tunisia-whisper/ (accessed February 3, 2012).

Ben Gharbia, Sami. "Blogs Tunisiens: Des Zones Touristiques!" (December 21, 2005). https://ifikra.wordpress.com/2005/12/20/blogs-tunisiens-des-zones-touristiques (accessed November 2, 2011).

Ben Gharbia, Sami. *Borj Erroumi*. http://samibengharbia.com/borj-erroumi-xl (accessed November 15, 2011).

Ben Gharbia, Sami. "Digital Activism: Arabs Can Do It Themselves." In *Perspectives II: People's Power—The Arab World in Revolt*, ed. Layla Al-Zubaidi et al., 86–89. Beirut: Heinrich Böll Stiftung, 2011. http://www.boell.de/downloads/Perspectives_02-13_Interview_with_Sami_Ben_Gharbia.pdf (accessed March 12, 2012).

Ben Gharbia, Sami. "I Blog for Tunisia, against the Maghreb" (June 1, 2007). http://samibeng-harbia.com/tag/blogsphere/page/2/ (accessed November 17, 2011).

Ben Gharbia, Sami. "The Internet Freedom Fallacy and the Arab Digital Activism." Nawaat (September 17, 2010). http://nawaat.org/portail/2010/09/17/the-internet-freedom-fallacy-and-the-arab-digital-activism/ (accessed April 4, 2011).

Ben Gharbia, Sami. "Second Arab Bloggers Meeting." *Global Voices*, December 5, 2009. http://advocacy.globalvoicesonline.org/2009/12/05/2nd-arab-bloggers-meeting/ (accessed December 16, 2012).

Ben Gharbia, Sami. "Silencing Online Free Speech in Tunisia." Nawaat (August 18, 2008). http://nawaat.org/portail/2008/08/20/silencing-online-speech-in-tunisia/ (accessed March 19, 2011).

Ben Gharbia, Sami. "Tunisian Prison Map" (September 29, 2006). (http://ifikra.wordpress.com/2006/09/29/en-tunisian-prisons-map/ (accessed November 24, 2011).

Ben Gharbia, Sami, and Astrubal. "A Glimpse at Internet Filtering in Tunisia." Nawaat (August 18, 2010). http://nawaat.org/portail/2010/08/19/a-first-glimpse-at-the-internet-filtering-in-tunisia/ (accessed June 21, 2011).

Ben Ismail, Hédi. "Massacre sur la Toile." *Attariq Al Jadid*, August 21, 2010. http://blogamiat-tariq.blogspot.com/2011/10/massacre-sur-la-toile.html (accessed February 8, 2012).

Ben Mhenni, Lina. "Comité de Protection des Blogueurs Tunisiens" (October 14, 2010). http://atunisiangirl.blogspot.com/2010/10/le-comite-de-protection-des-blogeurs.html (accessed January 17, 2012).

Ben Mhenni, Lina. "Flashmob Contre la Censure" (August 5, 2010). http://atunisiangirl.blogspot.com/2010/08/comme-tous-les-combats-qui-ont-fait.html (accessed June 13, 2011).

Ben Mhenni, Lina. "Mon Expérience avec la Censure et le Blogging" (November 9, 2010). http://atunisiangirl.blogspot.com/2010/11/mon-experience-avec-la-censure-et-le.html (accessed February 2, 2012).

Ben Mhenni, Lina. "The White Note Campaign against Cyber Censorship." Global Voices (December 30, 2009). http://globalvoicesonline.org/2009/12/30/tunisia-the-white-note-campaign-against-cyber-censorship/ (accessed March 19, 2011).

Ben Sassi, Samia. "Les Publinets de Tunis: Une Analyse Micro-Économique." *Netsuds* 2 (2004): 107–22. http://revues.mshparisnord.org/netsuds/pdf/424.pdf (accessed December 8, 2012).

Ben Sedrine, Sihem. "Monsieur le Président, Partez: Une Tribune Contre Ben Ali." *L'Obs*, December 11, 2009. http://tempsreel.nouvelobs.com/opinions/20091210.OBS0281/monsieur-le-president-partez-une-tribune-contre-ben-ali.html (accessed October 12, 2011).

Ben Sedrine, Sihem. "Tunisie Internet: La Navigation sous Haute Surveillance." *Kalima Tunisie*, October 3, 2001. http://www.kalima-tunisie.info/magazine/num1/Internet.htm (accessed June 1, 2011).

Bennett, Lance W., and Alexandra Segerberg. *The Logic of Connective Action: Digital Media and the Personalization of Contentious Politics*. Cambridge: Cambridge University Press, 2013.

Berger, Guy. "Empowering the Youth as Citizen Journalists: A South African Experience." *Journalism* 12, no. 6 (2011): 708–26.

Bernal, Victoria. "Diaspora, Cyberspace and Political Imagination: The Eritrean Diaspora Online." *Global Networks* 6, no. 2 (2006): 161–79.

Bernal, Victoria. "Eritrea On-line: Diaspora, Cyberspace and the Public Sphere." *African Ethnologist* 32, no. 4 (2005): 660–75.

Bettaïeb, Hajer. "Les Nouveaux Défis du Secteur Textile en Tunisie." *L'Année du Maghreb* 2 (2005–6): 419–25.

Big Trap Boy. "Action Speaks Louder than Words" (May 9, 2007). http://trapboy.blogspot.com/2007/05/blog-post_09.html (accessed November 17, 2011).

Big Trap Boy. "Le 1er Juin: Je Blogue pour un Maghreb Uni" (May 9, 2007). http://trapboy.blogspot.com/2007/05/le-1er-juin-je-blogue-pour-le-maghreb.html (accessed November 17, 2011).

Big Trap Boy. "Maghreb Blogging Day: Liste des Participants" (June 5, 2007). http://trapboy.blogspot.com/2007/06/maghreb-blogging-day-liste-des.html (accessed November 17, 2011).

Big Trap Boy. "The Tunisian Blogosphere and the Unspoken" (October 1, 2006). http://trapboy.blogspot.com/2006/10/la-blogosphre-tunisienne-et-ceux-dont.html (accessed June 11, 2011).

Bishara, Azmi. *Tunisia: The Diary of a Resplendent Revolution in the Making*. Doha: Arab Center for Research and Policy Studies, 2012.

"Bloggers May Be the Real Opposition: How the Authorities Are Being Nettled." *The Economist* (April 12, 2007). http://www.economist.com/node/9010890 (accessed June 17, 2012).

Boris, Tsar. "A Propos de la Charte." TUNeZINE 100 (October 10, 2002). http://www.tunezine.com/tunezine100.htm (accessed February 8, 2012).

Bouhlal, Saida. "The Phobia of the Net in Tunisia." *Assabah* (June 12, 2009). http://www.assabah.com.tn/recherche_details-21811.html (accessed August 22, 2012).

Bounenni, Bassam. "Dictatorship: Tunisia's Undeserved Fate." *The Daily Star*, May 18, 2009. http://www.dailystar.com.lb/Opinion/Commentary/May/18/Dictatorship-Tunisias-undeserved-fate.ashx (accessed March 4, 2012).

Boyle, James. "Foucault in Cyberspace: Surveillance, Sovereignty and Hardwired Censors." *University of Cincinnati Law Review* 66 (1997): 177–205.

Brahem, Rami. "La Tunisie, Première Cyber-Révolution: Interview avec Fœtus" (January 20, 2011). http://www.michelcollon.info/La-Tunisie-premiere-cyber.html (accessed May 23, 2011).

Bras, Jean-Philippe. "Internet au Maroc et en Tunisie: Entre Réglementation et Régulation." In *Le Maghreb dans L'Économie Numérique*, 163–80. Paris: Maisonneuve, 2007.

Bras, Jean-Philippe. "Ordre Public, Politiques Publiques et Internet en Tunisie." In *Mondialisation et Nouveaux Médias dans L'Espace Arabe*, ed. Franck Mermier, 247–60. Paris: Maisonneuve et Larose, 2003.

Braun, Célina. "À Quoi Servent les Parties Tunisiens? Sens et Contre-Sens d'une Libéralisation Politique." *Revue des Mondes Musulmans et de la Méditerranée* 111–12 (March 2006): 15–61.

Brik, Hedi. "Mercenary Tunisian Media Lash out at Al Jazeera." *Arab News*, November 3, 2005. www.alarabnews.com/alshaab/2005/11-03-2005/a13.htm (accessed January 24, 2011).

Brinkerhoff, Jennifer M. *Digital Diasporas: Identity and Transnational Engagement*. Cambridge: Cambridge University Press, 2009.

Bruns, Alex, and Joanne Jacobs, eds. *Uses of Blogs*. New York: Peter Lang, 2006.

Bsayess, Borhen. "The Other Dimension: On Monitoring the Internet." *Assabah* (September 25, 2008). http://www.assabah.com.tn/article-14204.html (accessed August 21, 2012).

Burkhart, Grey E., and Susan Older. *The Information Revolution in the Middle East and North Africa*. Washington, D.C.: Rand, 2003.

Bushnell, John. *Moscow Graffiti: Language and Subculture*. London: Unwin Hyman, 1990.

Camau, Michel, and Vincent Geisser. *Le Syndrome Autoritaire: Politique en Tunisie de Bourguiba à Ben Ali*. Paris: Presses de Sciences Po, 2003.

Carpe Diem. "Censure" (August 26, 2008). http://blogs.mediapart.fr/blog/carpe-diem/260808/censure (accessed February 11, 2012).

Carpe Diem. "(Mis)Using the Law to Manage the Internet?" (September 28, 2008). http://carpediem-selim.blogspot.com/2008/09/une-loi-pour-encadrer-la-toile.html (accessed July 17, 2012).

Carpe Diem. "Propagande 2.0" (December 20, 2008). http://carpediem-selim.blogspot.com/2008/12/propagande-20.html (accessed June 19, 2011).

Castells, Manuel. *Communication Power*. Oxford: Oxford University Press, 2009.

Castells, Manuel. *Networks of Outrage and Hope: Social Movements in the Internet Age*. Cambridge: Polity, 2012.

"Caught in the Net: Tunisia's First Lady." *Foreign Policy* (December 13, 2007). http://www.foreignpolicy.com/articles/2007/12/13/caught_in_the_net_tunisias_first_lady (accessed May 4, 2012).

Cavatorta, Francesco. "Geopolitical Challenges to the Success of Democracy in North Africa: Algeria, Tunisia and Morocco." *Democratization* 8, no. 4 (2001): 175–94.

"Ce Site a été Censuré par le Gouvernement Tunisien," *Takriz E-mag* 2, no. 3 (2000). http://takriz.tunezine.tn/archives/n2vol3.html (accessed May 23, 2011).

Chaâbane, Hanène. "La Presse d'Opposition en Tunisie entre Liberté, Censure et Autocensure: Le Cas d'*Attatiq Al Jadid*." *Horizons Maghrebins* 62 (2010): 30–34.

Chadwick, Andrew. *The Hybrid Media System: Politics and Power*. Oxford: Oxford University Press, 2013.

Chanfara. "Freedom" (July 2, 2008). http://chanfara.blogspot.com/2008/07/blog-post.html (accessed June 13, 2011).

Chanfara. "On Religion and Other Related Matters" (June 17, 2008). http://chanfara.blogspot.com/2008/06/blog-post_17.html (accessed June 13, 2011).

Chanfara. "To Achour Al Neji" (June 12, 2008). http://chanfara.blogspot.com/2008/06/blog-post_12.html (accessed December 18, 2012).

Chanfara. "To Ammar" (October 28, 2008). http://chanfara.blogspot.com/2008/10/blog-post_195.html (accessed June 13, 2011).

Charlton, Angela. "Tunisian Bloggers Win Online Media Award." *Washington Post*, March 11, 2011. http://www.washingtonpost.com/wp-dyn/content/article/2011/03/11/AR2011 031102643.html (accessed March 7, 2011).

Charrad, Mounira. *States and Women's Rights: The Making of Postcolonial Tunisia, Algeria and Morocco*. Berkeley: University of California Press, 2001.

Chebbi, Nejib A. "On the Rapprochement between the Islamists and the Secularists: The 18 October Experiment in Tunisia." *Adab* 11–12 (2010). www.adabmag.com/node/353 (accessed June 12, 2012).

Chebbi, Rym. "Communité en Ligne et Nouvelles Formes de Liens Sociaux: Étude de Cas de la Blogosphère Tunisienne." In *Les Nouvelles Sociabilités du Net en Méditerranée*, 63–74. Paris: Karthala, 2012.

Cherif, Rached. "Tunisie: Un Sheratongate pour le Ministre des Affaires Étrangères." Nawaat (December 27, 2012) http://nawaat.org/portail/2012/12/27/tunisie-un-sheratongate-pour-le-ministre-des-affaires-etrangeres-rafik-abdessalem/ (accessed April 21, 2014).

Chouikha, Larbi. "Autoritarisme Étatique et Débrouillardise Individuelle." In *La Tunisie de Ben Ali: La Société Contre le Régime*, ed. Olfa Lamloum and Bernard Ravenel, 197–221. Paris: L'Harmattan, 2002.

Chouikha, Larbi. "Pluralisme Politique et Presse d'Opposition sous Bourguiba." In *Habib Bourguiba: La Trace et L'Héritage*, ed. Michel Camau and Vincent Geisser, 341–55. Paris: Karthala, 2004.

Chouikha, Larbi. "Tunisie: Les Chimères Liberals." *La Pensée de Midi* 19 (2006): 29–37. http:// www.cairn.info/resume.php?ID_ARTICLE=LPM_019_0029 (accessed May 28, 2012).

Chouikha, Larbi. "Un Cyberespace Autonome dans un Espace Autoritaire: Le Cas de Tunisnews." In *Les Médias en Méditerranée: Le Pouvoir de Penser les Relations Internationals*, ed. Khadija Mohsen-Finan, 217–35. Paris: Actes Sud, 2009.

Chouikha, Larbi, and Éric Gobe. "La Tunisie entre la Révolte du Bassin Minier de Gafsa et l'Echéance Electorale de 2009." *L'Année du Maghreb* 5 (2009): 387–420. http:// anneemaghreb.revues.org/623 (accessed August 28, 2012).

Chourabi, Sofiene. "Tunisian Bloggers to Hold a Non-Blogging Day" (December 21, 2007). http://www.aafaq.org/news.aspx?id_news=3528 (accessed March 3, 2011).

Chourabi, Sofiene. "Violences dans le Sud Tunisien Suite à la Fermeture d'un Poste-Frontière entre la Tunisie et la Libye." France24 (August 24, 2010). http://observers.france24.com/ fr/content/20100820-violences-sud-tunisien-suite-fermeture-frontieres-entre-tunisie-libye (accessed January 7, 2011).

Comité pour le Respect des Libertés et des Droits de l'Homme en Tunisie. "Après Gafsa, la Répression Sauvage du Régime Tunisien s'Abat sur Ben Guerdane." *Tunisnews* 3739 (August 18, 2010). http://tunisnews.net/archive/18Out10f.htm (accessed March 1, 2012).

Comité pour le Respect des Libertés et des Droits de l'Homme en Tunisie. "Les Derniers Événements en Tunisie: Le Devoir d'Informer, le Droit à la Vérité" (January 9, 2007). http:// tunisie.over-blog.org/article-5211786.html (accessed October 5, 2011).

Commission Européenne. "Rapport de Suivi Tunisie" (May 12, 2010). http://europa.eu/ rapid/press-release_MEMO-10-184_en.htm?locale=en (accessed June 11, 2011).

Committee to Protect Journalists. "Without a Net" (June 2004). http://cpj.org/reports/2004/10/ yahyaoui.php (accessed May 18, 2011).

"Communiqué du 1er Novembre 2005." http://www.tounis.blogspot.com (accessed October 27, 2011).

"Conférence de TUNeZINE: Synthèse des Travaux sur la Logistique." Reveil Tunisien (June 12, 2002). http://www.reveiltunisien.org/spip.php?article35 (accessed June 5, 2011).

Couldry, Nick. "Theorizing Media as Practice." *Social Semiotics* 14, no. 2 (2004): 116–32.

Crowley, Philip J. "Statement on Protests and Website Hacking in Tunisia" (January 7, 2011). http://iipdigital.usembassy.gov/st/english/texttrans/2011/01/2011010819365 9su0.5481488.html#axzz3VKDVAJ8K (accessed December 2, 2013).

Cullum, Brannon. "Maptivism: Mapping Information for Advocacy and Activism" (September 29, 2009). http://www.movements.org/blog/entry/maptivism-mapping-for-advocacy-and-activism/ (accessed December 16, 2012).

Daguzan, Jean-François. "De la Crise Économique à la Révolution Politique?" *Maghreb-Machrek* 206 (2010–11): 9–15.

Dahmen-Jarrin, Zouha. "Les Aléas de la Libre Circulation de L'Information dans les Nouveaux Médias en Tunisie." *ESSACHESS: Journal of Communication Studies* 5, no. 1 (2012): 125–38.

Dakhlia, Jocelyne. *Tunisie: Le Pays sans Bruit*. Paris: Actes Sud, 2011.

Dbara, Ismail. "Ammar 404: Indiscriminate Shelling." *Elaph*, February 7, 2010. http://www.elaph.com/Web/opinion/2010/2/531784.html (accessed May 16, 2011).

Dbara, Ismail. "The Arrest of Fatma Arabicca Preoccupies Tunisian Bloggers on Their National Day." *Al Hayat*, November 23, 2009. http://international.daralhayat.com/internation-alarticle/79189 (accessed November 24, 2011).

Dbara, Ismail. "Internet Censorship in Tunisia Reaps the Wrath of Journalists and Users." Nawaat (June 4, 2008). http://nawaat.org/portail/2008/06/04/online-censorship-angers-journalists-and-users/ (accessed May 16, 2011).

Dbara, Ismail. "The Ministry of Interior Bans an Anti-Censorship Youth Protest." *Elaph*, May 22, 2011. http://www.elaph.com/Web/news/2010/5/563606.html (accessed May 15, 2011).

Dbara, Ismail. "Tunisian Internet Users Embarrass MPs with Anti-Censorship Letters." Alhiwar (July 22, 2010). http://www.alhiwar.net/ShowNews.php?Tnd=8510 (accessed May 15, 2011).

"Deadly Attack Keeps World on Alert." *The Guardian*, September 4, 2002. http://www.guardian.co.uk/world/2002/sep/04/september11.usa (accessed December 30, 2011).

De Certeau, Michel. *The Practice of Everyday Life*. Translated by Steven Rendall. Berkeley: University of California Press, 1984.

Dee, Philippa, and Ndiamé Diop. "The Economy-wide Effects of Further Trade Reforms in Tunisia's Service Sectors." *World Bank Policy Research Working Paper* No. 5341 (June 2010). http://www-wds.worldbank.org/servlet/WDSContentServer/WDSP/IB/2010/06/21/000158349_20100621084841/Rendered/PDF/WPS5341.pdf (accessed July 12, 2012).

Desmères, Marine. "La Société Civile Tunisienne en Otage?" December 2000. http://www.ceri-sciencespo.com/archive/Dec00/desmeres.pdf (accessed November 29, 2011).

"De Takriz à la France et l'Europe." www.takriz.com/emag/article.takriz-a-la-france-europe" (accessed April 27, 2011).

Diamond, Larry, and Marc F. Plattner. *Liberation Technology: Social Media and the Struggle for Democracy*. Baltimore: Johns Hopkins University Press, 2012.

Dickinson, Elizabeth. "The First WikiLeaks Revolution?" *Foreign Policy* (January 13, 2013). http://wikileaks.foreignpolicy.com/posts/2011/01/13/wikileaks_and_the_tunisia_protests (accessed October 12, 2012).

"Digital Battle between Authorities and Bloggers in Tunisia." Aljazeera.net (August 9, 2008). http://www.aljazeera.net/news/archive/archive?ArchiveId=1096460 (accessed March 19, 2011).

Dimasi, Hassine. "The Social and Political Significance of the Middle Class in Tunisia." In *The Tunisian Revolution: Causes, Contexts and Challenges*, 87–115. Doha: Arab Center for Research and Policy Studies, 2012.

Djbouzz. "Comment on Sami Ben Gharbia's 'Blogs Tunisiens'" (December 23, 2005). https://ifikra.wordpress.com/2005/12/20/blogs-tunisiens-des-zones-touristiques (accessed November 2, 2011).

Downing, John D. *Radical Media: The Political Experience of Alternative Media Communication*. Boston: South End, 1984.

Downing, John D. "Social Movement Theories and Alternative Media." *Communication, Culture and Critique* 1, no. 1 (2008): 40–50.

Dunne, Michele. "What Tunisia Proved and Disproved about Political Change in the Arab World." *Arab Reform Bulletin* (January 18, 2011). http://www.carnegieendowment.org/arb/?fa=downloadArticlePDF&article=42320 (accessed February 5, 2012).

Earl, Jennifer, and Katrina Kimport. *Digitally Enabled Social Change: Activism in the Internet Age.* Cambridge, Mass.: MIT Press, 2011.

Eickelman, Dale F. "New Media in the Arab Middle East and the Emergence of Open Societies." In *Remaking Muslim Politics: Pluralism, Contestation, Democratization,* ed. Robert W. Hefner, 37–59. Princeton: Princeton University Press, 2005.

Eickelman, Dale F., and Armando Salvatore. *The Public Sphere and Muslim Identities.* Bloomington: Indiana University Press, 2003.

El Bakkouch, Asma. "Is Facebook Innocent?" *Al Hadath,* January 28, 2009.

El Boughanmi, Tarek. "How Facebook Invaded Every Circle . . . and What Tunisians Use It For." *Al Bayan,* January 29, 2009.

El Heni, Zied. "Court Dismisses Case against Internet Agency" (November 27, 2008). http://journaliste-tunisien-29.blogspot.com/2008/11/blog-post_27.html accessed November 10, 2011.

El Issawi, Fatma. "Tunisian Media in Transition." Carnegie Endowment for International Peace (July 10, 2012). http://carnegieendowment.org/2012/07/10/tunisian-media-in-transition (accessed September 5, 2012).

El Nawawy, Mohammed, and Sahar Khamis. *Egyptian Revolution 2.0: Political Blogging, Civic Engagement, and Citizen Journalism.* New York: Palgrave Macmillan, 2013.

El Oifi, Mohammed. "Faire de la Politique par les Médias Arabes." *Maghreb-Machrek* 193 (2007): 81–108.

El Wafi, Samir. "The Facebook Virus." *Assarih* (January 31, 2009).

Eli'Coopter. "Quelle Twitter Revolution en Tunisie." Nawaat (January 19, 2011). http://nawaat.org/portail/2011/01/19/quelle-twitter-revolution-en-tunisie/ (accessed February 19, 2012).

Elyssa. "Comment on Ben Gharbia's 'Blogs Tunisiens'" (December 21, 2005). https://ifikra.wordpress.com/2005/12/20/blogs-tunisiens-des-zones-touristiques (accessed November 2, 2011).

"Emprisonné pour Avoir Critiqué: Zouheir Yahyaoui." Reveil Tunisien (March 16, 2005). www.reveiltunisien.org/spip.php?article1707 (accessed June 10, 2011).

"Enemies of the Internet: Countries under Surveillance." Reporters Without Borders (March 12, 2010). en.rsf.org/IMG/pdf/Internet_enemies.pdf (accessed 23 May 2012).

Entelis, John P. "The Democratic Imperative vs the Authoritarian Impulse: The Maghrib State Between Transition and Terrorism." *Middle Eastern Journal* 59, no. 4 (2005): 537–58.

Entelis, John P. "Republic of Tunisia." In *The Government and Politics of the Middle East and North Africa,* ed. David E. Long, Bernard Reich, and Mark Gasiorowski, 509–35. Boulder: Westview, 2011.

Epelboin, Fabrice. "Le Gouvernement Tunisien Passe à l'Offensive." Fhimt, May 22, 2010. http://www.fhimt.com/2010/05/22/le-gouvernement-tunisien-passe-a-l'offensive (accessed February 24, 2012).

Escribano, Gonzalo, and Alejandro V. Lorca. "Economic Reform in the Maghreb: From Stabilization to Modernization." In *North Africa: Politics, Religion and the Limits of Transformation,* ed. Yahya H. Zoubir and Haizam Amirah-Fernández, 136–58. London: Routledge, 2008.

Etefa, Abeer. "Transnational Television and the Arab Diaspora in the United States." *Transnational Broadcasting Studies* 12 (2004). http://tbsjournal.arabmediasociety.com/etefa.htm (accessed November 8, 2013).

Etling, Bruce, John Kelly, Robert Faris, and John Palfrey. "Mapping the Arabic Blogosphere: Politics, Culture and Dissent." Berkman Center Research Publication No. 2009–6 (June 2009). http://cyber.law.harvard.edu/sites/cyber.law.harvard.edu/files/Mapping_the_Arabic_Blogosphere_0.pdf (accessed March 21, 2011).

Ettounsi de TUNeZINE. "Merci Monsieur le Precédent," January 2002. http://omarkhayyam
.blogsome.com/2007/05/14/ (accessed October 15, 2011).

European Commissioner. "Tunisia and the European Union," March 25, 2010. http://ec
.europa.eu/commission_2010-2014/fule/docs/articles/article_tunisia_10-03-25_en
.pdf (accessed June 11, 2011).

"Facebook: Intervention du Président de la République." *Le Temps*, September 3, 2008. http://
www.letemps.com.tn/article.php?ID_art=19890 (accessed February 7, 2012).

Faes, Géraldine. "www.Takriz.org." *Le Monde*, September 13, 2000.

"False Freedom: Online Censorship in the Middle East and North Africa." Human Rights
Watch (November 15, 2005). http://www.hrw.org/reports/2005/11/14/false-freedom
(accessed February 14, 2012).

Fandy, Mamoun. *(Un)Civil War of Words: Media and Politics in the Arab World*. Westport,
Conn.: Praeger, 2007.

Faris, David. *Dissent and Revolution in a Digital Age: Social Media, Blogging and Activism in Egypt.*
London: I. B. Tauris, 2012.

Faris, David, and Patrick Meier. "Digital Activism in Authoritarian Countries." In *The Participatory Cultures Handbook*, ed. Aaron Delwiche and Jennifer Jacobs Henderson, 197–205.
London: Routledge: 2013.

Filiu, Jean-Pierre. *The Arab Revolution: Ten Lessons from the Democratic Uprising*. London: Hurst
& Company, 2011.

Fœtus. "L'Essence de Takriz" (January 2010). http://takriz.com/emag/article/essence-de-
takriz (accessed June 10, 2011).

Fœtus. "Quand ils ont Peur ils Censurent: Campagne des Censuré Contre Censure." *Takriz E-mag*
2, no. 3 (2000). http://takriz.com/gdim/archives/n2vol3.html (accessed May 23, 2011).

Fœtus. "Takriz en 2010." http://foetus.me/blog/2010/ (accessed May 24, 2011).

Foucault, Michel. *Discipline and Punish: The Birth of the Prison*. New York: Vintage, 1979.

Foucault, Michel. "A Preface to Transgression." In *Language, Counter-Memory, Practice: Selected
Essays and Interviews*, ed. Donald F. Bouchard, 29–52. Ithaca: Cornell University Press, 1980.

Foucault, Michel. "The Subject and Power." *Critical Inquiry* 8 (1982): 777–95.

Free Race. "The Blogosphere Is Fevered" (June 22, 2008). http://www.free-race.blogspot.com
/2008_06_01_archive.html (accessed June 13, 2011).

Free Race. "No More Fear after Today" (July 6, 2009). http://www.free-race.blogspot.com
/2009/07/blog-post_06.html (accessed May 29, 2011).

Free Race. "Non-Urgent News" (June 3, 2007). http://free-race.blogspot.com/2007/06/
blog-post_03.html (accessed June 30, 2012).

Free Race. "On That Which Makes You Laugh" (July 23, 2008). http://www.free-race.blogspot
.ca/2008/07/blog-post_23.html (accessed June 13, 2011).

Free Race. "On the Culture of Funnels" (June 13, 2007). http://free-race.blogspot.com
/2007/06/la-culture-de-lentonnoir.html (accessed May 30, 2012).

Free Race. "On the Question of Law Enforcement" (June 7, 2007). http://free-race.blogspot.com/
2007/06/blog-post_07.html (accessed June 30, 2012).

Free Race. "When the Censor Is Held Accountable" (March 9, 2010). http://www.free-race
.blogspot.com/2010/03/blog-post.html (accessed May 29, 2011).

Free Thoughts. "An Intellectual Genocide" (April 28, 2008). http://freethoughts-antiguerre
.blogspot.com/2010/04/blog-post_28.html (accessed December 17, 2012).

Gall, Carlotta. "Buffeted by Tumult, Jewish Population in Tunisia Dwindles." *New York Times*,
June 26, 2014, A6.

Gana, Nouri, ed. *The Making of the Tunisian Revolution: Contexts, Architects, Prospects*. Edinburgh: Edinburgh University Press, 2013.

Gantin, Karine. "Tunisie: Des Luttes Renouvellées pour des Droits Inextinguibles." Centre
Tricontinental (December 15, 2010). http://www.cetri.be/spip.php?article1469&lang=fr
(accessed August 29, 2012).

Gantin, Karine, and Omeyya Seddik. "Révolte du Peuple des Mines en Tunisie." *Le Monde Diplomatique* (July 2008). http://www.monde-diplomatique.fr/2008/07/GANTIN/16061 (accessed June 12, 2011).

Garon, Lise. *Dangerous Alliances: Civil Society, The Media and Democratic Transition in North Africa.* London: Zed, 2003.

Gause, Gregory F. "Why Middle East Studies Missed the Arab Spring." *Foreign Affairs* (July–August 2011). http://www.foreignaffairs.com/articles/67932/f-gregory-gause-iii/why-middle-east-studies-missed-the-arab-spring (accessed November 8, 2012).

Geisser, Vincent. "Les Blagues Tunisiennes: Analyse Socio-Politique." Forum Nokta (October 28, 2001). www.facebook.com/group.php?gid=61012075361, and reproduced on http://cosmauxpolis.com/2007/06/19/humour-satire-et-ironie-l'art-tunisien/ (accessed June 15, 2012).

Geisser, Vincent, and Éric Gobe. "La Question de L'Authenticité Tunisienne: Valeur Refuge d'un Régime à Bout de Souffle." *L'Année du Maghreb* 3 (2007): 371–408.

Gelvin, James L. *The Arab Uprisings: What Everyone Needs to Know.* Oxford: Oxford University Press, 2012.

"General Disappointment in WSIS-Host Tunisia." Digital Civil Rights in Europe (November 21, 2005). http://www.edri.org/edrigram/number3.23/Tunisia (accessed March 23, 2011).

Gerbaudo, Paolo. *Tweets and the Streets: Social Media and Contemporary Activism.* London: Pluto, 2012.

Geyer, Georgie Anne. *Tunisia: A Journey through a Country that Works.* London: Stacey International, 2003.

Ghannam, Jeffrey. "Social Media in the Arab World: Leading up to the Uprisings of 2011" (February 3, 2011). http://cima.ned.org/publications/social-media-arab-world-leading-uprisings-2011-0 (accessed February 26, 2012).

Gherib, Baccar. "Censure sur Internet: Qui est Ammar?" Les Amis d'Attariq (May 14, 2010). http://ahbebattariq.blogspot.com/2010/05/censure-sur-internet-qui-est-ammar.html (accessed June 12, 2011).

Gherib, Baccar. "Les Classes Moyennes Tunisiennes entre Mythe et Réalité." *L'Année du Maghreb* 7 (2011): 419–35.

Gherib, Baccar. "Mobilisation Contre la Censure sur Internet: De l'Officiel, du Virtuel et du Réel." Nawaat (May 29, 2010). http://nawaat.org/portail/2010/05/29/mobilisation-contre-la-censure-sur-internet-de-l'officiel-du-virtuel-et-du-reel/ (accessed February 8, 2012).

Ghorbal, Samy. "Comment les Salafistes ont été Neutralizés." *Jeune Afrique* (January 7, 2007). http://www.jeuneafrique.com/Article/LIN06018commessilar0/actualite-afriquecomment-les-salafistes-ont-ete-neutralises.html (accessed August 26, 2012).

Giglio, Mike. "Tunisia Protests: The Facebook Revolution." *The Daily Beast* (January 15, 2011) http://www.thedailybeast.com/articles/2011/01/15/tunisa-protests-the-facebook-revolution.html (accessed January 31, 2014).

Gladwell, Malcolm. "Does Egypt Need Twitter?" *New Yorker* (February 2, 2011). http://www.newyorker.com/online/blogs/newsdesk/2011/02/does-egypt-need-twitter.html#ixzz1CqneJJOu(accessed June 12, 2013).

Gladwell, Malcolm. "Small Change: Why the Revolution Will Not Be Tweeted." *The New Yorker* (October 4, 2010). http://www.newyorker.com/reporting/2010/10/04/101004fa_fact_gladwell (accessed June 12, 2013).

Gobe, Éric. "The Gafsa Mining Basin between Riots and a Social Movement: Meaning and Significance of a Protest Movement in Ben Ali's Tunisia." HAL-SHA (2010). http://hal.archives-ouvertes.fr/docs/00/55/78/26/PDF/Tunisia_The_Gafsa_mining_basin_between_Riots_and_Social_Movement.pdf (accessed February 13, 2012).

Gobe, Éric. "The Tunisian Bar to the Test of Authoritarianism: Professional and Political Movements in Ben Ali's Tunisia (1990–2007)." *The Journal of North African Studies* 15, no. 3 (2010): 333–47.

Gobe, Éric, and Michaël Bechir Ayari. "Les Avocats dans la Tunisie de Ben Ali: Une Profession Politisée?" *L'Année du Maghreb* 3 (2007): 105–32.

Gobe, Éric, and Larbi Chouikha. "Tunisie: Des Élections pour Quoi Faire?" SciencesPo-CERI (February 2010). http://www.sciencespo.fr/ceri/en/content/tunisie-des-elections-pour-quoi-faire-signification-et-portee-des-scrutins-presidentiel-et-l (accessed October 24, 2012).

Gonzague, Armaud. "Takriz Donne de l'Urticaire au Régime Tunisien" (February 1, 2011). http://www.transfert.net/Takriz-donne-de-l-urticaire-au (accessed May 12, 2011).

Gonzalez-Quijano, Yves. "The Birth of a Media Ecosystem: Lebanon in the Internet Age." In *New Media in the Muslim World: The Emerging Public Sphere*, ed. Dale F. Eickelman and Jon W. Anderson, 61–79. Bloomington: Indiana University Press, 2003.

Gonzalez-Quijano, Yves. "Trois Remarques à Propos du Web 2.0 Arabe." *Culture et Politique Arabe* (March 22, 2011). http://cpa.hypotheses.org/2587 (accessed February 8, 2012).

Gouverneur de Normalland. "The Blogging Movement Says No to Ammar" (December 27, 2010). http://normalland.blogspot.com/2010/12/blog-post_27.html (accessed June 13, 2011).

Granovetter, Mark. "The Strength of Weak Ties." *The American Journal of Sociology* 78, no. 6 (1973): 1360–80.

Graziano, Teresa. "The Tunisian Diaspora: Between Digital Riots and Web Activism." Fondation Sciences de L'Homme (April 2012). http://www.e-diasporas.fr/working-papers/Graziano-Tunisians-EN.pdf (accessed April 14, 2012).

Grira, Sarra. "Les Cyber Réfugiés en Tunisie: Un Contre-Poids à la Censure de Ammar sur Internet" (February 25, 2010). http://courantalternatif.blogspot.com/2010/02/les-cyber-refugies-en-tunisie-un-contre.html (accessed June 15, 2011).

Grira, Sarra, and Julien Pain. "Connaissez-vous Slimane Rouissi: L'Homme qui a Lancé la Révolution Tunisienne?" France24 (October 25, 2011). http://tunisie.france24.com/2011/10/25/connaissez-vous-slimane-rouissi-l%E2%80%99homme-qui-a-lance-la-revolution-tunisienne/ (accessed January 9, 2011).

Guaaybess, Tourya. *Les Médias Arabes: Confluences Médiatiques et Dynamique Sociale.* Paris: CNRS Éditions, 2011.

Hachicha, Neila Charchour. "Yezzi…Fock." Nawaat (October 3, 2005). http://nawaat.org/portail/2005/10/03/yezzi-fock-nch (accessed October 28 2011).

Haddar, Mohamed. "L'Économie Tunisienne: État des Lieux." *Maghreb-Mashrek* 206 (Winter 2010–11): 63–71.

Haddouk, Walid. "The Tunisian Revolution: An Exploration of the Socio-economic Background." In *The Tunisian Revolution: Causes, Contexts and Challenges*, 87–115. Doha: Arab Center for Research and Policy Studies, 2012.

Hafez, Kai. "Arab Satellite Broadcasting: Democracy without Political Parties." *Transnational Broadcasting Studies* 15 (Fall 2005). http://tbsjournal.arabmediasociety.com/Archives/Fall05/Hafez.html.

Hajji, Lotfi. "The 18 October Coalition for Rights and Freedoms in Tunisia." *Arab Reform Initiative Brief* (October 13, 2006). http://www.arab-reform.net/18-october-coalition-rights-and-freedoms-tunisia (accessed June 6, 2011).

Halavais, Alexander. "Blogging as a Free Frame of Reference." In *The Participatory Cultures Handbook*, ed. Aaron Delwiche and Jennifer Jacobs Henderson, 109–19. London: Routledge, 2013.

Hamdi, Sayed. "The Opposition Figure Moncef Marzouki Calls for a Popular Uprising." Al Jazeera.net (April 11, 2006). http://www.aljazeera.net/news/pages/f617e417-331f-4647-9e01-0295e30c1ea1 (accessed July 7, 2012).

Hand, Maud. "Il Fait Bon Vivre en Tunisie?" Association for Progressive Communication (April 1, 2005). http://www.apc.org/en/news/access/world/il-fait-bon-vivre-en-tunisie-state-human-rights-tu (accessed December 15, 2012).

Harrigan, Jane. "Did Food Prices Plant the Seeds of the Arab Spring?" SOAS Inaugural Lecture Series, School of Oriental and African Studies, University of London (April 28, 2011). http://www.soas.ac.uk/about/events/inaugurals/28apr2011-did-food-prices-plant-the-seeds-of-the-arab-spring.html (accessed May 4, 2012).

Hassanpour, Navid. "Media Disruption and Revolutionary Unrest: Evidence from Mubarak's Quasi-Experiment." *Political Communication* 31, no. 1 (2014): 1–24.

Haugbølle, Rikke Hostrup, and Francesco Cavatorta. "'Vive la Grande Famille des Médias Tunisiens': Media Reform, Authoritarian Resilience and Societal Responses in Tunisia." *Journal of North African Studies* 17 no. 1 (2011): 97–112.

Henry, Clement. "Tunisia's Sweet Little Regime." In *Worst of the Worst: Dealing with Repressive and Rogue Nations*, ed. Robert Rotberg, 300–323. Washington, D.C.: Brookings Institution Press, 2007.

Herrera, Geoffrey L. "New Media for a New World: Information Technology and Threats to National Security." In *Globalization and National Security*, ed. Jonathan Kirshner, 75–104. New York: Routledge, 2006.

Herrera, Linda. "Egypt's Revolution 2.0: The Facebook Factor." In *Mediating the Arab Uprisings*, ed. Adel Iskandar and Bassam Haddad, 47–53. Washington, D.C.: Tadween, 2013.

Herrera, Linda. "Youth and Citizenship in the Digital Age: A View from Egypt." *Harvard Educational Review* 82, no. 3 (2012): 333–52.

Herrera, Linda, and Asef Bayat, eds. *Being Young and Muslim: New Cultural Politics in the Global South and North*. Oxford: Oxford University Press, 2010.

Herzfeld, Michael. "Anthropology and the Politics of Significance." *Etnográfica* 4, no. 1 (2000): 5–36. http://ceas.iscte.pt/etnografica/docs/vol_04/N1/Vol_iv_N1_5-36.pdf (accessed September 22, 2013).

Hibou, Béatrice. *The Force of Obedience: The Political Economy of Repression in Tunisia*. Translated by Andrew Brown. Cambridge: Polity, 2011.

Hibou, Béatrice. "Tunisie: Économie Politique et Morale d'un Movement Social." *Politique Africaine* 121 (March 2011): 5–22.

Hijjawi, Aref. "The Role of Al Jazeera (Arabic) in the Arab Revolts of 2011." In *Perspectives II: People's Power: The Arab World in Revolt*, ed. Layla Al-Zubaidi and Paul Joachim, 68–72. Beirut: Heinrich Böll Stiftung, 2011. http://www.boell.de/publications/publications-perspectives-2-mai-2011-11961.html (accessed March 12, 2012).

Hirschkind, Charles. *The Ethical Soundscape: Cassette Sermons and Islamic Counter Publics*. New York: Columbia University Press, 2006.

Hofheinz, Albrecht. "Arab Internet User: Popular Trends and Public Impact." In *Arab Media and Political Renewal: Community, Legitimacy and Public Life*, ed. Naomi Sakr, 56–79. London: IB Tauris, 2007.

Hofheinz, Albrecht. "The Internet in the Arab World: Playground for Political Liberalization." *Internationale Politik und Gesellschaft* 3 (March 2005): 78–96.

Honwana, Alcinda. *Youth and Revolution in Tunisia*. New York: Zed, 2013.

Horchani, Mehdi. "The Policy of Impoverishment and Land Seizure in Regueb." The Tunisian Cyber Parliament, Forum for Rights and Freedoms (July 14, 2010). http://24sur24.posterous.com/23252863 (accessed January 3, 2012).

Houeidi, Fahmi. "The Crisis of Freedom in the Arab World: Tunisia as a Model." *Al Sharq Al Awsat*, November 23, 2005. http://www.aawsat.com/leader.asp?section=3&article=334 808&issueno=9857 (accessed March 22, 2012).

Howard, Philip N. *The Digital Origins of Dictatorship and Democracy: Information Technology and Political Islam*. Oxford: Oxford University Press, 2010.

Howard, Philip N., and Muzammil M. Hussain. *Democracy's Fourth Wave? Digital Media and the Arab Spring*. Oxford: Oxford University Press, 2013.

"Human Rights Watch, World Report 2011: Tunisia." United Nations Human Rights Watch Commission for Refugees (January 24, 2011). www.unhcr.org/refworld/docid/4d3e80261a.html (accessed March 16, 2011).

"Independent Voices Stifled in Tunisia." Amnesty International (July 13, 2010). www.amnesty .org/en/library/info/MDE30/008/2010 (accessed June 1, 2011).

Infinity. "Comment on Sami Ben Gharbia's 'Blogs Tunisiensr'" (December 21, 2005). https:// ifikra.wordpress.com/2005/12/20/blogs-tunisiens-des-zones-touristiques (accessed November 2, 2011).

International Crisis Group. "Popular Protest in North Africa and the Middle East: Tunisia's Way." Middle East/North Africa Report No. 106 (April 28, 2011). http://www.crisis-group.org/en/regions/middle-east-north-africa/north-africa/tunisia/106-popular-protests-in-north-africa-and-the-middle-east-iv-tunisias-way.aspx (accessed June 30, 2012).

"International Fact-Finding Mission: Tunisia and the World Summit on Information Society." FIDH, OMCT & ICHRDD Report No. 418.2 (May 2005). http://www.fidh.org/IMG/ pdf/tn418a.pdf (accessed January 31, 2012).

"Internet Filtering in Tunisia." OpenNet Initiative (November 2005). www. opennet.net/ studies/tunisia (accessed March 1, 2011).

"Intervenez pour Libérer Zouheir Yahyaoui." Reveil Tunisien (June 16, 2002). http://www .reveiltunisien.org/spip.php?article78 (accessed June 8, 2011).

"Je Blog pour l'Islam: L'Islam et Moi" (June 15, 2008). http://toreach-thegoal.blogspot.com/ 2008/06/je-blog-pour-lislam-lislam-et-moi.html (accessed June 17, 2011).

Jenkens, Henry. *Convergence Culture: Where Old and New Media Collide*. New York: NYU Press, 2006.

Jordan, Tim. *Internet, Society and Culture: Communicative Practices Before and After the Internet*. New York: Bloomsbury, 2013.

José, Garçon. "Tunisie: Des Jihadistes Contre Ben Ali." *Libération* (January 10, 2007) http:// www.liberation.fr/monde/2007/01/10/tunisie-des-jihadistes-contre-ben-ali_81526 (accessed February 2, 2012).

Jouët, Josiane. "Des Usages de la Télématique aux Internet Studies." In *Communiquer à l'Ère Numérique: Regards Croisés sur la Sociologie des Usages*, ed. J. Denouël and F. Granjon, 45–90. Paris: Presses des Mines, 2011.

"Journalist Faces Imprisonment for Covering Gafsa Unrest." Amnesty International (June 20, 2010). http://www.amnesty.org/en/library/info/MDE30/006/2010/en (accessed January 15, 2012).

Juris, Jeffery S. *Networking Futures: The Movement against Corporate Globalization*. Durham: Duke University Press, 2008.

Just an Illusion. "Comment on Sami Ben Gharbia's 'Blogs Tunisiens'" (December 23, 2005). https://ifikra.wordpress.com/2005/12/20/blogs-tunisiens-des-zones-touristiques (accessed November 2, 2011).

Kahlaoui, Tarek. "Ammar Censors the Blog Nocturnal Thoughts" (February 5, 2010). http:// tareknightlife.blogspot.com/2010/02/blog-post_05.html (accessed December 18, 2012).

Kahlaoui, Tarek. "Arabica and -Z-" (November 5, 2009). http://tareknightlife.blogspot .com/2009/11/blog-post_4092.html (accessed January 2, 2012).

Kahlaoui, Tarek. "A Brief Account of the Tunisian Revolution's Media Branch" (January 20, 2011). https://www.facebook.com/notes/kahlaoui-tarek/a-brief-account-from-my-perspective-of-the-tunisian-revolutions-media-branch-tar/101501205831658022 (accessed September 24, 2011).

Kahlaoui, Tarek. "Comments on Al Hiwar TV's Report on Tunisian Bloggers" (July 20, 2007). http://tareknightlife.blogspot.com/2007/10/1.html (accessed May 26, 2011).

Kahlaoui, Tarek. "Dotting the i's and Crossing the t's: On Exiled Blogs" (February 9, 2010). http://tkharbich.blogspot.com/2010/02/blog-post_09.html (accessed April 13, 2013).

Kahlaoui, Tarek. "Do We Need Democracy?" (July 9, 2007). http://tareknightlife.blogspot .com/2007/06/blog-post_09.html (accessed December 17, 2011).

Kahlaoui, Tarek. "How Tunisian Bloggers Reacted to the Arrest of Fatma Arabicca" Magharebia (November 17, 2009). http://www.magharebia.com/cocoon/awi/xhtml1/ar/features/ awi/blog/2009/11/17/feature-05 (accessed March 19, 2011).

Kahlaoui, Tarek. "Internet Control: Censoring Censorship." Nawaat (October 28, 2010). http://nawaat.org/portail/2010/10/28/ (accessed August 23, 2011).

Kahlaoui, Tarek. "Political Freedom of Expression and the Politicization of the Freedom of Speech" (June 11, 2007). http://tareknightlife.blogspot.com/2007/06/blog-post_2973.html (accessed December 17, 2011).

Kahlaoui, Tarek. "The Powers of Social Media." In *The Making of the Tunisian Revolution: Contexts, Architects, Prospects*, ed. Nouri Gana, 147–58. Edinburgh: Edinburgh University Press, 2013.

Kahlaoui, Tarek. "The Prospects of Democracy in the Arab World: A Historical Perspective." *Middle East Online* (September 27, 2007). http://www.middle-east-online.com/?id=52912 (accessed December 19, 2011).

Kahlaoui, Tarek. "Reflecting on Democracy" (June 17, 2011). http://tareknightlife.blogspot.com/2007/06/blog-post_9196.html (accessed December 18, 2011).

Kahlaoui, Tarek. "Selections from Gabriel García Márquez's *The Autumn of the Patriarch*" (December 14, 2007). http://tarek-kahlaoui404.blogspot.com/2007/12/blog-post_9183.html (accessed May 12, 2012).

Kahlaoui, Tarek. "Summer Reflections" (July 27, 2007). http://tareknightlife.blogspot.com/2007/07/blog-post.html (accessed December 18, 2011).

Kahlaoui, Tarek. "To the Blogger Ehmida" (November 15, 2009). http://tareknightlife.blogspot.com/2009/11/blog-post_15.html (accessed January 3, 2012).

Kahlaoui, Tarek. "Tunisia Censors Dozens of Sites in a Single Week…and Invites Ridicule of the Censor Ammar 404" (May 10, 2010). www.traidnt.net/vb/showthread.php?t=1557352 (accessed May 16, 2011).

Kahlaoui, Tarek. "The Tunisian Blogosphere: A New Horizon" (November 11, 2009). http://tareknightlife.blogspot.com/2009/11/blog-post_7663.html (accessed March 6, 2012).

Kahlaoui, Tarek. "A Vocal Blog on the Occasion of the National Day for the Freedom of Blogging" (October 12, 2008). http://radyountounes.blogspot.com/2008_10_01_archive.html (accessed September 18, 2011).

Kahlaoui, Tarek. "When the Debate Digresses" (March 11, 2008). http://tareknightlife.blogspot.com/2008/03/blog-post_11.html (accessed December 19, 2011).

Kahlaoui, Tarek. "When Tunisian Bloggers Decide to Write about Politics: Part One" (May 17, 2007). http://tareknightlife.blogspot.ca/2007/05/1.html (accessed June 25, 2012).

Kahlaoui, Tarek. "When Tunisian Bloggers Decide to Write about Politics: Part Two" (May 18, 2007). http://tareknightlife.blogspot.ca/2007/05/2.html (accessed June 25, 2012).

Kahlaoui, Tarek. "Who Is Islamophobic?" (June 6, 2008). http://tareknightlife.blogspot.com/2009/06/blog-post_06.html (accessed December 18, 2012).

Kalathil, Shanthi, and Baylor C. Boas. *Open Networks, Closed Regimes: The Impact of the Internet on Authoritarian Rule*. Washington, D.C.: Carnegie Endowment for the International Peace, 2003.

Kallander, Amy Aisen. "From TUNeZINE to Nhar Ala Ammar: A Reconsideration of the Role of Bloggers in Tunisia's Revolution." *Arab Media and Society* 17 (2013). http://www.arabmediasociety.com/articles/downloads/20130221104651_Kallander_Amy.pdf (accessed May 11, 2013).

Kamalipour, Yahya, ed. *Media, Power and Politics in the Digital Age: The 2009 Presidential Election Uprising in Iran*. Lanham: Rowman & Littlefield, 2010.

Kamoun, Farouk, Jamil Chaabouni, Sami Tabbane, and Asma Ben Letaifa. "Tunisia ICT Sector Performance Review, 2009–10: Towards Evidence-Based ICT Policy and Regulation." Policy Paper No. 12, Research ICT Africa, 2010. http://researchictafrica.net/publications.php (accessed June 10, 2011).

Kamrava, Mehran. *The Modern Middle East*. Berkeley: University of California Press, 2013.

Karim, Mona. "Singing against Internet Censorship." *Alrai*, February 8, 2011. http://www.alraimedia.com/Alrai/Article.aspx?id=255281&date=08022011 (accessed March 18, 2011).

Kausch, Kristina. "Tunisia: EU Incentives Contributing to New Repression." FRIDE (September 9, 2010). http://www.fride.org/publication/807/tunisia:-eu-incentives-contributing-to-new-repression (accessed May 7, 2012).

Khadraoui, Malek. "Interview avec Malek Khadraoui: Un Blogeur-Militant" (December 6, 2011). http://capharnaum-tremens.blogspot.com/2011/12/malek-khadraoui-blogueur-militant-la.html (accessed February 9, 2012).

Khadraoui, Malek. "Tunisie: Des Internautes en T-shirts Blancs Interdits de Flash Mob Contre la Censure." Nawaat (August 4, 2011). http://nawaat.org/portail/2010/08/06/tunisie-des-internautes-en-t-shirts-blanc-interdits-de-flash-mob-contre-la-censure/ (accessed June 13, 2011).

Khalaf, Samir, and Roseanne Saad Khalaf, eds. *Arab Youth: Social Mobilization in Times of Risk.* London: Saqi, 2011.

Khalil, Joe. "Youth-Generated Media: A Case of Blogging and Arab Youth Cultural Politics." *Television and New Media* 14, no. 4 (2013): 338–50.

Khalsi, Khalil. "Error 404 Not Found: 28 Mille Facebookers Tunisiens Privés d'Accès à leur Site Préféré." *Le Temps* (September 1, 2008). http://www.letemps.com.tn/pop_article.php?ID_art=19839 (accessed May 27, 2011).

Khanfar, Waddah. "At Al Jazeera, We Saw the Arab Revolutions Coming. Why Didn't the West?" *Washington Post*, February 25, 2005. http://www.washingtonpost.com/wp-dyn/content/article/2011/02/25/AR2011022503177.html(accessed September 25, 2012).

Khatib, Lina. *Image Politics in the Middle East: The Role of the Visual in Political Struggle.* London: IB Tauris, 2012.

Khayyâm, Omar. "À la Recherche d'une Espèce Perdue: Les TUNeZINiEns." *Tunisia Watch* (February 10, 2010). http://tunisnews.net/112010 (accessed October 14, 2011).

Khayyâm, Omar. "Les Maux de Tout les Mots." TUNeZINE 8 (July 8, 2001). www.tunezine.com/tunezine08.htm (accessed October 24, 2011).

Khechana, Rachid. "La Censure Paralyse mon Travail." *Tunisnews* 3739 (August 18, 2010). http://tunisnews.net/archive/18Out10f.htm (accessed March 1, 2012).

Khechana, Rachid. "Les Médias Tunisiens Face à la Prépondérance de l'État Partisan." *Confluences Méditerranée* 69 (2009): 99–105.

King, Stephen J. *Liberalization against Democracy: The Local Politics of Economic Reform in Tunisia.* Bloomington: Indiana University Press, 2003.

Kissa Online. "An Attempt against Free Thought" (May 2, 2010). http://kissa-online.blogspot.com/2010/05/un-attentat-contre-la-pensee.html(accessed June 15, 2011).

Kissa Online. "Censorship" (February 9, 2010). http://kissa-online.blogspot.com/2010/02/dico-15.html (accessed June 15, 2011).

Kissa Online. "The Centenary of Abou Al Kacen Chebbi" (February 23, 2009). http://kissa-online.blogspot.com/2009/02/blog-post_23.html (accessed May 12, 2011).

Kissa Online. "For the Youth to Laugh" (September 3, 2009). http://kissa-online.blogspot.com/2009/09/blog-post.html (accessed May 12, 2011).

Kissa Online. "The Tree" (September 18, 2009). http://kissa-online.blogspot.com/2009/09/pablo-neruda-larbre.html (accessed May 12, 2011).

Kissa Online. "Whenever You See It…You Know There Is Repression" (July 1, 2008). http://kissa-online.blogspot.com/2008/07/blog-post.html (accessed June 15, 2011).

Kraidy, Marwan. *Reality Television and Arab Politics: Contention in Public Life.* Cambridge: Cambridge University Press, 2009.

Kraidy, Marwan, and Joe Khalil. *Arab Television Industries.* London: Palgrave Macmillan, 2009.

Kraidy, Marwan, and Joe Khalil. "Youth, Media and Culture in the Arab World." In *International Handbook of Children, Media and Culture*, ed. Kristen Drotner and Sonia Livingstone, 330–44. London: Sage, 2008.

Kurzman, Charles. "The Arab Spring Uncoiled." *Mobilization: An International Journal* 17, no. 4 (2012): 377–90.

Labidi, Kamel. "Letter of Resignation as Head of Tunisia's INRIC." World Press Freedom Committee (August 14, 2012). http://www.wpfc.org/?q=node/485 (accessed April 5, 2014).

Labidi, Kamel. "No Place to Talk about Internet Freedom." *Internal Herald Tribune*, November 11, 2005. http://www.nytimes.com/2005/11/15/opinion/15iht-edlabidi.html (accessed March 23, 2011).

Lamloum, Olfa. "Entretien avec Tunisnews." In *La Tunisie de Ben Ali: La Société Contre le Régime*, ed. Olfa Lamloum and Bernard Ravenel, 249–51. Paris: L'Harmattan, 2002.

Lamloum, Olfa, and Bernard Ravenel, eds. *La Tunisie de Ben Ali: La Société Contre le Régime*. Paris: L'Harmattan, 2002.

"Launching the 'Freedom of Expression in Mourning' Campaign" (October 3, 2005). http://tounis.blogspot.com (accessed October 27, 2011).

Lecomte, Romain. "L'Amonymat Comme Art de Résistance: Le Cas du Cyberespace Tunisien." *Terminal* 105 (2010): 55–68.

Lecomte, Romain. "Révolution Tunisenne et Internet: Le Rôle des Médias Sociaux." *L'Année du Maghreb* 7 (2011): 389–418.

Lefebvre, Henri. *Everyday Life in the Modern World*. London: Allen Lane, 1971.

Lefebvre, Henri. *Fondements d'une Sociologie de la Quotidienneté*. Paris: L'Arche, 1961.

"Le 404 Not Found Nuit Gravement à L'Image de mon Pays." http://www.facebook.com/group.php?gid=191838240119 (accessed February 8, 2012).

"Le Journaliste Tunisien Fahem Boukadous Condamné à 4 Ans de Prison Ferme." *Libération* (July 7, 2010). http://www.liberation.fr/monde/0101645674-le-journaliste-tunisien-fahem-boukadous-condamne-a-4-ans-de-prison-ferme (accessed June 12, 2011).

"Le Mouvement de Protestation s'Étend à Ben Gardane, en Dépit de la Férocité de la Répression et des Promesses du Pouvoir." *Tunisnews* 3739 (August 18, 2010).

Lerner, Daniel. *The Passing of Traditional Society*. Glencoe, Ill.: Free Press, 1958.

Lerner, Melissa Y. "Connecting the Actual with the Virtual: The Internet and Social Movement Theory in the Muslim World." *Journal of Muslim Minority Affairs* 30, no. 4 (2010): 555–74.

Lievrouw, Leah A. *Alternative and Activist New Media*. Cambridge: Polity, 2011.

Lotan, Gilad, Erhardt Graeff, Mike Ananny, Devin Gaffney, Ian Pearce, and Danah Boyd. "The Revolutions Were Tweeted: Information Flows during the 2011 and Egyptian Revolution." *International Journal of Communication* 5 (2011): 1375–1405.

Lutz, Meris. "Tunisia: Online Activist Rally to Free Fellow Blogger." *Los Angeles Times*, November 6, 2009. http://latimesblogs.latimes.com/babylonbeyond/2009/11/tunisia-blogger-fatma-riahi-arrested-held-incommunicado.html (accessed December 11, 2012).

Lynch, Marc. "Blogging the New Arab Public." *Arab Media and Society* 1 (2007). http://www.marclynch.com/wp-content/uploads/2011/03/20070312155027_AMS1_Marc_Lynch.pdf (accessed October 6, 2010).

Lynch, Marc. "Globalization and Arab Security." In *Globalization and National Security*, ed. Jonathan Kirshner, 171–200. New York: Routledge: 2006.

Lynch, Marc. "Political Science and the New Arab Public Sphere." *Foreign Policy* (June 12, 2012). http://lynch.foreignpolicy.com/posts/2012/06/12/political_science_and_the_new_arab_public_sphere (accessed August 30, 2012).

Lynch, Marc. *Voices of the New Arab Public: Iraq, Al Jazeera, and Middle East Politics Today*. New York: Columbia University Press, 2006.

Mabrouk, Mehdi. "A Revolution for Dignity and Freedom: Preliminary Observations on the Social and Cultural Background to the Tunisian Revolution." *Journal of North African Studies* 16, no. 4 (2011): 625–35.

Mackinnon, Rebecca. "Tunisian Online Protest Blocked." Global Voices (October 4, 2005). http://globalvoicesonline.org/2005/10/04/tunisian-online-protest-blocked/(accessed March 17, 2011).

Madrigal, Alexis C. "The Inside Story of How Facebook Responded to Tunisian Hacks." *The Atlantic* (January 24, 2011). www.theatlantic.com/technology/archive/2011/01/the-inside-story-of-how-facebook-responded-to-tunisian-hacks/70044/ (accessed August 3, 2012).

Makhlouf, Zouheir. "Cyberspace under the Thumb of the Police." In *Tunisian Journalists Standing up to Dictatorship*, 123–49. Tunis: Tunis Center for Press Freedom, 2013.

Manenti, Boris. "Sidi Bouzid ou la Révolte Tunisienne Organisée sur Facebook." *Le Nouvel Observateur* (January 4, 2011). http://tempsreel.nouvelobs.com/actualite/vu-sur-le-web/20110104.OBS5680/sidi-bouzid-ou-la-revolte-tunisienne-organisee-sur-facebook.html (accessed January 23, 2011).

Manfila, Djeneba. "Facebook Censuré en Tunisie." Afrik (August 28, 2008). http://www.afrik.com/article15084.html (accessed June 11, 2012).

"Manifestation Contre la Censure sur Internet: Ça Bouge sur le Front de la Citoyenneté!" *Attariq Al Jadid* 181 (May 22, 2011). http://ahbebattariq.blogspot.com/2010/05/manifestation-contre-la-censure-sur.html (accessed February 8, 2012).

Mansar, Adnan. "The Tunisian General Labor Union: Socio-Political Dialectics." In *The Tunisian Revolution: Causes, Contexts and Challenges*, 271–98. Doha: Arab Center for Research and Policy Studies, 2012.

Marzouki, Meryem. "Pendant les Travaux, le Gâchis Continue." Alternatives Citoyennes (November 24, 2005). http://www.alternatives-citoyennes.sgdg.org/num17/dos-bilan-w.html (accessed May 25, 2011).

Marzouki, Meryem. "WSIS in Tunisia: The Reign of the Arbitrary." *Third World Resurgence Magazine* 184 (December 2005). http://www.twn.my/title2/twr184.htm (accessed June 8, 2011).

Marzouki, Meryem, and Rikke Frank Jørgensen. "Human Rights: The Missing Link." In *Visions in Process II: The World Summit on the Information Society*, ed. Olga Drossou and Heike Jensen, 17-23. Berlin: Heinrich Böll Stiftung, 2005.

Marzouki, Moncef. "Isn't It Time to Change the Discourse?" (January 24, 2008). http://moncefmarzouki.com/spip.php?article179 (accessed July 7, 2012).

Mazen. "Comment on Sami Ben Gharbia's 'I Blog for Tunisia'" (June 2, 2007). http://samibengharbia.com/tag/blogsphere/page/2/ (accessed November 17, 2011).

M.B.H. "Tunisie: Facebook Bat de Nouveaux Records." *Tekiano* (October 13, 2009). http://www.tekiano.com/net/web20/2-70-1196/tunisie-facebook-bat-de-nouveaux-records.html (accessed March 12, 2011).

McMillin, Divya C. *Mediated Identities: Youth, Agency and Globalization*. New York: Peter Lang, 2009.

Meddeb, Hamza. "L'Ambivalence de la Course à *el Khobza*: Obéir et se Révolter en Tunisie." *Politique Africaine* 121 (March 2011): 35–51.

Mihoub, Samia. *Internet dans le Monde Arabe: Complexité d'une Adoption*. Paris: L'Hamattan, 2005.

Mihoub, Samia. "Internet en Tunisie: Régulation, Usages et Conflits Émergents." *Horizons Maghrebins* 62 (2010): 105–10.

Mihoub, Samia. "La Question de l'Internet Arabe ou Quand les États se Trompent de Cible." *Africultures* (April 10, 2008). http://www.africultures.com/php/?nav=article&no=7494 (accessed February 10, 2012).

Mihoub, Samia. "Le Cyberactivism à l'Heure de la Révolution Tunisienne." *Archivio Anthropologico Mediterraneo* 12, no. 2 (2011): 17–31. http://www.archivioantropologicomediterraneo.it/?p=280 (accessed March 1, 2012).

Mihoub, Samia. "Particularités de l'Appropriation du Réseau Internet en Tunisie." Archive Ouverte en Sciences de l'Information et de la Communication (November 17, 2003). http://archivesic.ccsd.cnrs.fr/sic_00000804 (accessed June 1, 2011).

Miladi, Noureddine. "Tunisia: A Media Led Revolution." Aljazera.net (January 17, 2011). http://www.aljazeera.com/indepth/opinion/2011/01/2011116142317498666.html (accessed December 13, 2012).

Mirkin, Barry. "Population Levels, Trends and Policies in the Arab Region: Challenges and Opportunities." UNDP Research Paper Series, 2010. http://www.arab-hdr.org (accessed September 22, 2012).

Mnaouar, Maryam. "Internet: L'Inextinguible Soif de Liberté des Jeunes Tunisiens—Interview de Slim Amamou." Afrik (October 10, 2010). http://www.afrik.com/article20977 .html(accessed March 21, 2011).

Mnaouar, Maryam. "Takriz: La Violence était Légitime Face à une Dictature Meurtrière et Barbare." Afrik (June 2, 2011). http://www.afrik.com/article22996.html (accessed June 7, 2011).

Monshipouri, Mahmood. *Democratic Uprisings in the New Middle East: Youth, Technology, Human Rights and US Foreign Policy.* Boulder: Paradigm, 2014.

Morozov, Evgeny. "Freedom.gov: Why Washington's Support for Online Democracy Is the Worst Thing Ever to Happen to the Internet." *Foreign Policy* 34 (February 2011): 34–35.

Morozov, Evgeny. *Net Delusion: The Dark Side of Internet Freedom.* New York: Public Affairs, 2011.

Morozov, Evgeny. "Why the Internet Is Failing Iranian Activists." *Prospect* (January 5, 2010). http://www.prospectmagazine.co.uk/magazine/why-the-internet-is-failing-irans-activists/ (accessed December 18, 2012).

Mossberger, Karen. "Toward Digital Citizenship: Addressing Inequality in the Information Age." In *The Routledge Handbook of Internet Politics,* ed. Andrew Chadwick and Philip N. Howard, 173–85. London: Routledge, 2009.

Mugneret, Eric. "Le Web Censuré, à la Mode Tunisienne" (January 18, 2001). http://www .transfert.net/Le-Web-censure-a-la-mode (accessed May 22, 2011).

Muñoz, Ana Luz. "Le Rôle des Médias Comme Nawaat est d'Essayer de Changer les Choses," EMI (June 10, 2013). http://emi-cfd.com/echanges-partenariats/?p=2023 (accessed April 19, 2014).

Murphy, Emma C. *Economic and Political Change in Tunisia.* London: Palgrave Macmillan, 1999.

Murphy, Emma C. "Problematizing Arab Youth: Generational Narratives of Systemic Failure." *Mediterranean Politics* 17, no. 1 (2012): 5–22.

Murphy, Emma C. "The Tunisian *Mise à Niveau* Programme and the Political Economy of Reform." *New Political Economy* 11, no. 4 (2006): 519–40.

Murthy, Dhiraj. *Twitter: Social Communication in the Twitter Age.* Cambridge: Polity, 2013.

Nadia. "Tunisian Internet Citizens Protest against Censorship." *MidEast Youth* (May 20, 2010). http://www.mideastyouth.com/2010/05/20/7527/ (accessed May 8, 2012).

Noman, Helmi, and Jillian C. York. "West Censoring East: The Use of Western Technologies by Middle East Censors, 2010–2011." OpenNet Initiative (March 2011). http://opennet .net/west-censoring-east-the-use-western-technologies-middle-east-censors-2010-2011 (accessed December 12, 2012).

Norton, Richard August. "The New Media, Civil Pluralism and the Struggle for Political Reform." In *New Media in the Muslim World: The Emerging Public Sphere,* ed. Dale F. Eickelman and Jon W. Anderson, 19–32. Bloomington: Indiana University Press, 2003.

"Notre Article sur la Censure Censuré en Tunisie." France24.com (May 12, 2010). http://ob-servers.france24.com/fr/20100505-404-not-found-message-courant-internet-tunisie-censure-blogs-protestation-pacifique-ammar (accessed January 25, 2012).

Noyon, Jennifer. *Islam, Politics and Pluralism: Theory and Practice in Turkey, Jordan, Tunisia and Algeria.* Washington, D.C.: The Royal Institute of International Affairs, 2003.

O'Brien, Danny. "Tunisia Invades, Censors Facebook, Other Accounts." Committee to Protect Journalists (January 5, 2011). http://cpj.org/internet/2011/01/tunisia-invades-censors-facebook-other-accounts.php (accessed January 22, 2011).

Omrane, Nadia, and Meryem Marzouki. "Zouheir Yahyaoui, la Figure de L'Éclaireur." Alternatives Citoyennes (March 14, 2005). http://www.alternatives-citoyennes.sgdg.org/zouhair .html (accessed May 25, 2011).

"Open Letter to Kofi Annan" (October 1, 2005). http://www.worldsummit2003.de/en/web/ 21.htm (accessed March 23, 2011).

"Organiser une Manifestation en Tunisie" (May 23, 2010). http://larbieh.blogs.france24.com/ article/2010/05/23/organiser-une-manifestation-en-tunisie-0 (accessed January 15, 2012).

Orwell, George. "Funny, but Not Vulgar." http://orwell.ru/library/articles/funny/english/e_funny (accessed December 20, 2012).

Padania, Sameer. "Tunisia: Opening Prisons to the World." Global Voices (September 27, 2006). http://globalvoicesonline.org/2006/09/27/tunisia-opening-prisons-to-the-world/ (accessed July 2, 2011).

"Paris Préoccupé par l'Arrestation du Journaliste Tunisien Fahem Boukadous." *Jeune Afrique* (July 16, 2010). www.jeuneafrique.com/actu/20100716T141602Z20100716T141558Z (accessed January 15, 2012).

"Parties, Associations and Unions Support the 18 October Movement." *Al Badil* (November 14, 2005). http://albadil.org/spip.php?article595 (accessed November 21, 2012).

Perkins, Kenneth. *A History of Modern Tunisia*. Cambridge: Cambridge University Press, 2004.

Perlmutter, David D. *Blogwars*. Oxford: Oxford University Press, 2008.

"PES against Tunisia Receiving Advanced Status from the EU." European Forum (November 18, 2009). http://www.europeanforum.net/news/775/pes_against_tunisia_receiving_advanced_status_from_the_eu (accessed June 11, 2011).

Pintak, Laurence. "Satellite TV and Arab Democracy." *Journalism Practice* 2, no. 1 (2008): 15–26.

Pintak, Laurence, and Jeremy Ginges. "The Mission of Arab Journalism: Creating Change in a Time of Turmoil." *The International Journal of Press/Politics* 13, no. 3 (2008): 193–227.

Piot, Olivier. "De l'Indignation à la Révolution." *Le Monde Diplomatique* (February 2011). http://www.monde-diplomatique.fr/2011/02/PIOT/20114 (accessed January 30, 2012).

Piquard, Alexandre. "Zouheir Yahyaoui Libre, les Cyberdissidents Tunisiens Restent Harcelés par le Régime." Transfert.net (November 20, 2003). http://www.transfert.net/Zouhair-Yahyaoui-libre-les (accessed October 15, 2011).

"Pluralism in Tunisia's Virtual Parliament." Aljazeera.net (November 16, 2009). http://www.aljazeera.net/NR/exeres/7CA1232D-65AE-4C49-A1FA-191E6384A328.htm (accessed February 11, 2012).

Poell, Thomas, and Kaouthar Darmoni. "Twitter as a Multilingual Space: The Articulation of the Tunisian Revolution through #sidibouzid." *European Journal of Media Studies* 1, no. 1 (2012): 14–34. http://ssrn.com/abstract=2154288 (accessed September 4, 2013).

Poster, Mark. "Everyday (Virtual) Life." *New Literary History* 33, no. 4 (2002): 743–60.

Powel, Brieg, and Larbi Sadiki. *The EU and Tunisia: A Study of Democratization via Association*. London: Routledge, 2009.

Puel, Hélène. "Astrubal: La Révolution en Tunisie aurait eu Lieu sans Internet." *La Sentinelle de Tunisie* (March 11, 2011). http://www.01net.com/editorial/529946/astrubal-la-revolution-en-tunisie-aurait-eu-lieu-sans-internet/ (accessed February 9, 2012).

"Rapport Annuel 2008, Moyen-Orient et Afrique du Nord: Tunisie." Reporters Without Borders (2008). http://archives.rsf.org/article.php3?id_article=25310 (accessed March 13, 2012).

"Rate of Poverty Estimated at 24.7%." Tunisian Press Agency (May 28, 2011). http://www.tap.info.tn/en/en/society/2749-rate-of-poverty-estimated-at-247.html (accessed May 29, 2011).

"Reveil Tunisien, après 10 Ans." Reveil Tunisien (May 18, 2011). http://www.reveiltunisien.org/spip.php?breve4018 (accessed June 6, 2011).

Rheingold, Howard. *Smart Mobs*. Cambridge: Perseus, 2002.

Riahi, Olfa. "Fortes Présomptions de Malversation et d'Affaire de Mœurs—Urgence d'une Enquête Officielle" (December 26, 2012). http://tobegoodagain.wordpress.com/2012/12/26/rafik-abdessalem-bouchleka-fortes-presomptions-de-malversation-et-daffaire-de-moeurs-urgence-dune-enquete-officielle/ (accessed on April 21, 2012).

Richardson, Kay, Katy Parry, and John Corner. *Political Culture and Media Genre: Beyond News*. London: Palgrave Macmillan, 2013.

Rivère, Philippe. "Facebook: The Magic Mirror." *Le Monde Diplomatique* (January 16, 2011). http://mondediplo.com/2011/01/16facebook (accessed February 21, 2011).

Rivlin, Paul. "The Constraints on Economic Development in Morocco and Tunisia." In *The Maghreb in the New Century: Identity, Religion and Politics*, ed. Bruce Maddy-Weitzman and Daniel Zisenwine, 197–216. Gainesville: University of Florida Press, 2007.

Roberts, Joseph W. *How the Internet Is Changing the Practice of Politics in the Middle East: Political Protest, New Social Movements, and Electronic Zamizdat*. Lewiston: Edwin Mellon, 2009.

Rose de Sable. "Comments" (August 21, 2008). http://www.marhba.com/forums/actual-ites-3/que-pensez-vous-blogs-tunisiens-32642.html (accessed June 14, 2011).

Rouissi, Slimane. "Les Agriculteurs Tunisiens Manifestent pour Conserver leurs Terres." France 24.com (July 16, 2010). http://observers.france24.com/fr/content/20100716-agriculteurs-tunisiens-manifestent-conserver-leurs-terres (accessed January 3, 2012).

Russell, Adrienne, and Nabil Echchaibi, eds. *International Blogging: Identity, Politics and Networked Publics*. New York: Peter Lang, 2010.

Sadiki, Larbi. "Ben Ali Baba Tunisia's Last Bey." Aljazeera.net (September 27, 2010). http://english.aljazeera.net/indepth/opinion/2010/09/20109238338660692.html (accessed March 25, 2011).

Sadiki, Larbi. "Ben Ali's Tunisia: Democracy by Non-Democratic Means." *The British Journal of Middle Eastern Studies* 29, no. 1 (2002): 57–78.

Sadiki, Larbi. "Political Liberalization in Ben Ali's Tunisia: Façade Democracy." *Democratization* 9, no. 4 (2002): 122–41.

Sadiki, Larbi. *Rethinking Arab Democratization: Elections without Democracy*. Oxford: Oxford University Press, 2009.

Sadiki, Larbi. "Tunisia: The Battle of Sidi Bouzid." Aljazeera.net (December 27, 2010). http://www.aljazeera.com/indepth/opinion/2010/12/20101227142811755739.html (accessed May 10, 2012).

Saidi, Ali. "Interview with BBC Arabic" (August 20, 2010). http://www.youtube.com/watch?feature=endscreen&v=UrD-1nkM6Mg&NR=1 (accessed January 8, 2011).

Saïdi, Raoul. "La Pauvreté en Tunisie: Présentation Critique." In *La Tunisie de Ben Ali: La Société Contre le Régime*, ed. Olfa Lamloum and Bernard Ravenel, 11–35. Paris: L'Harmattan, 2002.

Samsoum. "Comment on Sami Ben Gharbia's 'I Blog for Tunisia, against the Maghreb'" (June 7, 2007). http://samibengharbia.com/tag/blogsphere/page/2/ (accessed November 17, 2011).

Samsoum. "First of July: I Blog for the Freedom of Expression" (June 12, 2007). http://samsoum-us.blogspot.com/2007/06/le-1er-juillet-je-blogue-pour-la-libert.html (July 12, 2007) (accessed May 28, 2011).

Samsoum. "Je Blogue pour la Liberté de la Parole!" (July 9, 2007). http://samsoum-us.blogspot.com/2007/06/je-blogue-pour-la-libert-de-la-parole.html (accessed December 17, 2011).

Samsoum. "Liberté d'Expression" (June 10, 2007). http://samsoum-us.blogspot.com/2007/06/libert-dexpression.html (accessed May 26, 2011).

Samti, Farah. "Eight Years Ago, When Leftists and Islamists Got Along." *Tunisalive* (October 18, 2013). http://www.tunisia-live.net/2013/10/18/eight-years-ago-today-when-leftists-and-islamists-got-along/ (accessed November 18, 2013).

Scott, James C. *Domination and the Arts of Resistance: Hidden Transcripts*. New Haven: Yale University Press, 1990.

Scott, James C. "Everyday Forms of Resistance." *Copenhagen Papers* 4 (1989): 33–62.

Seib, Philip. *The Al Jazeera Effect: How the New Global Media Are Reshaping World Politics*. Washington, D.C.: Potomac, 2008.

Séréni, Jean-Pierre. "En Tunisie, les Soubresauts de la Révolution." *Le Monde Diplomatique* (May 2011). http://www.monde-diplomatique.fr/2011/05/SERENI/20484 (accessed January 30, 2012).

Séréni, Jean-Pierre. "Le Réveil Tunisien." *Le Monde Diplomatique* (January 6, 2011). http://www.monde-diplomatique.fr/carnet/2011-01-06-Tunisie (accessed January 30, 2012).

"Seuls les Résultas Comptent!" Nawaat (December 20, 2005) http://nawaat.org/portail/2005/12/20/seuls-les-resultats-comptent/ (accessed March 19, 2011).

Shirky, Clay. *Here Comes Everybody*: The Power of Organizing without Organizations. New York: Penguin, 2008.

Shirky, Clay. "The Net Advantage." *Prospect* (December 11, 2009). http://www.prospectmagazine.co.uk/magazine/the-net-advantage (accessed June 12, 2013).

Shirky, Clay. "Reply to Malcolm" *Foreign Affairs* 90, no. 2 (March/April 2011). http://www.foreignaffairs.com/articles/67325/malcolm-gladwell-and-clay-shirky/from-innovation-to-revolution (accessed December 15, 2012).

Shirky, Clay. "The Twitter Revolution: More than Just a Slogan." *Prospect* (January 6, 2010). http://www.prospectmagazine.co.uk/magazine/the-twitter-revolution-more-than-just-a-slogan/ (accessed December 18, 2012).

Silver, Vernon. "Post-Revolt Tunisia Can Alter E-mail with 'Big Brother' Software." Bloomberg (December 13, 2011). http://www.bloomberg.com/news/2011-12-12/tunisia-after-revolt-can-alter-e-mails-with-big-brother-software.html (accessed February 11, 2012).

"Si on me Coupe Facebook je Résilie mon Contrat avec mon Fournisseur Internet." http://fr-fr.facebook.com/events/27877300142/ (accessed February 6, 2012).

Skalli, Loubna Hanna. "Youth, Media and the Art of Protest in North Africa." In *Mediating the Arab Uprisings*, ed. Adel Iskandar and Bassam Haddad, 54–59. Washington, D.C.: Tadween, 2013.

Skalli, Loubna Hanna. "Youth, Media and the Politics of Change in North Africa: Negotiating Identities, Spaces and Power." *Middle East Journal of Culture and Communication* 6, no. 1 (2013): 5–14.

Sorenson, David S. *An Introduction to the Modern Middle East: History, Religion, Political Economy, Politics*. Boulder: Westview, 2008.

Soudani, Seif. "Takriz: Quand les Hooligans Font de la Politique." *Le Labo Politique* (March 12, 2011). http://www.edupartage.com/web/labopolitique/magazine/-/asset_publisher/J9Zk/content/1641587 (accessed May 23, 2011).

Sreberny, Annabelle. "Television, Gender and Democratization in the Middle East." In *De-Westernizing Media Studies*, ed. James Curran and Myung-Jin Park, 63–78. London: Routledge, 2000.

Sreberny, Annabelle, and Gholam Khiabany. *Blogistan: The Internet and Politics in Iran*. London: IB Tauris, 2010.

Sreberny, Annabelle, and Ali Mohammadi. *Small Media, Big Revolution: Communication, Culture, and the Iranian Revolution*. Minneapolis: University of Minnesota Press, 1994.

Stupeur. "Is the Tunisian Blogosphere Dying?" (June 5, 2009). http://blog.kochlef.com/2009/06/05/dying-blogosphere/ (accessed June 19, 2011).

Suleiman, Mona. "Internet Censorship." *The Altar of Al Jazeera*. Al Jazeera Arabic Channel (May 22, 2010). http://www.aljazeera.net/NR/exeres/DC620C2A-9274-4C04-9D00-806DF9A986A3.htm (accessed February 8, 2012).

Sullivan, Andrew. "Tunisia's WikiLeaks Revolution." *The Atlantic* (January 14, 2011). http://www.theatlantic.com/daily-dish/archive/2011/01/tunisias-wikileaks-revolution/177242/ (accessed October 12, 2011).

Taki, Maha. "Beyond Utopias and Dystopias: Internet in the Arab World." In *The Middle East in the Media: Conflicts, Censorship and Public Opinion*, ed. Arnim Heinemann, Olfa Lamloum, and Anne Françoise Weber, 184–94. London: Saki, 2009.

Teib, Aicha. "The Socio-Economic Context of the Tunisian Revolution: A Sociological Reading." In *The Tunisian Revolution: Causes, Contexts and Challenges*, 57–85. Doha: Arab Center for Research and Policy Studies, 2012.

"The 10,000 Signature Petition against Internet Control and Censorship." https://www.facebook.com/Tunisie.libre.1714?v=wall&ref=ts (accessed January 25, 2012).

"Ten Worst Countries to Be a Blogger." Committee to Protect Journalists (2009). http://cpj
.org/reports/2009/04/10-worst-countries-to-be-a-blogger.php (accessed May 1, 2012).

"The Fellaga and the Information Revolution." Al Mutawassit TV Channel (September 27,
2013). www.youtube.com/watch?v=mbCN0ITZ9wc (accessed March 31, 2014).

"The Keyboard Revolution." Nawaat (August 30, 2005). http://nawaat.org/portail
/2005/08/30/the-keyboard-revolution/ (accessed March 3, 2011).

"The Maghreb Harvest Program." Al Jazeera Channel (September 19, 2010). www.aljazeera
.net/NR/exeres/F7AD880B-6860-461C-A035-5BB15E1756F1.htm (accessed November
16, 2012).

The Man Who Sold the World. "Comment on Free Race's 'A Foreign Body'" (December 5,
2007). http://free-race.blogspot.com/2007/12/blog-post_02.html?showComment=11
96844780000#c2326898256664877731 (accessed June 13, 2011).

The Man Who Sold the World. "Comment on Free Race's 'It Is a Matter of Reputation'" (September 16, 2007). http://free-race.blogspot.com/2007/09/blog-post.html (accessed June 13,
2011).

The Man Who Sold the World. "Comment on Sami Ben Gharbia's 'I Blog for Tunisia, against
the Maghreb'" (June 7, 2007). http://samibengharbia.com/tag/blogsphere/page/2/
(accessed November 17, 2011).

The Tunisian Revolution: Causes, Contexts and Challenges. Doha: Arab Center for Research and
Policy Studies, 2012.

"Third Annual ASDA'A Burson-Marsteller Arab Youth Survey" (2010). http://arabyouthsurvey
.com/wp-content/themes/arabyouth-english/downloads/2010-2011/ays-whitepaper-
2010.pdf (accessed October 3, 2012).

T.I.Z. "Opposant: Un Métier à Temps Plein!" Reveil Tunisien (May 21, 2003). http://www
.reveiltunisien.org/spip.php?article607 (accessed June 6, 2011).

"Tous Solidaires: Non à la Fermeture de Facebook en Tunisie." http://facebook.com/group
.php?gid=32550875030 (accessed November 11, 2012).

Tufekci, Zeynep, and Christopher Wilson. "Social Media and the Decision to Participate in
Political Protest: Observations from Tahrir Square." *Journal of Communication* 62 (2012):
363–79.

"Tunisia Aborts a Demonstration by Bloggers." Aljazeera.net (May 23, 2010). http://www
.aljazeera.net/NR/exeres/8C5BB7B5-2663-44DA-B044-137F6BFAF617.htm (accessed
March 21, 2011).

"Tunisia: Basic Demographic Indicators." World Bank. http://web.worldbank.org/WBSITE/
EXTERNAL/TOPICS/EXTGENDER/EXTANATOOLS/EXTSTATINDDATA/EX
TGENDERSTATS/0,,contentMDK:21438838~menuPK:4080892~pagePK:64168445
~piPK:64168309~theSitePK:3237336,00.html (accessed January 23, 2011).

"Tunisia: Bloggers and Censorship...Mocking Ammar 404, Re-Launching Blogs and Fighting
Legal Battles." Magharebia (November 5, 2008). http://www.magharebia.com/cocoon/
awi/xhtml1/ar/features/awi/features/2008/11/05/feature-01 (accessed November 10,
2011).

"Tunisia: Integrity Indicators Scorecard." Global Integrity (2008). https://www.globalinteg-
rity.org/global/the-global-integrity-report-2008/tunisia/ (accessed February 11, 2012).

"Tunisia: Internal Exile Used to Silence Dissent." Human Rights Watch (February 1, 2005).
http://www.hrw.org/en/news/2005/01/31/tunisia-internal-exile-used-silence-dissi-
dent (accessed June 30, 2012).

"Tunisia: Internet Usage and Marketing Report," http://www.internetworldstats.com/af/tn
.htm(accessed March 23, 2011).

"Tunisian Authorities Continue to Suppress Bloggers." The Arabic Network for Human Rights
Information (November 9, 2009). http://old.openarab.net/en/node/1548 (accessed
November 24, 2011).

"Tunisian Blogger Detained." Aljazeera.net (November 7, 2009). http://www.aljazeera.com/
news/africa/2009/11/2009117751273306.html (accessed December 11, 2011).

"Tunisian Government Severely Restricts Media Freedoms." Open Source Center (March 4, 2010). http://publicintelligence.net/ufouo-open-source-center-tunisian-government-severely-restricts-media-freedoms/ (accessed June 10, 2011).

Tunisian Internet Agency. "Internet in Tunisia." http://www.ati.tn/en/index.php?id=68&rub=26 (accessed February 5, 2012).

Tunisian Internet Agency. "Statistiques du Mois de Janvier 2011 sur l'Internet en Tunisie." http://www.ati.tn/en/index.php?id=90&rub=27 (accessed June 10, 2011).

"Tunisians Demonstrate Online Instead of Taking to the Streets." CNN (October 6, 2005). http://nawaat.org/portail/2005/10/06/tunisiens-manifestent-sur-internet/ (accessed May 17, 2011).

"Tunisian Web Journalist Jailed." BBC News (June 20, 2002). http://news.bbc.co.uk/2/hi/middle_east/2050453.stm (accessed May 22, 2011).

"Tunisia: Release Urged for Online Magazine Editor." Human Rights Watch (June 6, 2002). http://www.hrw.org/en/news/2002/06/05/tunisia-release-urged-online-magazine-editor (accessed February 14, 2012).

Tunisia's Global Integration: A Second Generation of Reforms to Boost Growth and Employment. Washington, D.C.: World Bank Publications, 2006.

"Tunisia's Global Integration: A Second Generation of Reforms to Boost Growth and Employment." World Bank Social and Economic Development Sector Unit for the Middle East and North Africa Region (May 2008). http://siteresources.worldbank.org/INTTUNISIA/Resources/Global-Integration-ReportSept08.pdf (accessed February 12, 2012).

"Tunisia's Media Landscape." *International Media Support* (June 2002). http://www.i-m-s.dk/wp-content/uploads/2012/11/ims-tunisia-assessment-2002.pdf (accessed July 7, 2012).

Tunisia: Understanding Successful Socio-Economic Development: A Joint World Bank-Islamic Development Bank Evaluation of Assistance. Washington, D.C.: The World Bank, 2005.

"Tunisie: Hommage au Cyber-Militant Zouheir Yahyaoui." *Tekiano* (March 11, 2011). http://www.tekiano.com/net/7-web-2-0/3451-tunisie-hommage-au-cyber-militant-zouhair-yahyaoui.html (accessed May 19, 2011).

"Tunisie: Le Courage d'Informer." Reporters Without Borders (February 2009). http://fr.rsf.org/IMG/pdf/Rapport_Mission_Nov_08_FR_PDF_-2.pdf (accessed March 1, 2012).

"Tunisie: On Assiste à une Cyber-Révolution" (January 12, 2011). http://www.youphil.com/fr/article/03370-tunisie-on-assiste-a-une-cyber-revolte-emeute-facebook?ypcli=ano (accessed January 26, 2012).

"Tunisie: Violents Affrontements entre Habitants et Forces de l'Ordre." *Le Nouvel Observateur* (August 15, 2010). http://tempsreel.nouvelobs.com/monde/20100815.OBS8521/tunisie-violents-affrontements-entre-habitants-et-forces-de-l-ordre.html (accessed January 6, 2011).

Ungerleider, Neal. "Tunisian Government Allegedly Hacking Facebook." *Fast Company* (January 10, 2011). http://www.fastcompany.com/1715575/tunisian-government-hacking-facebook-gmail-anonymous (accessed January 22, 2011).

United Nations Arab Human Development Report. New York: UNDP, 2009. http://www.arab-hdr.org/publications/other/ahdr/ahdr2009e.pdf (accessed January 23, 2011).

Van Dijck, José. *The Culture of Connectivity: A Critical History of Social Media.* Oxford: Oxford University Press, 2013.

Vaulerin, Arnaud. "Opération Tunisia: La Cyberattaque d'Anonymous aux Côtés des Manifestants." *Libération* (January 12, 2011). http://www.liberation.fr/monde/2011/01/12/operation-tunisia-la-cyberattaque-d-anonymous-aux-cotes-des-manifestants_706827 (accessed January 23, 2011).

Wacker, Gurdrun. "The Internet and Censorship in China." In *China and the Internet: Politics of the Digital Leap Forward*, ed. Christopher R. Hughes and Gudrun Wacker, 67–73. London: Routledge, 2003.

Waltzi, Mitzi. *Alternative and Activist Media.* Edinburgh: Edinburgh University Press, 2005.

Warner, Michael. "Publics and Counterpublics." *Public Culture* 14, no. 1 (2002): 49–90.

Wellman, Barry, and Caroline Haythornthwaite, eds. *The Internet in Everyday Life*. Malden, Mass.: Blackwell, 2002.

Werewolf. "Comment on Tarek Kahlaoui's 'Ammar Censors the Blog Nocturnal Thoughts'" (February 5, 2010). http://tareknightlife.blogspot.com/2010/02/blog-post_05.html (accessed December 17, 2011).

Weslaty, Lilia. "Entretien avec Sophie Piekarec." Nawaat (March 14, 2012). http://nawaat.org/portail/2012/03/14/entretien-avec-sophie-piekarec-la-fiancee-de-zouheir-yahyaoui/ (accessed March 12, 2013).

Weslaty, Lilia. "Les Cyberdissidents Tunisiens Rendent Homage à Zouheir Yahyaoui" (March 8, 2011). http://www.tunivisions.net/les-cyberdissidents-tunisiens-rendent-hommage-a-zouheir-yahyaoui,11604.html (accessed June 11, 2011).

Wheeler, Deborah L. *The Internet in the Middle East: Global Expectations and Local Imaginations in Kuwait*. Albany: State University of New York Press, 2006.

Wheeler, Deborah L. "Working around the State: Internet Use and Political Identity in the Arab World." In *The Routledge Handbook of Internet Politics*, ed. Andrew Chadwick and Philip N. Howard, 305–20. London: Routledge, 2009.

Wood, Christina. "French Foreign Policy and Tunisia: Do Human Rights Matter?" *Middle East Policy* 9, no. 2 (2002): 92–110.

"World Population Prospects: The 2008 Revision Population Database." http://esa.un.org/wpp/country-profiles/country-profiles_1.htm (accessed June 12, 2011).

"Yahoo! Still First Portal Call." *BBC News* (June 5, 1998). http://news.bbc.co.uk/2/hi/business/107667.stm (accessed December 15, 2012).

Yahyaoui, Mokhtar. "La Dictature Nuit à L'Image de Notre Pays: Letter Ouverte aux Blogeurs Tunisiens" (May 4, 2010). http://nawaat.org/portail/2010/05/04/la-dictature-nuit-a-limage-de-notre-pays-lettre-ouverte-aux-blogeurs-tunisiens/ (accessed February 9, 2012).

Yahyaoui, Mokhtar. "Open Letter to the President of the Republic." TUNeZINE (July 6, 2001). www.tunezine.comtunezine07.htm (accessed October 24, 2011).

Yahyaoui, Mokhtar. "Tunisie: Interpellation des Deux Jeunes Initiateurs d'un Rassemblement Contre le Blocage d'Internet à Tunis." Tunisia Watch (May 21, 2010). http://www.tunisiawatch.com/?p=2413 (accessed February 1, 2012).

Yang, Guobin. *The Power of the Internet in China: Citizen Activism Online*. New York: Columbia University Press, 2011.

Youssef, Olfa. "Lettre Très Objective à Ammar" (May 22, 2010). http://olfayoussef.blogspot.com/2010/05/lettre-tres-objective-ammar.html (accessed May 12, 2011).

-Z-. "Ce n'est pas Ammar qui Censure." Débat Tunisie (February 7, 2010). http://www.debatunisie.com/archives/2010/02/07/16819364.html (accessed June 30, 2011).

-Z-. "Indigestion de Brick au Thon à Carthage." Débat Tunisie (April 29, 2010). http://www.debatunisie.com/archives/2010/04/29/17724823.html (accessed December 23, 2012).

-Z-. "Jacques Doucinaud Sauve la Tunisie." Débat Tunisie (November 6, 2009). http://www.debatunisie.com/archives/2009/11/06/15699298.html (accessed February 7, 2012).

-Z-. "Nous Sommes Tous Fatma!" Débat Tunisie (November 6, 2009). http://www.debatunisie.com/archives/2009/11/06/15709603.html (accessed February 7, 2012).

Zamiti, Khalil. "La Question Syndicale: Contradictions Sociales et Manipulations Politiques." In *Tunisie au Présent: Une Modernité au dessus de tout Soupçon?* Ed. Michel Camau, 287–96. Paris: CNRS, 1978.

Zayani, Mohamed. "Al Jazeera and the Vicissitudes of the New Arab Mediascape." In *The Al Jazeera Phenomenon*, ed. Mohamed Zayani, 1–49. London: Pluto, 2005.

Zayani, Mohamed. "The Challenges and Limits of Universalist Concepts: Problematizing Public Opinion and a Mediated Arab Public Sphere." *The Middle East Journal of Communication and Culture* 1, no. 1 (2008): 60–79.

Zayani, Mohamed. "Social Media and the Reconfiguration of Political Action in Revolutionary Tunisia." *Democracy and Society* 8, no. 2 (2011): 2–4.

Zayani, Mohamed. "Toward a Cultural Anthropology of Arab Media: Reflections on the Codification of Everyday Life." *History and Anthropology* 22, no. 1 (2011): 37–56.

Zayani, Mohamed, and Sofiane Sahraoui. *The Culture of Al Jazeera: Inside an Arab Media Giant.* Jefferson: McFarland, 2007.

Zbiss, Hanene. "Qui est Derrière Takriz." *Réalités* (May 19, 2011): 46–48.

Zizou from Djerba. "Il est Temps de Censurer Facebook en Tunisie" (June 2, 2008). http://www.zizoufromdjerba.com/2008/06/il-est-temps-de-censurer-facebook-en.html (accessed December 19, 2011).

Zmerli, Aly. *Ben Ali le Ripou* (2011). http://kapitalis.com/fokus/62-national/2522-tunisie-ben-ali-les-annees-bonheur-les-annees-labeur.html (accessed June 1, 2011).

Index